John R Rice

John R Rice

"The Captain of Our Team"

VIOLA WALDEN

SWORD of the LORD
PUBLISHERS
P. O. BOX 1099, MURFREESBORO, TN 37133

Printed and Bound in the United States of America

JOHN RICHARD RICE (1895-1980)

John Richard Rice was born in Cooke County, Texas, on December 11, 1895, the son of William H. and Sallie Elizabeth LaPrade Rice. Educated at Decatur Baptist College and Baylor University, he did graduate work at the Southwestern Baptist Theological Seminary and the University of Chicago.

On September 27, 1921, he was married to Lloys McClure Cooke. Six daughters were born of that union, all of whom, with their husbands, labor in full-time Christian service.

Although Dr. Rice served as pastor of Baptist churches in Dallas and Shamrock, Texas—in addition to starting about a dozen others from his successful independent crusades—his primary work was as an evangelist. He was a friend and peer of Billy and Ma Sunday, Bob Jones, Sr., W. B. Riley, Homer Rodeheaver, H. A. Ironside, Robert G. Lee, Harry Rimmer and other leaders of that era. He himself held huge citywide crusades in Chicago, Cleveland, Buffalo, Seattle and numerous other key metropolitan centers.

Called "The 20th Century's Mightiest Pen," Dr. Rice authored more than 200 books and booklets circulating in excess of 60 million copies before his death, about a dozen of which were translated into at least 35 foreign languages. His sermon booklet, *What Must I Do to Be Saved?* has been distributed in over 32 million copies in English alone, 8 1/2 million in Japanese and nearly 2 million in Spanish.

In 1934 he launched THE SWORD OF THE LORD, which, by the time of his death, had become the largest independent religious weekly in the world, with subscribers in every state of the Union and more than 100 foreign countries. Thousands of preachers read it regularly, and it undoubtedly had the greatest impact upon the fundamentalist movement of any publication in the 20th century.

In 1959, Dr. Rice started the Voice of Revival, a 30-minute radio broadcast heard on 69 stations in 29 states, Puerto Rico and the Philippine Islands.

He died in Murfreesboro, Tennessee on December 29, 1980.

Introduction

Sometimes you discover a man after he is dead.

The world did not discover Jesus until after it had crucified Him.

John the Baptist was a fanatic and an agitator until his head lay safely reposing in the charger; then he was recognized as the greatest before Christ.

Saint Paul was a zealot and a disturber until the Roman prison saw the last of him; then he became the first and greatest missionary of the church.

Luther, while he lived, was a bigot and a self-righteous dogmatist; in fact, he was hounded as a lawbreaker; then he became the father of the Reformation.

Wesley was an insane enthusiast and a fanatical dissenter while he rode the highways of England. He happened to live long enough to see the beginning of the mighty movement he fathered; and yet it was only "long life and many days" that compensated for the reproach with which his whole life was attended.

Now we are discovering another man—after he is dead.

In every generation, a few men stand out as giants in their fields. Only rarely, however, does a man receive recognition as a giant in many fields. Our generation was blessed with such a man. None really knew the fullness of his greatness.

Some saw only his recent, more publicized achievements.

One group knew him as a scholar; but he was also a football player and coach.

To some, he was a revivalist; but he pastored and started churches, too.

Many knew of his "Hell-fire-and-brimstone"preaching; yet part of his life was spent teaching English.

Some viewed his many books and called him an author—and he was; but he was a composer as well.

All who knew him well knew of his soul-winning zeal; but few recalled his cowboy days.

None of these views—not even all of them together—describe what he was and did. He was so great that we could not comprehend his greatness.

Yet, sadly, for a few, his greatness was totally hidden. They viewed him simply as an old man with an out-dated message. They thought he was narrow, and somehow failed to see the love, the tears, the compassion. They overlooked his lifetime of giving, both of his time and his money. They saw only a fighter, a warrior, missing the balance of the man.

It is unfortunate that these people, blinded by his closeness, never really appreciated a man on whom future generations will look with awe. They missed a truly unique chance to know one of the greatest men of history. Perhaps, in time, they will recognize what they have missed and give his memory the honor his life deserved.

Someone has said, *"After a man is gone, men build monuments for him with the stones they cast at him during his life."*

Only from the distance of retreating years will most of this generation properly evaluate Dr. John R. Rice and his miraculous ministry.

What David was to Israel, Gladstone to England, Garibaldi to Italy, Lincoln to America, so John R. Rice was to the fundamentalist movement of the 20th century. Through his anointed preaching, his dynamic pen and his consistent example, this man blazed a trail across America and around the globe. He ignited fires of evangelism that may never be extinguished until the millennial dawn.

We pray that those who read this volume will not only laugh and cry, learn and be blessed, but that you will thank God for such a paper as THE SWORD OF THE LORD and for such a man who comes, perhaps once in a generation—the man, Dr. John R. Rice, the Captain of our Team!

The voice is now stilled; yet the influence of the man who owned it is destined to continue on, and on, and on. . . .

Sword of the Lord Publishers
September, 1990

Table of Contents

"Hold up your hand right now if you want forgiveness for your sins and Jesus in your heart," urged the preacher boy. He glanced down at the street-meeting crowd from the top of the old truck and scanned for response. The Lord was good—hands came up as June sunflowers after a rainy spring.

Then he saw him. The different one. The tall young man with Stetson hat and weather-beaten face. Oh, his hand was in action all right. Way high. Trouble was, his legs were in action too, as he headed away from the Tenth and Main Street corner toward the Fort Worth Depot.

"Just as I am without one plea," sang the crowd, but the cowboy outran the warm strains of the invitation. It was decision time all right, for both preacher AND hearer. The truck springs squeaked a protest when the minister vaulted the ladder and hit the ground depot-bound.

Quite a sight. There went the cowhand with a suitcase and here came the preacher with a Bible. "You held up your hand to show you wanted to be saved," he said, catching up.

"I do," puffed Cowboy, "but I've got to catch the Texas and Pacific Special in just ten minutes."

Well, the two hurried together down the street, jostling through the crowds, one talking, the other listening.

Before the T & P Express highballed out of the station that day, the Stetson came off and the Saviour came in.

Sure, it was a seminary student leading another sinner to Christ. But more than that: it was indicative of the "above and beyond the call of duty" type witnessing that would characterize the entire career of that young preacher, who proved for 60 years that anywhere is a meetin' place for Jesus.

1895-1932 Born December 11, 1895, he was named John R.— uncertain as to what the "R" stood for, but that is about the only thing in this world he was ever uncertain about! All who knew him know John R. Rice was a man of deep convictions!

Born of a preacher-rancher father—William H. Rice—and a country schoolmarm mother—Sarah LaPrade—he grew up on a Texas ranch.

Even before his birth, his parents had dedicated him to the Lord, his mother constantly referring to him as "my preacher boy."

Pastor "Will" Rice was so delighted with his new son that he opened his Bible to Luke 1:63 and heavily underscored the words: *"His name is John."*

Young John Richard was so impressed with his parents' hopes for his life that, when asked his name, his reply always was: "I'm John the Baptist preacher!"

Unfortunately, just before he was six, the lad's mother passed away.[1] On her deathbed she pled for all the children to meet her in Heaven. After her barely audible voice sang a verse of "How Firm a Foundation," she lifted her hands to Heaven and cried, "I can see Jesus and my baby now!" Moments later she was gone.

In a sermon in which he mentioned her death, Dr. Rice recalled:

> I remember the November day when we laid her body away. My father knelt beside the open grave. There was no white muslin to hide the raw dirt of the grave—like a wound in the earth. No fake, man-made carpet of grass was thrown over the clods.
>
> My father put one arm around his two little orphan girls, and one around his two little boys, and watched as they lowered the precious body in its dark casket into the bosom of Mother Earth.

---

[1] Will Rice's first wife died about 1889, leaving two children: a boy—Jesse; a girl—Jimmy. In 1892 he married Sarah LaPrade. To this union were born Gertrude, John R., Ruth, George and Baby Porter, who died soon after birth. In 1905 Will married Dolous Bellah. They had four children: Joe and Bill and two who died shortly after birth—both named William Henry.

The rain beat down upon us, and a friendly neighbor held an umbrella over our heads. . . .

This sorrow embedded itself in the personality of the child.

But as he grew into manhood, he became so busy playing football and working his way through college, that it seems he almost forgot that his mother had dubbed him her "preacher boy."

Years later he went to Amarillo to visit an aunt. While there, he found a faded letter written by his mother. Writing about her children, she referred to John as her "preacher boy."

"Did she really call me that?" he asked, lifting his eyebrows.

"Nothing else," replied Aunt Esse.

This discovery planted a seed in young John R.'s heart. Each day he thought about it; but his heart was set on doing important things in the teaching field—like becoming a college president; or even United States President! But John never forgot his mother's pleas to meet her in Heaven.

At age nine, after hearing A. B. Ingram preach on "The Prodigal Son," he slid off the pew at First Baptist Church, Gainesville, Texas, that Sunday morning and went forward to tell the preacher he would receive Christ as Saviour.

Three years later, after receiving assurance of his salvation by reading John 5:24, young John was baptized. He says about that day:

> I remember what a joy it was when I was baptized at Dundee, Texas, in a big artificial lake or water tank. It was a cold November day, but my heart was so warm as we were brought out of the water and lined up at the water's edge while everyone sang: O happy day that fixed my choice/On Thee, my Saviour and my God!/Well may this glowing heart rejoice/And tell its raptures all abroad.
>
> They wrapped a quilt about me and put me in the hack carriage, to drive home two miles. But I was not cold; my heart was so happy!

After finishing high school, he taught briefly in a country school. Read his early vow near this time:

> On a farm in West Texas, as a cold mist was falling, I went out by the woodpile on a January day, through the pea patch, crawled through the barbed wire fence and walked over the hill to a place

of prayer. In the "brakes" in a bare ravine under a chaparral bush I went down on my face and told God I would do anything He wanted me to do—preach, be a gospel singer or whatever He had in mind. I promised Him I would prepare myself and would look to Him to supply my needs to go through college.

Later Dr. Rice testified:

> How could I ever forget that holy hour when I made that holy vow! For God went with me as I saddled my sorrel horse and rode off to Decatur (Texas) Baptist College with about $9.35 in my pocket. I worked my way through Junior College and University. I played football. I was active in college debating. I was president of a literary society and of the University Christian Association. I took voice lessons and yet did enough outside work to pay my expenses. How I earned a scholarship and how there was always a job waiting me I could never explain except that I had a covenant with God, and I put Him to a test. And since then, I have had such a boldness on this matter that I have no trouble about daily provision.

At age nineteen, the young man left the ranch, got on his horse in the rain and made the 120-mile trip to enroll in college.

God gave him a job when the president told him first there was no job to be had. Soon he was milking cows and waiting on tables to pay his room and board. When tuition payment was due and he had no money, the president called him in and said, "John, can you teach a class in arithmetic to some backward boys who are not ready for junior college—courses in algebra and geometry?" Soon he was making enough to pay his tuition.

He had few clothes. He and his roommate prayed. Right away a long distance call came from an uncle, "John, how much money do you need for clothes?" Soon money for clothes, and a bit more, was on its way to the needy student.

God answered prayer again and again and again for whatever he needed.

It was at Decatur he met a beautiful Texas belle, Lloys Cooke.

When Lloys was preparing to go to college for premedical training, a wise evangelist told her father she ought to go to a Christian college, that she was likely to marry the wrong kind of man if she went to a state school. A few days later a surprised Lloys found herself on the campus of Decatur Baptist College.

As in all good fairy tale love stories, the very first person Lloys laid eyes on when she arrived on campus was—you guessed it!—John R. Rice! (What happened—later.)

(Dr. Ward, president of Decatur College, told John that he had known he was called to preach long before John himself knew it. Dr. J. B. Tidwell, professor of Bible in Baylor University, told his sweetheart, "Anybody who does not want to marry a preacher had better not marry John Rice.")

John Rice graduated in the spring of 1918. At the start of commencement week, he was drafted into the Army as a dental assistant, so a United States flag draped his empty chair at commencement. A case of mumps prevented his being shipped overseas with his Seventh Division.

After World War I and the signing of the Armistice, Mr. Rice immediately enrolled at Baylor University at Waco, Texas, and graduated with an A. B. degree in 1920 on an earned scholarship. As an intercollegiate debater at Baylor, he displayed the thorough preparation and simple, logical presentation of facts that made him world famous as a gospel preacher and writer.

Even though headed in the direction of becoming a college president, he often preached during the years he was pursuing his education.

After graduating from Baylor, he took a position at Wayland Baptist College, Plainview, Texas, teaching English and coaching football.

But Mr. Rice became restless and thought it best to work on a master's degree. So in the spring of 1921, he enrolled at the University of Chicago, taking graduate work in the school of education.

These were days of spiritual crisis for him. He was a Christian, and had been active in the Lord's work for a number of years. As field agent for the college one summer and as a gospel singer at revivals, he regularly worked at winning souls. However, Mr. Rice knew very little about the Bible and had absorbed a great deal of evolutionary teaching in a college course at Baylor.

He was brought face to face with his dilemma when William Jennings Bryan was brought to the University by the Y.M.C.A. When the crowds overflowed the space, the meeting moved to a church near the campus, where Bryan spoke on "The Bible and Its Enemies."

Dr. Rice's parents—Will Rice and Sallie Elizabeth LaPrade Rice

(L-R) John R., George, Ruth and Gertrude—about 1899

The Rice girls, 1935—Grace, Mary
Lloys, Jimmie Elizabeth, Jessie
Ruth, Joanna

Lloys and John R. Rice
in their early days

The address was a revelation. For the first time Mr. Rice saw that both evolution and the Bible could not be true and that evolution was a deadly enemy of true Christianity. He had nominally accepted this teaching without realizing that it contradicted Scripture. After hearing the powerful message by Mr. Bryan, he determined to pursue the truth and come to a definite decision. He resolved to put the Bible to an honest test. If it proved to be the infallible and lasting Word of God, he would believe, follow and defend it at any cost.

The University faculty arranged for a professor to reply to Mr. Bryan. Mr. Rice went to hear the case for evolution and against verbal inspiration and infallibility of the Bible and direct creation of man.

To his surprise, the learned professor had no proof of evolution: he merely advanced the same old theories and argument Mr. Rice had heard so often, even in his high school days, where he had been taught the evolutionary hypothesis.

At the close of the lecture, Mr. Rice went to the professor and asked him frankly, "Do you believe that Jesus Christ is the Son of God?" Smiling, the professor answered, "I see it would be useless to talk to you. I do not want to argue."

Mr. Rice saw then and there where evolution inevitably led, and his choice was made.

Leaving, he heard two freshmen on the steps—one, the son of a modernist preacher; the other, the son of a missionary, arguing.

The missionary's son at first hotly contended for the Bible; the modernist's son, that the Bible was a very good Book but not the Word of God and not accurate.

The conversation on the steps continued in Mr. Rice's hearing. The devout young man began to waver. Finally, interrupting, Mr. Rice urged the missionary's son to stay with the faith of his father and mother. But now, brushing the tears from his eyes and ignoring Mr. Rice's plea, the young man started down the steps, saying, "Well, I guess a fellow has to get his eyes opened sometime!"

Mr. Rice said, "I saw him walk away without his faith, arm in arm with the friend who had been taught by his infidel teacher-father not to believe the Bible but to believe the guesses of men who call themselves scientists."

This was a time of crisis for Mr. Rice. Standing there on the steps that spring afternoon, he felt a holy fire burning in him. Lifting his hand solemnly toward Heaven, he vowed: "I will at every opportunity smite this awful unbelief that wrecks the faith of men!"

That vow he tried to keep.

Later he declared: "I little knew then that the keeping of my vow would lose me some of the dearest friends I ever knew and brand me as an outcast, a fanatic, a 'non-cooperating Baptist,' a 'disturber,' a 'Bolshevik.' But I never regretted it. If there is anything at all to the Christian religion, there is enough to die for."

Dr. Rice would probably have risen to be president of a college, had he gone that route. He would doubtless have been a very successful businessman, had he chosen that field. To go high in the field of learning had always been his ambition. Indeed, he was attending the University of Chicago at the time with that goal in view.

But down at Pacific Garden Mission (where Billy Sunday had been converted), he was singing and doing personal work. A drunk came forward. Mr. Rice went to the altar to pray with him. And that experience changed everything.

Years later Dr. Rice remembered: "I got up from my knees beside this poor, dirty, unshaven but now converted bum, and found that all my ambitions for college teaching and the presidency were gone! I wanted nothing better than to win souls...."

As the preacher that night read Romans 12:1, 2 and the call of Isaiah (chap. 6), the ambitious college student presented his body to the Lord to be a preacher!

That one incident you might say constituted John R. Rice's call to the ministry!

Forgetting every other ambition, he was now ready to work at his new calling. He gently closed the academic doors behind him and leaped into the full-time ministry.

Mr. Rice left the university, resigned from an engagement with Montezuma Baptist College in New Mexico where he was to teach, and went back to Texas.

For four years Lloys Cooke and John R. had been engaged, and much of that time they were away from each other; their only contact was by daily letters. In the summer vacation during college days, then one year when he taught in Wayland College and she was finishing her work in Baylor University, then while he was in the army, Mr. Rice wrote her six times a week and got six letters from her each week (there was no mail on Sunday). How eagerly they watched for those letters!

"John's daily love letters in the time apart did a great deal to keep our romance alive," Lloys recalled.

Lloys McClure Cooke, to the casual observer, would not have seemed to have the background or qualifications for a typical preacher's wife. She was the only daughter of a prosperous Texas farmer, adored by her father and indulged by her four brothers. Her parents, determined that she would be reared in the best tradition of southern gentlewomen, saw that she learned music, along with cooking and sewing.

Texas farmland in those days was primarily a man's country, and Lloys often got lonely for the companionship of other girls. She occasionally would bribe a younger brother to "play house" with her for a little while by offering to play rough-and-tumble boys' games first, but she was not allowed to help in the fields because that was "men's work."

Her early love for books no doubt contributed to the excellent grades she made throughout her school career.

After Lloys' conversion as a young teenager, she set out to serve the Lord, not knowing exactly in what direction that service would lead. In later years when John R., busily pursuing a teaching career, suddenly felt he was called to preach, Lloys accepted the call to be wife and helpmeet to the man she already knew would be one of America's outstanding preachers.

They were married September 27, 1921, in the living room of her parents' farmhouse and set up their first home in a small apartment near the campus of Southwestern Baptist Seminary, Fort Worth, where both were enrolled in classes.

The years ahead were busy and happy ones, and Mrs. Rice shared uncomplainingly the life of sacrifice, deprivation, loneliness and dedication to which her husband was committed. While his revival work meant many long days of separation, she did, finally, discover the joy of feminine companionship. All six children born to the Rices were daughters, the last being Joy who arrived on their 16th wedding anniversary.[2]

With Lloys by his side, Dr. Rice entered Southwestern Theological Seminary, Fort Worth, Texas. While there he became a student pastor, conducting evangelistic campaigns and preaching in scores of jails.

---

[2] Grace (1922); Mary Lloys (1925); Elizabeth (1927); Jessie Ruth (1929); Joanna (1931); Joy (1937)

But it seemed evangelism was always in his heart. Even while pastoring, on his first stationery he put *"Evangelist John R. Rice."*

The name John R. Rice then and in later years was linked inseparably with evangelism. He did believe in defending the Faith, in sound Bible teaching, in missions—but evangelism was his strongest heartbeat.

Dr. B. H. Carroll, in his famous address on Evangelism at the Southern Baptist Convention in years past, reminds us:

> All that group of brilliant young men that constituted the staff of Paul *were evangelists, not pastors.* What a galaxy of stars are here: Barnabas, Mark, Luke, Silas, Erastus, Epaphras, Gaius, Clement, Tertius, Jason, Sosipater, Justus, Crescens, Epaphroditus, Achaicus, Stephanus, Fortunatus, Apollos and many others, were evangelists pure and simple.

Before the end of the 20s, Texas became aware of this young evangelist who preached with the boldness and fire and power of the Holy Spirit.

Dr. Rice was ordained October 9, 1921 at First Baptist Church, Decatur, Texas. The certificate was signed by three preachers: Dr. R. E. Bell, pastor of the church; Rev. William H. Rice, father of the candidate; and Rev. Thomas J. Doss, pastor of a neighboring church; and by the clerk of the Council, J. W. Bailey.

Dr. Rice left this word about his early ministry and having to be away from home:

> When I started out as a young evangelist, I left my wife with one baby and another on the way, in a tiny, two-room apartment on Seminary Hill, Fort Worth. She had no telephone. I could leave her almost no money for an emergency or extra food. I was gone for a two-week revival campaign, and my heart trembled. What would Lloys do if there were sickness of either her or the baby? She would have little money for food or medicine or anything else needed. And no car, no phone.
>
> I saw then that I must get this matter settled.
>
> That afternoon I walked away from the home where I was staying, down a country road to a schoolhouse, went inside and laid the matter out before the Lord. If I were to serve Him, I must have peace and assurance He would care for my family. I didn't leave that schoolhouse until I got that peace.
>
> From then to now, He has given me sweet peace about this lonely road I have traveled and about being away from home.

Early in his ministry and even in college days, Dr. Rice, himself a Southern Baptist, felt he must help rescue Southern Baptists from modernism. He saw the beginnings of it at Baylor. Evolution had been introduced into the university.

It was while at Southwestern that he watched a young preacher come to the pulpit to protest modernism and evolution in Baylor, and saw him banned from the platform without being allowed to finish his protest.

After this incident, Dr. Rice felt he must take a definite stand against modernism and evolution wherever he went. And from that time on, he boldly stood for the fundamentals of the Faith and against these two evils creeping into Baptist ranks.

Dr. Rice often preached for Dr. J. Frank Norris in his large church in Fort Worth and on his radio station, both having tremendous audiences. Dr. Norris, too, had made a bold fight for the fundamentals of the Faith, but he had been turned out of the county association and the Convention. He did a great work, but his methods were not always commendable.

After two years in Southwestern Baptist Theological Seminary, Dr. Rice accepted an assistant pastor's position at First Baptist Church, Plainview, Texas.

After one year there, he went to Shamrock, Texas, where he stayed two years and saw many great blessings. The church membership went from 200 to over 400. A new church auditorium was built under Dr. Rice's direction.

After he had launched into full-time evangelism, Dr. Rice went back to Southwestern, expecting to make that his base. He began to preach very plainly about some of the modernism in Texas Baptist schools where he had recently attended. It was a time of real testing, because he was such a thorough Baptist and wanted so badly the approval of the noble men of God who led the denomination. And you may be sure there was much criticism and some real persecution.

One day a committee came to see him. Two members were teachers in the Southwestern Baptist Theological Seminary, and a third was a pastor of the Seminary Hill Baptist Church. They laid the matter on the line very plainly, saying they represented a large group. "And if you continue as you are in allowing the denomination to be embarrassed by the way Dr. Frank Norris uses your testimony, then you will be blackballed in the denomination. The *Baptist Standard* (the state Baptist paper) will carry an open repudiation. The Tarrant County Baptist Association will ask every church to close its doors to you. If you expect to be an evangelist and preach the Gospel and educate your children, you must play ball with the denomination. You must no more appear on a radio station to discuss evolution and modernism."

Dr. Rice said he spent that night experiencing mixed emotions. He first had a tendency to laugh at the presumption of men who would come to give him such orders. But then he thought that, if they had made the same threats to ten young preachers, eight or nine would probably back down and leave their convictions in order to stay with the denomination.

So Dr. Rice said:

> If I am serving the kind of God who cannot open doors for me nor support my family nor bless my ministry without my bowing and scraping and kowtowing to denominational leaders, then I'll quit serving Him. But if I am serving the God I think I am, He can open the doors without the favor of men who try to cover up and hide sin. So the next day I went on the radio and openly and boldly told of the committee's coming to see me and their threats.
>
> My ministry was, it seemed, threatened with ruin. But God had a great ministry for me to stand clear and straight, to defend Christ and the Bible through the years. Satan knew that and wanted to ruin my ministry or shut my mouth.

So Dr. Rice's bold, firm reply was: "I will trust the Lord and follow His leadership."

And from that point on, though no one backed him, he had the backing of God and led literally thousands to the Lord in independent revival meetings.

That reminds me of this story:

> A local committee of a certain community called on an old Scot, a leading merchant, and threatened to boycott his store if he did not withdraw his support from a certain moral issue. His reply came back: "I want you to know, gentlemen, that my goods are on sale but not my character."

In these campaigns, Dr. Rice would go to a town, set up a tent on the square or in a public place, secure a piano and singer and begin the revival. He would stay in one place ten or twelve weeks and would not only see scores saved, but he would get these converts reading their Bibles and learning doctrine. Almost consistently he would leave some 300 or 400 people as members of a church for which he had found a pastor and provided a building.

In 1926, Dr. Rice stood on the steps of First Baptist Church, Mineral Wells, Texas, and passed out mimeographed sheets to Southern Baptist pastors who were meeting there—these sheets protesting liberal tendencies at Baylor University, Dr. Rice's alma mater.

He took his stand; then in 1927, sadly he left the Southern Baptist Convention and never changed his position.

Because of his Southern Baptist heritage, Dr. Rice loved Bible-believing Southern Baptist preachers and laymen—and there are still many of them. Yet he continually, up to his death, fearlessly exposed the liberalism and modernism in Southern Baptist institutions. (Scores of pastors and churches were led to leave the Convention as a result.)

"The meekest man who ever scuttled a ship or slit a throat," some said of him. As for the scuttling of ships and cutting of throats—that only happened if the ships be those of modernists who would steal the faith of honest, Bible-believing men and women and carry it so far over the storm-tossed sea of doubt that recovery was almost impossible, or if the throats be those of people who would hinder the cause of Christ and of evangelism, the cause for which he gave his life.

And as for "the meekest man" part—well, he was the meekest of men. Many other wonderful things could be said about him, but it would take hundreds of pages!

Let me say this: I have no idea to what heights of attainment he would have come had he chosen a profession in the world. But I do know that, wrapped in that body of flesh and bone were more energy, conviction, determination, purpose and grit than I have ever seen in any other man!

His next call will be to Dallas, Texas...

1932-1940

The Story of the Fundamentalist Baptist Tabernacle, Dallas

John R. Rice had been in full-time work as an evangelist since 1926, first holding revivals in churches, principally Southern Baptist ones, then beginning large independent campaigns without any local church sponsorship, in cities and towns in Texas and Oklahoma. These resulted in vigorous new churches in many cities.

For two years Dr. Rice had felt God would lead him to Dallas for the purpose of starting an independent, fundamental Baptist church in a growing metropolis.

So in 1932, through the newspapers, radio and printed handbills, it was announced meetings would begin July 12. Although the site had been chosen and announcements made, there were no seats and practically no money on hand. But God sent in the money needed and enough volunteers to make crude benches for that open-air campaign at Tenth and Crawford Streets in suburban Oak Cliff.

Everything was ready for the meeting.

And what a meeting it was! The crowds became larger and larger, until the lot and benches were completely filled.

Literally hundreds were saved during the duration of the revival, one block from where the Fundamentalist Baptist Tabernacle was later built.

It was in this open-air revival at Tenth and Crawford Streets that I became acquainted with Dr. Rice and his powerful ministry.

A circular had been delivered to my home announcing the meeting. I went the first night—and from then on nothing could keep me away!

Dr. Rice usually never gave an invitation for sinners to accept Christ the first few nights: he was getting Christians right with God so that they would not stand in the way of a revival. When he did begin calling for sinners to trust Christ and many were coming, he walked down to where I was sitting—a sixteen-year-old high school girl who attended a Southern Baptist church a block away—and asked if I would take the names of the new converts. I was thrilled to death!

A baptistry was built right behind the platform, out in the open. I was the first one baptized! I was also one of the sixty charter members of the new church.

What I was seeing and hearing from this man of God was entirely new. I knew nothing about separation. The pastor of the church I attended went to movies, smoked long cigars, and his daughter was a fashion model. I wanted what Dr. Rice was teaching about being separated from the world. So at this revival I wholeheartedly gave my all to Christ.

And it was here where I saw my first of many miracles!

We were—perhaps a thousand of us—sitting out in the open. We saw the clouds grow dark and stormy. Then it began to sprinkle. Dr. Rice, about to start the service, stopped and prayed that the rain would not hinder the revival nor hinder souls from getting saved.

As soon as he had stopped praying, the rain stopped, and he went on with the service.

Latecomers on their way to the revival thought, *They can't possibly have a service in this downpour,* so turned and went back home, not knowing God had "hedged that revival in"!

We learned the next day that within a block in every direction around the revival—North, South, East, West—it had literally poured for some time, but there we were—out in the open and dry as a bone!

Dr. Rice went from one revival to another, in several sections of Dallas and in the suburb of Oak Cliff, these revivals lasting two to three months.

Because there were so many new converts, a new church was organized with a clear-cut, fundamental Statement of Faith, charter members agreeing to membership if this evangelist would remain as pastor.

Within a year, there were more than 300 members. In twenty months of almost continuous revivals, the membership increased to 900.

A lot was bought and construction began on a great brick tabernacle, 90 feet x 145 feet, seating 1600. (After a disastrous fire, it was rebuilt several years later.)

The membership grew steadily through the 7 1/2 years of Dr. Rice's pastorate—to some 1700 members.

How mightily God had wrought in Dallas, Southern Baptist territory!

Besides the growth of this strong congregation, first called the Fundamentalist Baptist Tabernacle, then Galilean Baptist Church, thousands of the converts went to many churches throughout the area. It was not unusual to have people attending from fifteen or twenty miles away; and necessarily and perhaps properly, many found churches nearer at hand where they could take their families regularly.

When the Fundamentalist Baptist Tabernacle of Dallas began, there was not another independent Baptist church in the whole Dallas area; when Dr. Rice resigned in early 1940, there were fifteen to eighteen such churches, and many had as their principal workers and officials people who were won to Christ in these services conducted in the open air by Evangelist John R. Rice!

Dr. Rice's ministry in Dallas had to share time with many other activities. He was an evangelist. During those years, he held many revival campaigns, some one month or longer, all over America. The last twelve months he served as pastor of this church, Dr. Rice was gone eighteen Sundays, and an even larger proportion of the weekdays he was preaching in outside engagements.

Besides all this, his written ministry was extensive. Some years before, Dr. W. B. Riley, Dr. T. T. Shields and Dr. J. Frank Norris had planned to have Sunday school lessons through the entire Bible and had asked Dr. Rice to prepare notes on those lessons. It took five years, including the first years in Dallas, with a lesson prepared every week.

Then the weekly SWORD OF THE LORD began September 28, 1934, and that added much more labor.

During that Dallas time he wrote and had books published by Moody Press, by Fundamental Publishers and by Zondervan Brothers.

But in the midst of it all, God graciously blessed in saving thousands of souls and building up many Christians. Some 7,000 people claimed Christ under his ministry in seven and one-half years, with Dr. Rice baptizing many hundreds of them.

Next, let's find out more about that SWORD OF THE LORD magazine. . . .

1934—The Story of THE SWORD OF THE LORD

THE SWORD OF THE LORD was born in the midst of the bitter Depression when the winds of criticism were howling against evangelism, when financial empires were crumbling on every hand, jobs were hard to find, and everyone was asking: "Will the Depression end?

Will America go communist, socialist or fascist? Will there be war with Japan; or between Germany and France; or between Italy, Yugoslavia and Austria?"

What actually happened is now history and has been the subject of many books, but out of all the grief and trying times of the mid-thirties emerged THE SWORD OF THE LORD.

I was an eyewitness to the beginning of "America's Foremost Revival Weekly."

I can remember how distressed Dr. Rice was over editorials in leading magazines to the effect that *the days of mass evangelism died with Billy Sunday.*" I can still remember his saying that he, by the grace of God, would prove that it was possible to have as great revivals today as in the days of Finney, Moody, Torrey, Chapman, Sunday and others.

And Dr. Rice did conduct great revival campaigns in Dallas, with attendance sometimes 2,000 on weeknights and more on Sunday nights. He was totally convinced that what God could do in Dallas, He could do in Chicago, Los Angeles, New York, London or Moscow!

He felt someone should edit a paper, sound in doctrine, to advance the cause of evangelism in America; and he felt called of God to be that "someone."

Even as Spurgeon published *The Sword and the Trowel,* John R. Rice felt compelled to publish THE SWORD OF THE LORD.

So THE SWORD OF THE LORD was born when Dr. Rice was still pastor in Dallas.

I still remember the first edition of 5,000 copies that came out on September 28, 1934. The paper boldly stated then, and still does, that it stood for the verbal inspiration of the Bible, the deity of Christ, His blood atonement, salvation by faith, New Testament soul winning and the premillennial return of Christ; against modernism, worldliness and formalism.

It was a **revival** weekly—in the days when citywide campaigns and mass evangelism had disappeared. Dr. Rice referred to himself as an evangelist when the name was in disrepute and published revival and evangelistic sermons when others called printed sermons "addresses." Great soul winners of the past and their messages were featured. Such things as mass revival, preaching against sin, the public invitation, the evangelistic church and the fullness of the Spirit were promoted.

† † †

I remember that Dr. Bill Rice—just plain Bill Rice then—was the first circulation manager.[1] He "circulated" all around Dallas, putting THE SWORD in the hands of people, in doors of business houses and under car windshield wipers. Mrs. John R. Rice was his assistant! On Saturdays she would take her little girls and some other "little" people in her car, and Bill would dispatch them to streets in Dallas where they would personally deliver the papers from door to door.

As Mrs. Rice remembered it, there was no money in the deal; but at the end of a long Saturday, she would buy a five-cent ice cream cone for each child, report to Bill the streets on which they had worked and where they were sometimes chased by unfriendly dogs.

If there were still papers undelivered, then the "circulation manager" went downtown on Saturday night to finish the job.

Finally, Bill was promoted to advertising manager. Again he circulated all over Dallas by foot or streetcar to solicit advertising to pay for printing of THE SWORD.

Then, after a few months, when Bill was called to pastor a church in Gainesville, Texas, the old hometown of the Rice clan, Mrs. John R. Rice inherited his job as "advertising manager."

With the inauguration of THE SWORD OF THE LORD came an incessant demand for "copy, copy, copy!" With a deadline to meet each week, it was inevitable that a growing accumulation of his messages, old and new, should be born into written word. Their quality was so uniformly high that almost all of them later appeared in booklet form.

Back in those days we had no machines to take down messages, so Miss Lola Bradshaw and I took them down in shorthand; Lola for awhile, until she tired; then I took over; then she when I got tired. Thus we had messages to print.

Not only did we take down Dr. Rice's—and was he a speed-demon in those days!—but others—Hyman Appelman, R. G. Lee, H. A. Ironside—any of those "greats" who came to preach in our "Bible Schools" in Dallas (later called Sword of the Lord Conferences). Now it is easy to turn a switch, start a machine, record the message; but then it was hard, hard work by two faithful but tired secretaries!

When THE SWORD was launched, the subscription price was $1.00 a

---

[1] While Bill was "John's younger brother" and while he enjoyed the distinction, he didn't depend upon it. His background of experience in the "old West" and his straightforward, winsome, yet powerful manner of "speaking the truth in love" won for him his own high place in the field of evangelism.

year. On November 21, 1935, after we had gotten our second-class permit, it was: 4 pages, 35 cents per year, or 4 years for $1.00!

Dr. Rice used the paper in Dallas to promote the soul-winning ministry of the church, as well as for a preaching organ for this "sensational" preacher! The mailing was done in Dallas from tables set up in the Tabernacle. The addressing was done by a hand addressograph. Papers were wrapped separately and put in bags for the postman.

Some of the headlines in these first issues announced his fiery topics at the church:

"LOCKED OUT IN THE DARK!" with a subhead: *The Trumpet That Will Wake the Dead; the Angel's Voice Heard Around the World; and the Resurrection Shout When Jesus Comes.*

FLOODS! DROUGHTS! TORNADOES! FLU EPIDEMIC! JUDGMENT!

SOLD TOO CHEAP—YOUR SOUL

DISEASED, DECAYING BODIES WITH UNDYING MAGGOTS AND UNQUENCHED FIRE IN HELL

WHAT HAPPENED TO THE MAN WHO MISSED CHURCH ON EASTER?

ANGELIC VISIONS FROM STONY PILLOWS; PRINCELY TITLES THROUGH BROKEN LEGS; THRONES THROUGH SUFFERING, AND HEAVEN BY WAY OF DEATHBEDS

SHUT YOUR MOUTH BEFORE GOD SHUTS IT FOR YOU!

HEATHEN CHRISTMAS IN PAGAN DALLAS

GIANTS AND GRASSHOPPERS

His sensational subjects drew large crowds.

The paper became quite popular as the subscription list grew and it became nationally known. Approximately one year after its inception, it had reached a circulation which included subscribers in 41 of the 48 states, Canada, Mexico, Brazil and Norway.

There were times, however, when an unpopular stand has cancelled thousands of subscriptions. In crucial issues I have watched Dr. Rice lose friends of a lifetime by the stroke of an editorial pen—weeping but not swerving. But that was what made Dr. Rice unique. He stood for what he considered to be the truth, regardless of the cost.

The financial burden fell upon Dr. Rice's shoulders; and he carried this, along with the burden of the editor's work—and all this while

Getting SWORDs ready for post office in Dallas, 1936

Fundamentalist Baptist Tabernacle,
Dallas, Texas. Dr. Rice was pastor 1932-
1940. THE SWORD originated here,
September, 1934.

John R. Rice, 1939

Two of the first
few issues of THE
SWORD, 1934

carrying on the pastoral duties of a large church.

Dark days and years were to follow, days of prayer, of tears and of mighty hard work. Dr. Rice put most of the money he personally received from the congregation of the Fundamentalist Baptist Church into the printing of THE SWORD OF THE LORD, as well as his love offerings from revivals.

It was quite embarrassing when visiting ministers came home with him for meals or to spend the night and the table was set with old chipped or broken dishes. Pickle jars, jelly glasses and even milk bottles were their drinking glasses. The furniture was old, shoddy and rickety.

The guests never dreamed, I suppose, the money that could have been used for nice furniture, new dishes, kitchen cabinets, had gone into the forging of THE SWORD.

A publication must have a distinctive ministry to justify its existence. The justification of THE SWORD OF THE LORD is its evangelistic emphasis. Every issue is calculated to win souls, and the outstanding preachers of the continent are called into service to contribute to this end.

From the very first, the paper has been interdenominational in the sense that it publishes material by people of many denominations who are agreed on the fundamentals and has people of many denominations as its readers. Just as Dr. Rice's revival campaigns involved Christians of all groups of fundamental Bible believers, so does the readership of THE SWORD OF THE LORD.

It is impossible to estimate the influence on this nation wielded by THE SWORD OF THE LORD. In 55 years, it has never dipped its colors nor deviated from its original purpose.

Thousands have written of their salvation through its pages, and more thousands have been set straight on doctrine and their lives put back on track.

By the time of Dr. Rice's death, THE SWORD OF THE LORD had become the largest independent religious weekly in the world, with subscribers in every state of the Union and more than 100 foreign countries. Thousands of preachers read it regularly, and it undoubtedly had the greatest impact upon the fundamentalist movement of any publication in the twentieth century.

He put the fires of evangelism and soul winning into more preachers' bones than any other living man. Daring to be different in an age when

Hell-fire-and-damnation preaching was not emphasized, Dr. Rice simply did it because, as he noted, Jesus did it.

And never, in 46 years, was Dr. Rice paid one cent for his work as editor of THE SWORD OF THE LORD, nor as author of his many books.

The magazine has varied in length from its original 4 pages to 8, to 12, to 16, to 24. Now a biweekly, it has 24 pages and regularly features four or five full-length sermons by greatly used present-day preachers, and always one of the past.

And THE SWORD OF THE LORD is abrim with timely articles—an arsenal of information, instruction, inspiration on such areas as: Answers to Bible Questions, News and Views, With the Evangelists, Editor's Notes, Scrapbook Clippings, columns to children, to teenagers, to women, to soul winners.

Dr. Curtis Hutson is following in the steps of his predecessor. We have yet to see what God will do for this great soul winner and model for the thousands to whom he ministers through THE SWORD, in conferences and in speaking engagements.

The three mainstays in Dr. Rice's Dallas office were Miss Lola Bradshaw, Miss Fairy Shappard and I. A number of church members were donating their time weekly, helping mail out THE SWORD OF THE LORD; but we three gave ourselves continually to the work.

All three came to work as a matter of faith and in answer to prayer, asking Dr. Rice only for our bare needs. Remember—this was during the Depression years. I had changed my courses in high school to include typing and shorthand. In the year of my graduation, in the school yearbook under "Ambitions," was written, under my picture: *"To be personal secretary to Rev. John R. Rice."*

Dr. Rice did not ask me to give up a good-salaried job as a receptionist in a doctor's office until we both knew it was the Lord's leading.

The work was hard and the hours long. Many times we would finish copy for THE SWORD OF THE LORD around 1:00 or 2:00 in the morning, take it downtown, put it on a bus for Denton, Texas, where our printer was located, then go back home for a few hours' sleep.

We were not only responsible for all the correspondence, the preparing of labels and the mailing out of the paper; but we helped keep church records, did regular visitation and went to church ALMOST EVERY NIGHT!

Miss Lola was with Dr. Rice for about 19 years; Miss Fairy, until she died suddenly in 1985, and I'm still around after 56 years!

It was a busy, busy, busy seven and one-half years in Dallas, before moving on and up to Wheaton, Illinois, in 1940.

Perhaps this is as good a time as any to mention Dr. and Mrs. Rice's six girls.

The first girl, Grace, was born in 1922; the sixth, Sarah Joy, in 1937.

Dr. Rice loved each one of his babies dearly. When Grace was brought home from the hospital, it was he who gave her her first bath. The first night he took care of her all night. Mrs. Rice said about getting up the next morning: "I saw 12 diapers hanging on the string."

He liked to feed the small ones before they had learned to handle a spoon. And the first thing he taught them to say was, "I love Daddy."

Dr. Rice was a great father: that you will learn later on from testimonies of the girls. He stressed the importance of family devotions, and they were never missed. The Rices read the Bible through many times as a family. Dr. Rice would read two verses; and around the table each would read two verses, until three or four chapters were read.

Precious verses were memorized, and all prayed and talked about their problems. They were free to ask any questions. "Many precious truths were taught during those hours of family devotions," said Mrs. Rice.

Dr. Rice thought obedience was not obedience if it was not instant obedience. So they first taught them to obey. Then a second principle was: they were not allowed to ever fret, cry or pout. And soon after each was born, she was taught what "no" meant.

Both parents believed in spanking. Neither enjoyed doing it, but it was to protect their children from wrong. Dr. Rice emphasized, "Children need to know what is expected of them. They like a code of conduct. They like to know that it does not pay to do wrong. So the spanking was to protect them."

Both he and Mrs. Rice stressed that, in spanking, you get most of their wills settled in their first six years. "Only two of our girls were whipped after they were teenagers," Mrs. Rice declared, "and none ever rebelled against us."

Dr. Rice set the standards for the home, so they were never confused about what was expected of them and were convinced that Dad's standards were right, no matter what the rest of the world did or thought.

"Though Dr. Rice was away from home more than half the time on missions for the Lord," Mrs. Rice said, "he never left his children's discipline to others. He set the rules when he left; checked up when he got back. If things had begun to slide a bit in his absence, he took things in hand and set them on the right road again. He was determined that in the home of one evangelist, he would see that the children turned out right; he was determined under God to turn them out right."

She continued: "I could wish for every child a father like my children's father. While he was winning other children to the Lord, he did not neglect to win his own; he trained them for the Lord."

Dr. Rice insisted that "anyone who did not work was not worth his salt." So besides the work at home, they were expected to join their dad in his effort to get out the Gospel. Before they could operate a typewriter or addressing machine in the office, they could help give out circulars about revivals, they could fold sample papers for mailing, they could run errands or clean the office. By the time they were in junior high school, they were regularly helping in the office; and in high school they took courses in typing and shorthand, getting ready to be better helpers.

Highlights of His Ministry While Still in Dallas—1935

OF GREAT STATEWIDE INTEREST

The Rice-Oliphant Debate was announced for January 15-25, 1935, at Fundamentalist Baptist Church. For months Church of Christ preachers had yearned for a religious discussion with the Dr. John R. Rice. Finally he agreed to a debate.

They chose an experienced and well-known debater, Dr. W. L. Oliphant, minister of Oak Cliff Church of Christ.

Agreement about the details was signed:

1. The Scriptures teach that Jews, as a nation, will return to Palestine when Christ returns to the earth, and will then be converted to Christ. **Affirm—Rice; Deny—Oliphant.**

2. The Scriptures teach that Christ will establish a literal throne in Jerusalem, and will reign over the whole earth for a period of one thousand years. **Affirm—Rice; Deny—Oliphant.**

3. The Scriptures teach that baptism, to the penitent believer, is essential to his salvation from past or alien sins. **Affirm—Oliphant; Deny—Rice.**

4. The Scriptures teach that a child of God, one who has been saved

by the blood of Christ, can so sin as to be finally lost. **Affirm—Oliphant; Deny—Rice.**

In each session each speaker was granted two periods of thirty minutes each.

The interest was intense. Long before the first session, the building was jammed and packed. People were standing in the aisles, and scores were turned away. Probably 2500 were in the auditorium or about it.

People listened respectfully and, it seemed, with a sincere desire to know the truth.

The interest continued as the debate progressed, with no let-up in the crowds. People came from all over the state of Texas and from several other states, including hundreds of Church of Christ ministers.

The debate was taken down by another secretary and myself and published by Firm Foundation (a publishing company of the Church of Christ).

Much good came from the debate, as evidenced by testimonies. Dr. Rice was at his best.

Dr. Oliphant experienced many interesting "embarrassing moments" —and some funny ones, too!

I remember well that he refused throughout to call Dr. Rice "Brother," though Dr. Rice continually referred to him as "Brother" Oliphant.

Dr. Rice kidded him, asking why he refused to call him brother, calling attention to the fact that Ananias called Paul "brother" before Paul was baptized. Oliphant answered that Ananias must have called Paul "brother" because he was a "brother" Jew. To that Dr. Rice responded that "on the same basis, you could call me 'brother' because we are both Gentiles!" On the last night he finally broke and called Dr. Rice "brother"!

The speeches were warm, in fact, hot—and very earnest! Though they opposed each other, neither doubted the other's sincerity.

The debate ended in a fine spirit.

Of course Dr. Rice proved to be the scholar, the gentleman we knew him to be. I don't recall any other Texas Church of Christ minister wanting to debate him after that!

(Dr. Bob Shuler once said, "Dr. Rice and I stand in a rather unique position with reference to each other. I am a Methodist and he a Baptist. I believe that a man can possibly fall from grace—he doesn't; yet I would tremble in my boots should I have to meet him in debate. . . .")

We felt mention of this noteworthy because of the great crowds it drew to the Tabernacle.

† † †

Early, Dr. Rice felt a need to identify himself as a Fundamentalist, so wrote a remarkable article entitled "The Reproach of Being a Fundamentalist." I don't believe he could have stated himself more clearly. It is long, and I have no room for it here; but it was a masterpiece!

He called himself a Fundamentalist and never wavered from that biblical position. His direction was so carefully established by his literal interpretation of the Scripture that in his voluminous writings over the span of sixty years there is no change of direction or emphasis.

Hinderers Fail to Stop Revival at
Binghamton, New York—1936

The telegram read:

> BROTHER RICE BECAUSE A GRAVE QUESTION HAS ARISEN WE AS A BOARD OF DEACONS AND PASTORS ARE WIRING CANCELLING OUR ENGAGEMENT WITH YOU FOR JANUARY TWELVE LETTER OF DETAILS WILL FOLLOW PLEASE REPLY BY WESTERN UNION ON REVERSE CHARGES
>
> FRED R. HAWLEY
> GRACE BAPTIST CHURCH
> BINGHAMTON NEW YORK

Dr. Rice immediately wired asking that the objection be stated and its source.

In reply, a second telegram from Hawley stated that some of Dr. Rice's "friends" had accused him of "teaching and preaching McPhersonism and Pentecostalism."

Since Dr. Rice was already in print on this, he sent this printed material to New York to clear his position. He also asked about a dozen pastors who knew his stand on these issues to write to Rev. Hawley, which they did.

Now the background of the attack.

Dr. J. Frank Norris had written an article attacking Rev. Sam Morris, a long-time friend of the Rices and pastor of a fine Southern Baptist church at Stamford, Texas. Dr. Norris was in Detroit at the time, and the article had already been set in type in Fort Worth.

His secretary brought Dr. Rice the article to proofread. After reading it, he told Miss Jane Hartwell, "You tell Dr. Norris he must not publish that in THE FUNDAMENTALIST (the paper edited by Dr. Norris). It is not true. It will do Sam great harm, and it would be wrong to print it."

Miss Jane declared that it was already in type, but Dr. Rice insisted that she call Dr. Norris and tell him it ought never be published.

Dr. Norris did have the type killed on that article, but he wrote Dr. Rice a rather stern letter, saying that Sam Morris, John Rice and others must realize *"that no one can get anywhere in the North, East, or outside of Texas in this fundamentalist movement without the love and confidence of the First Baptist Church"* (of which Norris was pastor).

Dr. Rice kindly reminded Dr. Norris that he had worked with him for years as a matter of conviction; that he had worked with him to defend Christ and the Bible and the independence of the local church and the right of preachers to be free under God; he also reminded him that he had never worked with him for pay nor for promotion and never would, then quoted Psalm 75:6,7: *"For promotion cometh neither from the east, nor from the west, nor from the south. But God is the judge: he putteth down one, and setteth up another."*

Dr. Rice wanted Dr. Norris to know that no one need depend on his endorsement nor cater to him in order to receive it.

The story is long. But I saw what happened.

Well, that was just too much for Dr. Norris to take. He did not like opposition; nobody told him what to do or what not to do! So he had a few of Dr. Rice's "friends"[2] get in touch with the Grace Baptist Church who planned the campaign for Dr. Rice in Binghamton, New York. Then the pastor, with some evident pain, sent that telegram saying the campaign must be cancelled because Norris and others had said Dr. Rice had turned Pentecostal!

Dr. Rice had learned many years before that it took the blessing of God to have revivals, not the endorsement of men or churches.

Dr. Rice wrote Rev. Hawley he was leaving for New York. "If you and your church want the revival, I will go ahead with it as scheduled. If not, I will hold an independent revival in a large, downtown, central

---

[2] Many of those pastors later apologized for their false accusations, and Dr. Rice printed their letters in THE SWORD.

location and expect God to give His blessing since I feel clearly led to Binghamton." He also told him that there would be no way to get in touch with him in order to stop him.

Dr. Rice began the 2,000-mile journey by faith, taking with him his family and secretary. He had money only for the trip up, not the trip back.

He made several stops en route to preach; then when he finally arrived in New York, he found the pastor had counseled with other pastors, and they had urged Hawley to go ahead with the revival.

And what a hugging—when the pastor found there had been a frame-up! You would have thought they were long-lost buddies, though neither knew each other except by letter!

The revival spread and was then made citywide. Outgrowing the church, the big Binghamton Theater was rented for a month. Those "cold New Yorkers" warmed up in a marvelous way to Dr. Rice's ministry.

In spite of that February in Binghamton being the fourth coldest spot in the United States, with temperatures running 11 degrees below zero, approximately 1,600 people packed the Theater night after night.

What a blessed campaign, with 376 first-time professions of faith, besides many other decisions by Christians! A very great majority of those saved were adults.

Dr. Rice went back in memory "to that time in 1928 when I had put it to a test whether I could hold revivals and carry on my ministry in spite of the opposition and slanders of denominational leaders. God blessed us then. The same God has blessed us now. The greatest revivals I have ever had have been when I trusted in God and not in men, when we, by faith, began a revival in the face of opposition and indifference."

After such an attack, what was Dr. Rice's feeling toward Dr. Norris? He wrote this in THE SWORD:

> I urge friends everywhere to love and pray for Dr. Norris. He is a great man, has won many thousands of souls, and has stood for the fundamentals of the Faith in a way that has greatly honored God. He is human. I earnestly pray that no harm will come to his ministry, nor to these other good men who have followed him in attacking me. I don't want enmity and hatred aroused, nor anything to happen that would cause sinners to fail to hear these men.
>
> I know Dr. Norris well. His pride and his feeling that the Fundamentalist cause will fare better if he can absolutely control it, are very natural human temptations to which all of us are subject.

If we had such great blessings as Dr. Norris has had, we might be guilty of the same thing. Let no bitterness come in your heart toward this man of God who has, in this matter, acted so foolishly. Read his paper, *The Fundamentalist.* He will print some great sermons. Listen to him over the radio. His messages have blessed many. Pray for the two great churches he pastors, one in Fort Worth and the other in Detroit.

Dr. Norris is not as young as he once was, and he should have our sympathy and forbearance. May God bless him, his family, his churches, his paper, his radio work. I pray that no friend he has loved and been true to will forsake him, falsely accuse him, try to block his revivals and assassinate his ministry. And may the dear Lord deal with him in just such tender mercy as all of us so sorely need.

That was Dr. Rice! Always forgiving, compassionate, and I never knew him to hold a grudge, no matter how severely he had been hurt or mistreated.

How many of us would have urged the whole world to pray for one who had dealt us such a blow!

Dr. Norris' attacks kept on and accelerated, even attempting to stop the circulation of THE SWORD OF THE LORD.

The post office told us of the protest and asked for a report of our subscription list—how many subscribed at the full rate, how many at reduced rates, how many in clubs, how many subscriptions were paid for by others, etc. We gave them all the proof they wanted.

Isn't it strange that a minister of the Gospel should work so hard to block revivals, split churches and stop a religious paper by which thousands of readers were being blessed?

But God was for the great Binghamton revival and saved hundreds there, though Norris had tried to prevent it. God preserved our Dallas church wonderfully, though Norris tried to kill it. And the same dear God would not allow him to stop the gospel message going out in THE SWORD OF THE LORD.

We knew that years before, denominational leaders had tried to block Dr. Norris' revivals and stop his paper, *The Fundamentalist.* His complaints then were loud! Now he had tried to block Dr. Rice's revivals, split his church and stop his gospel paper from going out, since he would not boost him!

Dr. Rice's comment still was: "Age and success, envy and self-aggrandizement may lead any man to folly. Let every preacher observe and, instead of condemning Dr. Norris too harshly, consider lest we also be tempted."

What a man! But what an example for us all!

† † †

Beloved Gipsy Smith came to Dallas in September, 1936, with the nominal cooperation of 109 Dallas churches. Services were held in the great First Baptist Church auditorium where Dr. George W. Truett was then pastor.

Since the Fundamentalist Baptist Church was not represented in the Ministerial Association, it did not officially cooperate in the revival. However, Dr. Rice and many of the church members attended regularly, as if we were cooperating.

On the Sunday nights of the revival, as many people went away without seats as those who got in.

On commenting about the great Gipsy, Dr. Rice had these kind words to say:

> I suppose Gipsy Smith is not a great Bible scholar, though he loves his Bible passionately. My critical mind could pick flaws in his theology. He says he never had a day's schooling in his life. He learned to read from a Bible and a dictionary. The carping critic could find plenty to which his cold heart might object, I suppose, in the preaching of Gipsy Smith. But any day in the world I would gladly trade some of my worldly wisdom for some of what Gipsy Smith has—the tears, the compassion, the compelling love for Jesus Christ!

Then later he told "how Gipsy Smith won my heart," in these words:

> —with his love for sinners. His sermons leap from scorn, indignation and lashing attack on the church member's indifference to the salvation of sinners, to the tearful, pleading entreaty that they go out and win souls today.

Then, a great soul winner himself and always looking for "prospects"—Dr. Rice recalled how, as he witnessed to a man outside the First Baptist Church, he found he had just been won to Christ by the Gypsy man. Gipsy Smith had preached to the thousands, then upon leaving the building, had time and heart to win a black chauffeur!

This revival was a great "reviving" for all of us who got in to hear this great, loving preacher from England, who made famous the song,

> Let the beauty of Jesus be seen in me,
> All His wonderful passion and purity;
> Oh, Thou Spirit divine,
> All my nature refine
> Till the beauty of Jesus be seen in me.

1937

Now, after walking so long on a dirt floor at the Tabernacle, the cement floor made us feel like millionaires! We had not heretofore been able to enjoy that luxury.

Dr. Rice was still preaching tremendous sermons, and these were rushed into booklet form almost before the sound of his voice left our ears! He was still holding great revivals, still bringing great preachers to our Dallas Bible Schools, such as Dr. Harry Rimmer, Dr. William McCarroll, Dr. Roy L. Brown, Dr. Walter Lewis Wilson, Dr. H. A. Ironside, Dr. Harvey Springer, Rev. C. E. Matthews and the great Negro singer, Elbert Tindley. Every thought of these blessed days recalls many happy memories.

† † †

Dr. Rice gave this news on the progress of our church:

> With no budget, no pledge cards, no canvass of the membership, no personal solicitation of any kind, no suppers, socials or other devices for raising money, we count it a remarkable blessing of God that our large brick building could have been erected without debt, and maintain a group of seven full-time workers who live by faith, as well as sending the Gospel to the end of the world through THE SWORD, booklets, radio services and Bible conferences. NOT ONCE HAS HE EVER FAILED THOSE WHO PUT THEIR TRUST IN HIM!

Remember: this was in the heart of the Depression. One hundred dollars then was like a thousand dollars now. Money was hard to come by. Many people were without work.

As I have already mentioned, Dr. Rice had no regular salary, only offerings designated to him. And he also was solely responsible for the large printing bills and his radio broadcast. All this was a matter of continual prayer and faith.

† † †

In June, the Los Angeles Baptist Theological Seminary conferred upon Dr. Rice the degree of Doctor of Divinity.

† † †

And a box on the front page of THE SWORD read: "EDITOR HAS ANOTHER BABY GIRL!" (Sarah Joy was born on their 16th wedding anniversary.)

1938

In July Dr. Rice went to Navilla, Mississippi for a revival, invited by Rev. Robert Hughes, the pastor. There were 268 conversions and additions.

Then in September he was off to Waterloo, Iowa, for a three-week tent revival, with over 200 professions of faith. Dr. Robert Wells of Burton Avenue Baptist Church had made fine preparations for this great tent revival.

NOTE! Dr. Rice is venturing out of Texas more and more!

† † †

During our Bible school in October, our beloved and paid-for and uninsured building was destroyed by fire, the cause unknown. An unused church about two miles away was vacant, so the services were moved there. Later we moved to a larger building until a new church could be built on the same site.

1939

In February Dr. Rice went to Chicago to be with the Christian Business Men's Committee in the Grand Opera House, one of the largest and best-known theaters in the Loop, with the services broadcast daily over WJJD, Chicago's largest independent outlet. He was scheduled for one week but was urged to stay for three.

† † †

Back in Dallas, Dr. Rice had a blessed revival with Rev. P. B. Chenault, pastor of Walnut Street Baptist Church, Waterloo, Iowa. He had closed the meeting with the message, "Today and Tomorrow."

A few hours before Dr. Chenault's death

After a sweet gospel service Friday night, we sang, "God Be With You Till We Meet Again," and lined up to shake the hand of our beloved evangelist and to say good-bye.

Several of us went to a cafeteria with them for a late snack. After a happy time of fellowship and a prayer and good-byes, the Chenaults were on their journey northward: he was to begin a revival at Kewanee, Illinois, on Sunday.

About thirty miles out of Dallas, two drunk men crossed the middle line onto the Chenaults' side and sideswiped the car, killing Rev. Chenault instantly. Mrs. Chenault suffered a broken collar bone and a broken bone in one foot. Their little girl was not injured. An officer passing by took her to the hospital, and an ambulance picked up Rev. Chenault.

The McKinney Hospital called Dr. Rice, who drove to the hospital immediately.

At the request of Mrs. Chenault, Dr. Rice conducted his funeral in his church in Waterloo, Iowa.

The Waterloo Courier reporter wrote: "In a dramatic departure from usual procedure, Dr. John R. Rice concluded his sermon at the funeral service for Rev. P. B. Chenault Tuesday afternoon by asking all those in the audience who had not previously done so to accept Jesus Christ. About 25 persons rose from their seats in the large crowd and received the charge from Dr. Rice. . . ."

Many pastors from outside Waterloo attended the service, as well as Dr. W. H. Houghton, president of Moody Bible Institute, Dr. Robert Ketcham and others.

Dr. Rice was asked to remain in Waterloo for a revival. In thirteen days, some 150 were saved or reclaimed.

✝ ✝ ✝

On December 10, our new church re-opened; and, after almost seven years, we enjoyed standard church pews instead of hard benches. Now it is Galilean Baptist Church instead of Fundamentalist Baptist Church, but with no change in doctrine, organization or position.

† † †

Dr. Rice dedicated his first clothbound book, in 1939, to Mrs. Rice, with these words:

> *To my beloved wife, Lloys Cooke Rice, who for more than seventeen years has been my constant encouragement and help in revivals. Although burdened with the duties of home as the mother of six children, she is an ardent and successful soul winner, a diligent Bible student, my best critic, and my constant inspiration in revival efforts. She never said "STAY" but always "GO." Her husband's preaching is always fresh to her, and her joy in revivals never fades.*

1940-1963

Wheaton, Illinois

1940

Wheaton, Illinois

In 1936 Dr. Rice held his first citywide revival outside Texas—in Binghamton, New York. By 1940 the demand for such meetings was so strong that he felt led of God to resign his Dallas church and give full time to citywide meetings.

So on January 12, Dr. Rice told his members and the Sword audience, why he was entering full-time evangelism. For one thing, in 1939 he was away from his church eighteen Sundays, and more often in the week time than on Sunday. Second, he had more calls than he could possibly fill, even if he were already a full-time evangelist. Third, he felt the church would profit more by having a pastor on the field full time. He announced to his people:

> I have had real heartache at the thought of leaving my beloved people in Dallas, yet I am confident that it is the sweet will of God. The church is well established, has a commodious and beautiful new building, and is running in sweet harmony.
>
> May God send a mighty revival upon the church, send you His own choice for a pastor and make the church a great lighthouse of blessing in this town, more so than before.
>
> I will continue to act as pastor until a suitable one is chosen.

Soon Dr. Robert J. Wells was elected as the new pastor, to be on the field in March. He was an earnest and strong Bible teacher, a successful pastor, organizer and soul winner. His work in Waterloo, Iowa, at the Burton Avenue Baptist Church, had gone forward in a blessed, united way. But he now felt led to succeed Dr. Rice in Dallas. (Later on, he came to Wheaton to be Dr. Rice's assistant there, helping in editorial work and conferences.)

Dr. J. Frank Norris entered the picture again.

In his paper, *The Fundamentalist,* he stated that the Masons had run Dr. Rice out of Dallas. To that fake charge, Dr. Rice answered:

> No, alas, Masons did not run me out of Dallas. If it had been

1936:

L to R: Dr. Rice,
Dr. J. Frank Norris,
and Rev. Louis
Entzminger

the Apostle Paul, they probably would have. He was dragged out of a town, stoned and left for dead. Another time he had to run for his life, being let down over the wall of Damascus in a basket. Many a town Paul had to leave. He was that kind of a preacher. I am sorry to say that I am not that good a preacher. What an honor if I were!

I have no scars in my body for the Lord Jesus. My scars were gotten riding a young bull, playing college football, etc. I was never put in jail. I was never treated like Stephen. I was never treated like Daniel. I was never treated like Paul and Silas. I am not a good enough Christian and a good enough preacher, or I would be.

May God help us to mean business for Him and preach so powerfully against sin that we may sometimes suffer in Jesus' name. It is not to my credit that I have never been run out of any town. May God make us fit to suffer some for Him!

It happens that I was in Dallas nearly eight years. I preached the same when I went there as when I left. Many Masons and other lodge people, the modernists and the booze crowd and some others didn't like it the first year—or the eighth year. But many lodge members did quit their lodges, and many drunkards did quit their booze.

It was a happy time with between 7,000 and 8,000 professions of faith. But the widespread calls for revivals increased until the pressure became conclusive evidence it was from God. With the new church completed, the burden lifted, I got the Lord's clear leading to go to the wider field.

One cannot believe all that is published in *The Fundamentalist*. That is why I, Dr. W. B. Riley, Dr. Robert Ketcham and many others quit writing articles for it and why I didn't allow it in my home.

You remember Dr. Norris' threat: "No one can get anywhere in the North, East, or outside of Texas in this Fundamentalist movement without the love and confidence of the First Baptist Church."

When Dr. Norris died, he had still not made peace with those he had harmed by his poisonous pen.

You may think I'm just "picking" on Dr. Norris. No. He and I were friends—until he began his tirade in Texas against my boss and others. Dr. Norris was a great preacher, and many was the time I made a new start, a new vow, under his ministry.

The only time I remember there being a serious conflict in our Dallas church was when Dr. Rice wanted to pay cash as they built the Tabernacle, and four men, thinking the building program was going too slowly, conspired against it. They wanted to borrow money—and they also wanted to boss the pastor. AND NO ONE BUT THE LORD COULD BOSS DR. RICE!

These good men took a strong stand against a leadership that was being wonderfully blessed of God in the saving of thousands of souls.

Sadly, one of them—a prominent church leader—walked into a place of business and fell dead with a heart attack.

Another of the four was rushed to a hospital desperately sick. The doctors could not diagnose his trouble. He died within two days.

Another, strangely enough, a man with a large family, was suddenly drafted into the Air Force. When he was being moved from one camp to another, the plane crashed and he was killed.

All three gone in such a short time!

The blessed anointed ministry of Dr. Rice continued. People saw the hand of God at work. The whole community were talking about God's dealing with these individuals.

God intercedes for His own.

† † †

Now, after holding successful pastorates in Texas totaling some 18 years, the Sword and Dr. Rice's ministry prepared to move to Wheaton, Illinois, 30 miles west of Chicago, leaving behind 1700 beloved members and over 7,000 conversions, to go to cold Yankee country where we didn't know a soul. It was hard to leave all these warm surroundings, including our loved ones, and dwell in the land of a stranger; but Dr. Rice believed he had seen the cloudy pillar move and had heard our Leader's voice bidding him to "go forward"; so in trustful obedience we folded our tents and departed to the "place of which he has told us."

Wheaton was more in the center of the country, and Dr. Rice desired his daughters to be educated at Wheaton College, then the strongest and largest of the independent Christian colleges in America. It was outspokenly Christian and vigorous in its defense of the Faith and had the highest scholastic standards.

In Wheaton, population about 10,000, he set up his publishing business and attractive bookstore under the corporation name, Sword of the Lord Foundation. The new Sword of the Lord address became: 512 West Franklin Street, Wheaton, Illinois.

Miss Fairy, Miss Lola and I moved with the family.

Dr. Rice now gave himself to conducting revivals and conferences on revival and soul winning, still editing THE SWORD OF THE LORD from wherever his temporary location might have been as he traveled with his wife and secretary and revival staff. That soul-winning SWORD was always on his mind, wherever he was. Once he wrote:

> If these gray hairs which have frosted my head came because of the burdens of THE SWORD OF THE LORD, then I welcome

them and thank God! For the weariness, for the unceasing burden, for the tears spent in this holy cause, I thank God. Children are not born without travail, and a blessed work for God cannot be done without toil and prayers and tears and endless hours.

Dr. Rice held twenty-two meetings the year he left the pastorate and made his move north, all in Illinois, Indiana and Michigan, occasionally getting back to home base!

He bought a large house, and the Rice home for two years was also the office for the paper and the many Sword books. In 1942 a basement office was rented in the business section of Wheaton. This action was followed in 1946 with the purchase of a brick warehouse adjacent to the police station. In 1952 another brick building was purchased to take care of the growing ministry. Expansion plans continued with the purchase, in 1954, of the First Presbyterian Church properties. At that time it seemed advisable to obtain this strategic property for erection of the large, modern, efficient plant with all Sword offices and enterprises under one roof.

But God had other plans.... (Discussed later)

The front hall of the house at 512 West Franklin became the bookstore. In the dining room resided the Graphotype for making stencils of the subscribers and the addressograph for addressing labels for the magazine. Crowded into the adjoining sun room were desks for the secretaries, who shared bedrooms with the Rice girls. On the third floor (or attic) were stored the thousands of books waiting to be mailed out. And would you believe that, in order to get them down, someone threw the packages out the attic window to the second floor. Then the one there pitched them on down to the porch! That sure beat the long climb up and down stairs!

And every Rice girl had assigned responsibilities in the work, doing whatever needed to be done in order to get the paper out to a growing subscription list.

When asked, "Did you ever resent using your home and girls in this manner?" dear and beloved Mrs. Rice answered, astonished, "Certainly not! It was my ministry, too!" This great lady was totally absorbed in joining her husband in the ministry.

It did not take long for all of us to know that Dr. Rice had made the right choice in choosing Wheaton. The spirit of the town was different from anything we had ever known. Wheaton was known as *"Saints' Rest"* because so many missionaries retired there or came for refreshing and fellowship. Many of God's dear saints made this their home—I could not begin to call the roll. I know that Dr. Torrey's widow lived a few blocks from the Rices. Dr. Charles Blanchard's widow and daughter taught Sunday school classes at one of the churches. Dr. H. A. Ironside of Moody Church once lived there, as did many Moody Institute teachers and evangelists and other Christian workers. Consecrated Christian young people liked to gather there.

We were never lonely but felt we were among lifelong friends. I was astonished at the bond of love that existed among us who were in some sense strangers. The ties of blood—Christ's blood—were very strong; and sweet was the fellowship of His dear children.

We who worked in the office were highly esteemed in Wheaton because of our work for the Lord. Young people (we were young then!) were unusually kind, wanting us to take part in all the activities we had time for.

The spiritual blessings were not all. In early May the region became a veritable park; the spring season opened with a riot of color. The lilacs and tulips were gorgeous; then followed the bridal wreath and iris. After the iris season there came in a regular carnival of flowers—I could not begin to name them.

The trees were taller than the many two-story houses, and there were avenues of them. And there was a wealth of grass.

No one was allowed to fire a gun in Wheaton, so squirrels romped and played at the very doors of homes. Birds built their nests in the trees, unafraid, and the rabbits hopped about like pets. Then there were no beer parlors nor taverns in town. Liquor could not be delivered there. (This may still be true.)

The weather seemed about perfect. We sometimes wore spring coats on the Fourth of July! "Yes," but some said, "wait until winter comes and the thermometer registers zero and below; then you will wish for the sunny South." But there were storm windows, and a big furnace kept every room at a pleasant seventy degrees.

And I loved that deep, beautiful, white snow! Though it was sometimes heavy and lingered a few weeks, we prepared ourselves for it. And when we decided to move from Wheaton, Illinois to Murfreesboro, Tennessee, one regret was leaving behind all that beauty.

Mrs. Rice and I many times said, "Wheaton was the best years of our lives"—and we meant every word. Those twenty-three years there were blessed years, years I would enjoy living over again.

Dr. and Mrs. Rice's home at 512 W. Franklin in Wheaton, Illinois, where 6 little girls grew up and married

Mrs. Rice and her six girls in Daddy's absence: Libby, Mary Lloys, Grace, Joanna, Joy and Jessie. (Both Grace and Mrs. Rice are now with Dr. Rice in Heaven.)

1941

One outstanding event in 1941 was with Dr. Theodore H. Epp of Back-to-the-Bible broadcast fame.

In January and February Dr. Epp conducted a "radio revival" with Dr. Rice speaking for a month, the broadcasts going out from Grand Island, Nebraska; Yankton, South Dakota; and Shenandoah, Iowa.

Dr. Epp later reported:

> We can truly say the radio revival was the means of setting on fire a revival that is sweeping this whole north central section of the nation. The number cannot be definitely set. As in Christ's time, there was but one out of the ten who returned to thank Him. So we do not know how many made their confession, but we have heard from over one thousand. And the many who did not write in will be heard from in Glory! What a day of rejoicing that will be!

† † †

Returning from Grand Island, Dr. Rice spent a few weeks at home, turning down many invitations so that he could do a little catching up and get some rest, read and enjoy his family. But even while in Wheaton, he spoke in churches all around there and in the Chicago area. Miss Lola and I would go along and take down in shorthand his sermons and those of other men, to use in THE SWORD OF THE LORD. Never a dull moment!

While in Wheaton, each Sunday morning she or I would stenographically record messages by Rev. Charles E. Fuller of the Old-Fashioned Revival Hour, broadcast from Long Beach, California. In those early days, almost every week THE SWORD contained one of his sermons.

And often I was at a front table in my own Wheaton Bible Church with pencil and shorthand book taking down my own pastor, Rev. J. C. Macaulay's, sermons. Dr. Ironside was near, so we could record his messages. In those early days, the main sermons were those we "went after" week by week.

Soon Dr. Rice was on the road again, holding three- and four-week revivals in churches throughout the Northeast, and tent revivals.

His ministry was always colorful (he was often called the Will Rogers of the pulpit because of their great resemblance)—and he was controversial. His attacks on sin reminded one of Elijah and John the Baptist, but his sympathetic and tender heart was more like John the apostle.

He fought the vices of his day—and he did more. He kept on warning of the false teachings that were creeping into Southern Baptist schools and behind their pulpits—a prophecy which we are seeing come to pass today in the ranks of the SBC. Dr. Rice never bowed the knee to Baal, never sought to bend the truth to fit the whims and wishes of men. In his own words:

> Had Peter and Paul and Stephen been compromisers, they would never have won a martyr's crown. Had John the Baptist given in a little, no doubt he could have had the friendship of Herod. There was no compromise in those who were sawn asunder, stoned, imprisoned for Christ's sake. Indeed, they were radical and will not be sorry on that blessed resurrection morning that they gave up their lives rather than compromise. I too want to be in that number when the saints go marching in.
>
> The man who fears God fears nothing as far as this world is concerned.

Dr. Rice swung the sword of the Spirit, and he swung it hard. Indeed, he swung it with bowed head and with both shoulders. And as he swung it, he hadn't the slightest concern about who might be in the way. Many earnest Christians disagreed with him, but no one had the slightest doubt about where he stood. His feet were cemented firmly to the Rock, and no amount of money or pressure could persuade him to move—or even to lean. The only fear he knew was the fear of the Lord.

† † †

In the fall, he was at home pushing for subscriptions to THE SWORD OF THE LORD. A goal of 5,000 was set. In the office we put this figure in large letters on the wall and daily prayed for it. In those days, 5,000 subscriptions were a whole bunch!

Now Grace, a freshman in Wheaton College, had said to her dad, **"Daddy, don't you think we sometimes set our goals too high and do not reach them?"**

Dr. Rice often remarked to those looking over his books at the table, "I have read these books and find them to be sound...."

During his citywide revivals, he pounded home many a point.

That lay on Dr. Rice's mind and heart heavily. So he said to the Lord, "Lord, You heard my daughter's question. She hasn't tried You as often as I have. Lord, prove that goal is not too high. Strengthen her faith. Show her that You answer her daddy's prayers!"

Dr. Rice left for a meeting in Toronto. When the campaign ended, believe me when I say that we could write him, "Praise the Lord! He sent us exactly 5,000 trial subscriptions"!

Dr. Rice commented, "At this, my own faith was strengthened. And how happy I was for my children to see it! Big prayers, when answered, stop doubts, glorify God, strengthen Christians and convict sinners."

† † †

During these World War II days, Dr. Rice wrote a most popular book on war. Answering the question, "Should Christians fight?" it proved a blessing to our soldiers in the camps and to their families in the homes.

† † †

So vivid in my mind is an answer to prayer about *The Coming Kingdom of Christ* book. The type was being set; the printer sent word that he would have to buy more metal before he could finish the typesetting, so he needed money. We did not have it, but Dr. Rice called three of us in to pray with him about this particular need.

Before the day was over, enough money was on hand to buy the type metal and proceed with the typesetting.

† † †

Two years before the publication of Dr. Rice's *Soul Winner's Fire,* four of us agreed to pray that God would help him get ready a book on soul winning. And we asked that it be published in the Colportage Library Series of the Moody Press.

Dr. Rice commented: "That incident was forgotten until after the book was in print. Then one day while turning through the book of prayers recorded, I came across that request with our names signed to it, and I marked on the opposite page: ANSWERED AUG. 1941."

1942 Dr. Epp was ordering our booklets by the thousands—10,000 *Religious But Lost*, 10,000 *All Have Sinned*, etc., to be distributed to his daily radio listeners. The Soldiers' and Airmen's Christian Association of Canada used thousands of Dr. Rice's *"What Must I Do to Be Saved?"* among the soldiers. Chaplains and others in our own country wanted the same booklet for men in our own armed forces. These were going out free to servicemen.

† † †

July 19th, Dr. Rice was invited back to Dallas to help celebrate the Tenth Anniversary of the church he founded in 1932. A big paved lot beside the church was lighted, and great crowds assembled for four nights. Now this "mother" church had daughter churches in several parts of Dallas.

Dr. Wells, who succeeded Dr. Rice at Galilean Baptist Church, had done well in Dallas.

† † †

In October an eight-day Conference on Evangelism was held at Bethany Reformed Church, Chicago, with speakers Oswald J. Smith, Joe Henry Hankins, Harry Hager (the pastor), P. W. Philpott, Robert J. Wells, H. A. Ironside, Dr. Rice and soloist Elbert Tindley. The church had a seating capacity of 1,100, and it was filled to overflowing, with people present from many states.

It was during this conference that at 2:00 in the morning at a southside Chicago YMCA Dr. Rice discharged the burden on his heart by definitely committing himself to God to bring back mass evangelism and citywide campaigns to America. Watch and see what happened!

† † †

Summing up 1942: About 215 people wrote that they were saved this year through our books and THE SWORD OF THE LORD. There were

120 full-length messages printed in THE SWORD this year (4 pages), and we distributed one-third of a million booklets, *"What Must I Do to Be Saved?"*

1943 Dr. Rice borrowed J. Stratton Shufelt from Moody Church to help him in a four-week union tent revival in North Minneapolis June 27 through July 25, with sixteen churches cooperating. Night after night the big tent was packed, while some, unable to find a seat, sat in cars.

This was the first union revival in this city in twenty years.

He preached to great crowds on such searching subjects as: "An Old-Fashioned, Holy Ghost, City-Shaking, Soul-Saving Revival—How to Have It in Minneapolis"; "Is There a Bible Hell of Fire?" "Sins That Block Christians' Prayers"; "Blood on Your Hands"; "When Skeletons Come Out of Their Closets" and "When God's Patience Wears Out."

Scores of Christians were blessed, and many precious souls were saved.

† † †

Later, in Huntington, West Virginia, 20 churches united in an ambitious effort to win the lost. On many occasions the 1,324 opera seats in the East High School auditorium were filled, and some remained standing.

We know many were saved, though we did not receive the final report.

† † †

In October a PARTNERSHIP OF EVANGELISTS TO PROMOTE UNION CAMPAIGNS was formed, an organization to promote *citywide* union campaigns. The strictest code of professional ethics was adopted. Dr. Robert Wells was elected as the Executive Secretary.

In the years after Billy Sunday ended his mammoth revival campaigns, evangelism was in disrepute and evangelists were scorned. For years no great citywide revivals were held.

But Dr. Rice set out to bring back the day of revival to America. And by God's grace and with the help and prayers of a few others who took their stand, once again revivals could be seen in many of our great cities.

Perhaps more than any other living man, Dr. Rice was responsible for bringing citywide campaigns back to America in the forties and fifties—when such campaigns and mass evangelism had disappeared. When nobody else was doing it, he began conducting great united crusades and encouraged others to do it.

All over America, in England and in Canada, evangelists had been overwhelmed in the tides of modernism, worldliness, denominationalism and ultra-dispensationalism. Disheartened, abused and scorned, many of them lost their courage. Some went into the pastorate, while others founded tabernacles and Bible centers.

Evangelists began to be ashamed of the hated though scriptural title "evangelist," so started calling themselves "Bible teachers" and "world travelers."

But during it all, Dr. Rice was still calling himself an evangelist and was being used of God to hold great revivals, as evidenced by these reports and pictures.

He set about to encourage evangelists. He introduced thirty or forty to the public, who went on to be greatly used of God. He opened doors for evangelists and evangelism. Then he established a string of conferences on revival and soul winning designed to promote evangelism and revivals. In those early days they were called "Conferences on Evangelism." And he himself was setting an example in citywide campaigns and utilizing the power of the printing press.

Along with his own writing on revival themes, Dr. Rice selected the best writing of soul winners of the past and encouraged present-day leaders to contribute revival theme articles to THE SWORD OF THE LORD.

† † †

Through the first eleven months of 1943, a total of 666 wrote to say they had found Christ through Sword literature. We failed to print the December results. Foreign decisions were never recorded. We had been asked by missionaries to send all names to them for follow-up. Nevertheless, we rejoiced in every foreign soul who trusted Christ.

1944 Dr. Rice continually reported meetings held by evangelists, whether one-church or citywide, encouraging them every way possible. He used their messages in THE SWORD OF THE LORD. He printed their books. He wrote articles on evangelists and evangelism. By letter he encouraged them to hold citywide meetings. Very few were doing it. But ever on his heart were revivals and soul winning and bringing back great revivals to America.

Dr. Rice himself began getting more and more calls for citywide campaigns.

Knowing the importance of a good song leader, he secured J. Stratton Shufelt who for seven years had been director of young people, choir director and soloist at Moody Memorial Church, Chicago, where Dr. H. A. Ironside was then pastor. Mr. Shufelt was the successor of Ira D. Sankey, who sang in the same church in the former smaller building.

He soloed with marvelous winsomeness, directed the choir with mastery and led the congregational singing with such success as we have seldom seen.

"EVERETT FOR CHRIST"

Back in 1910 Billy Sunday conducted a stirring revival in the Pacific Northwest city of Everett, Washington. Reports were that no successful union campaign had been conducted in this Puget Sound port since that time, until Dr. Rice was invited by some twenty churches of many denominations to hold a similar meeting.

The Rice-Shufelt campaign met in the 2,200-seat spacious Civic Auditorium. Crowds assembled nightly to hear the forceful preaching.

Because of the extensive radio ministry broadcast direct from the platform, vast numbers of the unsaved came as well as Christians. Many delegations attended from surrounding communities. Officers and employees of the major industrial plants made up delegations to sit in special reserved sections.

The Rice-Shufelt party appeared at the State Reformatory in Monroe,

Washington. After a stirring message, hundreds of these men bowed their heads in prayer, and some trusted the Saviour. The team was invited into schools. Two whole nights of prayer were conducted.

The initiator of the campaign, Rev. Forrest E. Johnson, wrote:

> The Everett-for-Christ campaign is history now. But what a remarkable chapter of history it is! Never before has the discussion of a religious meeting been upon the lips of so many people. Never before have the Lord's people been so encouraged to "Press the battle e'er the night shall veil the glowing skies." Never before have preachers felt their responsibility to the lost and to the saved as in these remarkable days of visitation of blessing. . . .
>
> Dr. Rice, not one pastor cooperating in the campaign registered any major criticism. At the same time, all agreed that the Devil never took a greater beating in this city than during these three weeks. Oh, what victories were won! The fact that the messages were broadcast each evening, I am sure more than doubled the results. . . .
>
> The record of decisions of those whose record we were able to get totaled 292. But there were many more. I personally know of others who accepted Christ who were not in the inquiry room where a record would have been obtained.
>
> How we praise God for the great number of high school kids who were saved. I personally received thirty-nine cards from those who gave our church as their preference. . . .
>
> I am sure that you and Mr. Shufelt must have been persuaded that you were greatly loved by the people of Everett, when that crowd of over 300 gathered at the depot to say a fond farewell to ones who had been used of God to lift them into a newer and better relationship with Christ. They continued to sing and weep until the last coach of the Empire Builder swung around the curve and under the tunnel and out of view. Full well, many realized that they doubtlessly will never see your face again until "the day break, and the shadows flee away". . . .

The final count sent to our office was: "430 professions of faith."

Remember, people were not seeing great revivals in the forties and into the fifties. But Dr. Rice, under God, was getting them started once again. Won't you agree that he was beginning to prove that mass evangelism was not dead, as so many had been crying—probably mostly because they were not trying?

CHRIST FOR GREATER BUFFALO

Commencing with an Easter sunrise service and running for three weeks in April, the Rice-Shufelt team led a citywide crusade in the Kleinhan's Music Hall, Buffalo, New York, with 114 churches cooperating.

Great preparation was made prior to the revival. A huge sign was suspended across a principal downtown street, announcing the evangelist's coming. Nearly 200,000 blotters were put in practically every door of the city and in some homes outside the city, along with a copy of Dr. Rice's 24-page booklet, *"What Must I Do to Be Saved?"*

Great crowds came. Night after night scores walked forward to receive Christ. The last night, 3,759 jammed the Music Hall, with hundreds standing and many others not allowed inside because of firemen's regulations.

Chairman of the committee in charge of records, Rev. Donald Dibble, reported a total of 997 professions of faith, with 34 others surrendering to full-time service.

I will quote only one letter from a cooperating pastor, though many others wrote glowingly of the revival in their city.

All Brethren Interested in Union Revival Meetings:

In spite of Evangelist John R. Rice's high reputation throughout the nation, when a large union campaign was proposed for Buffalo, many local ministers desired to cooperate but had not met him. The enthusiasm of those brethren who knew him rapidly overcame the objections that naturally came to the surface, which summed up pretty much the sentiment that Dr. Rice was a fine, sincere, name-calling, Hell-fire southern evangelist, all very good and proper in the Bible Belt but quite too light for sophisticated Western New Yorkers, to whom must necessarily come a more "intellectual approach."

Frankly—I say it to the shame and added confusion of pseudo-erudite brethren in this area—Dr. Rice turned out to be a scholarly gentleman, lacking no depth nor charm, possessed of rare common sense and the finest cooperating evangelist we of the local promoting group have ever seen anywhere. Testimony is unanimous to this.

One way in which this cooperation was best exhibited was in Dr. Rice's complete submergence of his own financial program to that of the local committee. There is not a mercenary hair on his head.

As to Dr. Rice's preaching: People of all classes and church backgrounds frankly were delighted with it. Of course, a few heard, were hurt and stayed away; but for every one of those, there were a dozen whose scoffing turned to praise.

As to Dr. Rice's invitations: They are simple to understand, easy to accept and prolonged with tact only as long as the people respond. There is complete absence of hysterical bellowing and cajoling; rather the loving, patient entreaty of one whose obvious concern is for souls.

We have made a new Christian friend in John R. Rice, and we want him back in Buffalo in the Lord's time.

Walter Vail Watson, Pastor
Bethlehem Presbyterian Church

† † †

When Dr. Rice and Mr. Shufelt were not in citywide revivals, they were in many one-church campaigns throughout the year.

Dr. Rice's bold, fearless, yet compassionate preaching, coupled with Stratton Shufelt's heartwarming solos as well as the outstanding quality of his song directing, made a combination which could be ranked as one of the nation's effective evangelistic teams.

† † †

And THE SWORD OF THE LORD grew in spite of its being a "stepchild"!

Dr. Rice read assiduously, discarded and edited material—he was ever looking for articles to use. All the important matters of policy-making, long-range planning and the actual decisions as to what was to go into THE SWORD were done by him, whether on the road or at home. But to handle the myriad of details which came between that step and the actual reading of the paper, he had an efficient and dependable staff. Well aware of the importance of his staff, Dr. Rice often expressed his appreciation to each in person. He was well aware that no man, though superstar, works alone; it takes a team.

As the subscription list grew and as more and more books came off the press, more and more workers were hired. Soon there was a staff of fifteen, twenty, twenty-five. As we grew, so did the staff.

In expressing his deep appreciation for their loyalty and devotion, Dr. Rice once wrote to the staff:

My workers multiply my ministry many fold. When God begins to hand out rewards, you may be sure that the thousands saved through our literature will not all be accredited to me, but much of the honor and reward will go to you who "stay by the stuff," who do the drudgery necessary in getting out THE SWORD OF THE LORD each week and in getting out books and pamphlets to many hundreds of thousands.

One can do a little, but one hundred can do much. So you are very valuable to this ministry—with your time, your thoughts, your prayers, your LABOR and sometimes your tears.

† † †

Dr. Robert J. Wells had been pastor in Dallas for about five years—and a successful one. He had led in the founding of the Dallas Bible Institute and was president of the Dallas and East Texas Regional Association of the National Association of Evangelicals.

Dr. Wells had a special aptitude in setting up evangelistic meetings. Best of all, he was a great Bible teacher. His doctrinal position and Dr. Rice's were identical.

In September, Dr. Wells resigned the Galilean Baptist Church to become an evangelist and to be associate editor of THE SWORD OF THE LORD. But he actually did more. He was director of the Sword Book Club and director of the Sword of the Lord Conferences at Winona Lake and elsewhere.

When the evangelistic work became tremendously demanding, at the end of 1947 he resigned his Sword duties but remained as a Sword Book Club judge and consented to write more for THE SWORD than before and to continue to occasionally chair some Sword Conferences.

1945 Dr. Rice was invited for seventeen years to the Evansville Rescue Mission in Evansville, Indiana, headed by Dr. Ernest I. Reveal.

This was more than a rescue mission. It combined rescue mission work, relief work among the poor and a summer camp for boys, girls and mothers; handled employment cases, and was a center for this whole area for revival and Bible conference services.

White-haired Pappy Reveal was a cripple. He leaned against things when he prayed. Standing one day on the streets of Evansville, he looked at a building just vacated by the Chamber of Commerce, then walked over, leaned against it, took off his hat and said, *"O God, if You'll give me this building, You and I will do something in this town that will make Heaven glad."*

Within a few weeks Reveal had moved in and opened the Evansville Rescue Mission, now known around the world. The greatest evangelists of the world have preached from its pulpit.

Thousands upon thousands of dollars dropped, as it were, from Heaven for "Pappy's" mission in answer to prayer.

One day a director of a bank in Evansville phoned the president and said, "Do you know what's happening to our bank? Reveal is out there leaning against it with his hat in his hand. You know what that means!"

The president said he called all the directors and sent a large check without Reveal ever coming inside the bank and asking for one dime!

Evansville knew that a miracle-working God was working, hand in hand, with this simple though strange man of prayer.

So it was refreshing to go see Pappy and Ma Reveal!

Later, upon his death, Mrs. Reveal wrote:

"He made a quick getaway . . . and has now seen Jesus and is going up and down the streets of Glory fellowshiping with the many he knew, and hobnobbing with the angels."

† † †

CHRIST FOR GREATER CLEVELAND

Evangelists told them that everywhere they were greeted with the words, "Cleveland is a difficult place." Many in Cleveland were aware that Roger Babson had spoken of the area between Cleveland, Ohio and Erie, Pennsylvania as the coldest part of the United States spiritually.

Then, too, some of the pastors had heard Mrs. "Ma" Sunday relate that Cleveland was the only major city which refused to allow her husband to conduct an evangelistic campaign. Everyone owned that men like Moody, Torrey and others had said that Cleveland was the graveyard of evangelism. They had not had reviving since R. A. Torrey had held a campaign there thirty years prior to 1945.

But many of the good pastors, believing they served a living Saviour, refused to believe all they were hearing, but kept crying out with Habakkuk, "O Lord, revive thy work in the midst of the years, in the midst of the years make known; in wrath remember mercy."

The 100 clergymen who had met each Monday since 1944 to pray for revival said, "We had preached on prayer and seldom prayed. The worth of soul winning had been our subject, and we had not been subject to the command to win souls."

After putting their all on the altar and confessing their failures, they prayed on for an evangelist for a thirty-day period in February and March. Nine names were submitted, with Dr. John R. Rice's topping the list. They contacted him, saying, "Thousands of souls are dying without Christ in Cleveland, and we need an evangelist."

Dr. Rice, with Dr. Wells, went to them within the week to look things over and to make plans.

The dates were cleared, the place was set. The Rice-Shufelt team, sponsored by 118 ministers and several organizations, opened the campaign on February 11, 1945.

The Public Music Hall was secured, seating 3,000, and the meeting was on. Crowds were coming. The manager of the auditorium said, "Your Sunday night crowd was phenomenal. You are doing the impossible!"—the very one who had warned pastors ahead of time that such a campaign would not succeed in Cleveland! The revival influence began to spread over the adjacent part of Ohio.

Under the Spirit-driven messages of Dr. Rice and the singing by Mr. Shufelt, there just had to be results. It was not unusual to see elderly men and women, husbands and wives, sweethearts, many young people and

**3,767 by count March 11, 1945 in Union Revival Campaign,
Cleveland, Ohio. This was in the forties, when mass evangelism
had disappeared—they said!**

Many of Dr. Rice's early campaigns were in the open air.

A typical preaching
scene

The three preacher Rices—Bill, John,
Joe—at Cedar Lake, Indiana, 1950

serious-faced children streaming into the inquiry room.

The work of the personal workers was made easier by the clarity of the messages delivered and the clear-cut invitations.

I can't recall, in all the revival meetings I attended all over the United States, seeing so many gray-haired, tottering men and women come forward as in this meeting.

Then husbands and wives on the verge of separation were gloriously saved and reconciled.

Many Catholics of both Roman and Greek churches attended. The Lord had given great tactfulness to Dr. Rice to so preach the Gospel as to win many of these souls from the darkness of Romanism.

Only the records of Heaven contain the full story of those marvelous nights, but we shall have all eternity to hear of the wonders of His grace that were displayed in four weeks of Heaven-sent revival in Cleveland when so many souls found rest in the Lord Jesus!

Thank You, Lord, for allowing me to be there!

In these campaigns, usually Mrs. Rice and I, or his daughter Grace and I, were traveling with him. The office work had to go on. THE SWORD OF THE LORD had to get out every week. Letters had to be answered. Every day our Wheaton office sent a huge envelope of mail that had come that day.

Grace not only helped in office work, but she was the pianist. And Mrs. Rice sold books, cooked our meals and kept us happy. And we three had the joy of winning many to the Lord.

† † †

By May of 1945 the subscription list had grown to 43,000 circulation. And the price had increased to $1.50 a year. We were hearing so many good reports from readers about souls saved, lives changed; and many preachers were elated over the content of the paper.

† † †

By now, a renewed interest in evangelism and revivals was sweeping over the land. Great, stirring union evangelistic campaigns were being held in many of the largest cities of the nation, with many thousands turning to Christ. Individual church revivals were being held with greater interest than in many years. A tremendously effective evangelistic program was being blessed of the Lord for the young people of the nation under the direction of Youth for Christ movements through which hundreds of thousands were meeting on Saturday nights and multiplied hundreds were finding Christ. Thousands of sinners were responding to the gospel invitation as it was being given over the radio from coast to coast, while other thousands were being reached by the printed message of the Gospel which was going forth with more vigor and favor than at any other time in the history of our great country.

Yes, these were days of opportunity—but also days of challenge. We were witnessing only the beginning of what we had hoped might be one of the greatest revivals America had ever seen.

Of course THE SWORD OF THE LORD was vitally interested in what was taking place. This paper was founded for the purpose of promoting interest in revivals among God's people as well as for bringing the gospel message to the lost. The editor had solemnly vowed before God he would dedicate his life to proving that the days of great revivals, of sweeping mass evangelism, were not over.

Under God, he had been privileged to have no small part in helping bring about the greatly increased interest in evangelism.

Because Dr. Rice felt the importance of the challenge, because he felt his responsibility before God and man to have a greater part in the acceptance of the challenge, because of an overwhelming burden for the millions of lost people in sin-ridden America, THE SWORD OF THE LORD took the initiative in planning for great Sword Conferences which would reach thousands of needy preachers.

Once D. L. Moody planned such conferences on evangelism at Northfield, Massachusetts. Later J. Wilbur Chapman, Billy Sunday and William Biederwolf held such conferences at Winona Lake. But not for many years had there been any one program with so many outstanding successful evangelists on the program to preach revival, to tell how it is done, to demonstrate soul-winning passion and power and preaching and methods. And Dr. Rice was the first to sponsor such conferences on such a wide geographical scale.

Jesus spent most of the nearly three years of His ministry teaching, training, showing His disciples what it was all about. Perhaps others would have rushed about organizing churches. They would have put on big money drives. But Jesus did not. He got His disciples ready for the task that was theirs.

Dr. Rice felt that young preachers were the salt of the earth. In some sense they were pioneers, with all the courage that marked God's true servants of past generations. They worked hard and faithfully.

Once when it was reported that a professor felt it was his job to "take the starch out of young preachers," "No!" he was told. "They need to be encouraged and enheartened! The world, the flesh and the Devil will 'take the starch out' of them. Let us give them heartfelt love and admiration!"

Dr. Rice had a great love for preachers, as you will see as you read on.

Only Heaven's records will reveal the eternal worth of these conferences. The number of preachers who have had their visions lifted and enlarged, their hearts fired, their spirits revived, their ministries totally transformed in Sword of the Lord Conferences, is beyond comprehension. No doubt the conferences, in the years ahead, will prove to be one of Dr. John R. Rice's greatest accomplishments.

† † †

Winona Lake, Indiana

Who could ever forget July 15 through 21, 1945 at Winona Lake, Indiana, when the Sword of the Lord sponsored its first annual Conference on Evangelism! For three years this conference was held there, and additional conferences were sponsored in Toronto, Los Angeles and Chicago. Since then, Sword of the Lord Conferences on Revival and Soul Winning have been held in almost every part of the United States.

The theme of this Winona Lake conference was "REVIVAL, THE NEED OF THE HOUR," with all the messages centering around this theme to present the technical, devotional, inspirational and practical aspects of evangelism.

Who was on the first program at Winona Lake? John R. Rice...Hyman Appelman...Bob Jones, Sr....Joe Henry Hankins...Sam Morris...B. R. Lakin... Robert J. Wells...Jesse M. Hendley—to name a few. J. Stratton Shufelt and Rev. and Mrs. Elbert T. Tindley were in charge of the music. Dr. Robert J. Wells was director and presided with dignity and grace.

The crowds were immense. Practically every state and a number of Canadian provinces were represented.

Dr. Bob Jones, Sr., was such an authority on evangelism after 46 years of experience, that we were especially happy to have his comment on the Winona Lake Sword Conference:

> I have had a wide experience over a period of a good many years and have been in touch with most of the great evangelistic movements in this generation. But I have never witnessed more spiritual meetings than the meetings I have attended here this week. In the palmy days of evangelism I never heard greater or more powerful evangelistic messages than I have heard on the platform this week. I should also like to say that I have never heard a group of preachers who seemed to have such a passion for souls or who seemed to be so unselfishly interested in having a revival of "old-time religion."

"Ma" Sunday

Mrs. W. A. ("Ma") Sunday also wrote:

> "I thank God I have lived to attend the Sword Conference on Evangelism. I have been inspired and encouraged. I see the light breaking through the clouds. I can almost feel the fire of revival. I'm glad I've helped hold the ropes here at Winona through the years so a conference of this deep spiritual nature could be possible."

Winona Lake Conference ground was made famous by Billy Sunday and made dear to the hearts of thousands because of the blessings received there. It had become the world's largest Bible conference grounds, in some sense, the granddaddy of them all. There Homer Rodeheaver lived and made his headquarters until he took off for Heaven. There the Billy Sunday home is located.

The Sword held three great conferences at Winona Lake.

SWORD BOOK CLUB Announced on March 23, 1945

The latest service offered by the Sword of the Lord had been upon our hearts for some time. As we watched the progress of secular book clubs, influential in getting hundreds of thousands of people to read books—special, selected books, chosen by their committees and offered to the public each month—we felt impressed with the need for such a book club for Christians. We thought, "Why couldn't the Sword of the Lord provide such a club?"

It was not long until the desire became a purpose, and the purpose became a reality. We prayed, we planned, we trusted, we worked.

Our desire was to emphasize books of the highest caliber possible. We hoped to inform the Christian public of the most excellent books published from month to month, to encourage book reading and to provide them as inexpensively as possible. Our motto was: *"The Best Christian Book Each Month Selected by America's Outstanding Christian Leaders."* There is nothing better than the best, and we decided nothing but the best would do.

Our board of fourteen judges were: Dr. John W. Bradbury, editor of *Watchman-Examiner;* Dr. V. Raymond Edman, president of Wheaton College; Dr. Henry Hepburn, pastor of Buena Memorial Presbyterian Church, Chicago; Dr. H. A. Ironside, pastor of Moody Memorial Church, Chicago; Rev. Torrey M. Johnson, director of National Youth for Christ; Dr. Robert G. Lee, pastor of Bellevue Baptist Church, Memphis, Tennessee; Dr. Pat M. Neff, president of Baylor University and of the Southern Baptist Convention, formerly governor of Texas; Dr. T. Roland Phillips, pastor of Arlington Presbyterian Church, Baltimore, Maryland; Dr. Robert Lee Stuart, president, Taylor University, Upland, Indiana; Dr. Louis T. Talbot, president of Bible Institute of Los Angeles and pastor of Church of the Open Door, Los Angeles; Dr. Hyman Appelman, a converted Jewish attorney who was being greatly used in revivals; Dr. Z. T. Johnson, a prominent Methodist, a widely experienced speaker and president of Asbury College; Dr. Bob Jones, Jr., president of Bob Jones College and famous Shakespearean and dramatic scholar; and Dr. John R. Rice.

Dr. Robert Wells became director of the Sword Book Club.

Month after month the judges selected, the people joined, and the Sword ordered and mailed out the best books available, at the least possible price. (In one month, 524 joined. It averaged nearly 200 new members a month.)

This was another great but rewarding undertaking.

Members received the monthly Sword Book Club News.

The membership reached as high as 5,000 members.

After many people were getting behind in their payments and we were going broke, this service was discontinued. But it was a great venture as long as we could afford it.

† † †

November 4 through 25 found Dr. Rice in a union campaign in Seattle, Washington, sponsored by 52 fundamental pastors and churches. There were 497 public professions. One of note was an elder in the Mormon Church and grandson of Brigham Young, co-founder of the Mormon Church, who was happily converted.

† † †

And on Dr. Rice's 50th birthday—December 11—we reached 50,000 subscriptions! This was an exciting time! Six years ago it had less than 5,000 circulation. The growth was steady and solid, on the average doubling every two years.

A little background as to the 50,000 subscriptions.

Dr. Wells and others had carried on a subscription drive, keeping secret the number coming in. We were striving to get 50,000 subscriptions by Dr. Rice's 50th birthday.

On December 20 the staff gave a combined birthday-Christmas party on the second floor of the Sword of the Lord building in Wheaton. After a delicious dinner, some games and a brief devotional by Evangelist Bill Rice, Dr. Rice was presented with a birthday cake with 50 lighted candles and a beautifully lettered and framed plaque which read:

> We, your employees, on behalf of the many intimate friends, subscribers and supporters who have made this event possible, wish to present to you, Dr. John R. Rice, on this your 50th birthday, 50,000 SWORD OF THE LORD subscriptions.
>
> After years of earnest labor and in answer to your own prayers and the prayers of others during the recent subscription campaign, the Lord has seen fit to grant this petition, giving complete victory. I Corinthians 15:58.

Then a walnut office desk was given him on behalf of Sword workers. Dr. Rice had never had anything finer than a secondhand desk, which had cost $25.00, and he was then using an old desk left by a former inhabitant of the building before we purchased it.

So ended a busy but blessed year.

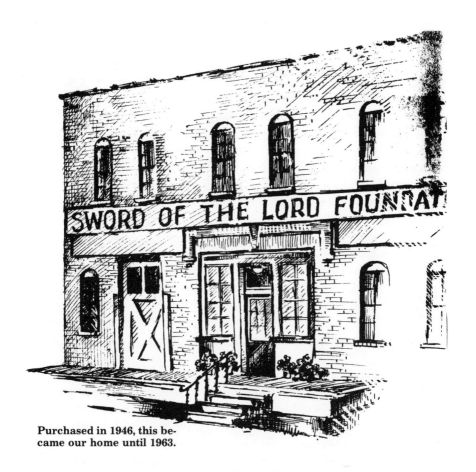

Purchased in 1946, this became our home until 1963.

1946 To those who staffed the offices at 214 West Wesley Street, Wheaton, Illinois, the Sword of the Lord Foundation was a building, a place of business where dedicated hands and minds got out the Gospel.

Though fond thoughts often ran "back home"—to the plains of Kansas or to the booming cities of Texas; to the redbuds of North Carolina or to the lashing whitecaps of Washington's Puget Sound—all came to feel very much at home in Wheaton, as, in reality, they were at home. While their abilities and talents varied as they filled positions as typists, printers, proofreaders, department heads, mail readers or file clerks, they came as consecrated servants of God, working to help Christians and to win lost souls just as surely as does any minister or missionary. Several Sword men were ordained ministers or trained mechanics; one was a doctor, and many of the women had had some training in Christian colleges or Bible schools.

Nearly all Sword of the Lord workers spent a great deal of their free time preaching, teaching Sunday school classes, holding services in missions and jails or helping in other work of the local churches—dedicated hands doing God's business the best they knew how.

This old warehouse, sitting back off the street and next to the police station, holds blessed memories of our 17 years of occupancy.

† † †

To have great union revivals required an enormous amount of organization, promotion, publicity and hard work. Long had we prayed that God would give Dr. Rice an advance man, a special representative with wisdom, training and experience to go into a community where a union revival was proposed, get the pastors and people united behind such a plan and work out the details of the cooperation, auditorium, committees and promotion.

Thank God, prayers were finally answered!

W. F. (Bill) Mann was a mechanical-production-construction engineer of wide experience. Although a comparatively young man, he was called to lay out a large part of the immense Dodge plant in Chicago, which made motors for the Flying Fortress. His engineering crew reworked the retractable landing gear on the Vengeance dive bomber and replaced 700 parts with 12.

Graduate of the University of Pennsylvania, Bill was for a season the head of the archeological and historical work of the state of Pennsylvania Department of Education.

Dr. Rice had met Mr. Mann and had laid on his heart his need for an advance man. When God began dealing with him, the business world lost much of its appeal. So in March this splendid construction and mechanical engineer left his profession to help Dr. Rice set up union revivals.

He at once went to Miami, where he spent a month preceding and during the Rice union campaign there.

Then followed weeks of helping Mr. Willis Haymaker, Dr. Bob Jones' advance man, in the promotion work of the great Chicago united campaign.

I enjoyed so much working with this genius! But he did have one flaw. Having his mind on a thousand other things, he might just open the car door and step out while driving down the highway! So usually his sweet wife Arla or I drove when traveling with him.

What a blessing he was to Dr. Rice the years they worked together!

(Bill, you know how much I love you! And you know I have always thought you were the smartest man I ever knew, with the exception of our Boss!)

Dr. Harrison M. Pierce of Santa Barbara, California, was a physician and surgeon for twenty-two years. At the same time, he was very active in Christian work. Dr. Rice prayed him to Wheaton also to help Bill Mann set up citywide union revivals for him, Dr. Wells and others who desired their superior knowledge in this field.

Having these two advance men proved to be a mighty asset to large-scale revivals.

MIAMI, FLORIDA

In March of 1946, Dr. Rice was officially sponsored by the forty-four churches of the Miami Baptist Association in a 15-day crusade. Decision cards recorded over 600 public professions of faith in the inquiry room; then there were an estimated 400 other professions when the evangelist spoke in the public schools.

We never know all the results at any time, but God's recording angels keep the record, and we rejoice in every soul that was saved there.

† † †

"LIFE BEGINS" Campaign in the Arena in Chicago
With Jones—Rood—Rice

The greater Chicago Evangelistic Campaign—"Life Begins"—opened April 28 in the 7,000-seat Chicago arena, with some 200 churches and organizations cooperating. Dr. Bob Jones, Sr., was the speaker for the first two weeks, followed by Dr. Paul Rood for another two weeks; then Dr. Rice had the final two weeks. Mr. Shufelt was in charge of the music.

This was the first citywide union evangelistic campaign in Chicago since Billy Sunday's 1918 meetings twenty-eight years before.

Those saved totaled some 2,000 plus 400 young lives dedicated to Christ. Homes were re-established, separated husbands and wives were reunited, and a new vision was given to all to win the lost at any cost.

† † †

In June Dr. Rice wrote an extended review of a book written by Dr. Lewis

Sperry Chafer[1] called *True Evangelism*,[2] a book that had already done enormous harm. It was written during the heyday of R. A. Torrey, J. Wilbur Chapman, Gipsy Smith and Billy Sunday and was a direct attack on mass evangelism as they practiced it—an attack on their message and methods.

The book was not a protest against men who were false in doctrine or over-commercial or immoral in life. No; it was against *evangelism* itself as known and practiced in America by the greatest soul winners.

Many prominent pastors resented this book, though they had no publication in which they could voice their disapproval.

For twenty years evangelism had had hard sledding, and few people cared to stand up for mass evangelism, as already stated. However, since Dr. Rice was working hard to bring back mass evangelism, he began an all-out attack on *True Evangelism*, published by Moody Press.

At a Sword Conference at Winona Lake, the matter was discussed, and a resolution regarding *True Evangelism* was adopted and signed by forty-seven evangelists present, asking Moody Press to drop this book from their publications.

Others not present had also objected to the book: Dr. P. W. Philpott, Dr. W. B. Riley, Dr. John Brown of John Brown Schools, Dr. H. A. Ironside. Even Dr. Will Houghton, president of Moody Bible Institute, confessed to Dr. Rice that he disagreed with the book's teaching.

When the final word came from Moody Press that they decided to go ahead and reprint the book, Dr. Rice kindly wrote the publishers: "With love for my brethren, with malice toward no one, but simply putting soul winning first, I rest my case with God and with Bible-believing people."

Throughout the long controversy with Moody Press, Dr. Rice was ever so kind. Wasn't that just like him! What an example he was to us all!

---

[1] Dr. Chafer wrote several books, founded the Dallas Theological Seminary and was pastor of Scofield Memorial Church, "but," said Dr. Rice, "he was so largely influenced by John Nelson Darby that he was a hyper-Calvinist and an ultradispensationalist, and this viewpoint made it impossible to have much success as a soul winner. Under his leadership, the church dried up, few souls were saved, and pressure compelled him to surrender the pastorate."

[2] *True Evangelism* was published first by an independent publisher, who lost money and dropped it from his list. Then Sunday School Times published it, letting it go out of print after finding it unprofitable. Then Moody Press took it on and advertised it very widely as a "revolutionary book" which evangelists needed. After Dr. Rice's unfavorable review of the book and added pressure put on them after valiantly fighting for it, they finally disposed of the book and others by Dr. Chafer. Then it was taken over by Van Kampen Press in Wheaton. After losing thousands of dollars, finally they went out of business. Then Dunham Publishing Company in Findlay, Ohio, took it. Dr. Rice, strongly feeling the curse of God was on this book, suggested this: "Watch to see what God will do with Dr. Dunham and his publishing company." We have not heard of this company in years, and likely it is no longer in existence.

CHICAGO, ILLINOIS— "Life Begins" crusade sponsored by more than 200 churches and Christian organizations. Dr. Bob Jones, Sr., was the speaker the first two weeks; Dr. Paul Rood the third week; and Dr. John R. Rice the final fifteen days.

Part of choir at Rice-Shufelt meeting, Cleveland

Stratton Shufelt, who
worked two years with
Dr. Rice in great
meetings; formerly
of Moody Memorial
Church, Chicago

Harry Clarke, who for 8 years
was Billy Sunday's song leader,
joined Dr. Rice in 1946.

Dr. Rice and Mr. Bill Mann,
his advance man

Elbert Tindley, whose father
wrote such songs as "Take
Your Burden to the Lord and
Leave It There" and "Nothing
Between My Soul and My
Saviour." I was never so
moved by singing as by Elbert
Tindley, who sang often in
Sword Conferences.

Dr. Bob Wells, Conference
Director in earlier days

(Left) Albert Lane, our
Four-Star, brilliant pianist

(Below) Viola Walden and
Grace Jean Rice (Dr. Rice's
eldest daughter and
marvelous pianist) who
traveled with the team

Dr. Rice's booklets were being mightily used during wartime by chaplains in the armed forces. For instance—and this letter is just one of scores received—:

ARMY SERVICE FORCES
SEATTLE PORT OF EMBARKATION
Seattle 4, Washington
Port Chaplain's Office
11 May 46
Rev. John R. Rice
Wheaton, Illinois

Dear Brother Rice:

Let me thank you for your literature. Your booklets are the best and most popular of any literature I have had.

Coming back from Yokohama with over 1500 troops it was my privilege to conduct a ten-day revival. God's Word still packs an atomic punch, and the Holy Spirit was attendant. The troop mess hall was packed each night. Men who had committed adultery, fornication, thievery, murder, were pricked by the Sword of the Gospel.

After each service I passed out your books which were on the subjects of the sermon. Every night they cleaned me out of literature. They are so hungry for the truth as set forth in such booklets of yours as: *Hell, "What Must I Do to Be Saved?" Trailed by a Wild Beast* and *A Good Man Lost and a Bad Man Saved.*

There were 105 professions of faith and over 200 rededications in this meeting.

Sir, I want you to know that at the last day of harvest, you shall have a share in the salvation of men you've never heard of or seen. A young Army captain, graduate of West Point, was made to think of his lost condition while reading your tract, *A Good Man Lost and a Bad Man Saved.* A Negro lieutenant with a master's degree felt the call to preach in this meeting.

For myself, let me say, my heart has been lifted by reading your sermons which are being used of God to the salvation of many souls. May God bless you in your ministry in the days ahead. I would certainly appreciate receiving an assortment of anything you wish to send.

> Yours fraternally,
>
> Elmer V. Webb
> Chaplain (1st Lt.) U.S.A.

You may be sure Dr. Rice filled his request.

Just one other among so many:

S. S. "MARINE DEVIL"[3]
S.E.P.E.
Seattle, Washington
16 September 1946
Dr. John R. Rice
Wheaton, Illinois

Dear Dr. Rice:

Your literature was picked up by the men almost exclusively on my last trip, just finished. Especially *Trailed by a Wild Beast* and *A Good Man Lost and a Bad Man Saved.* I am very happy to report that 157 souls were saved. So you see, God uses your pen when you are not even conscious of it! We carried over 1800 men and brought back 2400.

Now can you spare some more literature? I could use 500 each of the above named booklets, plus a great deal other of your gospel literature—if you can spare it. God knows how it is needed, as many of these men have never heard the Gospel before. Is this program supported by free-will offerings?

In His precious name, yours,

Racy L. Akins
Chaplain (1st Lt.) U.S.A.

Somehow Dr. Rice got those requested books to Chaplain Akins. I do not remember one time his saying "no" to such requests, be they large or small.

I'll just think ahead a bit and say that shortly after the German surrender at the end of World War II, the Chaplain General for the American forces in Europe ordered $5,000 worth of free booklets. Since the treasury was nearly exhausted, Dr. Rice could have replied with a polite letter mentioning the fact. But this was not his way. After

---

[3] On October 27, 1965, the Nashville *Tennessean* ran a picture of the "Marine Devil" and told that, while it was in drydock in Mobile, Alabama, being remodeled for the Matson Line, an explosion blew a 15-by-25-foot hole in its forward portion. The freighter was being converted for the Matson Line of Hawaii and was to be renamed the Hawaiian Queen.

Immediately the name "Marine Devil" rang a bell because we knew that ship had been used during the Korean War to carry troops from Seattle to Japan and return. We had provided thousands of dollars' worth of Sword literature to chaplains, and the chaplain had told of many being saved through our literature, both in taking new troops from Seattle to Japan and returning with them coming home.

consulting Mrs. Rice, he mortgaged their Wheaton home for $6,000, put the money into free literature and mailed the booklets, paying the monthly mortgage payments as they came due out of their own pockets.

This was an investment he never regretted. In his book, *All About Christian Giving,* he mentioned some of the results that came to his ears.

> ...hundreds of men in our armed services wrote to say how they found Christ as Saviour through these booklets. Later word came that missionaries DeShazer and Glenn Wagner had won to Christ the Japanese Naval Commander who had led the attack of three hundred and sixty planes on the American fleet at Pearl Harbor, December 7, 1941. They went over my booklet, *"What Must I Do to Be Saved?"* with him. Then this man took that message in the little booklet we have spread by the millions and gave it on his lecture tour to one group of eleven hundred men!
>
> I have sweet assurance that, in the long, beautiful eternity of blessing in Heaven, I will have sweet fellowship with many souls who were kept out of Hell because of money that we gave to get out the Gospel....

A total of 8,489,000 copies of *"What Must I Do to Be Saved?"* were printed and distributed in the Japanese language during the war years, most of which were financed by Dr. Rice and the Sword of the Lord.

† † †

After Stratton Shufelt felt called to another field, Dr. Harry Clarke, musician/song leader/soloist/preacher, joined the team.

Born in Cardiff, Wales, he came to study at Moody Bible Institute. While in charge of the Practical Work Department, he worked closely with President James M. Gray and led singing for R. A. Torrey and many other famous men. And for the last eight years of Billy Sunday's ministry, Dr. Clarke was this famous evangelist's song leader.

Feeling as did Dr. Rice, that it was of the utmost importance to establish again great union campaigns, Dr. Clarke joined Dr. Rice.

Warm, radiant, "whole-souled," he didn't have to prime folk to make them sing—they just couldn't help it in his presence! And some of the most devoted and spiritual singing that I ever heard came from his choirs.

† † †

At DAYTON, OHIO, September 8 through October 6, 100 preachers cooperated in a campaign in Memorial Hall under the leadership of the Rice-Clarke team.

In charge of the inquiry work was Rev. Peter Quartel, who for thirty-four years had been superintendent of the City Rescue Mission. He wrote:

> ...Dayton hasn't seen such a revival in more than twenty-five years. It was indeed inspiring to see about 500 accept Christ in the regular services, besides some 350 others who took a stand for Christ in our schools.
>
> Figures cannot measure the value of a campaign like this. It brought about a wonderful unity among the cooperating pastors. The spiritual blessings from this campaign are going to be felt in Dayton for many years.

† † †

$10,876.44 in literature was given away the first ten months of 1946, and a reported 469 came to Christ through Sword literature in the 12 months.

A beautiful letter came from a young German doctor in the Church of St. Lucas in Munich, who had found a copy of Dr. Rice's *"What Must I Do to Be Saved?"* He knew it was intended for American soldiers; but rather apologetically he told how he, too, found the Saviour through its message. Read it in his words:

> d. 22.9.46
> Dr. med. Robert Arnholdt
>   Kempfenhausen
> Krankenhaus Der Stadt Munchen
> Post Percha/Obb. bei Starnberg/
> Oberbayern
>
> Dear Mr. Rice:
>
> Excuse my bad style, but I am a beginner in your language. You will wonder, that a young German doctor write to you. The reason is, that I saw yesterday in the Church of St. Lucas at Munich your little writing, *"What Must I Do to Be Saved?"* I was very glad to find such a writing destined for the soldiers of the U.S.A.
>
> Excuse me when I as young German man confess you, that I trust Jesus Christ as my Saviour, too. I know that I am a sinner

and believe that Christ died for my sins. If all the men in all the world believe on the Lord Jesus Christ and one is the brother of the other, then it will never be war in the world.

I am an assistant doctor in a hospital of Auberkulosis and I am many years member of the German Bekenutuiskirche. Our patients here know what the Word of the Lord means. Our daily bread give us today. The food is here, the daily speech. And we thank the American people for all the generous help, what it has given to the German people. My hope is that all the men of the world recognize Christ is the Lord and Saviour and do what God will.

I would be very glad to get a little letter from a young man in America. I want to learn better the language.

> With best regards, I am
> Yours respectfully,
> Dr. R. Arnholdt.

In the same mail came a letter from a German boy, Wolfgang Muller in Nurnberg where German war criminals were tried and hanged. After reading a number of Dr. Rice's pamphlets, he penned: "I'm so happy that I've found the way to Him after we had been taught for many years to idolize criminals."

† † †

Dr. Rice kept on promoting evangelists, kept on writing articles on evangelists and evangelism, bound and determined that they have their rightful place. He kept on promoting union revival campaigns. Dr. Bob Jones joined him with a strong article, "Evangelism Is Orthodoxy on Fire."

1947 Though Sword of the Lord had been a nonprofit Christian business, it seemed best that the work be incorporated as a nonprofit corporation under the laws of Illinois. We applied for and were granted a charter; now the corporation would be handled and safeguarded by a Christian board of directors. This also made it so any gift to Sword of the Lord Foundation would be deductible from income tax.

Our buildings, our office fixtures and equipment and many thousands of dollars' worth of books were transferred to the nonprofit corporation.

Dr. Rice could easily have accepted royalties from his books and retired to a comfortable home. But this he refused to do. Unswerving in his devotion to the Lord, he set up this nonprofit corporation. All the assets of the publishing company were turned over to this Foundation. Thus, his writings never earned him a penny. He never accepted a salary from the paper. His livelihood—all of it—came from revival meetings and from support of those who believed in his work.

One of the purposes of Sword of the Lord Foundation was to distribute Christian literature. And this it did in Dr. Rice's lifetime, and it is still the purpose today.

† † †

To carry on THE SWORD OF THE LORD as the mouthpiece of reputable, Spirit-filled, successful evangelism in America; to publish the best revival literature; to carry on the Sword Book Club; to put on great conferences on evangelism; to try to defend the evangelists and evangelism against infidels and misguided Christians—these were tremendous tasks. So Dr. Rice needed good men around him. And this he had in song leader Dr. Harry Clarke, in Dr. Robert Wells, in Bill Mann and in Dr. Harrison Pierce. He hoped soon to employ two or three other such men to help carry the load.

† † †

SAN PEDRO, CALIFORNIA: Some twenty-five churches and religious groups united in this meeting which touched the whole harbor area: San Pedro, Wilmington, Lomita, Harbor City, with people coming from other nearby cities.

The big tent seating 1500 was located within two blocks of the area which Robert Ripley called "the most wicked spot on earth."

Personally, we were moved to see how cosmopolitan the meetings were—different denominations, different races, different languages and peoples. The singing, the listening, the praying, the rejoicing together—this was like Heaven.

A parade several blocks long got the attention of the city. Dr. Rice led it in gallant style astride a fine horse.

Night after night Harry Clarke carried the great crowd along on the waves of Christian melody, and Mrs. Clarke played the piano with fine musical skill.

Most all of Dr. Rice's union campaigns received wide newspaper publicity, much as in the Billy Sunday campaigns.

There were recorded some 600 conversions. No spot is too hard for God to work!

† † †

WINSTON-SALEM, NORTH CAROLINA: In July Dr. Rice, Harry Clarke and the team were in Winston-Salem in the Liberty Warehouse for a union campaign with thirty-five churches.

Winston-Salem is one of the two great Moravian centers in America. All the Moravian churches in town (nine) and some in nearby communities cooperated.

Every night scores walked the aisles to confess Christ. Only Heaven could record the results, but we saw enough on earth to cause abundant rejoicing! There were more than 600 registered decisions for Christ here also.

Let me add this: Dr. Rice had no cheap methods of getting people to make a profession in order to count numbers. He insisted that no person's profession of faith be counted until some competent personal worker sat down with that one and showed him/her from the Bible how to be saved. That was true in every campaign he conducted. He was much more interested in people understanding how to be saved than in recording numbers to enhance his ministry.

In his church bulletin, Rev. T. C. Keaton made this comment:

> Dr. R. A. Torrey had more people reading their Bible than we

**Just a portion of the great crowd that came night after night
to the Liberty Warehouse, Winston-Salem, North Carolina**

Gipsy Smith did much to sweeten and tone up the lives of Christians; but it remains to say that Dr. Rice preaches more Gospel and with greater demonstration of the Spirit's power than any of these world-famous and valiant servants of God. . . . Eternity alone will reveal the full results of the great work he is doing in our midst.

And there were many other reports by pastors in later issues of THE SWORD. All were of the general opinion: "Outstanding evangelist of America."

Were I to take time to tell about each campaign, I could get nothing else in this book. So I mention only those with unusual results.

† † †

The GREENVILLE, SOUTH CAROLINA campaign, held in November in the large Textile Hall seating 5,000, saw scores saved. I was greatly impressed that the preaching had caused many to right wrongs they had committed—more in this revival than usual. Even the daily newspaper reported a "strange spirit for good working in North and South Carolina."

The widespread conviction for sin throughout the community was illustrated by two reports in that same local newspaper. The *Piedmont* told how two boys walked into a drugstore and asked for the manager. The older one confessed, "I took some gum two years ago and didn't pay for it." The younger fellow chimed in, "And I helped my friend chew that gum, so I'm guilty, too."

When the manager directed him to the cashier, he walked over to her, explained that he wished to pay for some gum he had stolen two years before—"nine packs"—deposited the money on the counter and, with his friend, walked briskly from the place.

Another clipping appeared two days later telling that the manager of one of Greenville's largest department stores had received a "conscience letter" from a young woman who said she had worked at the store in 1922-23 and on one occasion took a compact without paying for it. Now that she had been converted, she enclosed payment for the stolen compact.

"What kind of spirit has gotten to work in upper South Carolina in the last few weeks?" the manager of the store asked.

Numbers of people came to the evangelist privately and to other team members to tell of sin confessed and forsaken or of some restitution made.

Many revivals we have heard about are like the one that two Indians were talking about down in Oklahoma. One went up to the other and said, "I heard you had a revival at your church. How did it come out? How did you like the preacher?"

In characteristic Indian fashion, the other one answered, "Ugh; big wind, heap dust, no rain." A lot of revivals are like that—big wind, heap dust and no rain.

This was not merely an evangelistic campaign; it was really a revival!

Dr. Rice showed that God was still able to rain down the showers of blessings upon us.

† † †

From October 1947 through January 1948 he was grievously afflicted with sciatic rheumatism, and much of the time Dr. Rice used crutches and stood on one foot to preach at Greenville, South Carolina; Lewistown, Pennsylvania; and at the Evansville Rescue Mission in Evansville, Indiana.

† † †

There were 314 reported conversions in 1947 through Sword literature.

1948 Because of the sciatic condition, Dr. Rice took time off from campaigns; but in the office he was planning for Letter Month (12,000 wrote during April); a subscription campaign; three conferences—at Siloam Springs, Arkansas; at Toccoa, Georgia; and at the Chicago Gospel Tabernacle (the famous Paul Rader Tabernacle seating 2,800)—gathering more good material for THE SWORD OF THE LORD, preparing his book, *Power of Pentecost,* and contracting for a Sunday afternoon radio broadcast on a Chicago station.

† † †

As time went by, Dr. Rice began conducting more Sword of the Lord Conferences on Soul Winning and Revival than actual revivals. He saw that, if America would be saved, pastors would have to be inspired and trained. Speakers were used who were being greatly blessed of God and knew how to get the job done.

Dr. Bob Jones, Sr., and Dr. Rice traveled the country together putting on these conferences. Both are in Heaven now. I love to envision Dr. "John" and Dr. "Bob" sitting on a golden park bench in the shade of the Tree of Life talking over their many experiences in those days when they were showing young preachers "how to do" the work of the ministry, "how to" have power and "how to" get their prayers answered!

After Dr. Jones' death, Dr. Jack Hyles joined Dr. Rice as conference director; also, he was one of the main speakers.

The Sword of the Lord Conferences at Church of the Open Door, Los Angeles; at Massey Hall, Toronto; three at Winona Lake, Indiana; at John Brown University, Siloam Springs, Arkansas; thirteen years at Lake Louise, Toccoa, Georgia; at the Paul Rader Tabernacle in Chicago—all resulted in scores of Spirit-filled preachers going back to their churches to start revivals. They made evangelists, set preachers on fire, turned cold, formal, scholastic ministers into Spirit-filled firebrands for God.

Dr. Rice's hardest decision was to share his time between citywide campaigns and Sword Conferences. But when you hear of so many men being set on fire in such Sword Conferences, you come to realize his decision was the right one. The list who attribute their start in their ministry to Dr. Rice's influence is astounding: Jack Hyles, Jack Hudson, Jerry Falwell, Bob Gray, Curtis Hutson, to name only a very few.

† † †

Dr. Rice began a Sunday afternoon radio broadcast over WAIT, a Chicago station, adding two more stations later. Then C. O. Baptista made several twenty-minute sound pictures of him preaching: "The Dying Thief," "He That Winneth Souls Is Wise," "When God Is Deaf," "Come Unto Me" and "Missing God's Last Train for Heaven." These sermons had packed large auditoriums and stirred thousands.

In September this telegram came from Billy Graham, who was chosen president of the Northwestern Schools, Minneapolis, after the death of Dr. W. B. Riley:

> YOU HAVE BEEN UNANIMOUSLY ELECTED TO THE BOARD OF TRUSTEES OF NORTHWESTERN SCHOOLS FOR A PERIOD OF THREE YEARS. WE ARE COUNTING ON YOUR ADVICE COUNSEL AND HELP IN COMING DAYS.

† † †

So ends a most productive 1948.

Right: Dr. Rice and
Dr. Hyles. Over 2,200
times these two sat
together on the same
conference platforms
across America.

Left: Dr. Bob Jones and
Dr. John Rice—no two
people ever loved each
other more. They spoke
on many a platform
together!

1949 Paul said, "I am made all things to all men, that I might by all means save some." With that ever on his mind, Dr. Rice entered into a contract with Radio Station XENT, a 50,000-watt Mexican border station reaching 46 states, to broadcast daily at 11:00 p.m. This is in addition to his three weekly broadcasts on Sunday on Chicago stations.

What more would this man take on!!!!

† † †

SPRINGFIELD, MISSOURI: A tent seating 3,500 was rented for the Springfield, Missouri, tent revival May 8 through June 5. Preceding the opening, the city was completely covered with handbills and with Dr. Rice's gospel tract, *"What Must I Do to Be Saved?"* Also posters, billboard and newspaper advertising were employed. Everyone in the phone book was called and invited to the big tent.

During the one month of revival effort, Evarett Mills, song leader for the campaign, conducted with great success special services for children in schools and churches in various sections of the city.

This revival was well attended, and hundreds were saved. Wherever Dr. Rice went, we could expect to see scores walk the aisle for salvation.

† † †

In an article, "It Cannot Be Done...but Let's Do It!" Dr. Rice wrote:

A few years ago it seemed impossible that mass evangelism could ever return to America. When I insisted that we could, by God's grace, bring back great citywide campaigns, the best Christians in America said it could not be done.

Beloved "Ma" Sunday, widow of the princely Billy Sunday, showed me great scrapbooks of clippings, newspaper notices of tremendous tabernacle campaigns in principal cities. But the best-known evangelists in America said to me that never again would newspapers give much space to revivals, and never again would such campaigns be possible.

One of my dearest friends said, "Brother John, if you have

revivals, you will have to go without the help of pastors and churches in large campaigns." But I went on holding citywide campaigns, helping to prove it can be done.

We have a long way to go before we make the impact on American society that ought to be made, but God has done the impossible.

Got any rivers you think are uncrossable?
Got any mountains you can't tunnel thro'?
God specializes in things tho't impossible;
And He can do what no other power can do.

Do you know what happened to that fellow who said, "It can't be done"? He was run over by Dr. Rice who "was doing it!"

LAKE LOUISE, TOCCOA, GA—a million-dollar conference ground built by the industrialist, Christian layman R. G. LeTourneau. The large air-conditioned hotel, with wings spaced around the big steel dome of the auditorium seating 1500 is where many Sword Conferences were held.

CHANCES ARE, YOU'RE THINKING ABOUT VACATION TIME RIGHT NOW. MAYBE YOU HAVEN'T ACTUALLY LOOKED OVER ROAD MAPS AND PLANE OR TRAIN SCHEDULES YET, BUT YOU PROBABLY HAVE STARTED TO WONDER WHERE YOU WILL GO AND WHAT YOU WILL DO FOR YOUR SUMMER'S VACATION. MAY WE MAKE A SUGGESTION?....

Then we sold you on attending another Sword Conference. But it didn't seem to take much persuasion back in those days. People came every year from far and near.

"East is East and West is West, And never the twain shall meet"—so the poet affirmed, but he hadn't attended a Sword Conference!

Every one was well attended. And at some, unless you got in an early reservation, you had to wait until next year.

It was true again this particular year at Lake Louise, in northern Georgia. People came for a blessing and were never disappointed.

This is when Dr. Bob Gray's ministry was made over.

This is when another preacher returned home and put a big ad in the local paper:

"COME HEAR THE NEW PASTOR OF FIRST BAPTIST CHURCH!"

Many of his own people wondered if he had resigned, gone crazy or hired an assistant; but found that none of these were correct. He had come home from the conference a new man. And we find that his work and ministry from then on were changed completely.

† † †

On the heels of Lake Louise followed a Sword Conference at Cedar Lake, Indiana. More soul-stirring sermons I have never heard. These men brought messages that would have wakened the dead to life—in fact, they did!

Here was evangelism at work; here was a demonstration of revival itself. Evangelist John Linton, who spoke, expressed it well: *"Evangelism won't die in America while John R. Rice is with us."*

Though Cedar Lake Conference Grounds was not as large as Winona Lake, that did not hinder the blessing that came down.

All had a splendid time—except one was heard to say, "But we didn't SEE DER LAKE!"

Still another Sword Conference in 1949 was held at the Arkansas Baptist Assembly Grounds in Siloam Springs, Arkansas, which Dr. Bob Jones said was the best Sword Conference on Revival he had been in of all those conducted at Winona Lake, Chicago, Los Angeles, Toronto and Lake Louise. And who would ever doubt Dr. Bob! Each one seemed to get "gooder" and "gooder"! There was a freshness, an eagerness, a richness of blessing in this conference that in many respects was beyond anything we had seen in such conferences on revival and soul winning.

Sometimes, the smaller the crowd, the greater the blessing.

Each speaker brought us from laughter to tears again and again. They sowed for eternity when they preached into the upturned faces of those preachers and Christian workers from far and near.

When services were not in session, many went from house to house doing personal work.

Let me add this. Mrs. Bill (Cathy) Rice used to help register people. That "work horse" didn't shy away from doing anything that needed to be done.

One day her deaf girl, Betty Ann, came into the cabin crying. When Cathy asked her (by signs) what was wrong, Betty Ann signed, "All these people love the Lord!" When her mother inquired further about why she had said this, Betty signed, "I can feel it here [pointing all around her], and it feels good."

Remember, she could not hear, but the Spirit of God was so manifest that this little twelve-year-old could feel the difference and tearfully expressed her feeling to her mother.

Siloam Springs will always have a hallowed spot in my heart. Oh, the facilities were not the best, but that didn't matter; this conference was actually a bit of Heaven on earth. I wish every preacher in America could have been there that holy week! One was heard to say: "I want the throb of this man's anguish to touch my own soul. I've spoken to great masses without turning a hair, unmoved. I've preached the Gospel these 30 years with dry eyes."

After reading in THE SWORD the many testimonies from this Siloam Springs conference, it seemed to many to be the best ever of all our conferences.

Dr. Bob Jones testified at the Siloam Springs Sword Conference:

> In my lifetime, for fifty years I have known no paper that is doing as much along a certain line as THE SWORD OF THE LORD. It is doing more to stimulate interest in soul winning than any other periodical that has ever been printed in my lifetime.
>
> Of the 3,000 students at Bob Jones University, some 1,000 are ministerial students. I am going to require every preacher boy at BJU to read THE SWORD OF THE LORD every week for the 36 school weeks as a part of his course of study. I do this because this periodical is the only one in America where they can get the outstanding sermons of outstanding preachers—all of them with

the evangelistic emphasis. They will read the paper, then write a review of every sermon.

This requirement was in effect from that time until a short while after Dr. Bob Jones' death in 1968.

You will enjoy hearing about this that happened during the conference.

Dr. Rice took along his little dog Flicka, who "sat" up front or lay on the floor near the front. When he was making a point and bent over and moaned as if he had been hurt, like a bolt of lightning Flicka rushed to the platform and to Dr. Rice! When he assured her he was all right, she sheepishly went back to her resting place!

† † †

When you have to find a man who can cajole an oil furnace back into working order, handle the finances of a company with business acumen, keep 50 employees happy and at top efficiency, have good judgment and faith in himself and yet be willing to listen to counsel and defer to others—brother, that's a big order!

But all these qualities—and many more—were just what was needed in a general manager for Sword of the Lord Publishers. And when Dr. Rice came to know Walter E. Handford, Jr., something inside him said, "This is the one!"

Before entering Wheaton College, Walt was with Pan-American Airways as a radio operator; and during the war he installed radar for Boeing Aircraft.

Walt started working at the Sword part-time while in college, sandwiching in ad writing and Sword promotion with a busy college career as a varsity debater and honor student.

What's more, he wooed, won and married the Boss's daughter, Elizabeth, in 1948!

After graduation in 1949, he became general manager and vice-president of Sword of the Lord Foundation—a place he filled in a wise and capable way for eight years. In 1955 he announced his plans to become a full-time evangelist, and he was relieved of his duties as general manager, though he remained as vice-president.

Walt had been Dr. Rice's right-hand man for these years and was sorely missed around the office. This genius had earned the affectionate respect of all who worked with him.

In 1960 Dr. Rice, upon unanimous vote of the church, asked Walt to succeed him as pastor of Calvary Baptist Church and to help in the promotional work at the Sword of the Lord. Now he was vice-president and assistant editor.

After the Sword moved to Murfreesboro in 1963, Walt stayed on in Wheaton for a year, then became pastor in Greenville, South Carolina, where he has remained these twenty-six years.

† † †

At the end of the year, the circulation of the paper approached 75,000.

† † †

There were 307 reported conversions through Sword of the Lord literature in 1949.

Springfield, Missouri, May, 1949. Choir not shown.

**Right: Evangelist Bill Rice,
Director—Sword Staff of
Evangelists, Associate Editor,
and Dr. John Rice's companion**

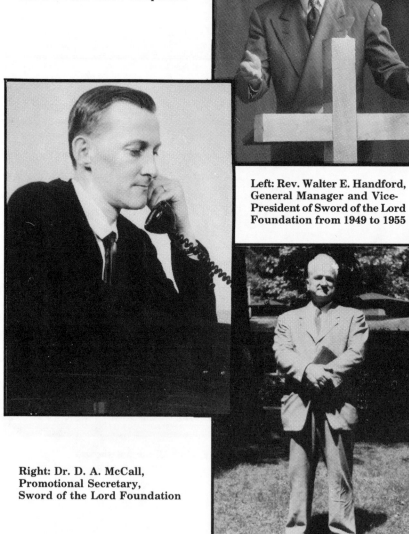

**Left: Rev. Walter E. Handford,
General Manager and Vice-
President of Sword of the Lord
Foundation from 1949 to 1955**

**Right: Dr. D. A. McCall,
Promotional Secretary,
Sword of the Lord Foundation**

1950 Dr. Rice chose a cold time—March—for a meeting in Presque Isle, in northern Maine! West is Quebec; east, New Brunswick and Nova Scotia. We drove three hard days, the last day through a heavy snowstorm. And a snowmobile rescued us a time or two when the car refused to climb hills or when the road was blocked with five feet of snow.

Crowds came to this union campaign, packing the building nightly (see photo). And what a revival!

The last report gotten from the committee was that there had been 300 decisions for Christ in the first nine days. But soon we were receiving letters from cooperating pastors telling how the revival fires were still burning, how churches were still being blessed, and how individuals were continuing on in their new-found faith.

Rev. Philip C. Hughey wrote: "One week after the meeting closed it was our delight to receive forty-three into the membership of our church, thirty-nine by baptism and four by Christian experience. These represent about one-third of the cards referred to our church. Many more of those who made decisions will be added to the church."

Rev. Bill Powell stated: "The dust you stirred hasn't settled as yet, for many are making professions of faith. There have been responses to every invitation....We baptized sixty-nine on Easter Sunday."

Rev. Herman A. Grant, head of the inquiry room, stated among other things, "...The spirit of revival is still in the air. The Holy Spirit is still calling sinners to repentance. There is no way to measure accurately the full results of these meetings...."

These reports, and others in similar vein, caused us to rejoice even more.

† † †

From there we went to Grand Manan Island, New Brunswick, in the Bay of Fundy. We could get there only by boat. God gave a breaking out of revival among those lobster-scallop-herring fishermen.

Here Dr. Rice dictated the book, *We Can Have Revival Now,* lectures to be given at Bob Jones University.

† † †

Joining the John R. Rice evangelistic party in March was Albert A. Lane, a four-star brilliant pianist. I had heard many pianists, but there is no way to describe his technique on the keyboard.

† † †

JAPANESE ATTACKER OF PEARL HARBOR CONVERTED
was the headline in June 9 SWORD.

Mitsuo Fuchita, Chief Flight Officer in command of the armada of 360 planes that bombed Pearl Harbor, had shortly before been saved through the ministry of missionaries Glen Wagner and Timothy Pietsch. This man led the attack, dropped the first bomb on our fleet and was credited with sinking the battleship *Maryland.* He was the sole survivor of the thirty-two officers who participated in the battle.

Having been given a copy of Dr. Rice's booklet, *"What Must I Do to Be Saved?"* he carefully studied it. This seemed to open his eyes, and the missionaries were able to lead him to Christ. The next week after he was saved, he was invited to give a lecture to a culture club. Instead of speaking about his wartime experiences, he gave the message from Dr. Rice's booklet, in the Japanese edition, to a group of about one thousand men.

† † †

This year we began flooding Japan with this booklet mentioned above, and from January 1950 through February of 1970 we had provided them with 8,489,000 copies, costing $59,966.97. At the same time we were also supplying *"What Must I Do to Be Saved?"* to scores of other countries—some 12 million distributed in 32 languages.

This resulted in many thousands of conversions, some of them most remarkable, as the local missionaries in those lands reported to us.

† † †

Facing three thousand students at Bob Jones University, approximately one thousand of them ministerial students, along with faculty and guests, Dr. Rice gave ten lectures on "We Can Have Revival Now."

† † †

Presque Isle, Maine, March 1950

In August Dr. Rice announced: "The circulation of THE SWORD OF THE LORD is now equal to the leading interdenominational fundamental Christian magazines in America, and larger than all but one or two." He was pleading for 100,000 circulation by the first of 1951.

† † †

The Sword staff of evangelists was composed of young men who, like the first deacons in the book of Acts, were men of good report. Each was well-trained, clean of mind and body, and each had been definitely called of God to do the work of an evangelist.

These men were doctrinally sound to the core. Everyone believed in the inspiration of the Bible, the virgin birth, the deity of Christ, the blood atonement, salvation by faith alone, etc. They did not major on minors but were always striving to unite and bless a church rather than cause divisions and dissension. None were money-minded. Each was very modest in his financial requirements. And each made soul winning his major business.

Dr. Bill Rice was the director, and Mr. Ralph Mucher, the field representative.

The number of evangelists who represented THE SWORD OF THE LORD on the field varied. But there were many.

The extension department arranged revival dates for them, handled a multitude of correspondence back and forth with the pastors, and provided help and encouragement to these men of God. Through them thousands were saved.

Not only did Dr. Bill head this department; but also he became assistant editor of THE SWORD OF THE LORD; was one of the judges of the Sword Book Club and one of the assistant directors of Sword Conferences—and one upon whom Dr. John leaned continually for counsel. Dr. Bill and Dr. John, though half brothers, were very closely knit together. Hear Dr. Bill[1] say,

"I GOT IT FROM JOHN!"

I have been a full-time evangelist ever since I graduated from Moody Bible Institute in 1941. It has been my happy privilege to preach from coast to coast here in the States and to conduct revival meetings in many foreign countries. I have preached to men and women dressed in fur-lined parkas and heavy boots in

---

[1] Dr. Bill passed away in 1978; Dr. John, in 1980.

temperatures way below freezing; I have preached to thousands of near-naked natives of the Belgium Congo. I have preached Christ to lumberjacks in Maine, to fishermen in California, to plantation workers in Jamaica, to turbaned men in Egypt, to the daring horsemen of the Arab Legion in Palestine, to the bearded Bedouins of the desert and to robed men and women in Bethlehem and Jerusalem.

And just about everyone who has heard me preach has heard me say, "I got it from John!"

That's right, I did get it from John Rice. Almost everything I know about the Bible, about preaching, about leading singing, about soul winning, about gospel advertising, about planning and promoting a revival, about writing—I learned from my splendid big brother. Ever since the day I surrendered to preach, he has been the big man in my life.

Perhaps that is not surprising since he is my own brother; but I have been utterly astounded to learn that there are literally hundreds of thousands of others, not only in America but around the world, who can say the same thing. I have never preached to any congregation in any country in the world but that someone in the congregation had heard John Rice preach in person or had seen him preach in a gospel film or had heard him on the radio or had read something he had written in a book or pamphlet or THE SWORD OF THE LORD.

I remember one day in Africa two other white men and I, with six or seven natives, entered a little village of mud huts. We had traveled three days through the African "bush," and I wondered if civilization in any form had ever touched these people in the heart of the Dark Continent. But an old fellow who could neither read nor write a word of English or anything else, showed me a tattered, yellowed copy of THE SWORD OF THE LORD!

Years before someone else had "got it from John" and had given the Gospel to the people of this little African village.

✝ ✝ ✝

Statistics can be dry, dull figures. But with what anticipation we waited for each year's results of the letters we had from those who wrote that they were saved through some book or booklet of ours or through the pages of THE SWORD OF THE LORD! So we again rejoiced when the figures were in: 527 during 1950.

1951

A news note in February:

"Dr. and Mrs. Rice and Miss Viola were the guests of Dr. Billy Graham and his party after the Saturday night mammoth rally in the KRNT Theatre, Des Moines. A 'midnight' dinner was served to them by Billy Graham at the Kirkwood Hotel."

† † †

Beginning in March a ten-week revival was carried on through THE SWORD with the following features: 1. a strong sermon to the unsaved each week with a decision form for those who wanted to turn to Christ; 2. an earnest message on soul winning in each issue; 3. special promotion of tracts with the hope that we could get out a quarter of a million *"What's. . . ?"*; 4. a special prayer list of unsaved people for whom the Sword staff and our readers were to pray daily.

This brought marvelous results.

† † †

D. L. Moody, it is said, used to spend several weeks in the New England hills each summer. His only companion—his Bible. His only statement regarding the fact that he read it through during that period every year: *"The instrument needs retuning."*

So Dr. Rice continued holding Sword of the Lord Conferences on Revival and Soul Winning in various sections of the country so that pastors and laymen alike could tune their instruments. This year three more conferences were planned at the same places as last year, with the addition of Latham Springs, Texas Baptist Assembly Ground.

† † †

The pessimists, the doubters and the skeptics who proclaim that the days of revival are past and gone forever, should have visited Moncton, the city in the Hub of the Maritime Provinces of Canada, from May 20 through June 8.

During this period, several Baptist churches united in a citywide Crusade for Christ Campaign with Dr. Rice, which Rev. Arthur R. Pyke, chairman, said "was one of the greatest spiritual awakenings in the history of this area. . . . Many of the oldest saints testified that they had never witnessed anything like it. Moncton and its suburbs were shaken. In the offices, in the factories, in the schools and in the streets, people were talking about the unusual demonstration of God in our midst! . . . ."

Dr. Rice spoke an even fifty times with no rest day. He had seventeen radio services, two shop meetings at the Canadian National Railroad shops, and the rest were all major services when he spoke from forty-five minutes to an hour. All that besides our office work and two nights of all-night prayer!

The crowds in the high school auditorium were large, and people were hungry to hear the Gospel in that part of the country.

In his closing message, "The Harvest Is Past, the Summer Is Ended, and We Are Not Saved," he stressed the fact that the opportunity for salvation passes away; that youth, the best chance to be saved, soon passes; times of special dealing by the Spirit of God pass away; times when there are loved ones to warn and pray pass; that the wooing of the Holy Spirit may cease; revivals come to a close; life itself slips away.

After such a moving sermon, people came streaming down front to take Christ as their Saviour.

Approximately 453 people, we were told, came forward publicly in the fifteen days.

As we drove the 1600 miles back to Wheaton, the scenery was beautiful and the contact with French-speaking people delightful.

When Mrs. Rice and I traveled with Dr. Rice, our travel was usually by car. The most knowledgeable man I ever knew took time to explain the countryside, the monuments—just anything he thought would be of interest to us. We stopped to go on top of Pikes Peak, rode a cable car down the Royal Gorge, went inside Carlsbad Cavern; we rode mules down the Grand Canyon, took a boat to Catalina Island, drove into Yellowstone Park to see "Old Faithful," rode "Maid of the Mist" at Niagara Falls. And of course there were our many trips to the Holy Land and a Bible conference trip to Hawaii.

On and on I could relate places he wanted us to enjoy amid his heavy preaching schedule or en route to the next revival. He always wanted those with him to see and learn everything they could, to eat new foods, to see new places. Being with him on such trips was a high school-college-seminary education.

Yes, Dr. Rice loved life, people and a good time.

† † †

By now three of Dr. Rice's precious daughters had joined the office staff: Mrs. Grace MacMullen took Mr. Lampman's place; Mrs. Elizabeth Handford was secretary to her husband Walt, the general manager; and Jessie Ruth headed the art department. Joanna was already working part-time; and Sarah Joy, only thirteen then, did odd jobs while getting ready for a full-time office position later. Mary Lloys Himes was a pastor's wife in Treece, Kansas.

All these trained girls were wonderful help. And of course Dr. Rice was delighted to have five of them near him and in the work.

† † †

In June Dr. Rice wrote to 1800 Japanese pastors offering them THE SWORD OF THE LORD for one year, to be paid for by American friends, if they read English and if they requested the magazine. Immediately we got back some one thousand replies asking for the paper. "I feel this is a wonderful way to mold the lives of young Christians in Japan," said Dr. Rice.

Here is just one sample of the scores of "thank-you" letters which later came:

> Dear Dr. Rice:
>
> Thank you very much for THE SWORD OF THE LORD which you are sending me since March. I tell you honestly, I did not pay much attention at first. I asked you to send it to me because you send it free of charge. But when I read, "Going After Sinners," I am struck. It thrusted my heart. It gave me new diction [decision]. Of course I knew the idea, but the other idea is very common among Japanese which those who wish to be taught must come to the teacher hundreds of miles without saying far. You may laugh at me. I feel like to explain more to avoid it, but I can not write it in English. But anyway it was the point.
>
> I am glad that I can tell you my new pastoral life will begin from today. Because I wished to share my thanks to God, I wrote this letter to you. I am forty-nine years old pastor. Thank you very much and will be thanking all the time.
>
> (Signed) John Y. Yamamura

P.S. As I wrote in the letter, I did not much care for the paper at first. I have lost the others. I beg you send another paper under the article, "Going After Sinners," if possible air mail. I wish to look it quickly.

I found your picture on the paper. I am going to put it on my desk all the time.

Folks, you have no idea what influence this paper has had on lives around the globe!

† † †

Mr. Ralph Mucher, field secretary of Sword staff of evangelists, reported in August that there had been 1,800 first-time decisions in the first six months since the staff was organized. Many good men were now on the field, and others were being added as they applied and were approved by both Dr. Bill Rice and Mr. Ralph Mucher.

† † †

My head gets dizzy every time I look back at Dr. Rice's schedule. For every revival or conference mentioned, he was in ten or more. I have to skip so many for lack of room. But wherever he went, people could expect a blessing.

Dr. Rice's preaching was such as none ever experienced: it was humble, marvelously kind, bold—often **very** bold—most positively biblical and without any ranting. It sought revival of Christians and the conversion of sinners, and it accomplished both of these objectives.

† † †

It was this year that my many years of travel, long hours and pressure, caught up with me. I informed Dr. Rice, in a down moment, that I could not take the travel any longer. This was of great concern to him because of the volume of work we were able to do on the road, in a makeshift office, transcribing machine and typewriter on a chair, letters on the floor, SWORD copy on the window sill.

So when we returned to Wheaton, he saw to it that recreation was fitted into our schedule. He would regularly take several of us golfing or skating or bowling or to play tennis. Now if I needed it, imagine how much more he needed it!

I do not know anyone who worked as hard or such long hours as Dr. Rice. He dearly loved to be with a group for a picnic, but his outings were few. He was an excellent horseman, a good tennis player and fond of golf; but I doubt if he rode horseback after ranch days more than a dozen times before he moved to Murfreesboro and had a farm. And he hardly ever found time before for tennis and golf. Now he was doing these things and seeing that we did them, too. And this regular schedule of recreation was a great tonic to us all.

The one who says you don't work up a sweat playing golf has never gone nine holes with Dr. Rice! That man hit the little ball, then took off like he was trying to catch the commuter train that just pulled out of the station.

With much prayer, less pressure and more play, little by little my health was completely restored with a new lease on life. Of course I am ever mindful that God was gracious, and I hope He felt I was still needed in His work.

That "illness" was nearly forty years ago; I am still very busy in His vineyard. (And when was I born? This little bit of handy information can best be secured at the reading of my obituary at your convenience and at my departure!)

Let me hasten to say that Dr. Rice was free from any blame. He was always trying to get me to get more help while I was in the office, which then was very seldom. I did have excellent office secretaries who were hard workers and such a comfort in the work.

I keep urging Dr. Hutson to more recreation; for I know Dr. and Mrs. Rice, Miss Fairy and I were able to do much more and had better health because we took time out to play.

† † †

Dr. Rice received this card in December from Mrs. W. A. Sunday, widow of the immortal Evangelist Billy Sunday:

> Christmas is over—I am at the home of my younger grandson, Paul Haines, Helen's only child. We had a wonderful Christmas— nine of us here Christmas Eve, and also at dinner. Today one goes back to the Navy and others are on their way back to Chicago, driving. I am staying on a few weeks. Have plans to be in Washington, D.C. during the last week of Billy Graham's campaign there.
>
> May your blessings be multiplied.
>
> Mrs. W. A. Sunday

Dr. Rice again in 1951 made it clear that:

The work of the Sword of the Lord is interdenominational. That means we work with all Bible-believing groups of Christians. One who knows the Lord Jesus as his personal Saviour is our brother. We are glad to promote revivals among all groups. The large cooperative revival campaigns the editor conducts are often sponsored by churches and pastors of many denominations.

However, let it be known that we are not for the uniting of Bible believers with modernists, in a super-church organization. We believe in cooperation of denominations, but not union.

We do not encourage any group of sincere Bible believers to throw away great convictions. Those who agree on the great fundamentals of the Faith. . . can cooperate in many things.

We do not want to be thought on the side of church union. We do not believe it pleases God to play down doctrine, to ignore convictions, to compromise principles earnestly held by good Christians.

There are some great Bible principles for which Christians ought always to contend, like the inspiration of the Bible, the blood atonement, salvation by faith in Christ, Heaven, Hell, etc.

There are lesser doctrines on which people can disagree while having brotherly fellowship.

For example, I think salvation is much more important than baptism. I believe that Christ's atoning death on the cross is more important than whether His second coming will be pre- or posttribulation. I must break fellowship with one who does not believe that Jesus is the very Son of God which He claims to be; but I would not break fellowship with one who believes all the Bible and loves the Lord and is saved by the blood, but who may have been mistaught on baptism. I will love him and fellowship with him while I tell him I think he is wrong.

We are for interdenominationalism, if it means working with sincere, born-again, Bible-believing Christians. But we are not for church union, not for any compromise with modernism.

1952 All the work was prospering. Nearly 100,000 sermon-filled, Bible-teaching papers a week were going out...the Sword Book Club presenting the best in books...the Sword Bookstore bringing in many customers...the impact of soul-winning revivals, evangelists, evangelistic conferences was being felt over America...tracts and books were going all over the world.

Such things I did not just hear about; I saw with my eyes, I handled much of it with my hands, I felt the throb of it in my heart.

How blessed to be in such a work!

† † †

Dr. Rice kept on the road much of the year in revivals and in Sword Conferences.

† † †

We were always glad to report any good revival in the paper, including those held by Dr. Billy Graham, who then was in the fundamental camp, preaching the pure Gospel and obeying its command.

† † †

It seems that whatever the organization did, the Lord prospered. During a 100-Subscription-Club campaign, where people agreed to send in 100 subscriptions, 45,545 were received! This was an enormous amount! It brought the total near the 100,000 mark. Dr. Rice said, "It puts THE SWORD OF THE LORD even further out in front of all the other independent, fundamental Christian magazines in America, in circulation."

† † †

In July Dr. D. A. (Scotchie) McCall became promotional secretary at Sword of the Lord Foundation. He had been for eleven years executive secretary and director of evangelism for the State Board of the Mississippi Baptist Convention, where he had leadership of over 1500 Baptist churches. His strong leadership there made history. "Preaching...Power...Promotion"—his weekly SWORD column—was widely read. He had unbounding energy and was running over with ideas.

Mrs. Margie McCall came as assistant director of the Sword Book Club, which she increased to over 4,000 members. She had a charming personality, a brilliant mind, a lively imagination and the most gracious manner one can imagine. Orchids to Mrs. McCall!

The McCalls stayed with us two years and did such an important work for the Lord.

† † †

Another very important department at the Sword of the Lord was the advertising department, headed by Miss Fairy Shappard.

In a John R. Rice revival in Waxahachie, Texas, she committed herself to the service of the Lord; and while the Sword was still in Dallas, came to work at any job available, just as I did and just as Miss Lola Bradshaw did.

In 1938 she went to study at Bob Jones University and stayed two years. Then when we moved to Wheaton, Illinois, she came back to the Sword as advertising manager. In this capacity she knew all the "greats" in a personal way. And how they loved her!

What a great asset she was to Dr. Rice and the Sword Foundation in her standards, in making new friends for the work and in the amount of ads gotten and money brought in.

Miss Fairy was also available to be with the Rice girls when it was necessary for Mrs. Rice to be away with her husband. She knew well the rules of the family and held the girls strictly to them. They dearly loved her.

Those who worked under her almost "revered" her. Although she demanded perfection from herself and from those who worked with her, yet they had lots of fun, too, both in the office and out.

Miss Fairy traveled widely in search for advertising. Sometimes her office would put a letter on her desk and the "pretended" answer such as:

Dear Mr. Advertiser:

Your letter today did come but to Miss Shappard you rite it and from the office she is away. In the absence of her, your ad I care take of.

You desire date of May 8 but now is too late for ad to appearance on date of May 8. That paper has in it all ads that in it can be printed because May 8 paper is already now been printed.

Scheduling we are your ad for May 15 date. If that date satisfy not you, let please us no by mail return.

The ad you send be two much copy for the space designate. It be needing 4 inches because it be two much for 2 inches. Let please us no is this satisfy?

If questions do trouble, do hesitate to write not as Miss Shappard soon back will be and glad will be to questions clear up.

Cincerely,

(ssiM) lleD'O

(This is Dr. Al Byers' wife now, who worked many years for Miss Fairy. Her name before marriage was Marcella O'Dell!)

After Dr. Rice's death in 1980, she continued on as advertising manager under the new SWORD OF THE LORD editor, Dr. Curtis Hutson.

On February 6 of 1985, when Miss Fairy was suddenly taken from us, Dr. John Reynolds took over her duties.

I shall forever reckon it among the rich providences of my life to have known Miss Fairy from the time she was 24. She and I shared years of happy times together—in play, in work and in seeing God work miracles.

Her life was a beautiful blend of love, loyalty and leadership.

† † †

Because of the rapid growth of the soul-winning ministry at Sword of the Lord Foundation, the last few years had been filled with "growing pains" for all the work and workers.

The following pictures are worth a thousand words to describe our *status quo.* And, we hasten to remind you, *status quo* is Latin for "the mess we were in"!

BUILDING #1: Counting basement, it was 3 stories—and jammed with more than 50 workers. A big brick warehouse, originally built by a large moving and storage firm but now converted into offices, it had become totally inadequate. It had been purchased in 1946 for $7,000.

BUILDING #2: Just one block south of Building #1. We would take a short cut through an alley and parking lot to save time. Purchased from Al Smith of Singspiration Music Publishers in 1952 for $52,500, the first floor housed the Sword Book Room and Retail and Book Club departments. Upstairs were the editorial offices and art department.

Though the 2-story building with full basement and strategic location was a good investment, it was not at all large enough to fill the ultimate needs. But it did make possible the enlargement of the work until the larger and final new plant should become a reality. It was not the final word, because not only was it not large enough, it divided the workers and departments.

For over a year the Sword Board of Directors had been praying and planning for the future. Much time was spent investigating the possibilities of moving our headquarters to other parts of the country. Then one day the Lord seemed to speak very definitely about a piece of property.

The Presbyterian Church group had announced their plans to build a new church and sell their present lot in the heart of town. The ready acceptance of a reasonable offer for the property gave us the proof of God's leading.

Twelve years before, the Sword of the Lord was in Dr. Rice's home. As God prospered the work, an office was rented in the basement of a downtown building. The bookstore was on the first floor. In 1946 that old warehouse building was purchased and remodeled. Then in 1952 that other office building was purchased to facilitate things for our growing staff.

We had not stopped growing!

The Presbyterian property seemed ideal for our needs: near the bank and post office, convenient for our workers and close to the old warehouse building, which we thought we would later use for book storage, shipping and some printing. To let such an ideal lot go by without buying it surely seemed to limit God's plans for our work.

The price for the property, which included a church building and two two-story houses, was $66,000, or in measurements, $2.50 per square foot.

Left: BUILDING #1

Right: Artist's cartoon conception of the over-crowded warehouse in Wheaton. Finally the staff divided, and Editorial and Book Room went to Singspiration Bldg. one block away.

Left: This is not a "bird's eye" view of the crowded condition we were faced with; it was a "full" window view!

Right: Neither was this scene in the crowded aisle of the Sword building overdrawn. I know that from personal experience! I have obligingly "backed up" to let someone pass.

Above: Presbyterian church property, which included two 2-story houses at right and left, purchased as Sword's future home. Sold all when we moved to Murfreesboro, Tennessee, 1963

BUILDING #2, purchased for editorial offices and book room. On Main Street, downtown Wheaton

God laid it on the hearts of thousands of our friends around the world to help purchase the new property. The final payment of $44,000 on the $66,000 full price was made in the summer of 1954.[1]

† † †

In August of 1952 Missionary C. R. Hillis, who worked with us in the great island of Formosa in the printing and distribution of Dr. Rice's *"What Must I Do to Be Saved?"* in the Chinese language, sent a glorious report of 2,483 writing to them saying they had found Christ through 44,000 booklets distributed. He added, "If the results from the rest of the printing of 100,000 follow the same proportion, some 5,000 souls will have found the Lord through our distribution of the booklet in Formosa."

Praise the Lord, and print more booklets!

† † †

Will you believe it!!! Dr. Rice takes a vacation, the first one since 1935! The head of the Christian Sportsmen's Association of Cody, Wyoming, had invited him for a fall hunting trip.

He made his plans, he chose his companions: Dr. McCall and two of Dr. Rice's sons-in-law, Walt Handford and Allan MacMullen. Bill Rice was unable to go.

The four loaded Dr. Rice's car with sleeping bags, red jackets, hunting knives and rifles, piled in, then headed West—preaching on the way, of course. Arriving at their destination, they went by jeep and horseback into the Shoshone Mountains looking for deer, bear and elk, with perhaps some fishing and game-bird shooting on the side.

Later: All they bagged were three elk! But it was a vacation enjoyed by all.

† † †

A SWORD COOPERATING BOARD WAS FORMED with America's most influential Christian leaders agreeing to serve:

Dr. Richard V. Clearwaters, dean of Northwestern Seminary, Minneapolis;

Dr. Bob Cook, president of Youth for Christ International, Chicago;

---

[1]   In 1963, the Presbyterian property buildings were sold for $100,000 and an adequate building in Murfreesboro, Tennessee, was purchased for $100,000. See later explanation as to why the move.

Dr. M. R. DeHaan, Radio Bible Class broadcast, Grand Rapids;

Dr. V. Raymond Edman, president of Wheaton College, Wheaton, Illinois;

Dr. Billy Graham, evangelist;

Dr. J. H. Hunter, editor of *The Evangelical Christian,* famous novelist, Toronto, Canada;

Dr. Bob Jones, Sr., and *Dr. Bob Jones, Jr.,* of Bob Jones University, Greenville, South Carolina;

Dr. Sam Morris, "Voice of Temperance" broadcast, San Antonio, Texas;

Dr. Lee Roberson, president of Tennessee Temple Schools and pastor of Highland Park Baptist Church, Chattanooga, Tennessee;

Dr. Merv Rosell, evangelist, Montrose, California;

Dr. Bob Shuler, pastor of Trinity Methodist Church, Los Angeles, California;

Dr. Jack Shuler, evangelist, Baldwin Park, California;

Dr. Oswald J. Smith, pastor of People's Church, Toronto, Canada, and international leader;

Dr. Louis T. Talbot, president of Bible Institute of Los Angeles;

Mr. Pat and Mr. Bernie Zondervan, publishers of Grand Rapids.

Each was to promote the work of the Sword of the Lord and join heartily in our program of stirring revival fires.

† † †

The staff had grown to 65 workers. Some were part-time students from Wheaton College. New workers weren't at the Sword long before they realized this place was where we depended implicitly on the Lord for all our needs. They saw God work literal miracles in providing for our needs.

How well do I remember once when we had a $6,900 bill to pay for a carload of paper which we had contracted for when newsprint was very difficult to obtain. The very day the bill had to be paid, we still did not have the money.

But God, in a very wonderful way, sent that morning a letter from a godly man in California who had some money he wanted to invest for the Lord—$7,500 for this work of faith!

Time and again when we called on God, He airmailed our need from Heaven!

† † †

In October Dr. and Mrs. Rice and I took a train North, going through Toronto, Montreal, Quebec, on up the St. Lawrence River to Mont-Joil,

Moncton, New Brunswick, Canada, revival

then on to Moncton, New Brunswick, in the Bay of Fundy.

Eighteen months before, Dr. Rice had held a wonderful revival at Moncton. Urged to return, he did so with fear and trembling.

But God gave another gracious outpouring. There were some 344 public professions of faith. Catholics, Anglicans, people from the United Church of Canada, old and hardened sinners, walked forward for salvation.

The crowds came—some 2,000 people—to hear God's man, and the power of God again fell in New Brunswick.

† † †

At year's end and after deep searching of heart and waiting on God, Dr. Rice came to the conviction that he must spend at least half of his time in the Wheaton office editing THE SWORD OF THE LORD and promoting the work of the Foundation in general.

These he felt God wanted him to do through the paper: (1) fight the battle for evangelism and soul winning; (2) help restore great Bible preaching to the pulpits of America and the English-speaking world; (3) set out anew in a great defense of the Faith; (4) constantly watch and warn of the heresies and false cults of the day; (5) oppose worldliness and give clear Bible teaching on separation and holy living; (6) stand for brotherly love and fellowship among Bible believers.

I believe he fulfilled to the letter what God had laid on his heart to accomplish, before he was called Home at the end of 1980.

It is hard to decide which letters to use as proof, but perhaps Dr. Bob Gray and Dr. Jack Hyles can convince the doubter the worth of THE SWORD OF THE LORD to the ministry of preachers:

> Only eternity will reveal the souls that have been won to Christ and the Christians who have been helped to serve the Saviour in a better way through the outreach that God has given through this channel of blessing. Missionaries have told me personally how much THE SWORD OF THE LORD has meant to their lives and hearts while serving Christ on foreign soil.
>
> And we must remember that all of this tremendous work being accomplished through the Sword of the Lord Foundation is the lengthening shadow of a spiritual giant—Dr. John R. Rice. In my opinion, no man in America has had the influence for soul winning and revival like God has entrusted to him. Fundamental Christianity in our generation owes a debt of gratitude to Dr. John R. Rice that we will never be able to repay.

† † †

I well recall the day in college when I stumbled over a newspaper on the floor, picked it up—only to see THE SWORD OF THE LORD and one of Billy Sunday's messages. I subscribed to THE SWORD, joined the Sword Book Club, began to purchase Dr. Rice's books, and my ministry was molded through the Sword Foundation and its work.

I shudder sometimes to think of America without THE SWORD OF THE LORD. . . .

† † †

509 wrote to say they trusted Christ through Sword literature in America alone in 1952. And this year 63,165 new subscriptions were enrolled, 15,649 renewals advanced and 3,006 preachers and missionaries were added to the list through our Ministers and Missionaries Subscription Gift Fund.

1953

Dr. Rice was an animal lover. The family owned a beautiful small sheep dog named Flicka. I don't think I have seen a prettier dog, and I know there was never one more obedient.

Dr. Rice taught Flicka many tricks. It was routine for her to watch for his car to pull into the driveway each day. When he walked into the hall, she ran and got on the piano bench; and while Dr. Rice played with one hand, "Whispering Hope," Flicka turned her face toward Heaven and "sang" in a loud whine! Mind you, this was an everyday thing with her and Dr. Rice.

I say the piano bench was routine. But if she had disobeyed Mrs. Rice or had gone out without permission, she would run upstairs and under the bed when she saw his car pull into the driveway. Of course, Dr. Rice right away knew Flicka had been a bad girl!

Once when he had been gone for six long weeks, Flicka decided she had better contact her master and see why. Here was her letter (with help from Miss Fairy):

October 19, 1961

Dear Boss and Master:

I thought I'd just write and tell you how things are. I know I took you "for better or for worse," but I didn't know how "worse." Six weeks is a L-O-O-O-O-O-O-ONG time! Of course we didn't discuss the length of time you'd be gone, but I'm sure six weeks never entered into my young mind when I came to be your young dog twelve years ago.

Course I'd rather be your dog, six weeks and all, than to be anybody else's dog—even if he be the richest man in all the world. Even if he came home every day at five o'clock, I still wouldn't trade you for him.

But I did feel I must tell you—six weeks is a long time!

Sometimes people drive up in the driveway, but I know even before I leave my couch that it isn't you. The car doesn't come in right. And I look at the piano bench when they come in—but

they act like they never saw a piano bench and didn't know a dog was supposed to jump up on it and greet her master with a song.

Sometimes I run and get under the table, but nobody comes to eat. They are all too busy!

The nights are the worst. I can't hear you call Jesus' name during the night when I'm on my couch, though someway I feel He likes dogs, don't you?

Miss Fairy takes me for walks, and we have a right good time. But when I get back you aren't in your lean-back chair, and I can't get up there on your lap like I do when you're here.

We didn't talk about Mrs. Rice being gone either. But I guess if it means either you must be by yourself or me by myself—I'll take being by myself.

Well, you preach good—and I'll take care of things at home 'til you get here.

Your ever lovin' and faithful

FLICKA

P.S. Next time just don't make it six weeks!

P.P.S. I do have a sad tale (or tail)! You know there comes a time in everyone's life when he has a strong desire to cast off all restraint. Would it not be rather ideal for one to come and go at one's own choosing every once in awhile, especially when her master has been gone so long?

Well, this past Saturday, I went out without explicit permission. It seems no one knew when I left or where I went. After checking the local hospital, bureau of missing dogs, bus station, train station and airport, Miss Fairy located me at the city jail! And she wasn't about to bail me out until a day later. And do you know what! She had to pay a fine of $5, charged against me for traveling at late hours without a human being fastened to the opposite end of my leash!

What is this town coming to if a cultured lady dog like myself can't even step out for a breath of fresh air? Besides, I think it was pretty nervy to take the $5 out of my allowance.

Shall we talk about that when you get back?

† † †

The first item to catch our attention in THE SWORD was:

1. Youth for Christ in Japan Asks for One Million More *"What Must I Do to Be Saved?"* for Nationwide Evangelization This Year;

2. Portugal Exhausts First Edition of *"What Must I Do to Be Saved?"* Asks for One-Half Million More;

3. India Begs for New Printing of *"What Must I Do to Be Saved?"* in Four Languages;

4. Japanese Braille Edition of *"What Must I Do to Be Saved?"* for Blind Winning Many;

5. Check for $6,125 Sent January 6.

We prayed in the money, then sent it on its way in these cases and in scores of others, trying by all means to win some.

† † †

In March Dr. Rice announced that his *Prayer—Asking and Receiving* was listed in the large Sears Roebuck catalog.

† † †

The Bill Rice Ranch was added to the growing number of conference grounds for Sword Conferences.

Since Dr. Bill was so close to his brother and was being so greatly used in revivals, why was his name never on these conference programs? Let me tell you why.

Conferences? Phooey!

About six years ago when I began receiving invitations to speak at summer conferences, I turned down every invitation. Conferences? Phooey! I was an evangelist. My job was winning souls and teaching and inspiring others to do so. I even refused John Rice's gracious invitations to speak at Winona Lake. Flattered—but not at all interested.

I thought that conferences did no real good, were aimed at

nothing. It seemed no speaker had a definite constructive purpose in view. One might talk about the wheel within a wheel,
the horns of the beast, or whether or not saints would go through
the Tribulation! Good, perhaps, but none especially constructive
and calculated to inspire Christians to win souls.

And from the very few conferences I had attended, I formed my
opinion of the whole.

Finally when my big brother persuaded me to go to a SWORD
Conference, it was an eye-opener! Every speaker on the same
track: how to preach for results; how to win souls from house to
house; how to give an invitation; how to pray. It really amounted
to a seminar on evangelism.

Now he was inviting Sword Conferences on Revival and Soul Winning to Cumberwood Christian Retreat in Murfreesboro.

CUMBERWOOD IN 1953:

You've heard of Lookout Mountain at Chattanooga where on top they
claim you can see seven states? So what! On top of Scales Mountain at
the Bill Rice Ranch (Cumberwood Retreat) you could see in seven
directions—and it was free if you could make it up that steep mountain!
To say the least—IT WAS THE MOST!

Once Dr. Bill took Dr. and Mrs. Rice and me in the Scout over places
you just don't go over in a car. We went over the pass, saw pioneer
graves, ancient log cabins, Indian altars, remains of old log cabins, and
heaven only knows what else! No one but Dr. Bill would attempt to take
us where we went. Even my motorcycle ride with him didn't match this!

Mind you—there were no roads on this here mountain, except those
made by Dr. Bill and the cattle! This was territory—much of it
unexplored—on the Bill Rice Ranch.[1]

Only once on that day did we have to stop and pull a tree out from
under the hood! And Bill had his pistol along in case we saw Indians—
or rattlesnakes. They killed 'em by the dozens then—rattlesnakes,
I mean.

I understand that when Dr. Jack Hyles rode with Dr. Bill on this trip
some time before our famous ride, he was thrown out of the Scout three
times! For some reason, he was reluctant to make this trip with us!

---

[1] Nowadays there is not a more up-to-date conference ground in America—two large dining
halls, air-conditioned John R. Rice Tabernacle, Cowboy Town, nice accommodations, wonderful recreation facilities, etc. Thousands of young people and the deaf come to the Bill Rice
Ranch every year, and many are saved there.

And a certain one in our small party was heard to say, "I want to get in the same place coming back because I have already made dents in the top of the Scout to fit my head!"

Large crowds attended the Sword Conference each year at the Bill Rice Ranch, held around the first week of July so as to pull for a huge Fourth of July rally.

† † †

Dr. Rice kept on going to a two- or three-day conference or a one-night speaking engagement or a week of Sword Conferences. But he was spending more time in Wheaton writing articles, promoting books and pulling for subscriptions.

Now the Sword had added some special features: Noteworthy News Notes and Sword Thrusts (Bill Rice); Merv Rosell Presents Illustrations and Quotes; Preaching...Power...Promotion (D. A. McCall); Grace Notes (Grace Rice MacMullen); Uncle Walt's Thrilling Bible Stories for Young Folks and News Flashes From Christian Schools (Walt Handford); Book Reviews; as well as columns on the staff of evangelists and Editor's Notes. We were also running chapters from well-known children's books, a chapter a week.

† † †

NEWS NOTES:

$2,000 go to Japan for more *"What Must I Do to Be Saved?"* to be printed and to be used particularly in the Youth for Christ World Congress in Tokyo.

And Portugal gets half million *"What Must I Do to Be Saved?"* booklets with Sword check of $1,100.

† † †

In September Mrs. R. A. Torrey, a neighbor in Wheaton who lived three or four blocks from the Rices, died at the age of 94. She was a lover of THE SWORD and a lover of revivals. Her famous husband died in 1928.

† † †

Mrs. W. A. (Billy) Sunday was a tremendous influence for good and our greatly treasured friend. From her home at Winona Lake, Indiana, she wrote in August, 1953: "Dear John: Read your editorial, and it is a fine plan. I sincerely hope people will respond. I'm going to send in 25 subscriptions as fast as I can. These 6 at $1.50 each make $9, which I enclose."

SWORD EMPLOYEES PROMISED 5,070 subscriptions on the 200,000 goal we were seeking by our 20th anniversary, September 28. Time and time again the employees got deeply involved in getting subscriptions, which meant their heart was in the work.

673 people wrote us that they trusted Christ through Sword literature in 1953. We believe that these 673 who were so certain and so bold in claiming Christ represent thousands of others who were turned to Christ largely through THE SWORD OF THE LORD and Sword literature who did not write to say so.

1954

"YESTERDAY I GAVE AWAY $4,101.90," read the bold headline.

When Mr. Ellsworth Culver of the Orient Crusade visited the office, he told about three million people, some fifty years before, leaving the Catholic Church in the Philippine Islands and forming the Independent Filipino Church. Unfortunately it got into the hands of the Unitarians and for years did little and lost about a million adherents.

But a few years back some strong leadership arose in the Independent Filipino Church. They adopted a new Statement of Faith which held to the deity of Christ and salvation by faith.

This Independent Filipino Church, with 339 priests and approximately two million adherents, had no libraries, no Bible institutes, no Christian colleges or seminaries in which to train preachers or their uneducated priests.

After holding evangelistic services in some of their churches and seeing many saved, the presiding bishop asked Brother Culver to provide a Gospel of John for each of the two million adherents and to help get libraries of sound Christian books for the priests.

"Brother Rice, can you help?" our friend pled. Another man would furnish the two million Gospels of John, but Culver wanted to match him with two million *"What Must I Do to Be Saved?"* He asked also for some books for the library and a subscription to THE SWORD OF THE LORD for each of these 339 hungry-hearted priests who had left Romanism. Most read English there.

So that is the way it came about that Dr. Rice gave away $4,101.90 and obligated himself and the Sword of the Lord for $12,000 to $15,000 more.

† † †

Some have but to hear that a new version of the Scriptures has come out, and they are off to the bookseller to pick up a copy. As Ponce de Leon knocked about the world looking for a nonexistent fountain of youth, some continually look for new versions for one reason or another.

But in most cases, you pore over the new awhile, put it aside and return to your first love, the famous King James Version.

Dr. A. W. Tozer said that it had been his experience that the new versions make at least one mistake for every one they correct.

When the Revised Standard Version was released after a tremendous publicity campaign, literally thousands of preachers were taken in and actually believed it would make biblical truth easier to understand.

THE SWORD at once took the lead in exposing the work of modernists, the slanting of the translation[1] by the enemies of Christ with the deliberate intention of discounting the fundamentals of the Faith.

Week after week Dr. Rice unfavorably reviewed the Revised Standard Version, calling attention to its errors. "Any modernist translating the Bible cannot be trusted," he pointed out. "And where there was a difference of opinion, they had a tendency to put in the modernistic viewpoint."

When appeared, chapter by chapter, *Methodism and the Bible,* by Newton Conant, THE SWORD opened the eyes of literally thousands of Methodists to the dangerous trend away from God and the Bible that so many Methodist churches had taken.

When infidel Nels Ferre wrote his modernistic book, *The Sun and the Umbrella,* THE SWORD exposed it in a review.

In that book he denied the bodily resurrection of Jesus and affirmed it to be unreasonable, unreliable and untrue. He declared that nobody knew what actually happened. He virtually declared that the disciples manufactured the resurrection story of whole cloth. He says, "Mystery religions got sucked into the resurrection story." On and on he preached his infidelity.

Doubtless by Dr. Rice's exposure, thousands of eyes were opened to the truth about this sneaking wolf who had been masquerading as a sheep.

Yes, THE SWORD became a mighty weapon to defend all against modernism.

Then skepticism was taking a large toll among our young people of high school and college age. Then, as now, many teachers of zoology, biology, geology, anthropology and other kindred sciences spoke

---

[1] We who grew up on the grand old King James Version of the Bible, as did our fathers, grandfathers, mothers and grandmothers; we who learned to say, "Blessed are the pure in heart"— let's keep it that way!

blatently about evolution as though it were a proven fact instead of a discredited theory.

Many parents, without proper schooling, felt themselves inferior to the learned (?) professors. When Junior came home with the news that Professor Know-it-all said the story of Jonah and the whale could not possibly be true, and Sister added that Dr. Out-of-this-world said it didn't matter whether Jesus was born of a virgin or not, just so He was a good man—many parents were at a loss to know what to say.

Well, what did Dr. Rice do? He printed sermons and articles by scholarly scientists proving the authenticity of the Scriptures—articles by Dr. Harry Rimmer and Dr. Arthur I. Brown which presented facts that would stand up in the Supreme Court of the United States—of the reliability of the biblical record.

Yes—THE SWORD OF THE LORD was a mighty weapon to defend our young people.

He ran messages on false cults when Watchtower people were selling their papers on the street corners and Seventh-day Adventists were posing as Bible teachers. Literally thousands of homes were being invaded with these and other heresies. The Devil is the father of liars; and the propagators of these false cults follow in their father's footsteps, often using the Bible itself to "prove" their false doctrines.

Irvine's book, *Heresies Exposed,* was published chapter by chapter, and many similar works showing from Scripture the wickedness of the isms sweeping our country. Wimbish's *Jehovah's Witnesses* was printed, then put in a pamphlet and widely used. It is still in print.

And THE SWORD OF THE LORD was a mighty defender against worldliness. Plain, common sense articles showed young people the dangers of petting. There were articles on mixed bathing, the danger of the modern dance, gambling, Hollywood movies and other matters plaguing our youth.

We had every reason to believe that thousands were changed by such articles. Maybe you were—or someone you knew.

† † †

New editions of *"What Must I Do to Be Saved?"* were ordered in Korea, Japan, Formosa, the Netherlands and Africa—totaling $2,897. The Sword picked up the tab.

† † †

"Whad bakes you tink dis is da Hay Fever seasud?" How much this
'fever' affected some of us during August-September! But the work had
to go on, so we went around with boxes of Kleenex, nose spray, pill bottles, and did our best, determining, "We shall overcome!"

† † †

Through the years, thousands of wonderful letters came to the Sword.
We liked best those which told of being saved through our efforts. Dr.
Rice delighted to hear from preachers who had been blessed by his books
or THE SWORD. Letters were our lifeline, our contact with the outside
world.

So many of them were read in devotions. But let me quote a most
touching one from a child:

> Dear Rev. Rice:
>
> I thought I would writ you and tell you about our trouble. My
> daddy is a shurf [sheriff] and him and another shurf went into
> the woods to get some stills and the drunks shot at them. And
> the next night they came and blased [blasted] our car up with
> a dymite and I was a sleep and it scared me and I jumped. My
> grandma jumpup and said what was that fuss. I want one of your
> books "What Must I Do to Be Saved?" I'm nine years old and want
> to be.
>
> Your friend Brenda

† † †

With some book orders we had to use more than our imagination! We
liked to believe that "the customer was always right," but after having
to answer such queries as, "Please tell me what I ordered on my last
order," and not give a name, we were convinced that it just always
'ain't' so!

1955 In April Dr. Rice flew to Scotland to be in the Billy Graham campaign, the trip provided for by a Christian businessman. Dr. Rice felt he could better report the campaign in THE SWORD OF THE LORD after seeing it firsthand.

Since he was promoting evangelists and evangelism, he continually ran pictures of the Graham campaigns, with long articles about the crowds and results. (This was still before Dr. Graham appointed liberals on his committees and recognized leading modernists in the setup of his campaigns.)

† † †

Dr. Rice's love and concern for ministerial students and preachers everywhere was well known. In every way he sought to help them where he could. Out of a burdened heart he once wrote:

> It is said that before her death, Mary I, Queen of England, said, "If, when I die, you open my body and look at my heart, you will find engraved upon it the word CALAIS!" (Calais, across the channel in Europe, had been owned by England but was lost to France, causing Queen Mary great grief and continual mourning.)
>
> If one could read the deepest pages of my heart, he would find written thereon the preachers of the world! My most fervent prayers, my hottest tears, my most earnest exhortations, my hardest work for these many years, have been for preachers. I live from day to day to be a blessing to preachers, to help them understand the Bible, to show them how to have God's power, to keep them from false doctrine and unbelief.

It had been a year or so since Dr. Rice had given, upon request, $1,000 worth of his books to students of New Orleans Baptist Theological Seminary and *Prayer—Asking and Receiving* to Philadelphia Bible Institute.

Now desiring to make another investment in ministerial students all over America, he wrote to some 200 colleges, enclosing a form for ministerial students to fill out. If they would promise to read a select group of his books ($7.28 worth), these would be sent upon request.

This was a $34,216 investment, for some 4,700 returned the order form! While making this offer, Dr. Rice explained:

> I have thanked God a thousand times for the men who put in my hands R. A. Torrey's *How to Pray* when I was in my teens and, a little later, *George Mueller of Bristol,* by A. T. Pierson. Another gave me *In His Steps, or What Would Jesus Do?* by Charles M. Sheldon, and still another, *The Autobiography of Charles G. Finney.* Only eternity can tell what these books did for me in teaching me how to pray, how to win souls and to see the price one must pay to be a good Christian. So I know what these books will do to young preachers.

Many of the SWORD readers helped by sending money earmarked for MINISTERIAL FUND.

† † †

Many of us, including Dr. and Mrs. Rice and family, were members of Wheaton Bible Church, since the Baptist church in town was in what was then the Northern Baptist Convention. We enjoyed our church, which included professors from Wheaton College, from Moody Bible Institute, and many returned, retired missionaries.

How gracious all were to Sword employees! The fellowship was indeed sweet. I was editor of the church paper, working under my journalism teacher at Wheaton College, Mr. Robert Walker. The memories of those days are mighty blessed!

For fifteen years Dr. Rice had lived in Wheaton, had prayed for Wheaton, but had seen very few saved in the good churches there. We Christians had separated ourselves completely from the lost around us.

Now, after all these years, when the Wheaton Bible Church officials decided that the pastor would not publicly baptize any longer, Dr. Rice started Calvary Baptist Church in the old Presbyterian Church building which the Sword had purchased and would in the future tear down and there build a new plant.

We went out to find the lost—something we hadn't had a burden to do for years. It was our own fault, of course, but no special burden had been laid on us to get those saved around us.

One example:

In this town, known as *Saints' Rest,* a bartender had lived for many years. Then he moved to Miami. There he was contacted, went to church, got saved and said, *"As long as I lived in Wheaton, not once did anyone invite me to church"*—not a missionary, not a teacher at Moody or Wheaton, not one from Youth for Christ headquarters nor one from Scripture Press nor one from Sword of the Lord Foundation!

Now we determined to do something about Wheaton, to "begin at Jerusalem . . . ."

God prospered Calvary Baptist Church.

† † †

At 7:45 each Tuesday morning the bell rang at the Sword of the Lord. This was the day when some fifty or sixty workers from both buildings met together for combined devotions for 25 or 30 minutes. The other mornings, Mr. Handford led Building #1 group in a few minutes of devotions and prayer, and when Dr. Rice was home, he led at Building #2.

Tuesdays were looked forward to with real joy. We began by singing a couple of verses of a song; then we heard choice letters read—letters telling of conversions, of particular blessings one way or another—all directly connected with the work we did at the home base. This was the time when our work was rewarded—when we heard answers to our prayers, when we could actually see what part we were having in changing lives and winning souls.

Then after a brief word of exhortation from the Scriptures and several short definite prayers made to God, asking Him to save more the coming week, we were dismissed for the day's work. Our feet were much lighter as part of us walked those 240 steps from Building #1 back to Building #2. After our spiritual stimulus for another week, it seemed not nearly so hard to wrap those books, file those stencils, type those letters, answer that mail and open those nearly thousand letters a day!

Praise the Lord, we, week by week, awaited to hear God's blessings in our 7:45 Tuesday devotional period! We began the day with daily devotions.

† † †

McCormick Theological Seminary in Chicago (Presbyterian), one of the most prominent liberal seminaries, asked to buy back copies of THE SWORD OF THE LORD from the first issue on. And if all copies were not available, would they be allowed to photograph and put on microfilm every page of every weekly issue since it began? These copies of THE SWORD were wanted, the writer of the letter said, "because THE SWORD OF THE LORD is somewhat the mouthpiece for fundamental Christianity and represents the whole fundamentalist movement in a way no other known magazine did." For future study by their students, they required these copies as an authoritative source on the fundamentals of the Faith and the fundamentalist movement and what out-and-out Bible-believers stood for.

This liberal seminary knew THE SWORD OF THE LORD was, in some sense, the voice of Fundamentalism in America and in the world, as it is in some sense, and to multitudes, the voice of evangelism.

† † †

In October, SWORD OF THE LORD print order was 117,000, and 12 pages weekly.

1956 The passing of another year reminds us we have a job to do, that can be done only in time; and our section of time is limited. It is true that with every day we get closer to our meeting with the Saviour; but it is also true that with every day our opportunity of doing the job He has given us to do is more curtailed.

Time is a treasure;
How shall we use it?
We can make useful,
Or can abuse it!
Only the Giver
Can make our hearts wise,
Teaching us daily
The New Time to prize.
Time is a treasure,
So view it, my soul!
Keep all its spending
'Neath watchful control;
Employ each moment
In God's holy fear,
And He will ensure thee
A Happy New Year.

† † †

"Entering into 1956," said Dr. Rice, "I felt led of God to seek out some blessed promises on which I might expect to have the greatest year's ministry and the greatest year's blessing of my ministry thus far. My heart seized upon two Scriptures: Isaiah 40:28-31 and Ephesians 3:20."

† † †

"Ma" Sunday wrote Dr. Rice:

Dear Friend:

Thanks for your fine Christmas greeting. No doubt by now you know that Rody took off for Heaven Sunday at 11:20 [January 14, 1956].

Now Rody [Homer Rodeheaver, for twenty years with Billy Sunday] is in Heaven, singing and shining there, along with Moody, Torrey, Billy Sunday, Gipsy Smith, Sankey, P. P. Bliss and Charlie Alexander!

† † †

January 29, 1956, Calvary Baptist Church's first anniversary: 183 in Sunday school.

† † †

38,000 preachers, 1,500 missionaries, people in 81 foreign countries—many peoples and tribes who read English—delight with weekly visits from THE SWORD.

† † †

March 2 issue reported 323 churches observing SWORD Sunday either on February 2 or a Sunday close to that.

† † †

The office staff called for volunteers to form a riot for the purpose of demonstrating! The chant: "BURN THAT CARD! BURN THAT CARD!" Dr. Rice had been gone too much, too long, too often. We were ready to burn his air travel card and keep him home!

What's this? You say Dr. Rice is leaving soon for Japan and Korea?

The Evangelical Foreign Missionary Fellowship had invited him for its annual Bible Conference at Karuizawa, 95 miles from Tokyo, to speak six times to missionaries from many nations and from 25 denominations, but all evangelical Bible believers. "It is a tremendously important group, the key to the future of the Gospel in Japan," Dr. Rice was told.

After a week there, he flew to Korea, where he spoke to some 400 servicemen in Seoul and Inchon. Then back to Tokyo for another week, to speak to national pastors and others.

While there he promised to try to raise money for one million copies of his booklet, *"What Must I Do to Be Saved?"* in Japanese each year for the next three years. "We definitely agreed to provide $2,500 for the first 1/2 million copies within the next few weeks," he said.

It was very hard for him to say "no" to any request for literature; so, the Sword tried to fill all orders as money came in, including 100,000

"What Must I Do to Be Saved?" in Hindi, for India. Previously we had furnished money for some 150,000. Other calls came. These too were provided for.

† † †

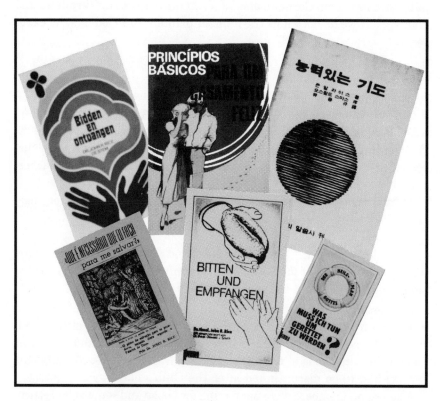

A soul is a soul regardless of the color of the skin which houses it. The world is to be our parish. God loved the world. Jesus died for the world. The Holy Spirit convicts the world. Boundaries, geographical lines, oceans, continents and hemispheres are all to be crossed in the spreading of the Gospel.

The separation of the world into TWO fields—home and foreign—is a master stroke of the Devil. It's all "foreign" to God, and on this Jesus had this to say, "The field is the WORLD."

We kept receiving the strangest-reading pamphlets, all "foreign" to us. We will never know how many millions of *"What Must I Do to Be Saved?"* were translated and printed outside America, but our records do show 16,576,245, which included the countries of Japan, Korea, Germany, Italy, China, Africa, Finland, Holland, eight languages in India, the Philippines, Spain and other countries.

We do know that his book, *Prayer—Asking and Receiving,* has been published in Dutch, German, Japanese, Spanish, Korean, Ukrainian and Danish, but we do not know the number printed. But God has the exact record!

† † †

He had several speaking engagements in Canada in 1956, including a blessed campaign in Calgary, Alberta; Edmonton and Vancouver.

Dr. Rice noted: "It was a joy to have a phone call from Premier E. C. Manning of Alberta while in Edmonton. Besides being a very successful premier or governor of that province, he is a true gospel preacher, greatly respected and loved."

There was no letting up in conferences and two- to three-day meetings.

† † †

It was Job who said, ". . . the Lord gave, and the Lord hath taken away; *blessed be the name of the Lord,"* after learning of the loss of his possessions and the death of his seven sons and three daughters.

We were trying to say the same thing around the Sword of the Lord Foundation in the midst of our grief over the loss of "one of the family." We did not feel we could continue month after month and year after year losing hundreds of dollars on the Sword Book Club; so sadly this service had to be discontinued after the Club's eleven-year history.

When some members were not paying for books and some were returning those they had allowed to come under the automatic shipment plan, we changed to the "cash" plan with fifteen percent discount on every order, hoping to put the Club on a paying basis. But only about 400 out of 3,000 members were ordering. So we felt we could not continue its existence, with so few participating.

Only God knows and eternity will reveal the good done in this time through the Sword Book Club and the good books distributed.

† † †

Please read this remarkable letter from Iraq, with his spelling left as he wrote it:

Dear Dr. Rice:

I beg to apologise for not replying your so precious and inspiring letter dated March 19.

I have to confess, that I was a poor sinner and while being fully occupied with future business prospects while receiving your letter it sounded as fiction to my narrow Christian mind and felt reluctant to reply it. Meanwhile my people, being in old and fanatic Christian faith, became an obsticle of discurragement. In fact I was also at first agreeable to their point of view.

As I was receiving from you my weekly magazine THE SWORD OF THE LORD at first I forced myself to look at it but reluctantly, while devil was doing his utmost to divert me from looking and reading this Christian and inspiring magazine; then I realized that it was the voice of Jesus Christ who invited me to find interest in the containts of the magazine, and I found myself attracted to read every part of it.

From time to time I used to interprate some important parts of it to my wife whose English knowledge is a bit poor and I also used to speak and interprate parts of it to my relatives and friends whenever they happened to visit us. After completion of each edition I am passing it to my friends as a Christian gift.

Hoping it will interest you to know that I am working as Chief Clerk at Accounts Dept., with Iraq Petroleum Co. K3 Station and I am for twelve years in my present position; besides I am also a certified Dental Mechanic for which I run a private Dental Clinic after working hours.

I wish to add that my people, specially my wife Anna, joins me in thanking your Christian endeavoury which dragged us from darkness where Satan is ruling to light of eternal and promising life . . . .

> In international friendship, yours,
>
> (Signed) Baba Talya

† † †

742 converts wrote us in 1956 of their conversion through Sword literature distributed in the United States.

1957 Rev. Kenny Joseph led in the distribution of 500,000 copies of a special holiday edition of *"What Must I Do to Be Saved?"* in Japanese (a separate printing from the one in 1956).

It is reported that sixteen missionary vehicles, some fifty Japanese students and workers from Japan Christian College, from Youth for Christ, Navigators, servicemen and cooperating churches, joined in helping distribute them at shrines during the Japanese New Year.

Mr. Joseph said:

> Through the kindness of your thousands of readers who sent in $2,890, we were able to print 1/2 million copies of a special edition adaptation of your world-famous tract, with an appropriate New Year's cover.
>
> Early on the morning of January 1st (Japan's most significant religious festival called O-Shogatsu—the honorable opening of the New Year) we took off for the famous shrines in Tokyo and vicinity, namely, *Meiji* (dedicated to the worship of their former emperor); *Kyujo*—the Imperial Palace (where resides the present emperor, Hirohito); *Yasukuni* (where are enshrined the dead soldiers of World War II—regarded as gods after their death); *Narita San* in Chiba Ken (very famous Shinto Shrine which attracts many almost fanatical believers); and the *Asakusa Pleasure District* (the goddess of mercy temple where millions of people daily flock during the New Year's holidays).
>
> We had to receive written police permission to distribute these tracts since the crowds were so large as to present a hazard. So with red bands on their arms and prayerful hearts, the workers went forth, instructed that each tract was to be given out prayerfully and courteously.
>
> The crowds exceeded those of last year, and once again the workers were inadequate. Over 200,000 tracts were distributed the first day, mainly at Meiji Shrine where over three million people attended.
>
> We concentrated in front of the Palace the second day, where

the Emperor made seven appearances to the throngs who shouted "vanzai" (long live the Emperor) and spontaneously sang the national anthem (supposedly abolished by MacArthur). The third and final day we spent mostly at Asakusa where we were not even able to give one out of every twenty persons a tract—the crowds were so dense.

Mr. Joseph enclosed pictures of the distribution, but time has caused us to misplace them.

It is hard to realize NOW just how much free literature we were supplying THEN. Praise the Lord that we had so many open doors to the world!

JEHOVAH JIREH—so Abraham named the place where God stayed his hand and provided a lamb for the sacrifice instead of his son Isaac—meaning "the Lord will provide."

As we look back over the years, we ask in wonder, "How was all this possible?" There is only one answer: without fanfare or too much drive, God tenderly provided. Dr. Rice and his staff simply carried out the task given—reaching everyone possible with the Gospel.

† † †

Mrs. Helen (Ma) Sunday, wife of the famous Evangelist Billy Sunday, died in her eighty-eighth year on February 20, 1957. She was buried in Chicago, next to her husband.

What a good friend she was, often writing Dr. Rice about events or happenings in hers or her husband's life or ordering subscriptions or thanking him for some blessing.

† † †

In March Zondervan Publishing House of Grand Rapids, Michigan took over all publishing and wholesale distribution of Sword books, relieving Sword of the Lord Publishers of a very heavy burden. Of course we continued to sell the editor's books, but those who bought wholesale had to order directly from Zondervan.

With the transaction with Zondervan, the Sword turned over a stock estimated at nearly $250,000 in retail value.

Both Pat and Bernie Zondervan were on the Sword of the Lord Cooperating Board and were our beloved friends.

Royalty on Dr. Rice's books went directly to the Sword of the Lord to be used to send the paper to missionaries, ministerial students, ministers and others who could not pay for their own subscriptions but had requested the paper.

✝ ✝ ✝

As he finished two radio recordings on tape on April 6, Dr. Rice started to leave the editorial office building through the dark back door and accidentally fell down eleven basement steps, his head hitting the concrete floor.

He got up, found his package, locked the door, drove automatically to the post office, mailed the radio tapes (although he did not recall doing this), then drove home.

When he walked into the living room, head covered with blood, there was pandemonium and bedlam!

His doctor was immediately called. Not knowing how seriously Dr. Rice was hurt, Dr. Wyngarden said he would meet him at his office. There he sewed up Dr. Rice's head and sent him home.

Later, X-rays showed a long fracture from the back of his head down near one eye. The tremendous sickness which followed indicated that he had a very close call.

When he fell, he may have lain unconscious for a time. Later, a six-inch pool of blood was found where he had fallen; and when he arrived home, the blood on his head and clothes seemed dried.

After nine days, he was able to feed himself, after lying flat on his back and not moving.

At Dr. Rice's insistence, the doctor let him remain at home, but no visitors, three weeks in bed, and two more for recuperation. Dr. Wyngarden spent hours with him. What a beloved brother and friend!

Dr. Rice said, "Satan tried to kill me, but Satan can do nothing but what God allows. I think the saint was right who said, *'The Christian is immortal until his work is done.'*"

He completely recovered—except he never regained his sense of smell. After about 6 weeks, he was going full steam!

✝ ✝ ✝

"Thank God for over 25,000 subscriptions which came in during our summer 'OTHERS' Subscription Campaign. God reward everyone who helped spread the Gospel, the defense of the Faith, and revival fires" (Dr. Rice).

✝ ✝ ✝

"God bless Billy Graham in his services at _____. Bless his workers—Cliff Barrows, Bev Shea, Grady Wilson, Jerry Beaven and Paul Maddox."

That prayer I heard prayed hundreds of times.

Then came the serious challenge to Dr. Rice's dream of bringing back great citywide revivals to America.

Dr. Graham was a member of the Board of Directors of Sword of the Lord Foundation and holding large citywide revivals, and Dr. Rice was on the Board of Northwestern Schools when Dr. Graham was president. Happy to see his dream coming true more and more, Dr. Rice was wholeheartedly boosting Dr. Graham in THE SWORD.

Dr. Rice reported Dr. Graham's campaigns before they were popular; defended him when he was attacked by men and when the attack was quoted favorably in *Moody Monthly* and *Evangelical Action* magazines. He commended him and built confidence in him among Southern Baptists when Southern Baptist papers publicly opposed him. None of the great evangelists had ever before accepted the sponsorship of modernists, so why would he believe Dr. Graham would?

With wide publicity came much criticism. Some were critical of mass evangelism in general; others, including Dr. Bob Jones, Sr., felt Dr. Graham was wavering a bit from his early fundamental stand. But as an editor, Dr. Rice was reporting the facts made available to him. When Dr. Graham kept on assuring him that he had not changed his position on sponsorship, Dr. Rice kept staunchly defending him.

But then came the New York City crusade of May, 1957 and Dr. Graham's public statement to the National Association of Evangelicals: *"I intend to go anywhere, sponsored by anybody, to preach the Gospel of Christ. . . . "* This was certainly contrary to what Dr. Graham had been assuring Dr. Rice. There Dr. Graham, for the first time, had known liberals on his sponsoring committee. Then each campaign followed the same pattern, the same rules.

Dr. Rice went to Dr. Graham with this, but to no avail. They talked long distance again and again. All the counsel Dr. Rice could give him was ignored.

Dr. Rice tried to show Dr. Graham how wrong his policy was in refusing to hold a revival unless all the modernists in town were invited to publicly cooperate; how wrong it was having unconverted men on his committees or to lead in prayer; how wrong it was to send inquirers back to churches which were against New Testament Christianity, even Roman Catholic churches!

Then there came the time when, according to his own letter to Dr. Rice, Dr. Graham could not sign the doctrinal statement which each Sword Board member must sign yearly, because it stated: "... opposes modernism, worldliness and formalism."

Sadly and with a broken heart, Dr. Rice withdrew his support of Dr. Graham's now compromising ministry and through THE SWORD OF THE LORD helped many preachers and others see the serious problem involved with ecumenical evangelism.

No one could possibly know the heartbreak this caused Dr. Rice. The price paid was unbelievable in friends, subscriptions and personal grief. I know—I saw the letters, the heartbreak.

Yet in it all, I never saw my Boss turn mean nor vindictive. In fact, in my judgment, herein lay Dr. Rice's great strength. He had rock-ribbed convictions for which he would die—but with the Christian charity and kindness which enabled him to be a help to those who needed encouragement and direction.

He felt he must warn the 22,000 preachers who read THE SWORD OF THE LORD of Dr. Graham's compromise. "While we love and pray for him," he said, "we cannot be a party to fellowship with unbelievers in Christ and the Bible."

Dr. Rice kept on praying for and loving Dr. Graham—and kept on warning him and the public of the error of his way. Dr. Graham kept justifying his compromises with, and concessions to, the enemies of historic Christianity on the ground that these compromises and concessions were producing the greatest revival movements in modern times.

Dr. Rice later said:

> Dr. Billy Graham is only an incident. Any other man, friendly or unfriendly, well known or unknown, is only incidental in this matter of compromise. There are eternal issues at stake much more important than any man. The authority of the Word of God, the integrity of gospel preachers, the welfare of Christian institutions, the cause of evangelism—these are all wrapped up in being true to Christ and the Bible on the matter of separation from modernism.
>
> It would do tremendous harm if THE SWORD OF THE LORD should stop any discussion of the question of yoking up with

modernists and should let the matter ride and people go their own way without warning.

Yet Dr. Rice continually rejoiced over the many saved in Dr. Graham's crusades.

In closing this sad part about Dr. Graham: Dr. Bob Shuler, great Methodist pastor and also a defender of the Faith, tells how God gave him grace to stand alone, as it seemed Dr. Rice was called upon to do:

> I have come, thank God, to where I believe I could stand up and vote my convictions if I were the one lonely man on my side of the question. I recall one instance when one man and one only stood up and voted with me. I confess that it is more pleasant to be with the majority than with the minority, but the joy of taking a conscientious stand and feeling that you are right is far greater than the thrill of multitudes who agree with you.
>
> I most certainly do not compare my humble battles with those of men concerning whom I now write. But I have read of Luther, who at one time was so utterly friendless that one historian speaks of him as "a lone fox chased by the whole pack of the countryside."
>
> I cannot forget that Wesley was denied a church in which he might preach and was forced to make a platform and pulpit of his father's tombstone. He died an Episcopalian, but the problem when he died was finding an Episcopal clergyman who would conduct his funeral.
>
> I might tell the story of friendless John Knox and Savonarola and scores of other immortals of the centuries whose friends—if they had any—deserted or stood dumb, as Peter, who denied Christ outside Pilate's court.
>
> Such are times when men need to know their own souls and to be fortified with a loyalty that is to God alone. If standing true and courageous amid the storms that now assail they can look up and go forward, it will matter little whether other men are their friends or their foes. If friends gather about them, well and good. If their fellowmen desert them, their hearts will still be warm with purposeful resolve and they will be none the worse!

Bless the memory of Dr. Shuler!

Remember this: when we appear before the judgment seat of Christ to be judged for the deeds done in the body, Christ is not going to look for medals, but for *SCARS!*

Had every friend turned against him, had he lost every subscriber to

THE SWORD OF THE LORD, Dr. Rice would still have followed his convictions and done what he thought was right in opposing liberals and modernism and the compromising of Dr. Billy Graham, for whom he prayed regularly even long after denouncing his compromise.

Some people suppose that, when a man fights sin and stands up for his convictions, his heart must be of stone and his skin of leather.

Let it be understood that, when good men slandered Dr. Rice, it still hurt. He was still human. It still hurt to be slandered by enemies, shunned and sometimes betrayed by friends, suspected by those who ought to be the first to commend, not condemn, his stand for Christ. He delighted in and was comforted by any word of encouragement, just as any man.

This reminds me of Shylock in Shakespeare's *The Merchant of Venice.* Abused and despised because he was a Jew, he said, "Hath not a Jew eyes, hands, organs, dimensions, senses, affections, passions? Is he not fed with the same food, hurt with the same weapons, subject to the same diseases, healed by the same means, warmed and cooled by the same winter and summer, as a Christian is? If you prick us, do we not bleed? If you tickle us, do we not laugh? If you poison us, do we not die?"

So as an editor, as an evangelist, as a preacher of righteousness, a defender of the Faith, Dr. Rice had feelings, too, just as all people do. Loss of friends caused him great grief.

† † †

What a "Letter Month" we had in 1957! 15,960 letters; 2,919 *Sermons From the Saddle* booklets (Bill Rice) given away; 1,934 plastic Bible cases (with orders, subscriptions or gifts of $5 or more); sold 214,215 copies of *"What Must I Do to Be Saved?"* at $1 per hundred; and total retail sales were $5,162.18.

† † †

And we say it's hard to win them!!!

A man in prison pled:

> Dr. Rice, I'm writing in regard to being a Christian. I have been Hell-bound for about 22 years and I would like to turn to the Lord and serve Him. If you can and will, forward any advice as to what to do. I am a sinner, and I would like to repent before it is too late. And sir, I know just as sure as I'm writing this letter that,

if I don't repent, I'll spend eternity in Hell. So what would you advise me to do?

Scores—perhaps we could say hundreds—of hungry sinners "approached" the Sword by letter asking to be shown how to be saved. And we say it is too hard to win them!!!

Wrote another: "It was your booklet, *'What Must I Do to Be Saved?'* that opened my eyes to salvation. Thank the Lord for it."

And another: "My brother was won to Christ last week by one of your booklets, *'What Must I Do to Be Saved?'*"

And another: "I sent my brother near his birthday your booklet, *'What Must I Do to Be Saved?'* Surprisingly, it was my sister-in-law who read it, became convicted and surrendered to Christ in her home."

Still another: "Yesterday in my place of business I gave one of the booklets to an old man 82 years old and told him to please read it. He promised he would. Last night my pastor and I went out to visit him. As soon as we got in his home, he told us he had read the little booklet— *twice,* he added quickly. And before we left, we had won both him and his 77-year-old wife to the Lord."

I just must quote two more letters from the 1957 mail bag.

A good doctor from Miami related:

> Enclosed find my check for 500 *"What Must I Do to Be Saved?"* booklets. I gave one to one of my patients who has now gone on to be with the Lord. She said to tell you that she had been baptized twice before she was saved once. After reading your pamphlet she received Christ and died a victorious "born-again" Christian.

A prisoner in Missouri State Penitentiary got saved and wrote:

> Brother Rice, this is just to tell you I have taken Jesus to be my Saviour this Sunday, April 28. I lived in sin all my life but now I know my Saviour, Jesus Christ. I got down on my knees this morning and asked Jesus to forgive me. I feel deep down in my heart He saved me from sin because I feel like a new man after asking Him to forgive me. My dad is a preacher. He told me time after time, "Son, ask God to forgive you of your sin." I said, "Dad, I ain't ready yet." But today as I am writing you I have found my Saviour.

Such letters come from all over the world. Oh, there are hungry hearts everywhere! People are out there to be won.

These are only a drop in the bucket. Scores of others told of getting saved, or they knew of others getting saved after reading this soul-saving literature.

† † †

Mr. Alvin Byers came to the Foundation on July 15, after graduating from Bob Jones University with both an A.B. and Master's degree. Dr. Rice discovered his exceptional abilities and qualities of leadership, and it was not difficult for any of his fellow-workers to recognize the same.

Amiable personality, precise statistician, competent executive, Mr. Byers was God's man for the responsible position as office and business manager and treasurer of the Foundation.

And if you knew Al, as we came to know Al, you would see how wise Dr. Rice was to designate him treasurer of the Foundation!

At the Sword we had a LITTLE SWORD, put out by and for the staff. In it we could speak our minds, be as silly as we wanted to be—in other words, let down our hair. This gave us opportunity to find out the talent each had, and many more things! Dr. Rice was its most avid reader! Dr. Bill Rice, to whom we mailed copies, sent many hilarious articles for the LITTLE SWORD.

While looking through a few issues recently, I came across one item: **"Can of corn with pimento below cost. See Al Byers."** Another told how Al used to wait for his neighbor (me) to burn her trash; then he would pile his on top while hers was still smoldering in order to save a match! I could go on and on, and you would laugh and laugh.

Miss Viola, broom in hand: "Do you suppose Al would buy us a new one?"

Max: "No, not until the last straw falls out!"

Dr. Rice had no doubt that he could count on Al to save the company every penny possible.

After awhile, this bachelor romanced and won Marcella O'Dell of the advertising department.

The Lord gave them three wonderful children (the fourth died after living only a few days). And how much they loved Dr. Rice! Little Rebecca thought the Scripture, "I was glad when they said unto me, Let us go into the house of the Lord," said, "I was glad when they said unto me, Let us go into the Sword of the Lord"! She would come with her daddy on Saturdays to Dr. Rice's office. This was not mail pick-up day, but since Dr. Rice might be leaving, Al would kindly get Saturday's mail. And how little "Becky" looked forward to those Saturday visits. Of course Dr. Rice fussed over her.

Al and Marcie reared their children by the rules set by Dr. Rice for his.

At this writing, Dr. Byers has been with the Foundation for thirty-three years and is still invaluable as vice-president and general manager. His devotions at 7:00 each morning, when Dr. Hutson is not in the office, are very pointed and get our day started right.

Al is my very personal friend, and I often go to him for advice, counsel and encouragement. He still comes back to my office, which is next to Dr. Rice's, and says, "I'd like to talk with Dr. Rice, please." He quotes him in devotions and visits his grave at the Bill Rice Ranch. Dr. Rice could have had no better friend.

It is a delight to work with him and under his supervision and to daily observe his witty, wise and winsome mannerisms.

† † †

Dr. Rice announced his new novel, *Seeking a City,* a descriptive and moving story of the most interesting of all Old Testament characters—Abraham. It was published by William B. Eerdmans Publishing Company.

✝ ✝ ✝

759 people were saved through Sword literature in 1957. These were
not vague and indefinite reports from people who said they knew someone else who had been saved through our Foundation; these were actual letters and decision forms with clear-cut testimonies of saving faith
in Christ. This figure is the more remarkable when you consider that
it probably represents but a fraction of those who were saved. Of the
ten lepers Jesus healed, only one returned to thank Him. It seems there
undoubtedly were several thousand others who were saved through THE
SWORD OF THE LORD or our books but did not write to tell us.

1958

In January a list of 90 evangelists and pastors signed a pledge not to work under the sponsorship of modernists nor to support any program contrary to the Gospel. That list included Bob Jones, Sr., Bob Jones, Jr., John R. Rice, Bill Rice, Monroe Parker, Jack Shuler, James Mercer, Joe Henry Hankins, Tom E. Berry, Tom Malone, Clifford Lewis, Fred Brown, Harry McCormick Lintz, Oliver B. Greene, Hugh Pyle, Hal Webb, Merle Fuller, John E. Zoller, E. J. Daniels, Michael A. Guido and a host of others—90 in all.

† † †

Dr. Rice took out his note pad and began making check marks.

"What are those notes you are making?" Mrs. Rice asked.

"Oh, I'm praying for my evangelists—one by one."

"But what do those check marks mean?"

He explained that twenty-six of the seventy had some problems and had left the evangelistic field.

Seven had left revival work to go into the pastorate; still he could not give them up and kept praying for them, along with the other evangelists.

Three had left evangelism to go into other work: two to become college presidents and one to assist a college president.

Ten others he had checked with a sad heart. Each had in some very definite way sold out by: catering to denominational leaders and shunning the fundamental group or endorsing the Revised Standard Version of the Bible or ceasing from fighting modernism, hoping to gain the endorsement of men or for some other reason leaving the fundamental camp. But could Dr. Rice take them off his list of evangelists? No. He would not give them up, so kept on praying for each by name.

Billy Graham was on that list, of course, and it was he who had influenced some of these ten. "Lord, help them to see the right way; help them to overcome the harm Billy has done," was his prayer now.

In the case of one particular, Dr. Rice always paused when he came to his name. This one had been tempted by Satan and had fallen into a grave sin. "But God, he is still dear to You!"

Three others—he also paused when he came to their names. These had debts unpaid. Because of this, one was seeking a pastorate. Another, well-trained and gifted, had gone into secular work in order to catch up on back bills.

Another, a good preacher, whose offerings had been small because he lived in an area where evangelists were not popular, had a wife who insisted on helping with the finances. On the job she met and became enamored with another man. Oh, how earnestly Dr. Rice cried to God for that preacher and his family when he prayed and checked his list of evangelists!

Another name on his "evangelist" list sadly had to be removed. That was Dr. Rice's brother Joe who had recently gone to Heaven.

There were twenty-six check marks by those evangelists who were no more on the field. Now Dr. Rice was praying for God to raise up others to take their place: "O God, provide support for men and encouragement to the lonely, isolated and persecuted ones who still have a burden for souls! O God, send some great evangelists to fill the shoes of these who have laid down the burdensome work of evangelism."

Each morning some seventy evangelists were named and prayed for. God seemed to bring their names before him. I would have forgotten the names of many of them, but not Dr. Rice. He loved each on that list and never failed them—month in and month out.

† † †

We started something this year that almost got out of hand!

To all who correctly worked the weekly puzzles, we offered to send a free booklet, which was described alongside the puzzle. In addition, we gave a Scofield Bible to all who sent in fifty correct answers during the year.

They enjoyed working the puzzles, but mostly they wanted the good booklets we were offering each week.

Well, we felt we could handle the expense—perhaps 300 or 400 would send correct answers. And that wouldn't be too much to handle.

WERE WE IN FOR A SURPRISE! Everybody we could call in was checking 2,000 to 2,500 puzzles every week!

Dr. Rice came to the startling conclusion that the puzzles would, at that rate, cost us from $12,500 to $15,000 a year! This included: free booklets, workers' time checking the puzzles sent in, mailing, postage, envelopes, etc.

Since I had suggested to Dr. Rice that we send a free booklet to those whose puzzles were correctly worked, it seems I was the one designated to come up with a quick solution to stop up the hole!

We got our heads together and decided that through THE SWORD we would ask the puzzle worker to enclose a dime each time a person sent in the worked puzzle. This would help on the heavy expense—and perhaps keep me at the organization a while longer!

Besides my already bunch of headaches, I was causing more work for others. Mrs. Elizabeth Handford had to provide the puzzles every week. Others had to search for good premium booklets and call the publishers to see if they had at least 2,000 in stock. Many didn't but some did. And this went on—not monthly but weekly!

With appeals in almost every issue, our "fuzzle pans" responded well. The readers had contributed $5,300.22 by year's end, leaving a deficit of $9,729.96 to make up.

What now should we do? Close down the department and discontinue the puzzles? We were most reluctant to do that since it was such a worthwhile pastime, and very useful booklets were reaching the public, helping Christians in their spiritual lives. Some even went to the unconverted. Only eternity will fully reveal the good that department was doing. To stop it seemed out of the question and would remain in our minds only as a "last resort."

So we kept on asking for help so the puzzles could continue.

To show the interest in puzzles, one wrote, "I just had a healthy baby girl this morning, so please excuse this paper." Also there were some funny letters including: "Please do not **degrade** me because of the error in the puzzle clews"!

† † †

Attention, All "Fuzzle Pans"!

When things got so bad the Boss began muttering to himself with incoherent phrases, *it was surely time to start some action!*

The puzzle department started out as an innocent little diversion for SWORD readers. However, this little pet grew into a monster which about completely disrupted the entire equilibrium of Sword of the Lord Foundation!

One day the Boss (that's Dr. Rice), after figuring out what this puzzle department was costing the company, was heard to exclaim somewhat frantically, "We're getting so many *fuzzle pans,* we're just going to have to do something!"

This picture summarized pretty well the situation in the Sword editorial office. Confusing, isn't it? We were literally "swamped" each week with thousands of puzzle entries.

† † †

Dr. Rice had been invited to speak two weeks on WMBI, the voice of Moody Bible Institute in Chicago.

Feeling a great urge to get out his popular *Bible Facts About Heaven* book, he offered it free to the radio audience.

Orders began coming in. A total of more than 7,000 copies of *Bible Facts About Heaven* went out absolutely free those two weeks! The Sword furnished the books, and Moody Bible Institute furnished the postage.

In the next six months, some 200 people wrote that they had found Christ through this 64-page book of 8 chapters; most got the copy during the two weeks on WMBI.

At the time of the death of Edsel Ford, someone sent a copy of *Bible Facts About Heaven* to his mother, Mrs. Henry Ford. She took time to write a lovely letter on black-bordered paper to tell Dr. Rice of the comfort she had received from reading it.

† † †

Another evangelistic sermon contest was announced. For five years the Sword of the Lord had been giving $1,600 in awards for the ten best evangelistic sermons submitted: first prize—$300; second, $250; third, $200; three prizes of $150 each and four at $100 each. You have no idea how hard it was then to find top-notch evangelistic sermons by *living* preachers, and this offer brought in many blessed messages.

These contests stimulated interest in preachers writing out their sermons, and the great value in this is that it clarifies the logic, brightens the style and gives a degree of polish and freedom otherwise frequently missing in preaching. Then, too, writing out one's message preserves it in printed form.

Unbiased judges passed on the sermons and declared their choices.

This certainly got preachers to working. Hundreds of manuscripts came in during each contest. Those sermons not selected were returned.

† † †

By October, a total of $5,250 had been sent out for the printing of 700,000 copies of *"What Must I Do to Be Saved?"* in Portugal and 100,000 copies to be used among Portuguese-speaking people in Brazil. Now could the Sword supply $580 more for 100,000 additional copies?

Dr. Rice never said "no" to such requests, so the check was soon on its way.

† † †

What a thrill to receive this letter of the year from an infidel who had found Christ through only one message in one issue of THE SWORD OF THE LORD:

> Twelve years after returning from the army, my heart was filled with hate, my mind with infidel doubts and arguments, such as, "How do you know Jesus is the Son of God?" "How do you know there is a god?" "How do you know that we are not the descendants of an ape?" which had come from one of Roy Chapman Andrews' books.
>
> As a career I planned on getting rich writing murder fiction, which I had hoped would be taken over by some movie company. My infidelity brought no happiness, no assurance, and I was driven to the thoughts of taking my own life. But if there was life beyond the grave, I would be in Hell, so I was afraid to take the chance of going to Hell.
>
> An aunt had loaned me a lot of old issues of THE SWORD. And I had read a lot of them. With nothing to do, I decided to look over the book advertisements while lying in the bed one night about ten, when my eye caught a catchy sermon by Joe Hankins entitled, "Why Half of the Preachers and Church Members I Know Should Go to Hell for Twenty-Four Hours." I started reading it. I thought I was tough and hard-boiled, but was soon weeping like a baby as it seemed I was falling straight into Hell. I cried, "Jesus, save me!" He did.
>
> A few months later I surrendered to the ministry while helping my grandfather, went to church Sunday, told the pastor and made it public.
>
> My doubts had vanished. After becoming a member of your Sword Book Club, my faith was strengthened by Dr. Rimmer's book, *The Theory of Evolution.* Your book, *Is Jesus God?* helped me understand more about the deity of Christ.
>
> By this one issue of THE SWORD, my whole life has been radically changed from infidelity, immorality and debauchery to hope, life and faith.
>
> > Yours in Christ Jesus,
> >
> > S. Allen Van Horn
> > DeWitt, Arkansas

One message in one issue of THE SWORD OF THE LORD!!

† † †

The discontinuing of the Sword Book Club three years before and the selling of the book publishing and wholesale trade to Zondervan Brothers made it possible for us to move our Sword office work back into one building. Now we did not have to furnish storage space for $250,000 worth of book stock, and we had no need to provide office space for the wholesale book business and the Sword Book Club.

Not only did this cut down on telephone, lights, heat, janitor, etc., but we could rent Building #2, which would add to the building fund.

This combining under one management simplified problems and saved duplication of effort and made our work more efficient and economical.

† † †

"Joe B. Rice Dies Suddenly" was the headline in March 14 issue. He had spent Monday with his brother John in Wheaton, then upon his arrival in Oklahoma on Tuesday morning, died suddenly on the street from heart failure.

Brother Joe was in his early fifties.

† † †

Other news of interest:

March Letter Month brought an amazing total of 22,000 letters.

The average circulation increased by 10,391 per week over 1957. There were 17,578 new subscribers added to the list.

All Wheaton Sword property had been paid in full.

Exactly 450 people wrote during the year that they had found Christ through sermons in THE SWORD or through other Sword literature. Praise the Lord!

1959

. . . A mighty revival is coming this way,
The very revival we're needing today,
It's coming from Heaven; believe while you pray,
. . . A mighty revival is coming this way.

And so the Voice of Revival theme song went out over the air waves from coast to coast every Sunday. This opening theme was written by George Bennard, who also wrote "The Old Rugged Cross." The closing theme was from one of Dr. Rice's own songs, "Open Your Heart's Door."

I saw a radio broadcast born!

I suppose there is nothing particularly spectacular about some twenty people assembling in a studio to record a tape for the first half-hour broadcast. There was no great crowd to inspire us. But this long recording session was an exciting two hours, for we felt the presence of God as we sang and announced and preached and prayed; and we fully expected this to grow into a worldwide ministry in a short period of time.

The program, entitled "The Voice of Revival," was designed to fill the need for old-fashioned revival preaching.

When the radio work began, Grace suggested to her father that she knew someone who might help with announcing for the broadcast. The man was then associated with a youth ministry in Rockford, Illinois, but he and Grace had worked together in radio at Bob Jones University several years before.

The man was called; and for the first six months drove to Wheaton, Illinois, twice each month for recording sessions. Then, as the work load grew, Dr. Rice asked him to move to Wheaton to be his radio assistant.

So the voice of Rev. Leslie "Bud" Lyles had been a part of the broadcast from the very start.

Bud majored in speech at Bob Jones University and did extensive work in radio with the University station, WMUU. His duties at Voice of Revival included supervision of production of the broadcast as well as handling all of the business. He kept close contact with the John M. Camp Agency which handled Voice of Revival from the beginning in 1959.

Bud also helped with the music, singing bass.

An ordained preacher, Mr. Lyles conducted 20 to 25 revivals each year and often led singing for conferences and camps as well.

Bud for many years wrote a weekly column in THE SWORD, "Teen Talks." Later these were put in four volumes.

Although a number of people and a variety of parts were involved in the production, the backbone of the radio ministry was always the sixteen-minute message by Dr. Rice.

Certainly he was no newcomer to radio, for he started back in the days of the crystal set and earphones. Then for years he had a daily thirty-minute broadcast in Dallas and later was on several other stations.

With his long years of experience in citywide revivals, his touch with the common people and his Spirit-filled preaching, Dr. Rice was needed in America. In my opinion, no other living man had a more pungent, easy-to-listen-to style. His voice was excellent and his delivery powerful and convincing. And by means of radio, this message could be sent to vast areas quickly.

After airing the Voice of Revival a few Sundays, letters began coming in—wonderful letters—from the unsaved. Here is but a sample or two:

"I am a young man 24 years old and single. I seem to be caught in all the evil vices of the world—drinking and smoking—the worst. Please help me find the spiritual guide that has led you to the light, so that I may find myself and God."

Another: "We have heard you over the air several times. . . . Will you pray for our family? We are not Christians and would like so much to be. That's the only way to live. With so much sin within reach, it is hard to do. I would like to get everything I can read about the Gospel of Christ. I know He died for us all."

One more: "Yes, I heard you yesterday over Station CKLW. Did you ever hear of—or know of—a hard heart? I mean *hard*? It dwells within this bosom. I have a desire to read the booklet you mentioned." It was signed, "An old reprobate, whom God is drawing near."

What an encouragement!

GOD WORKED MYSTERIOUSLY ON MANY HUNGRY HEARTS. Broadcasting is a rather strange business. All of Voice of Revival programs were tape recorded, the master tape was edited, then duplicated by a high speed process, then mailed to the stations about two weeks in advance of the date on which they were heard.

featuring...
Dr. John R. Rice

Above: Bud Lyles, coordinator and announcer

The Voice of Revival Choir in rehearsal, under direction of Don Sandberg. Every verse was rehearsed and sometimes re-rehearsed! We met twice each month and did two or three broadcasts at each session.

Right: Mr. Walter Super was in the control room.

Here is something else that is strange: we spoke and sang into a microphone; the sound was recorded on magnetic tape; the tape was mailed to a distant radio station; the station played the tape out over its equipment, and electrical impulses were carried through the air. We did not know who would hear the broadcast! We could not tell whether it would be heard by anyone. Strangely, in thousands of homes, people turned a radio dial and presently heard the music and message which were prepared and recorded many hours before and many miles away.

How could it be that these songs and this particular message seemed just suited for a hungry heart in the Midwest? How could we have known that in California a man would be listening with a burdened heart? How could it be that the duet by the Rice sisters was just what a poor, lonely shut-in needed in North Carolina? We did not know there was a man in Chicago who had lost his dear wife and was struggling to rear his children without God. Yet, again and again letters came from precious souls telling us that the message by Dr. Rice was "just what I needed" when they heard it on the broadcast. Isn't that strange?

There is no way of explaining such things without God. But before any broadcast, the Voice of Revival choir, the speaker, the announcer— all sought from God the right message, the right song. We prayed for the power and blessing of God upon this ministry. We prayed that He would cause those to listen who needed the message, the song.

That, no doubt, is why Voice of Revival brought salvation to many a soul, and peace and comfort to troubled hearts. There is no doubt that His hand was upon this program. The cost was great, but when measured in the light of souls kept out of Hell forever, it seemed so little.

† † †

Another year at Lake Louise, Toccoa Falls, Georgia, and this July seemed to have been the greatest, including the largest attendance.

Dr. Rice determined that the speakers would stress soul winning, organize for soul winning, and, along with speaking at the conference, spend much of the afternoons in soul winning.

A few lost people who were on the grounds got saved. After Dr. Hyles had given careful instructions about house-to-house visitation, on Thursday and Friday afternoons, some sixty were divided into five teams and carefully assigned streets.

Souls were won all over the city and nearby—a total of 167! And we believe that, as people drove back home, others were saved because of the burden placed upon individuals.

Though we had been going there many years, scores came up to say this was their first time at the conference. "But I'll be back next year for sure!"

Sword Conferences were held at Lake Louise for fifteen weeks in thirteen years (sometimes the conference was twice a year).

During this time the Sword of the Lord had the largest crowds of anyone year after year. There had never been a complaint about the music, the preaching nor the behavior of our great crowds. No one claimed that anyone had been unkind or unchristian in attitude or that any false doctrine was preached. Many times the accommodations were full.

Now, to the surprise of everyone, we were not invited back. Why? Dr. Rice said, "Those who are supposed to know say it was the influence of Dr. Graham and his friends and some Southern Baptists."

In October, after the manager of the Lake Louise Conference Grounds had expressed his regrets by letter, Dr. Rice wrote most kindly to R. G. LeTourneau, owner of the ground, outlining all the Sword had done to advertise the grounds, the great crowds and the good the conference had done each year and asking him for an explanation. But to this day—31 years later—no word has come from Mr. LeTourneau.

Sadly, Dr. Rice announced the cancellation in THE SWORD, saying, "While we are sad not to go back to Lake Louise, where many of you had a mountaintop experience with the Lord, yet we take it as from God, and He will open other doors to us."

Both Dr. Rice and Mr. LeTourneau are now in Heaven. No doubt they have settled any differences now!

Mr. LeTourneau is the one who had sent Dr. Rice and the Sword the first $1,000 ever received, back in the 1930's, when a $740 printing bill was due and there was no money to pay it. What rejoicing this gift brought to all connected with the Sword and the printing plant!

† † †

In Dr. Rice's Wheaton office hung a rare Crusaders' sword, shipped from Germany and purchased through a museum in Miami, then beautifully silver plated, with ivory handle from the Belgian Congo. The plate read: "THE SWORD OF THE LORD AND OF JOHN R. RICE." The sword was given Dr. John from Dr. Bill's loyal and generous heart. (It now hangs in the Sword auditorium in our Murfreesboro plant.)

**Crusader's Sword presented to Dr. John by Dr. Bill
on the 25th Anniversary of the Sword**

This ancient two-edged sword seems to have been made in the Holy Land for one of the Crusaders. It has Sanscrit lettering on the steel blade.

It has a bit of the Bill Rice Ranch flavor since the sword is held by silver-plated spurs and since the plaque itself is suspended from two gold-plated horseshoes taken from the feet of the Arabian stallion given Dr. Bill by the king of Jordan, King Abdullah Ilen Al Hussain, when Dr. Bill was in Palestine some years before.

† † †

Missionary Fred Jarvis wrote: "To date our records show that we have received 1,631 responses from the last half-million tracts, *What Must I Do to Be Saved?*" which we printed for you. Unfortunately, we have only 2,200 of these tracts left. If the Lord should make it possible for you to let us do another printing, we would certainly thank God." Then he added: "The above number of responses represents only what has come to our office—not to churches, etc."

These figures do not include thousands of decisions for Christ made in the first 3 million copies spread abroad before.

Dr. Jarvis enclosed many testimonies from those who were saved through the booklet, or wanted to be saved, and wrote in to ask how.

"I am twenty years old. I was saved by reading the tract."—Aoki Takeo.

"I am a wife and have had a hard time and a difficult life. I want to believe in Christ and be saved."—Furuike Chiyoko.

"I am a high school student and want to depend upon Christ to save my soul."—Shimizu Yoko.

"I would like to have peace in my heart and know my sins are taken away."—Nakagawa Iwao.

"I have no person to depend on and no hope or reason to live. I am a very unhappy girl. Can I believe in God?"—Suzuki Reiko.

"We are writing Dr. Jarvis, saying we will undertake to pay for the printing of another half-million. *What Must I Do to Be Saved?*'" said Dr. Rice. That amount of several thousand dollars would need to be raised—either by Dr. Rice personally or through the Free Literature Fund.

† † †

Billy Graham came to Wheaton for a revival September 27 through

October 4. Of course, the Sword organization could not cooperate. The newspapers reported large crowds. We never knew the number saved, but for each one we thank God.

Dr. Rice said he hoped there would be a good survey made of the actual results. "There has been no report of increased Sunday school and church attendance among the Bible-believing churches with which I am familiar. There has been no evidence of moral revolution in the town. But for every word of the Gospel preached, we rejoice; and for every good resolution made, whether an actual conversion or not, we thank God."

Dr. Rice went on in a SWORD article to mention one noticeable result following the Graham Crusade:

> Before the Billy Graham campaign, the ministerial association elected a committee to bring in a constitution and a strong evangelical statement of Faith. After the Billy Graham campaign, they turned down that plan by an overwhelming vote. Now any stand for the fundamentals of the Faith in Wheaton will be much more difficult, after good men cooperated with modernists because Dr. Graham asked it.

† † †

In 1959 exactly 350 people wrote to tell us they had been saved through the Sword of the Lord literature. These are only the ones who took time to write us that they had been saved. Actually there were undoubtedly many, many times that number who were saved and never wrote to tell us. We don't know of another magazine in the world that gets people saved like THE SWORD OF THE LORD does, week in and week out.

1960 WHILE HE MUSED, THE FIRE BURNED! When Dr. Rice began thinking of the goodness of God and how He had supplied for the work of the Sword for twenty-six years, he made this observation:

While trying to count my blessings, it recently dawned on me how much God has really helped me get out the Gospel!

I have been richly blessed in reading the life of George Mueller of Bristol, England, who built orphans' homes and cared for as many as 2300 with food, clothes and education—without asking man for money—plus sending free literature around the world and helping send to the field several missionaries.

So I have rejoiced to tell people that George Mueller prayed down an estimated 7 1/2 million dollars for the Lord's work.

Now God called Mueller for a particular work. And God called John R. Rice for a different work. George Mueller felt impressed never to tell his needs nor ask for money because he wanted to give testimony that God answered his prayers.

Well and good.

On the other hand, according to the Scriptures, it is sometimes wise to let your needs be known to God's people. Paul was a good example. He wrote those at Corinth of the need of the poor saints at Jerusalem and how he was collecting money.

It is neither wrong to take collections nor to tell of the needs of God's work. George Mueller was led to do it another way for a particular purpose; I have been led to use the method more often used in New Testament churches and in God's work around the world.

While counting up, I discovered this amazing fact: The Lord has caused His people to put into my hands something over $7 million, too, for getting out the Gospel! As I felt that was a tremendous blessing in the case of George Mueller, so I am overwhelmed with joy and a sense of gratitude and thankfulness that He has mercifully blessed me likewise.

Surely everyone knew that Dr. Rice was what would be considered a "poor" man. His $8,200 home in Wheaton had a mortgage on it. It had been paid out once, then mortgaged again to send free literature to men in the armed services. He was driving an old Buick with many miles on it. He had no money laid by, no property, no stocks and bonds, no life insurance, no annuities, no Social Security, no old-age pension. But the Lord saw that his six daughters got a college education and that his family had no need.

His great joy was that God enabled him to get the Gospel out which would affect and change the lives of thousands, yea, millions. By 1960, the Lord had helped him get out over 20 million copies of his books and pamphlets in more than twenty-eight languages. (At his death, it had reached 44,812,720 million.) And THE SWORD was reaching a multitude. Dr. Rice was preaching over the radio and in great auditoriums, as well as in churches great and small all over America, Canada, Scotland, Japan and Korea.

On one occasion we are told that Rowland Hill was given one hundred pounds, or about the equivalent of $500, with the instruction that it be used to help a certain preacher who had been overtaken with financial reverses and perhaps some failure in health.

Mr. Hill sent the poor preacher five pounds or about $25, dropping in the envelope with it a slip of paper bearing the words, "MORE TO FOLLOW." He did this repeatedly at intervals of a few days until the needy minister had become familiar with the cheering words, "MORE TO FOLLOW."

I use this illustration only to tell you how the heavenly Father took care of Dr. Rice's ministry through the years, not through gifts from Mr. Hill but from God's hand in direct answer to prayer. Sometimes money seemed to be air-mailed from Heaven when he prayed.

† † †

After we had used, by permission, Dr. R. G. Lee's famous sermon, "Payday—Someday," he wrote Dr. Rice these facts:

> I gave it as a twenty-minute talk at the First Baptist Church, Edgefield, South Carolina, February 1918. One of the deacons— a rather old man—said to me, "Son, if you will elongate that talk and elaborate somewhat on it, you'll have something really worthwhile."

I did what he suggested.

That sermon has been preached thirty-two times in my own pulpit in Bellevue Baptist Church—and several times at other churches in Memphis. I have preached it in forty states of the United States, in Honolulu, in Canada and in the Baptist Church in Nazareth, Israel, on a day when twenty-five people made confession of faith under the two sermons I preached that day. Of course, I preached through an interpreter.

I have preached it to congregations of 12,000, in small churches, in big churches, in baseball parks, in college and university chapels, etc. I preached it by request before the Tennessee State Legislature. Many have been saved under the preaching of this sermon through the years. I have preached it to date 666 times [this was back in 1960].

I pray that your publishing of it will result in some accepting Christ, and cause Christians to rejoice in the truth that, through Christ, they have been saved from the wrath to come.

"Payday—Someday" was one of the most used and most famous sermons of this generation.

† † †

Over 300 Miles to Find Someone to Win Her Sons! A good woman had written to find out when Dr. Rice would be in town. "My three sons are unsaved, and I do not know where else to go to find someone to tell them how to be saved. I read THE SWORD OF THE LORD, and I know you are a man of God whom I can trust."

Father, mother and three sons drove from southern Ohio to Wheaton.

The youngest was about twelve.

After Dr. Rice had carefully gone over the plan of salvation with them, all three boys happily trusted Christ as Saviour.

Then, to Dr. Rice's surprise, the mother pointed her thumb to her husband, then to herself and said, "We are not saved either!"

So he began again at the same Scriptures and taught them the plan of salvation. They, too, trusted Christ.

Now there was a happy family! All were assured they were now God's children, and now together they were on their way to Heaven.

That night they went to a motel where they had already reserved rooms. The next morning they came by the office for a good-by. All were still happy in the Lord. Dr. Rice had prayer for them. Then they got in the car and drove back across half the state of Illinois, across the state of Indiana and across part of Ohio to their home 50 miles from Dayton.

After they were gone, Dr. Rice said: "I closed the door of my office and walked to and fro in some distress of mind as I prayed, 'Lord, didn't You have anybody in the state of Ohio who could tell anybody how to be saved?' " Then he said, "The Lord seemed to answer back, 'Oh, yes, there are many saved people who are not over five or ten miles from that Ohio home, who know the plan of salvation; but they are not talking about it, so nobody knows who can tell them how!' "

† † †

She Lived Among a Hundred Christian Women, With Christian Neighbors, Yet Unsaved!

When Dr. Rice resigned the pastorate of First Baptist Church, Shamrock, Texas, to enter full-time evangelism, he moved his family to Fort Worth, to the Seminary Hill addition, near Southwestern Baptist Theological Seminary, where he had had two years of training and where he had many friends.

When he was in revivals, Mrs. Rice and the babies attended Gambrell Street Baptist Church, which was just across the street from their little home. Mrs. Rice attended a Sunday school class of a hundred women or so, taught by Mrs. L. R. Scarborough, wife of the president of the seminary.

Once when Dr. Rice returned home, Mrs. Rice said, "There is only one unsaved woman in our Sunday school class, as far as I know. I have a burden to see her. Will you go with me?"

Dr. Rice agreed.

Mrs. Rice hired a baby-sitter, and she said to her, "Now she's a pretty hard case. Probably she is Gospel-hardened. We may be gone for some time."

Dr. and Mrs. Rice went across Seminary Hill, down by the little business district, turned left at the big home of President Scarborough. Three doors below lived this unsaved woman. Seminary students lived on each side of her. And the Sunday school teacher, Mrs. Scarborough, lived three doors away.

Now Dr. Rice will tell you the rest of the story.

> We knocked timidly. I should not have been surprised if the woman had met us with scorn. I supposed many had urged

her to turn to Christ and she perhaps had refused every opportunity. I expected her to be a difficult case.

But when she came to the door, she was so friendly and kind.
"Why, Mrs. Rice! How nice of you to come! And is this Brother
Rice? Come in! Come in!"

After chatting a bit, I sought for some tactful approach to this
matter of salvation. (Sometimes we are so tactful that we do not
make contact!)

I saw a morocco-bound Bible lying on the table, so I said, "That's
a lovely Bible."

"Yes," she replied, "Mother gave us that for Christmas."

"Well," I said, "I understand you are not a Christian. If you
were a Christian, you and your husband could read a chapter in
that Bible together every day."

Very quietly she answered, "We already read a chapter every
day together, and have since we got it."

"But," I continued, "if you were Christians, you could kneel
down together and pray, after reading it, and ask God to bless
your home and thank Him for His blessings."

"We already do," she said. "We read a chapter in the Bible;
then he kneels down by his chair there, and I kneel down by my
chair here, and we both pray."

Now I had courage to ask the plain question, "Why, then, are
you not a Christian?"

Through choked sobs she answered, "I don't know how to be. We
do everything we know, but we don't know how to be Christians."

"Well, I am going to take this new Bible and show you. You
will certainly know how in a few minutes."

And so I turned to John 3 and went over the simple plan of salvation. In just a little bit she was so glad to trust the Saviour and
claim Him and was so happy. We rejoiced together and thanked
God and went on our way.

Mrs. Rice told the baby-sitter, "Never mind about staying so
long. She wasn't as hard as we thought."

Many a lost sinner is not so hard as the Christians around him.
Many a sinner would be open to the Gospel if people, with loving
kindness, would press the matter of salvation!

They are lost everywhere and wanting someone to tell them
how to get saved!

† † †

Five days there, three days here, one night here, a week in Florida—

so went Dr. Rice's 1960 schedule, the same as always, though now the nationwide radio broadcast had been added to his myriads of other responsibilities. Wasn't God good to give him strength for his multitude of labors!

† † †

For years the Sword Conference had been at Lake Louise Conference Grounds in Toccoa, Georgia, the week of July 4. Since it was not permitted to return (explanation under 1959), Dr. Bill Rice graciously offered the facilities of the Bill Rice Ranch; so the July 4th week was Sword week there for many years, drawing great crowds. (We had not yet moved to Murfreesboro.)

† † †

In July Mrs. Jessie Rice Sandberg started her column in THE SWORD, "From My Kitchen Window," and it has run for thirty years. She has never been late with her copy, and the content is unquestionable.

Miss Jessie is always so practical, so helpful, so understanding in her writings. Not only is the column interesting, but it is heart-moving and indeed helpful. She is daughter #4, a graduate of Wheaton College, and was, until she married, full-time artist at the Sword. Don, her husband, was president of Wheaton College Chapel Choir, a schoolteacher, director of Voice of Revival choir and the choir at Calvary Baptist Church.

Jessie, in her first column, invited women to suggest what sort of thing they would like to see dealt with—favorite dishes of famous preachers, economical recipes for church dinners, time-saving suggestions for sewing or housekeeping, discussions on the use of time, relationships with neighbors, problems with children, etc.

Later a good many, we found out, were reading "From My Kitchen Window" before "Editor's Notes." This started a little "feud" between father and daughter. In other words, the editor just didn't like hers before his! So when Jessie would bring her column in to him, you could hear all kinds of "threats" being made on her life—I mean, on her column!

Thanks, Jessie, for these beautiful thoughts you've shared with us these thirty years.

† † †

By the end of November, 49,739 booklets had gone out in 1960 as free prizes in the puzzle department!

1961 SWORD OF THE LORD IN PORTUGUESE! "Choice articles are selected from THE SWORD OF THE LORD and republished in A ESPADA DO SENHOR—a Portuguese edition," says Missionary Manuel S. Matthews of Lisbon, Portugal. He adds that it was going to North and South America, Africa, Europe and many islands as well as being distributed to preachers and Christians in Brazil.

(Some thirty years later, it is still being published and a copy of each issue is sent to our office.)

† † †

After Rev. John Wilder of Harlingen, Texas had used thousands of *"What Must I Do to Be Saved?"* booklets, this happy word came from him in January:

"This past cotton-picking season we gave out some 12,000 of these tracts to Mexican nationals. Already I have received some forty confessions of faith from all over the Mexican nation, and before the year is over, I believe we will get well over one hundred replies, as we did last year."

† † †

"I'M FROM MISSOURI." Perhaps you have heard people from every state in the union say, "Well, I'm from Missouri—you'll have to show me." And that's only a natural and very human trait, confined by no means to Missouri alone.

The nice thing about THE SWORD OF THE LORD is that it convincingly meets that challenge. Time and again people have written, saying they had been sent the paper by a friend and didn't expect to enjoy it at all, then found to their surprise that it became the mainstay of their spiritual reading!

So we recommend THE SWORD OF THE LORD just for that kind of people—the shrewd, discerning Missouri kind who have to be shown.

Coming to us this year from some "show me" people were letters from those who read THE SWORD and were convinced:

> ...I can truly say that I have enjoyed receiving the paper and have received many times my money's worth from it—although I'm probably as far removed from you as to opinions concerning "things religious" than any man could be. I'm a Methodist minister and perhaps the type of minister you would label "modernist." I'm not entirely sure if that word describes me or not— but from the articles in your paper I'm afraid that I must come under that category!
>
> The reasons that I say that I'm probably one of those "modernists" is that I have the *Interpreter's Bible*—which has been condemned in your paper; I use the R.S.V. version of the Bible— which, I understand from some of the articles in the paper—is not accepted by you. I believe in the virgin birth but do not feel it is absolutely necessary to believe in it to be a Christian. I do not believe that Christ will visibly reappear in the clouds at the second advent and so on—I could probably name a hundred other items that would "separate" us as far as opinions are concerned....
>
> However, in spite of this difference in opinions I feel that you are probably as sincere and devoted a Christian as any man I know—with the exception of my father.... He is eighty-eight years old now and as hale and hearty as you seem to be with your amazing schedule of preaching, evangelizing and teaching. I cannot but admire you for it. I wish you many more years of good work and a long and healthy life!
>
> Keep the paper coming! The sermons in it are worth many times the three dollars....

Rev. Homer Reid
Carrizozo, New Mexico

> May the Lord bless you for your fearless stand against spiritual wickedness in high places. Never is it easy to stand against sin, but it is so much harder when you have to stand and rebuke the religious leaders of our day....
>
> Your paper and books were used by the Lord to keep me out of the snares of modernism while I attended a Baptist school....
>
> In 1956 Jack Hyles was my guest at this school and he asked, "Where did you boys get your fundamental beliefs, since there is not much help here?"
>
> ...I thought of your paper and books, so replied, "From John R. Rice, I guess."

He said, "I thought so. Dr. Rice has done more for young preachers than any other man I know."

Only eternity will reveal the thousands of men and women who were not swept under the raging tide of modernism, simply because you were faithful to Christ and His Word.

Rev. Leland Maples
Uvalde, Texas

Your articles in THE SWORD OF THE LORD pointing out the trend in fundamental ranks toward liberalism, and more particularly the dangers of unscriptural alliances with the liberals, have *our wholehearted support....*

I am a graduate of Indiana Central College, which is sold out to liberal trends. I was a philosophy major, graduating in 1938. Your paper was sent to me in 1942. It helped me and Mrs. Sale to sort out the right position for us to take. We felt led to withdraw from preaching in the United Brethren pastorates due to certain trends toward liberalism in the U. B. Seminary. Other policies of the church we could not support nor urge our congregation to support. In 1948 I graduated from Grace Theological Seminary with the B. D. degree. The only reason I am telling you this is to let you see the part you have had in our lives.

Be assured of our prayers and support of your bold leadership in this important struggle against the Devil. A voice needs to be heard these days and we are confident the Lord has led you in the Sword ministry to be that voice.

Mr. W. R. Sale
Cinda, Kentucky

† † †

"MY ONLY FRIEND." From Korea came this pleading letter from a war orphan who borrowed a copy of THE SWORD while in the army and called it "my only friend." I hope you can understand it:

Sir:

How are you?

In Korean War, I was left a orphan of war. But when I get used to courage, I went to army. In my army life, I lent [borrowed] SWORD OF THE LORD from my higher officer and read it. Ever since, SWORD OF THE LORD became my only friend in the war.

News of orphan and confession of faith made me truly saint. And I devote in the church at now.

Since I was discharged from army, in the same previous day I cannot read it that was my only friend.

So here is country that I am very isolation and loneliness. Please send me SWORD OF THE LORD.

(Signed) J. Kim.

Wouldn't anybody have been glad to send this young man a subscription to THE SWORD OF THE LORD, "my only friend"!

Six college students from the Philippines encouraged Dr. Rice with this letter:

We, the students of Luna College, Tayug, Pangasinan, have read some issues of THE SWORD OF THE LORD and we are inspired to accept our Lord Jesus Christ as our personal Saviour. We were the devoted Roman Catholic before, but now our mind and belief has changed.

We are then requesting you to please send us THE SWORD OF THE LORD, for we are very interested.

One from Java, Indonesia, wrote him a deeply moving letter:

I receive your SWORD OF THE LORD every week, but these last weeks I never receive more your paper. Week after week I am waiting, but THE SWORD never visits me again. O Dr. Rice, give me THE SWORD OF THE LORD again. For my Christian friends accept THE SWORD is the one most independent Christian weekly in all the world.

Dr. Rice, I always translate the sermons in the Indonesian language. The other Christian people belong to the wonderful sermons and lessons that are written in THE SWORD.

Please, Dr. Rice, give me your SWORD again.

Forever waiting the coming of THE SWORD OF THE LORD to my address.

Such requests came so frequently. Do you wonder that Dr. Rice could never turn down such urgent calls for his books or THE SWORD OF THE LORD, even if he had to mortgage his home to supply their need!

We should be ashamed of ourselves for even entertaining a thought that people are so hard and cannot be reached. They are out there! Why don't we go out there and find them!

Here is another tear-jerker from one burdened soul:

I am writing concerning my own spiritual condition. I have been Sunday school superintendent, teacher, trustee and treasurer for nearly thirty years. But now I have come to the eventide of my life—seventy-eight years—and I must say like Jacob of old, 'Evil have been my days.'

There has been too little concern over my spiritual condition, too many compromises, too much complacency. My prayer life has become a tragedy. The heavens seem to be as brass, and the echo comes back, Lost! Lost! This is my reason for asking for *"What Must I Do to Be Saved?"*

My parents were fine Christians—my brother is a minister; my three uncles were Methodist ministers; my granduncle was a bishop (Baptist) in Australia. Thus I am not of stock that is other than Christian.

I thank God for THE SWORD that has awakened within me a desire to be a Christian.

A. H ____ S ____ of Los Angeles

As Dr. Rice read such letters and dictated an answer, many times he wept.

† † †

I have worn many hats over the years. At Wheaton College I took two strong courses in journalism, better preparing myself for writing. And you may believe I have had plenty of opportunity to use that talent!

For awhile I was responsible for retail sales, and was forever thinking up ways to promote our many publications. I learned in journalism that "the first 10 to 20 words are the most important of everything you write. Catch 'em early or kiss 'em goodbye." I have tried this method over and over again, and it does indeed work.

Here is one case which brought in scores of orders! And I made thousands of friends over the years by being homey, and just "talking to them" in this manner—getting their attention and keeping it.

Dear Sword Friend:

S'POSE YOU COULD HELP ME GET TO THE ROCKY MOUNTAINS?

This is vacation time and I should be thrilled over the trip I plan to take. Believe me, I enjoy seeing the country as much as the next gal—but it looks like I may never make it to Arizona. I have a real five-feet, eleven-inch problem. His name is Dr. John R. Rice and he's running me ragged!

For weeks I've been trying to get the August sale ads out of the way so I could go on my vacation with a clear conscience. They tell me the mountains of the West and all the lovely scenery enroute is more beautiful this year than ever. But I doubt if I'll ever find out for myself. Just as I tackle those ads in earnest, the hubbub grinds into high gear:

"Viola, can't we get this book ready for the sale?. . . Viola, you'd better plan about offering my novel, *Seeking a City*, during August sale. . . . Viola, we have several new titles this year—better push those hard. . . ."

That's bad enough, but his enthusiasm is so catching that I

forget all about Arizona and Colorado for maybe a whole hour at a time.

It's what I get for having an emotional nature, I guess. Just because he thinks it's terrific to have a special sale is no reason for me to get my blood pressure up! But this morning really did it. It was the earnest glow that got me as he leaned over my desk.

"Viola, have you really thought about this?" (something I'd been laboring over for weeks!)

"A time or two," was my masterpiece of understatement.

"Last year we sold nearly $50,000 worth of my books through retail by mail; we should do better this year. And the August sale—with every book and pamphlet cut 20% or more—gives people a chance to stock up on these books which God has blessed to so many hearts. Since the Lord has already helped us get out over 20 million copies, let's hurry with another million, then you can take that vacation.

"And why not offer a special special! Since we have only 800 copies left of *The Ruin of a Christian*, let's let this $2.50 book go at $1. Are you agreeable?"

I'll tell you, this starry-eyed boss of mine has me so keyed up I don't know whether I should tackle those Rocky Mountain curves even if I *do* get the August sale ads written.

So what about giving a frustrated secretary a break? Just sit down and write Dr. Rice a letter and enclose a great big August sale order. That will keep him happy for *at least a little while*— and I can get my work done, particularly the ads for the last two issues.

Do this for me, and I'll let you know how the trip turns out.

Hopefully,

Viola Walden
Editor's Assistant

And I kept my word. To every person who sent an order, I mailed them this postcard.

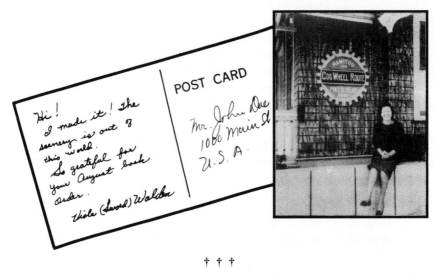

POST CARD

Hi! I made it! The scenery is out of this world. So grateful for your August book order.

Thila (David) Walden

Mr. John Doe
1000 Main St
U.S.A.

† † †

While in a meeting at Garland, Texas, in January, we found—and Dr. Rice bought me—the cutest little Chihuahua, the rowdy of the litter. On our way back to Wheaton, Mrs. Rice named MY baby "Dixie." It was a good Southern name. On her registered paper, we had to add another name, so she was "Dixie Carmelitta."

Dr. Rice loved her, and she loved him back. Her little wicker bed was under his desk, where she stayed when she "came to work," that is, unless she was in his lap, helping him dictate letters or articles!

Occasionally she went with us to meetings; when she couldn't go, she stayed with her "Aunt Hilda," my secretary who lived with me.

Once she "wrote" this letter to a pastor in Ohio (with some help), begging to be invited:

Dear Uncle Bob:

Plees pardon my Eengleesh. She ees not so pretty good. You see, I have come from a long line of Mexican ancestors. I am from Chihuahua.

The reeson I am write to you, senor, ees becaus I have hear that my gardin, Mees Viola, is go to your town for a veeseet. Seence I have come to Wheaton, I have stay weeth Mees Viola. She very nice to me. . . feex me totilla, enchilada. . . take me for walks. We very close friends. Eef she go away I don't know what I do.

Plees, senor, do not theenk me too bold, but eet would be so nice eef I could come veeseet your town weeth Mees Viola, Doctor and Mrs. Rice. I promise, I weel be no troble. I eet but lettle. I not take up mush room. . . can sleep in a corner, or in a lap.

Plees to write me a ladder and say ees Hokay!

Weeth Luff,
Carmelitta

Fun, mixed with lots of hard work, kept Dr. John from growing weary!

† † †

In a full-page ad, in bold headlines—Dr. Rice: "MY PREACHER BROTHER, DO WITHOUT FOOD IF YOU MUST—BUT GET THESE BOOKS WHICH MOST INFLUENCED MY LIFE," and he named them and commented on a few:

George Mueller of Bristol and His Witness to a Prayer-Hearing God (Arthur T. Pierson): One of the great books which, falling into my hands as a young Christian, has had an unusual influence all these years.

In His Steps (Charles M. Sheldon): I first read it when I was fourteen. More than all the preaching I had ever heard, this simple, fascinating gospel story of how a group of Christians, led by their pastor, started out to settle every decision by the simple question, "What would Jesus do?" has led me to long to follow in the steps of Jesus, to crucify self and live just as He would do if He were in my place.

Jesus Is Coming (W. E. Blackstone): I had been preaching about five years when there fell into my hands a copy of this little book. I believed that Jesus was coming, but I had a very hazy idea of what would happen when He did. I had been taught in Sunday school, college and seminaries the general postmillennial idea, and sadly enough, I had never had any consecutive, thorough Bible teaching.

Several things about this book gripped me, stirred me, convinced me, and made clear the fundamental facts concerning the premillennial coming of Jesus. One thing is the enormous amount of Scripture it contains. Next, every objection is answered carefully. Third, it proved that the Bible has a clear line of teaching—

from the first book to the last on the subject. It is absolutely one of the best single volumes on this subject outside the Bible.

How to Pray (R. A. Torrey): When I was about seventeen, a friend loaned me this remarkable book. So clearly and simply written and every point so proven by the Scriptures makes it easy to read. I, a young Christian, was moved to the depths by it!

I would read a few pages, then feel compelled to go to a place of prayer. How many times, during the couple of days I was reading the book, I had gone to the barn, or through the pea patch and over the fence to my secret nook, under a chaparral bush on that West Texas farm! The Holy Spirit taught me to pray and take the Bible at face value concerning these holy promises of God. From that time to this, I have read everything I could find that Dr. Torrey wrote.

Then Dr. Rice listed these also, without room for comment:

All About the Bible (Sidney Collett); *Autobiography of Charles G. Finney; Finney's Revival Lectures; The Holy Spirit: Who He Is and What He Does* (Torrey); *How to Work for Christ* (Torrey); *How to Bring Men to Christ* (Torrey); *What the Bible Teaches* (Torrey); *My Daily Prayer* (F. B. Meyer); *Matthew Henry's Commentary.*

† † †

"These notes are being dictated to Miss Viola as we cross the panhandle of Texas and near the New Mexico border...." We were on our way to Albuquerque, New Mexico, for a Sword Conference. These words were dictated so many times—only the town and state were different.

So much of our work was done while traveling. But when there were twelve pages of THE SWORD every week to get ready, and scores of letters to answer, Dr. Rice had no other choice.

And as was the case so many times, he flew back to Wheaton, "leaving the driving to us." But Mrs. Rice and I always enjoyed our times together. She said that she and I had spent more time together through forty-six years than she had spent with her husband and children. And, come to think of it, she was right!

† † †

We could have started a JOHN R. RICE ADOPTION AGENCY and had good success. There seemed to be so many babies needing a home.

Many mothers, and even the daughters themselves, were asking Dr. Rice if he knew of any good Christian who wanted to adopt a baby born to—or about to be born to—an unwed mother.

"Oh, Dr. Rice, let me adopt this one!" I would plead after almost every such letter. Now this was in the days before single girls started adopting. But even if it hadn't been, Dr. Rice would have said, and did say, "No; you are too busy in the Lord's work to take on such a gigantic task of rearing a baby."

But there was one experience I shall not soon forget.

Knowing that our good Christian doctor in Wheaton had a childless nurse wanting a baby so badly, when one became available, immediately Dr. Rice discussed it with Dr. Wyngarten. He was elated at this prospect.

Dr. Rice contacted the mother of the unwed girl and said his secretary would fly up to Maryland to get the baby, who then would be placed in a Christian home.

I will not go into all the many details involved in picking up a baby from out of state; but I flew to Maryland in August, 1961, spent the night in a motel with the baby's mother, won her to the Lord, then she and her parents, avid readers of THE SWORD, went with me the 90 miles to the foster home where the baby had been placed a few days after birth in a Florence Crittendon home. (The real mother had never seen her baby until now.)

When I saw her dressed so beautifully and waiting, my heart melted! How could I give her up, when she could be mine!

Since I had flown from Illinois into Maryland, I was carefully watched by authorities. At the Baltimore airport I was put on the plane ahead of others, and was met by men in uniform when I arrived in Chicago. (They wanted to be sure I was not a kidnapper, I guess.)

Friends picked me up, and I held "Ann"[1] as we drove the 30 miles west to Wheaton. After keeping "my" baby for a few hours, I delivered her to our doctor, who waited at his office. He checked her over, kept her for the night, and the next day turned her over to a delighted nurse.

I am still in contact with those involved, and they have become such precious friends.

Yes, we could have had an adoption agency, because so many were looking to Dr. Rice for help when they were in trouble.

---

[1] At birth, the mother had named the baby Ann; the adopted parents, not knowing this, named her Ann!

1962

Up to January of this year, 10,666 people reported they had found Christ as Saviour through THE SWORD OF THE LORD and through other literature distributed through the Sword of the Lord in the English language. That does not count thousands who claimed Him in foreign countries as reported to Dr. Rice by missionary committees.

† † †

"May God make 1962 the best year of my ministry, the best year of a happy life, since I was converted fifty-six years ago," wrote Dr. Rice in "Editor's Notes."

† † †

It was announced that this year we could no longer afford sending free gifts to those who worked the crossword puzzles, nor the labor cost of grading the nearly 2,000 entries. But fans were urged to make a habit of working them, since it was a wonderful way to get familiar with the Bible.

† † †

When Dr. Rice and Dr. Bob Jones, Sr. were at Decatur, Alabama, Dr. Rice commented: "What a joy to hear Dr. Bob speak with vigor, although he is seventy-eight. He retains much of the eloquence, the literary beauty, the sparkling wit as well as the prophetic power which made him next to Billy Sunday in great crowds and seeing hundreds of thousands saved during a tremendous ministry as an evangelist."

He took notes as Dr. Bob preached. I quote from his notes:

DR. BOB: " 'The dead shall be raised incorruptible,' says Paul. Abraham will get up and brush the dust off his shroud and say, 'Get up, Sarah; didn't you hear the alarm go off?' David will awake and ask for his harp. 'I can play it now better than ever.' The wanderers in the desert will unwrap their winding sheets of sand, ocean waves will swell and from the storm-tossed deep will rise the bodies of saints, and every country churchyard will seem like a camp meeting when Jesus comes!''

DR. BOB: ''The drunkard and harlot will have an easier time getting into Heaven than the preacher who denies the virgin birth, the incarnation and the blood atonement.''

DR BOB: ''Don't play with sin! If you want to be daring, go out West and take up a rattlesnake and play with it. Do you want to strut your stuff? Then go out to a storm cloud and seize the bolts of lightning in your bare hands. Rather that than fool with sin!''

DR. BOB: ''When a man says, 'Every man has his price,' he means he himself is for sale.''

DR. BOB: ''If you have never had any trouble, let me tell you how to have some. Be a Spirit-filled Christian and your neighbor will say, 'Fanatic! He's a fundamentalist.' ''

I pity those who never heard that great man of God preach. He was one of the greatest preachers of our age, and the best living example of the era of great revivals from Sam Jones to Billy Sunday.

† † †

RESOLUTION OF APPRECIATION

Because Dr. John R. Rice has served as Editor of THE SWORD OF THE LORD these 27 years without pay, working long hours every week, and,

Because he has diligently served, also without pay, as President of the Sword of the Lord Foundation since its inception, working hard to promote its various gospel literature missionary endeavors around the world, and,

Because he has sacrificed his own valuable time, which might have been used in great revival campaigns, in order to serve the best interests of this Foundation, and,

Because he has put thousands of dollars of his own money into this work, and,

Because of his uncompromising faithfulness and dedication to Truth, even at the cost of friends and supporters, some of them the warm, personal friends of a lifetime,

BE IT RESOLVED that we, the members of the Sword of the Lord Foundation Executive Board, meeting in annual session at Wheaton, Illinois, this twenty-third day of January, in the year of our Lord, nineteen hundred sixty and two, publicly express our heartfelt appreciation for the services he has rendered, by publishing this resolution on the front page of THE SWORD OF THE LORD, thereby showing our love for and our confidence in the man and his ministry.

He always had a melody
in his heart.

By 1962, Dr. Rice had written the words to twenty-five songs and they were published in *Revival Specials*. Before he died in 1980, the total was 85—all with the old-fashioned revival flavor.

On music, Dr. Rice had this to say:

> The best songs must come out of great revival fires. How many came from the Moody-Sankey, Torrey-Alexander, Sunday-Rodeheaver revivals and from the great revival age! Then when great revivals passed, Christian songs tended to lose the soul-winning fire and be simply nice songs with testimony and devotion.

> In ten thousand churches next Sunday, when the pastor gives an invitation to the unsaved, the songleader must go back 140 years or more to Charlotte Elliott's time to sing, "Just As I Am." And it is about as far back to "I've Wandered Far Away From God, Now I'm Coming Home," or, "Softly and Tenderly Jesus Is Calling." It is nearly a hundred years since "Let Jesus Come Into Your Heart," was copyrighted—not a single invitation song except those more than a hundred years old!"

> Where are the songs like "Tell Mother I'll Be There," "Must I Go and Empty Handed?" "The Great Judgment Morning," "Ye Must Be Born Again," "Will There Be Any Stars in My Crown?"

> We need a new emphasis on revival and soul winning in our gospel singing. Songs like this are needed:

59   So Little Time

by John R. Rice

and   that   He'll say, "Well   done!"
en,   lost   ones not   re   born.
we'll have   but   for   our   sin.   To - day   we   reap,   or
to   face   the   slack - ers' blame!
and   love   and   pray and   go!

miss   our   gol - den   har - vest!   To - day   is   gi - ven   us

lost souls   to   win.   Oh then   to   save   some dear ones from the

burn - ing.   To - day   we'll   go   to   bring some sin - ner   in.

Dr. Rice, wanting to get out a million copies of his booklet, *"What Must I Do to Be Saved?"* in English, in 1962, was offering to churches, rescue missions, Bible institutes and schools 10,000 copies for $200. Each could prepare his own copy for the back page, advertising the church or mission, picture of church or whatever. And he was urging everyone to order at least 100 copies.

✝ ✝ ✝

On February 11, Mrs. Rice told us this:

My husband is always teasing me about "riding on his coattail."

It was forty years ago last October 10 when I heard him preach his first sermon. That morning six people came out to claim the Lord publicly. That afternoon I saw a council of good men lay hands of ordination on the head of my husband who had already been ordained of God.

It has been good to "ride on his coattail." I have been blessed because he has been blessed. I have heard him pray a long time every morning for some seventy-five to one hundred evangelists and soul-winning pastors. And when he prays, "Lord, bless Mother," I say, "And I shall be blessed."

† † †

One hundred and forty-six sermons were entered in this year's Evangelistic Sermon Contest, from thirty-five states and six foreign countries.

† † †

THE WINNAH!

Final Results of Epic Battle Between Sabers and Scimitars

Thursday, June 28, 1962. The sun crept slowly over the eastern horizon, as though fearful of what its light might reveal.

A terrible battle had surged across the tiny stronghold of the Sword of the Lord. Again and again Abou Ben Al Byers had hurled his *Saber* warriors into the conflict with Sheik Abdullah Walt Handford's brave *Scimitars*. It was a knockdown, drag-out, no-holds-barred struggle. This was the fateful day when the arbiter, Dr. John R. Rice, would announce the winner!

Some six weeks before, Sword Vice President, Dr. Walter Handford, had solemnly read two lists of names during the devotional period which began every workday at the Sword office. The twenty-seven members of the office staff, the field staff, the board members, and the cooperating board, became either a Saber or a Scimitar.

The teams were challenged to work to outdo one another in a contest to get subscriptions to THE SWORD OF THE LORD.

What scheming and secret planning took place! What effort was expended! Letters were written. Forms were printed. Everything imaginable was done to get former subscribers to renew and to locate new subscribers.

We could get them by hook or by crook. We could write friends and loved ones, which resulted in secret mass overtime projects. Sometimes we worked into the wee hours of the morning on our secret mailings.

There were prayer meetings. There were progress report meetings. There were skits and stunts. There were songs. There were yells. There were signs and posters planted strategically about the office. The competition was ferocious and at times the atmosphere seemed thick enough to cut with a—*sword*. It was one of the most heated subscription contests ever held by Sword employees.

The deadline for the contest was set at midnight, June 20, 1962. In order to allow for last-minute subscriptions, the date for announcing the result was set for June 28. It had been made clear that the losing team would provide dinner for the winning team on July 17 at the Cedar Lake Bible Conference Grounds. This would be in conjunction with the Sword Conference which would be in progress there.

There was a perceptible hush upon the Sword staff as we gathered that June morning. The team captains—Al Byers of the Sabers and Walt Handford of the Scimitars—presented to Dr. Rice sealed envelopes containing the total number of subscriptions obtained by their respective teams.

With obvious delight, Dr. Rice tore open each envelope and silently looked at the results. He then turned to the group that sat waiting impatiently. After expressing his appreciation for the loyalty and devotion of all the staff, with a bit of quick addition he announced—

SABERS 4,463

SCIMITARS 4,387

a total of 8,850 subscriptions as a result of the contest (besides others that came in the campaign and took no side).

Then with a big smile he heartily congratulated the winners—THE SABERS.

Truthfully the contest was very close. The difference in total numbers of subscriptions for each team was only seventy-six. And when you come right down to it, there are no losers in a contest like this one.

AND NOW THE PAY-OFF!

The Scimitars, who were to "fix" the dinner for the winning Sabers, posted this inviting

MENU

Appetizer:	Chocolate Covered Ants
	Spider Soup
Choice of:	Fried Scorpion Legs
	or
	Golden Brown, Tasty Green
	Tomato Worms—fried in Fuel oil
Choice of:	Molded Fly Salad
	or
	Grasshopper Salad
Drink:	Green Olive Juice
Dessert:	Buttermilk Sundae Topped
	with dill pickles

That was our printed menu, but the real thing was like unto nothing you have eaten before. Comfortingly, Dr. Rice said to the Scimitars: "If the Sabers don't thank you properly for that delicious meal, you see me! After all, you worked hard, too!"

I was a Scimitar—and proud of it!

✝ ✝ ✝

CROP FAILURE! Every farmer knows the sickening headache, the sorrow, the unspeakable misery and woe wrapped up in those two words. Any number of things individually or combined—drought, hail, pestilence, fire, wind, insects, etc.—can bring tragedy and loss to the farmer. Frequently total crop failures occur several years in succession, bringing ruin and bankruptcy in their wake.

Why, then, do farmers continue plowing, harrowing, sowing? Why do they labor so diligently fighting bugs, plant diseases, weeds and other enemies of their crops? Why are they apparently so willing to risk so much?

The answer is simple: they know not "whether shall prosper, either this or that, or whether they both shall be alike good" (Eccles. 11:6).

The farmer is willing to take the risk because he knows the value, the profit of the crop which comes to harvest. Experience has taught him that it *pays* to sow seed.

The same is true with the gospel seed. "The seed is the word of God," says Luke 8:11. The faithful sower never knows in advance when or where his seed will produce a harvest. How frequent are our crop failures! How many times the Devil's stink bugs get our spiritual cabbages and his boll weevils ruin our cotton!

Yet God repeatedly encourages us to sow beside all waters, to ignore hindering circumstances, and to "withhold not thy hand." Repeatedly He assures us that "in due season we shall reap, if we faint not" and that the faithful sower of gospel truth "shall doubtless come again with rejoicing, bringing his sheaves with him." *It pays to be faithful.*

For twenty-eight blessed, fruitful years THE SWORD OF THE LORD had been proving the truthful trustworthiness of the plain promises in the Bible guaranteeing that "they that sow. . .shall reap."

Just a few more letters that came in 1962 to prove the point:

She Bought Subscriptions Instead of Flowers: "I Now Have More Flowers Than $23 Could Buy!"

I had $23 and wanted some flowers for my backyard, but my husband said no. So I sent it to you for subscriptions, figuring it was selfish to want those flowers when people were going to Hell.

Since then, almost every week some neighbor has given me a root or some seeds of a flower. Now I have more flowers than $23 could ever buy, and still more are promised to me this fall! The Lord will never let us get in debt to Him.

—From a Toronto reader.

An interesting letter indeed. But we got so many sometimes I feared we grew callous and failed to rejoice as we should have.

I don't have but one arm—my left—to write with, and I work seven nights a week night watching. I don't have words to express what I think of THE SWORD. I love Dr. Rice, his family and all connected with the Sword with a holy love. Every time I pray, I thank God for the first SWORD I ever picked up and read. It led me to know and love a man, a great teacher, preacher, servant. . . YOU, Dr. Rice.

I like THE SWORD so well that this makes twenty-nine subscriptions I've paid for. It has already led one precious soul to the Lord through my puny efforts. He died two weeks ago. A wealthy man—3,000 acres of fine timberland and a number of white-faced cattle—and hard to approach. When preachers talked to him, he would ask them to show him a technical reason why he should be saved, and look at how old he was—67!

I like the blessed books ordered from your ads. *HOME: Courtship, Marriage and Children*—if it had only been placed in my hands when I was 17, it would have saved me thirty years' living in sin, heartache, disappointment, confusion, walking with the living dead—a sin-scarred, wasted life. And it would have saved me from $30,000 to $40,000 wasted money.

Believe it or not—you have the only three checks I ever wrote in my life. Have made good money, but spent it as fast as I got it. But it is wonderful what the Lord can do. I met my dear Saviour just 2½ years ago. . . .

—Mr. G. B.

Then this one:

Last Saturday I had laid down due to what seemed to be an oncoming of the flu. After sleeping awhile, my wife Marj referred to Dr. Hyles' sermon in THE SWORD, "Digging God's Wells." Again and again she said, "Listen to this." She read on and on, pretty near reading the whole message.

One of our daughters heard it and she feels her life has been different since then.

I got up, put my shoes on and Marj said, "Where are you going?"

"Out to the car. I've got to be alone."

Though it was cold, that didn't matter, for out there it seemed like my soul turned over. God gave me sorrow for my sins. I repented of my lukewarm Christian living. I, too, like my wife and daughter, have noted a real change. Jesus has become precious again and real. Now only His will is important.

The remarkable thing about that and so many other messages in THE SWORD is, they are so simple, yet so heart-stirring.

—D. S.
Arlington, Virginia.

Oh, there are heartaches galore out there!

In my hour of darkest despair I found your booklet on the seat of a city bus. My wife had just left me, and I had turned to alcohol for solace. After reading your booklet I realized how wrong I was and that I must trust the Lord.

So I joined a group taking instructions before joining a local church. The change brought about was so dramatic that now, a month since I read your booklet, my wife has returned and we are starting a new life together with the help of the Lord. When I find myself slipping into the old ways, I remember your booklet and pray for strength and faith to carry on. Life has never been so good as in the past few weeks.

—R.M.B.
Cedar Springs, Ontario

We are touched continually by the sacrifice made for the Sword's work. Some fine unknown friends wrote:

We decided last winter we would pick up all bottles on the highways and roads; so we got nearly all beer bottles and cashed them in. We do believe through your work every dollar will bring one more person to Christ, so please use this $6.00 where it will do the most good. . . . By the end of the year we expect to get a little more together.

WE WATER, GOD GIVES THE INCREASE. BUT WHAT IF WE HADN'T WATERED?

Always those who are most blessed of God have to fight the indifference which familiarity with holy things may bring. "Familiarity breeds contempt," a proverb says. But if we are not moved by the stories of people saved, then we are not like the Lord and those in Heaven, for 'there is more joy in the presence of the angels of God over one sinner that repenteth than over ninety-nine just persons which need no repentance.'

Where we quote one letter, there were a hundred more. There just is not room for them; but all are remarkable.

Dr. Bob Jones, Sr. called this "just clipping coupons" on a lifetime investment.

† † †

This year Dr. Rice was campaigning against some teachers in Southern Baptist seminaries who were writing bad books and teaching bad doctrine. June 8, 1962, he wrote:

How to Defeat the Modernistic Poison
of Southern Baptist Seminaries

My heart is made heavy at every evidence of the inroads of unbelief and modernism, open infidelity ofttimes, in Southern Baptist seminaries that were once sound in the faith. What will we do in the next twenty-five years if all the preachers coming out of these seminaries are tainted with their unbelief? What can we hope but utter ruin for America, with God turning us over to communists or war or pestilence and a cesspool of immorality, if all preachers come to doubt the virgin birth, to believe the Bible is not truly the infallible Word of God, come to teach salvation by human merit instead of by the blood of Christ! For I warn you now, at least three out of every four seminaries in America are largely controlled by liberalism, wicked unbelief and open opposition to the essentials of the historic Christian Faith.

There is only one way: we must see that preachers get THE SWORD OF THE LORD. If every ministerial student in America could be sent this paper, then I am certain that literally thousands of them could be saved to preach the true Gospel. Already literally scores of them have testified that they were taught the fundamentals of the Faith, were taught to win souls, were warned against modernism, were brought out of false cults, through THE SWORD.

I do not wonder, then, that one ministerial student in Indiana spent his whole summer one year working, then spent his entire summer's wages in sending THE SWORD to his denomination. I assure you, this is a missionary product of first importance to try to save the preachers of America.

Below is proof of the above.

Rev. Tom Wallace, then of Elkton, Maryland, wrote Dr. Rice in 1962:

I think I probably would have been a modernist or a liberal except for THE SWORD OF THE LORD. I yielded to preach shortly after I was saved and knew absolutely nothing about the Bible or its doctrines.

I heard you preach several times and became interested in your books. I bought almost every book you had written or published. I cut my spiritual teeth on them and strengthened my foundation. The matters of security, separation, soul winning and so many, many others were settled for me.

Since then we have ordered many hundreds of dollars' worth of books, tracts, subscriptions, etc., through THE SWORD for our work.

As I look around me and see the many young preachers my age yielding to modern thinking and pouring themselves into the molds of the new evangelicals, modernists and social programs, I am ever grateful to the Lord for raising up THE SWORD OF THE LORD....

Dr. Wallace is today a well-known preacher in fundamental circles.

A Mrs. Birch of Macon, Georgia, talked to a young fundamental preacher's wife. During the conversation she asked where her husband had gotten his training. When told it was at Mercer, "How could he be a graduate of Mercer and still be a fundamental preacher?" questioned Mrs. Birch. The wife said, "Back in my husband's college days he heard Dr. John R. Rice speak at Macon.... It was then he learned what had been bothering him about the modernistic teaching he was receiving. Then and there he became a different ministerial student. He could never be the same. He studied his Bible more and more."

"...Only eternity will reveal Dr. Rice's influence in this generation. I am studying for full-time Christian work, and one of my teachers testified that Dr. Rice's stand against modernism saved him from liberalism," wrote C. B. of Chattanooga.

When a critic wrote, "I would rather read about the faults of Southern Baptists in Southern Baptist papers," Dr. Rice answered him:

Doubtless the Jehovah's Witnesses would rather nobody show them their false doctrine except Jehovah's Witnesses officials. Doubtless Catholics would far rather hear a discussion of their doctrine from the pope than from Bible-believers. Christian Scientists do not like it when we show the errors of that Christ-denying heresy.

But when Jesus commanded us to "beware of false prophets, which come to you in sheep's clothing, but inwardly they are ravening wolves," He did not mean for us to be callous or indifferent about false prophets that arise among our neighbors, loved ones, friends— the people of God anywhere.

All spiritual people surely rejoice in the great heritage of Southern Baptists and feel an obligation to protect them from enemies of Christ and the Bible. In fact, the work of Southern Baptists is so important to the cause of Christ that it is every Christian's business how Southern Baptists go.

† † †

Scores of letters praised the sermons by great men of the past as published in THE SWORD OF THE LORD—sermons by Moody, Torrey, Truett, Talmage, Sunday and others.

But people have a tendency to miss the fact that the greatest sermons being written today are also published in THE SWORD OF THE LORD. All of us have a tendency to kill the prophets that now live and to garnish the tombs of those who are gone.

In 1932, in Dallas, when an old mansion was torn down to build the Galilean Baptist Church, a corner cupboard had been sealed up when the house had been remodeled and repapered. And in that old cupboard, shut up for many years, were found copies of *The Christian Herald* magazine of about the years 1895 to 1898.

One editorial greatly lamented that all the great preachers were dead and that now there were no more!

In those current issues of *The Christian Herald* were sermons by men **then living:** D. L. Moody, Charles Spurgeon, R. A. Torrey, Billy Sunday, T. DeWitt Talmage and other giants of the pulpit! Imagine! In the years of these men, the editor was saying there were no more great preachers!

In another generation people will still be rejoicing over the great ministry of some of the men whose sermons are printed in THE SWORD OF THE LORD: Lee Roberson, Jack Hyles, John R. Rice, Bob Jones, Sr., Curtis Hutson and others.

† † †

The August headline read:

67,927,918 copies of THE SWORD in 91 countries in 28 years; 22 million copies of books and pamphlets by editor scattered around the world in 35 languages; over 11,000 letters from people saved through English language edition of Sword literature.

In these 28 years the Sword had greatly influenced perhaps 50,000 preachers and had led thousands of young men into the ministry. Tens of thousands of sermon outlines and illustrations had been taken from THE SWORD OF THE LORD by preachers all over the world. Not only had it published more sermons than all other fundamental magazines in America put together; it had published more Bible teaching, settled more questions of doctrine and stirred more revival fires wherever it had gone, than any other Christian magazine, according to thousands of witnesses.

As we looked back, 28 years didn't seem to be a very long time. In fact, it didn't seem possible that a quarter of a century, plus three years, had slipped by since we first started THE SWORD OF THE LORD with a couple of typewriters and a printer who couldn't spell any better than the stenographers!

That these have been interesting years, no one can deny.

† † †

Richard B. Clearwaters...W. E. Dowell...Bob Gray...Jack Hyles...Bob Jones, Sr. and Jr., Tom Malone, Monroe Parker...Ford Porter...Lee Roberson...Bob Shuler...Harold Sightler...Louis Talbot...G. B. Vick...G. Archer Weniger: on our 28th anniversary (September 28) Dr. Rice reminded SWORD readers of these great men on our Cooperating Board who represented the backbone of Bible-believing, soul-winning, church-building defense of the Faith in America.

In ten institutions they were training over 6,000 college and seminary students;

Over 2,000 ministers and missionaries were under their instruction;

Ten pastors on our board had over 50,000 members combined and pastored some of the largest churches in the world;

They baptized some 4,000 converts each year;

They had the greatest influence on the ministry, defending the Faith, speaking to thousands of preachers yearly.

† † †

Up to this time, no active employee of the Sword of the Lord Foundation had ever died, though one incident in our history could have been tragic.

The large press was being moved by elevator from basement to loading dock in Wheaton, Illinois. Al Byers and Bill MacLeod were in the basement; Walt Handford was on floor 1. Suddenly the cable broke and the press fell. The two men were under the elevator as it went up; when it came down, the Lord had moved them or they would have been crushed to death. Walt did not know the fate of the two, and we think he froze and could not call down to them! When finally Mr. MacLeod said, "All is well down here!" what a relief to us all!

† † †

For 28 years THE SWORD had, most of the time, only two printers, Mr. McNitzky of McNitzky Printers, Denton, Texas and G. H. Willms of Herald Book and Printing Company of Newton, Kansas. After the office was moved to Wheaton 22 years before, the McNitzky printers continued printing THE SWORD for four years. Then for some 12 years, Herald Book and Printing Company, with Mr. G. H. Willms at the head and his strong corps of helpers, cared for the printing and mailing.

Mr. Willms sent his greetings on the Sword's 28th anniversary:

> It is obvious that we as printers are dealing mainly with the technical aspects of THE SWORD OF THE LORD business. Dr. Rice is specializing in evangelism, using most effectively the printed page. But in addition to this, Dr. Rice is a good businessman. His home office is operated very efficiently. He has surrounded himself with a capable staff of department heads. In this respect, it can truly be said that he is implementing most effectively the following five-point program: visualize, organize, deputize, supervise and evangelize.
>
> To publish for 28 years a large-circulation, tabloid-size weekly, with the main emphasis on evangelism, is not only an accomplishment of magnitude proportions, but it is a singular achievement in the field of Christian publications in America.

† † †

Dr. Rice announced in December that Dr. Hyles was to become not only Assistant Editor of THE SWORD OF THE LORD but Director of Sword Conferences. For some time Dr. Hyles had been on our Board of Directors.

No one knows the heavy burden of securing the right speakers, making out the program, seeing to the publicity, the enlisting of pastors, etc., which are necessary at every conference. And this is all the more serious because there are only a handful of men in America especially fitted to transform the lives of preachers and teach them to win souls, hold revivals, build evangelistic churches.

Thank God for Dr. Hyles!

† † †

Dr. Rice had a very interesting note on how it felt turning 67, an event which took place December 11, 1962:

> It is often true, though sad, that when preachers get to be as old as this editor, they preach old sermons, not wanting to do the study and planning and praying to make new ones. It is often true that an older preacher softens in his preaching against sin, in his fight and defense of the Faith, because he feels he is too old to make new friends, or he does not want his children to suffer for his convictions. Many a man tempers his message as he grows old, to maintain his retirement pay from the denomination or to feel sure in his golden years.
>
> Some of the greatest preachers have in later years become so absorbed in building institutions or serving their denomination, that they are not used to stir great crowds and turn many to Christ as they once were.
>
> Some of us who are older remember how tremendous was the ministry of Dr. George W. Truett in the years when he was a great soul winner. His book, *A Quest for Souls*, revival sermons preached in Fort Worth in 1917, is one of the greatest books of sermons ever printed. How heartwarming and blessed they are! But in later years Dr. Truett was largely occupied with raising money for denominational causes, serving on denominational boards, etc. And his preaching, while still blessed, seemed not as powerful and tremendous as in his earlier years. The book of sermons of his later years, edited by Powhatan James, his son-in-law, and published by Eerdmans in a series of books, are not nearly as heartwarming and powerful as *A Quest for Souls*.
>
> But in Bible times Moses was at full strength when the Lord took him to Heaven at age 120. His eyes were not dim, nor his natural force abated.
>
> Caleb and Joshua are other examples of men still mighty for God in old age. "Paul the aged" was still a good enough preacher to be in jail. And the hand of God upon him was mighty until his death.
>
> God has plenty of compensations for old age. "He giveth power to the faint; and to them that have no might he increaseth strength. Even the youths shall faint and be weary, and the young men shall utterly fall: But they that wait upon the Lord shall renew their strength; they shall mount up with wings as eagles;

they shall run, and not be weary; and they shall walk, and not faint" (Isa. 40:29-31).

There may be an enthusiasm and liveliness in youth, but the strength of youth, the wisdom of education, the influence of prestige—God does not need these. Those who wait upon the Lord get renewed strength.

† † †

The Sword Tours to Bible Lands began in 1962 and for seventeen years Dr. Rice spent from fifteen to twenty-one days a year walking where Jesus walked, with as many as 160 pilgrims a year.

One of the reasons for the tour's popularity was Dr. Rice himself and his nightly briefings on the places to be seen. His knowledge of the Bible was far beyond that of the guides and of most tour directors, so that made his descriptions of the places discussed more vivid and rich.

It was my privilege to go on many of these as his assistant. Time and again I heard some tour member say that Dr. Rice's talks, and the tour itself, were much like a spiritual revival.

Many were saved through the years—a guide here, a tour agent there, or an Arab hungry for someone to show him the way to Jesus.

† † †

Our print order for the last issue in December was 17,700 more than the print order for the last issue in December of 1961. That meant a net increase in regular circulation of that many in a year's time.

514 were saved by mail by the end of 1962, making 11,500 who had written they had found Christ through Sword literature.

—At Baalbak in Syria

Yes, he took 17 tours to Bible
Lands! People wanted his
teaching, his description
of the lands of our
Lord. How many were
blessed on their
pilgrimages
with him!

Dr. John and Dr. Bill on
a Caribbean cruise

Ron Ormond produced Dr. Rice's
THE LAND WHERE JESUS
WALKED. Here they are discussing
a scene.

1963

Sword of the Lord Foundation Moves to Murfreesboro, Tennessee

1963

One of the oldest towns in Middle Tennessee and truly one of the most beautiful, is Murfreesboro.

Located 30 miles southeast of Nashville, this community of some 40,000 is a pleasant blend of modern industry and old southern charm. Founded in the early 19th century, it has been the site of several important Tennessee historical occurrences, including the tragic Battle of Stones River during the Civil War. A second battle, the Battle of Murfreesboro, was fought in and around the beautiful courthouse, now over 125 years old, that still stands proudly in the center of the square.

Murfreesboro was, at one time, the state's capital (1818-1826).

Many interesting and exciting sites

The Rutherford County Courthouse, built in 1859, is one of six pre-Civil War buildings still in use in Tennessee.

depict the heritage of that area: Stones River National Battlefield and Old Fort Park; Oaklands Mansion, one of Murfreesboro's oldest homes. Cannonsburgh, a replica of the early 19th century village, has a dozen restored or reconstructed buildings typical in early settlements. Murfreesboro is also one of the major antique centers in the South. And Middle Tennessee State University is located here, with over 13,000 students.

In the last few years the residential growth has been phenomenal.

The Move to Murfreesboro, Tennessee

God seemed to be in this move all the way. One day Dr. Rice had a call from a man wanting to buy the Presbyterian church property at a greatly increased value over what we paid for it. Then within a day or two, he had a call from Murfreesboro, Tennessee—would he be interested in buying a large, adequate plant for $100,000?

So in March two important business deals were negotiated: 1. The Presbyterian Church property in Wheaton was sold for $100,000. 2. The Westvue Baptist Church, Murfreesboro, Tennessee, was purchased for $100,000. The Murfreesboro property included the brick and concrete block tabernacle 84' x 143', two-story front, with some 25,000 square feet of floor space; also in that price was included an older church building of brick, seating 400, a five-room brick home and a two-apartment brick building.

Why had the the Sword of the Lord Foundation decided to move to Murfreesboro?

1. Many employees had come to Wheaton from the South;

2. Warmer climate and lower living costs;

3. In Wheaton we would have to pay at least $200,000 to build an adequate plant, with its rigid building codes and union labor—a lot of money to raise in the '60s.

4. And Dr. Bill and the Bill Rice Ranch were just nine miles west of Murfreesboro.

In 1940 Dr. Rice had moved the Sword of the Lord to Wheaton to be near the Chicago train and plane center for his work as a traveling evangelist, and to have his girls in Wheaton College. Now the plane service in Nashville was greatly improved, and the Nashville airport was about the same distance from Murfreesboro as the Chicago airport was from Wheaton. And his girls were now through college and married.

† † †

Mr. Byers and I and my secretary made a couple of hurried trips to Tennessee to plan the remodeling of this beautiful church building, fitting it for offices. Some 300 seats were removed from one side of the auditorium to make room for a row of offices on floor one. The front of the building is two stories. The editorial offices were to be on floor two, so with carpenters we planned what partitions to remove; stairs to the attic were taken down; rooms were repainted and drapes were hung.

In April, prior to the move, the daily newspaper, the radio, the Chamber of Commerce and the business people sponsored a luncheon to honor Dr. Rice. Some eighty prominent civic, business and Christian leaders came, with welcoming words from the mayor, the county judge, the Chamber of Commerce officials, etc.

† † †

On June 10, the Sword loaded up for the 525-mile move to Murfreesboro, leaving our beautiful Wheaton. Dr. and Mrs. Rice had lived in one house there for twenty-three years. Here their six daughters grew into womanhood; from here they were married.

Goodbye with happy memories—to Sword building; to Calvary Baptist Church; to Wheaton College; to the Wheaton community where we had lived, worked and played for twenty-three years.

**Old-timers from Wheaton—1963—most of whom
moved with us to Murfreesboro**

I suppose Mrs. Rice and I were more sad about leaving Wheaton than the others. She said: "I have shed a few tears at the thought of leaving our home at 512 W. Franklin to strangers, every little nook is so full of happy memories. I try to keep in mind the admonition, 'Forgetting the things that are behind and pressing forward...,' but 512 is the site of so many exciting activities of our big family. If the Lord had asked me about it, I would probably have told Him this place was good enough, but He evidently knows there is something much better for us ahead, and I gladly follow where He leads."

Twenty-three of our 29 employees made the move with us. Dr. Handford stayed with the church. They had already broken ground for a new church building in a nearby suburb, since Calvary Baptist Church was part of the Presbyterian property, which was no longer Sword property.

✝ ✝ ✝

Business manager Al Byers, our walking IBM computer, came up with some figures on the word "move":

> The four freight trucks brought 141,500 pounds. Of the four, one was machinery and three were printed matter. The six moving vans brought 104,800 pounds. The ten trucks brought 246,300 pounds. This is almost 123 tons, or ¼ of a million pounds.
> Dear friends, let us not soon move again!

To which I said a loud AMEN!

Our extra activities of moving and entertaining our visitors increased from a whirl to a tornado! We had some 300 visitors in two months! And this number did not count the townspeople who came for some "Get-Acquainted" services when we first moved in.

To each was given a tour of a "building as big as a football field," as it had been described.

Even after providing all the office space we needed, some 600 opera seats were still intact in the huge auditorium, plus 78 chairs in the choir on the large platform.

How proud Dr. Rice was of his office with 36 feet of windows, and room for his library of 6,000 books, which had been scattered in three offices in Wheaton.

On either side of the office building, great concrete platforms were built for trucks to back up on, then unload on a hoist, which is lowered to the basement.

Above: Building #1, oldest of the three buildings

Above: Building #2, facing the east, was built onto the old building in 1974

Left: Building #3 houses Sword books

Another church building at the side which had seats for 400, was used for storing household goods of some of the workers until they could get permanently located. Later it was used for book storage.

† † †

For twenty-three years our address had been "Wheaton," Illinois—easy to spell and remember. And we are slow to get familiar and to remember a totally new address, especially one that is hard to spell.

But it spells just like it sounds—MUR-FREES-BORO.

Three cheers for the Murfreesboro post office for getting our mail to us. We wondered how it got here, and you will, too, when you read the following ways people spelled the name for awhile:

Murphyboro	Murphysborough	Mufferybour
Murffersburle	Murpheesboro	Murphyborrow, Tennesy
Murphy'sboro	Murphysboro	Murphy's Borough
Murphybery	Murfeboro	Murphreesboro
Murfreesburo	Murfrey Barg	Markersbour
Muffaburl	Murfreesbore	Merkers Burg
Murphrysboro	Mercuries Borou	Memphisborought, Tennessi
Murosboro	Murfysboro	Murfresier Boro, Tenniesie
Murfreeseeboro	Murpheesville	Murphy's Boro
Murphreysboro	Murifriburgs, Tenesee	Murforbur
Murfresboro	Mufferbore	Mursfreezebrug
Murfeyboro	Murphresboro	Murpharysborought
Murphesboro	Murphy Burro	Mirfees Barrow, Tennecy
Merphys Burro	Murfressboro	

When Dr. and Mrs. Rice came to Murfreesboro to consult a builder about a new home, Dr. Bill Rice met them with the good news he had found a farm of 44 acres just a mile from the city limits, which he thought they would like.

They found it a fascinating place.

At the corner of the side yard was a lovely spring with its clear flowing water. The owner, a professor at the state college of Murfreesboro, told the Rices something of its history.

At this particular spot the first shot of the Battle of Murfreesboro was fired. The Confederate soldiers were on the east facing the Federal troops on the west. They both had planned to attack at seven in the morning.

The Rice home for 27 years. The old farmhouse is located to the right

While the Federals were at the spring washing up and getting ready for breakfast, at early dawn the Confederates made a surprise attack, and the Federals never had a chance that sad day to have their breakfast.

The battle was long and costly to both sides. There is a great cemetery in Murfreesboro (Stones River Battlefield) with thousands of white crosses showing how heavy the cost to both sides, though it was claimed a victory for the Confederates at the time.

The professor told how they had picked up and dug up on this farm many relics of that battle. His father had collected many mementos of the battle on the place and sold or given them away.

On the lawn were remains of an elegant flower garden which was said to be a showplace in its early days. There were signs of a lovely Japanese garden, with rock formations and Japanese pottery.

Mrs. Rice fell so in love with the old place that she asked her husband for it. She wanted to restore the farmhouse to some semblance of its early beauty, while building a new house at the side of the famous spot.

So Route 2, Franklin Road, was the address as long as they both lived in Murfreesboro. (Of course we know their new address!)

Mrs. Rice said after moving to Murfreesboro, "Flicka [their dog] and I had looked forward to a sort of retirement to 'middle-age,' but with all the work facing me, I'd better get a drink at the Fountain of Youth, roll up my sleeves and get to work! I had thought of getting to go barefoot and stretching out in the sun for long spells of rest—southern fashion—

but there will be no time for that comfortable-looking rocker on the front porch."

The brick home, in which Dr. and Mrs. Rice lived out their years, was built beside the farmhouse. Dr. Rice died at the end of 1980, and Mrs. Rice, at the end of 1989.

† † †

This Evangelist Learned to Preach Through THE SWORD!

Evangelist Jack Van Impe who, with his wife Rexella, make the evangelistic team, "Ambassadors for Christ," wrote:

Dear Dr. Rice:

Greetings in the name of the Lord!

I just feel led of the Lord to write you today to send a few roses along the way while you can appreciate them. Many times I have felt like doing it, then did not find the time. However, I feel I must say in a few lines how much I thank the Lord for your ministry.

I started in evangelism some fourteen years ago and did not really know how to go about it or what type of message was needed. Through reading and rereading your messages, the Holy Spirit showed me the type of sermons needed for this day.

I started to preach against sin and name the sins and have continued to do so. In earlier days when criticism came, I would reconsider and wonder if I should be a little softer. Then THE SWORD OF THE LORD would come and I would make a new dedication to preach it hotter and stronger.

What has been the outcome? We have seen some 17,000 conversions in these fourteen years and thousands of other decisions. The Lord has been so pleased that we have some 500 churches on file for future meetings. In fact, we are not taking them in succession anymore, but praying for guidance as to which ones we should take. I feel that you have a great part in all of this and again *I want to say thank God for a man who will take a stand so that the boys going into the ministry have a real leader and know the issues of the day.* The Lord bless you for all you have done for me. . . .

We pray for you often.

In Christ,
(Signed) Jack Van Impe

† † †

MANY A LITTLE MAKES A MUCH. Back thirty years or so ago most homes had at least one radio, and some had several. Shops, stores, business places, even some factories, used radios to set a happy atmosphere for employees and customers. Some towns had loudspeakers along the streets to entertain shoppers. It seemed as though radios went everywhere people went.

The stations on which Voice of Revival were heard had a potential listening audience of many millions of Americans. One station claimed that in the area it served, the average cost per one thousand listeners was less than 5$^¢$. One little nickel to get a message to one thousand precious souls! In those days, that was real purchasing power for the lowly nickel.

Many were tuning into the Voice of Revival to hear the sweet singing and the powerful fifteen-minute message.

† † †

Dr. Rice reported that nearly 600 people wrote after hearing Voice of Revival during December. "And you would be surprised at how many letters were from the unsaved."

A man in Bonnyman, Kentucky wrote: "I listen to your program every Sunday night. I am a sinner and would like to be saved. Please send me a booklet telling me how I can be saved."

From St. Thomas in the Virgin Islands one who was "a constant listener" wrote: "I am not saved, but I have an eternal desire to be . . . ."

From Cocoa, Florida: "I am not saved, but I believe through reading your booklet, it will help me more to the way of life. My wife is saved and I am happy about that. Pray for me . . . ."

From Hazel, Kentucky: "Tell me how to be saved. I heard you on the radio."

From Chicago came this: "My mother always says one has to be born again to be saved. I want to be saved . . . ."

Another man from Chicago wrote: "I heard your program and would love to have your booklet. My home is broken and I would love to be saved . . . ."

† † †

And in the twelve months, 401 people had written that they had trusted Christ through Sword literature.

1964

REVIVAL IN A FILE DRAWER. Maybe that sounds strange to you, but it isn't really. It may sound strange because there's nothing very exciting about filing cabinets. There are filing clerks in some places who do nothing but put things away in file folders all day long. Their jobs are routine and monotonous—far from what Christian people would call revival atmosphere.

But here was a row of filing cabinets. One secretary pulled out a drawer, reached inside and extracted a manila file folder. "Here are the monthly record sheets for 1963," she said, "and the letters are filed alphabetically in this same drawer. These other drawers are for all the other years."

I thanked her, and she went on about her business.

I took the file folder and began to thumb through the reports. For each month there was listed a row of names with cities and states. There was an indication at the side as to what booklet brought this person to Christ. Repeatedly there was the notation, *"What. . . ?"* (Dr. Rice's famous tract, *"What Must I Do to Be Saved?"*) There were notations for sermons which appeared in THE SWORD. Other books were listed, and "Radio" appeared on some.

Though I had worked at the Sword for these many years, this was the first time I felt like shouting over a file drawer! I looked at all those names—nearly every state in the Union was represented. Here were names I couldn't begin to pronounce, and addresses in Africa, Indonesia, New Zealand. Many foreign countries were mentioned. There were more than 400 names of real, live people who had been saved in 1963 through the various ministries of the Sword Foundation and had written to tell us about it. Probably there were that many more who were saved but did not write.

THAT'S BIG BUSINESS!!! That was enough to make even my old, cold heart rejoice.

Why, there are many good gospel-preaching churches where they did not have that many converts in 1963. Some churches get really happy and all excited if they meet the commitments of their budget. The missionary circles count the bandages they wrapped. The sunshine committees report how many cards were sent and how many baskets of fruit were given.

When you come right down to it, the main business of every church and every Christian is trying to keep folks out of Hell—and most of us aren't even in business! 1964 was the first spiritual birthday for at least 400 people who the year before were dead in trespasses and sin. This because of THE SWORD or books put out by Sword of the Lord Foundation.

GLORY!!!

More than 22 million copies of books written by Dr. Rice had already been printed and circulated around the world by 1964. These books made lasting impressions upon the lives of multitudes. They were read in about 35 languages. White men, black men, yellow men and red men read his books in their own tongues and experienced the blessing of God through them.

Many read Dr. Rice's books who never saw him nor heard him in person. Hundreds and thousands of them came to trust Christ as Saviour. One day they will meet the "Captain of Our Team" in Heaven. Can you imagine what it will be like!

Here comes a man from India to shake hands with him and to say, "I was saved through reading your book translated in my own language."

Another—this one from Japan—says, "Me, too. I read that same book in my own language and trusted the Lord."

Then there is one from Finland, another from Denmark, one from England and one from Africa—all crowd around to greet him and shake his hand. They never met him in this life, but in Heaven they will meet and rejoice together.

In Heaven we will know all of the stories. Here we only know a few. We are thrilled when we read letters from those who take time to write and share with us the blessings which have come to them through Sword literature. When the Lord calls us Home, what rejoicing there will be when all the stories are told!

Already you have read scores of letters to prove what I am saying. This is just to remind you of the ministry Dr. Rice's books have in the lives of untold millions.

† † †

While preaching in a town in Texas, Dr. Rice had strongly urged parents to discipline their children. One woman came up to him after the service fuming: "I'll never come back to hear you preach again!"

Suddenly this woman fell over as if dead. Dr. Rice casually called for someone to call her husband, then went on shaking hands with those leaving the service.

Now that woman came back the next night and the next, and every night of the revival, taking in and enjoying every word! But when she got near Dr. Rice, she began to stutter (which she had never done before)!

God has a way of dealing with rebellion, doesn't He!

† † †

Dr. Rice's book sales were phenomenal. Moody Press published in 1964 a list of over 10,000 books in print from 57 publishing companies. The author who had the most published was JOHN R. RICE, with some 142 titles—more than double that of the second place entry, Dr. H. A. Ironside, with 65.

† † †

Dr. Hyles made this prediction: "If the Sword of the Lord ended its ministry and circulation today, its influence would still be felt until Jesus comes."

† † †

Dr. Rice was again saying why he must spend time promoting and pushing a Christian magazine which defends the Faith, exposes modernism and false cults, and continually presses against formalism. "The Sword of the Lord has a holy commission from God," said he. "We must publish the inroads of modernism and oppose the blandishments of 'false brethren,' as the Scripture calls them, and we must oppose the coldness, the formalism in the church and call people again and again back to the fervor and bold preaching and house-to-house visitation and soul winning of New Testament churches.

"Had it been left to my own choice," he added, "I would have preferred to spend all my time in great revivals, but through THE SWORD OF THE LORD I must now make a climate for revival. I must promote evangelism and evangelists. I must hew at the worldliness and powerlessness of Christians. I must insist upon Christians' seeking and having the fullness of the Spirit as in Bible times."

He went on to say, "God has given me a willingness to suffer shame and reproach for Him."

† † †

Dr. and Mrs. Rice's small shepherd dog, Flicka, a member of the family for fourteen years, had gotten old and stiff. Her hearing and eyesight were poor, she could eat very little, and she seemed to be in pain and had fever. The veterinarian thought it best to have her put to sleep. Dr. Rice commented: "We will miss Flicka terribly."

† † †

Keep in mind: Dr. Rice was now 68 years old, and would be 69 in three months. In "Editor's Notes" he revealed that that day he had caught Mac and gone for a good ride, had come in and was eating supper, when Pete Rice called: "Some of us are going to play tennis; would you come along with us?"

"I donned tennis shoes, sports shirt, trousers and left. Dr. Bill and I played against his two sons, Bill III and Pete. We beat the boys in a seven-to-five game set! Then home, a little weary, a good night's sleep and now to work."

† † †

RICE NEW HOME GOING UP. For over a year, the Rices had lived in a little four-room house moved onto the property in back of the place designated for a permanent home. With its tiny rooms, it was totally inadequate. There was no room for a piano, and the dining room furniture had been stored.

In 1937 in Fort Worth they had drawn their own plans and built a beautiful little brick home, with an "Upper Room." Famous song leader B. B. McKinney, their friend, had come, prayed and dedicated every room.

Both Dr. and Mrs. Rice told the Lord then that they would gladly leave this dream house anytime He said to.

The Lord led them to Dallas in 1932. Since the Fort Worth house had not sold, they just walked out and left it.

In Wheaton they rented, then purchased a large old frame house about seventy years old, where they lived the twenty-three years they were there.

Now again they had in Murfreesboro drawn up their own plans and let out the contract. The house would be brick veneer with five rooms besides baths, carport and a utility room.

MOVING TIME. They moved in three days before Christmas. Most of the children and grandchildren came for the holidays. Dr. Rice commented: "Of course I enjoy the comfort of the new home, the tile bath, the wall-to-wall carpet, the automatic electric heat and plenty of room. But I enjoy it more for Mrs. Rice who deserves it and for our children and workers who are proud of it.

"And we promise the Lord that, as in other homes, the Word of God will be read and family prayer, as well as private devotions, held. And we promise Him that we will leave the home in a moment to please Him, as we have done before."

† † †

On September 27 Dr. and Mrs. Rice celebrated their forty-fifth wedding anniversary. The following poem was written by daughter Jessie Sandberg with this note: "In a gentle conspiracy with Dad's faithful secretary, Miss Walden, I hope to sneak this past Dad's sharp editorial eye to share it with you. It has no great literary value, but because the occasion and subject are worthy of whatever honor I can bestow, I take the liberty of presenting it in this way."

> *Full forty years ago, plus five (so long ago!)*
> *You stood before the solemn company*
> *And pledged before the Lord that you two would be one.*
> *(It was a sad occasion for the family—*
> *Was not this bridegroom some young dreamer full of hope*
> *With little else to merit someone dear as she?)*
>
> *You claimed by sacred vow that you would jointly share*
> *Whatever part of poverty or wealth,*
> *Whatever came of highest joy or deepest pain,*
> *Reproach or fame, disease or glowing health.*
> *That faith was not betrayed by hard, determined will,*
> *Nor broken by temptation's subtle stealth.*
>
> *Within the providence of God, the days and years*
> *Brought measured portions of the good and bad,*
> *And you, young dreamer, by your pen and voice and prayers*
> *(Whose partner shared the vision that you had),*

Helped shape the course of countless thousands' destinies
And by your fruit made even God's heart glad.

Whatever accolade or praise the world may give,
However grand the monument may seem,
Let this reward of faith stand tall among the host
Of well-earned honors, and your friends' esteem,
The thanks of thousands whom you two have helped and blessed—
Your children bring their love, and share your dream.

† † †

Dr. Rice: "Mrs. Rice saved up her money, and after I found the horse I wanted, she bought him for me—a beautiful Tennessee walking horse that I have named 'General of the Army's Douglas MacArthur II'—'Mac' for short." Dr. Rice was quick to add, "The horse was not expensive."

Below: Dr. Rice always had time for his pet, Flicka.

Above and below: Such typical scenes! He loved children, and they loved him. No matter how busy he was, there was always time for them. He was everybody's father.

Said Dr. Hyles: "I remember one day in Milford, Ohio, when after the service Dr. Rice couldn't be found...he had just disappeared. Later he was found playing hopscotch with some children down the street!"

1965

Dr. Rice wrote: "You will remember that Dr. Jack Hyles is Assistant Editor of THE SWORD and Director of Sword of the Lord Conferences. In a recent board meeting, Dr. Bill Rice was elected first vice-president and Dr. Hyles, second vice-president of Sword of the Lord Foundation."

† † †

While Cumberwood Christian Retreat (the Bill Rice Ranch) was in the building stage, Dr. John Rice kept calling men to come and help; he kept asking for tools; he kept seeking for plumbers, electricians, block layers to give a few days' time. But not only was he calling for help; many of the "work weeks" Dr. Rice himself was out there nailing nails and sawing lumber along with the rest.

† † †

Every succeeding pastor at the church Dr. Rice founded in Dallas in 1932 wanted him back for special services whenever he was available.

† † †

Galilean Baptist Church

In April he returned to the Galilean Baptist Church for "Dr. Rice Day." Twenty charter members were present who were in the organization of the church thirty-three years before. Scores of others, who had been members under Dr. Rice's leadership, attended the conferences during the week.

"How they blessed my heart by their greetings and fellowship," he commented.

† † †

The August 25 issue listed Sword Conferences for a year ahead, and there were twenty-four of them! And as I look back, it seems that was the way it had been for many years.

† † †

"Dr. Rice, you talk like you could ask the Lord for a barrel of pickles and get them," said a critic who did not believe God would answer our prayer for personal things.

His reply was, "If I needed a barrel of pickles, I would certainly ask God for them."

† † †

EDITOR NOT FOR SALE. The world is looking for men who are not for sale, men who are honest, sound from center to circumference, true to the heart's core, men with conscience as steady as the needle to the North Pole; men who will stand for right if the heavens teeter and the earth reels; men who will tell the truth and look the world right in the eye; men who neither drag nor run, men who neither flag nor flinch; men who can have courage without shouting it; men in whom courage of everlasting life runs still, deep and strong; men who know their message and tell it; men who know their place and fill it; men who know their business and attend to it; men who will not lie, shirk or dodge; men who are not too lazy to work nor too proud to be poor; men who are willing to eat what they have earned and wear what they have paid for; men who are not ashamed to say "no" with emphasis and who are not ashamed to say, "I can't afford it."

Few people are subject to more pressures, psychological, obvious, subtle and brutal, than an editor of a periodical like THE SWORD OF THE LORD. Many "lobbyists" on either side try to make editors say what they would like them to say: "Buy this or sell that. . . Promote this or don't promote that. . . Don't mention his name or communism or TV or pacifism or new evangelicalism, evangelicalism, British Israelism or tongues. Carry secular ads. . . . THE SWORD should be printed on a better grade paper. . . Promote baptismal regeneration," etc., and one hundred other special requests subtly given.

What says Dr. Rice? You probably already know!

> This is to announce that the editor is not for sale to the highest bidder or to the loudest caller or to the longest letter-writer. Nor are we in the business of presenting a "symposium of ideas" to read the truth by a majority vote.
>
> THE SWORD is also not in a beauty or popularity contest with any other magazine; we are just one voice in the wilderness crying out for noncompromise in mass evangelism, to reinforce evangelists and pastors, without fear or favor. As David said in Psalm 119:63, "I am a companion of ALL them that fear thee, and of them that keep thy precepts."

† † †

Dr. Bob Shuler, 86, went to be with the Lord September 11, 1965. The funeral service was held at Trinity Methodist Church, Los Angeles, where he had served as pastor from 1920 to 1953.

Dr. Shuler was on the Cooperating Board of the Sword of the Lord, and our wonderful friend. When his book of sermons, *What New Doctrine Is This?* was put "under the counter," as he said, in Methodist bookstores and the Methodist publishing house did not want to republish it, Sword of the Lord did. Then later we published his books, *Some Dogs I Have Known* and *I Met These on the Trail.*

Dr. Shuler called Dr. Rice "one of the best friends I have ever had."

He was an ardent fundamentalist, a crusader for righteousness and editor of *The Methodist Challenge.* Some years after his retirement he turned over his subscription list to THE SWORD OF THE LORD, and we finished out the subscription obligations.

† † †

Bill Harvey, with Dr. Rice in a 15-day united crusade near Seaford, Delaware, observed:

> Reflecting on the meeting, I think of Dr. Rice "at work" and of the priceless experience and storehouse of campaign know-how he has gained through the years. Praying, studying and a

multitude of other duties behind him, Dr. Rice went to the platform knowing what would "work" and what would not.

One of the first "orders" given when he got up to preach was
the gentle-but-firm demand that the ushers come in and be seated
so there could be a "total participation." Incidentally, they com-
plied immediately and beautifully. Wouldn't you?

Dr. Rice had his finger on the crusade pulse, constantly
challenging, changing, arranging and adjusting under the leadership of the Holy Spirit, ever mindful of the revival temperature.

To encourage continued large crowds, Dr. Rice unselfishly offered $25 worth of his books to the library of any church that
would have at least 75 percent of their Sunday school enrollment
present on a given night. Five churches proved equal to the
challenge.

One thing about Dr. Rice stands out in my memory, and I know
I shall long cherish it. He had each seeker come to him personally. "Have you ever been saved?" he might ask them. "Do you
want to ask Jesus to come into your heart?" was another question. Each question was asked with tears, with deliberation, with
sincerity; then Dr. Rice would turn them over to an able personal
worker.

Many times after the services a personal worker would bring
a new convert to Dr. Rice and introduce him as having just trusted
Christ, and Dr. Rice could be heard from a good distance, saying,
"Wonderful!" then call to me, "Oh, Bill...come and meet this
fine young man! He has trusted Jesus tonight as his Saviour!"
Then to the convert: "Is it all settled? Aren't you glad? And now
you must be sure to read God's Word (and he tells them where)
and pray and...here (we were nearly always close to the book
table), let me give you something to read."

Suggestions, demands, arrangements, adjustments—whatever
Dr. John R. Rice did in that fine campaign, his sights were zeroed
in on that truck driver, that high school girl, that sailor lad, that
tender child, that desperate woman, one at a time, to walk forward for salvation.

Every church in that campaign was surely strengthened. Every
pastor certainly must have discovered "it can be done."

I have never seen any finer harmony on the part of participating
pastors in any previous campaign in my experience.

The crusade as such came to an end with so many wishing we
could go on another two weeks at least.

That part of Delaware will never be the same. There's one thing of which I'm sure: I never shall be.

† † †

One of our best-loved contributors, Evangelist John Linton, went Home to Heaven on December 7, 1965. He died while preaching—as he would have wanted it had he had his choice.

† † †

Our annual Sword of the Lord Board meeting was held in Chattanooga, Tennessee. It was a thrilling experience to hear reports of the wonderful way God had blessed the Sword ministry in 1965.

On the Board were: Dr. John R. Rice, president; Dr. Bill Rice, Dr. Jack Hyles, Dr. R. L. Sumner, Dr. Tom Malone, Al Byers, Evangelist Bud Lyles, Rev. Paul Raker, Mrs. John R. Rice, Miss Fairy Shappard and I, Viola Walden.

Each year all members and directors of the Board must sign the Statement of Faith of Sword of the Lord Foundation, which reads:

I BELIEVE

1. In the verbal inspiration of the Scriptures and the absolute reliability and authority, without error, in the original manuscripts.

2. In the virgin birth, atoning death, bodily resurrection and deity of Jesus Christ.

3. That man is a fallen creature, sinful by nature and choice, can only become a child of God by regeneration by the supernatural work of the Holy Spirit.

4. That salvation is by penitent faith in Christ as our Substitute, on the merits of His atoning death and shed blood.

5. In Christ's premillennial second coming (by which we mean the pre-tribulation rapture position or the imminent return of Christ).

6. In the eternal blessedness for the saved, and in the eternal punishment in Hell for the lost.

7. In the need for a personal enduement of power by the Holy Spirit, who already lives in the body of each Christian.

8. In the duty of each Christian to live a holy life, to make soul winning the main end of all Christian work; that God's great commission never changes as the principal obligation of churches and Christians, and that this includes mass evangelism as well as

personal soul winning and soul winning through other means and agencies.

AGREEMENT WITH ABOVE STATEMENT OF FAITH AND PRINCIPLES

I solemnly affirm that I sincerely believe the above Statement of Faith from my heart, without mental reservation or evasion, and I promise, God being my helper, that as long as I am associated with the Sword of the Lord Foundation in any capacity I will faithfully try to live by the moral and spiritual standards for which the Foundation stands, and to support these standards. Before all I promise on my sacred honor, that if ever I find myself in disagreement with the above Statement of Faith and principles, I will immediately offer my resignation from membership, directorship or any position under Sword of the Lord Foundation.

For Christ's sake, I will endeavor to safeguard the welfare of this Christian organization and the work to which it is dedicated, by helping to enforce this agreement on the part of all directors and members, by every Christian means.

† † †

When we offered as a premium for a Sword subscription, Dr. Bill Rice's *Cowboy Boots in Darkest Africa,* one lady from Iowa sent in three subscriptions and said, "I do not want those cowboy shoes as I can't wear them."

 **GIVEN TO JESUS.** We were very much touched to receive this lovely letter from Miss Florence H. Waid in New York State:

Dear Dr. Rice:

There it stood, a thing of beauty, a large vase of honey amber glass. It was a perfect example of applied glass, for amid heavy enameling of apple blossoms and leaves a master glass blower had applied a ruffle of electric blue glass at the top, a bluebird, a nest of eggs and four feet.

As I stood admiring it an inner voice said, "Give it to Jesus." This is just what I'm doing, giving it to you, Dr. Rice, to give to our precious Lord. May this comfort and encourage you as you so faithfully serve Him.

(signed) Florence H. Waid

P.S. A friend took a picture of it recently, but she failed to capture its beauty.

The colored photo of the vase is beautiful; we can only reproduce it in black and white.

The gift was applied to help pay radio broadcast time, and this letter and receipt were sent to our dear sister.

Dear Miss Waid:

It was wonderfully kind of you, and I know it was your devotion to Christ that caused you to give up that beautiful large vase. I could tell by the picture something of how beautiful it is.

I remember that, when Mary brought an alabaster box of ointment, "very precious," worth 300 days'

wages, Jesus was greatly pleased. I am sure your loving gift pleases Him in the same way. I am more grateful than words can express.

A receipt goes along with my heartfelt thanks.

In Jesus' name,

John R. Rice

† † †

I found this interesting short article by Dr. Rice in early 1966, "We Try to Follow the Steps of D. L. Moody"—and truly he did.

> Moody, Torrey and their helpers spread revival fires so widely through conferences at Northfield, Massachusetts and through stirring the hearts of preachers and teaching them, that there arose a great evangelistic generation following them.
>
> J. Wilbur Chapman, R. A. Torrey, Sam Jones, George Stuart, Billy Sunday, Bob Jones, Biederwolf, Mordecai Ham, L. R. Scarborough and many others arose to preach the Gospel in great revivals. At one time, some forty years ago, there were a thousand evangelists in great citywide campaigns over America, in an association of evangelists with headquarters at Winona Lake, Indiana. These thousand evangelists preached to a million people every night in tabernacles, tents, city auditoriums and other meeting places.
>
> So with revival literature and reaching 8,000 to 10,000 preachers a year with great conferences and over 20,000 preachers a year with THE SWORD OF THE LORD, we are stirring revival fires, training soul winners, teaching men how to build great evangelistic, soul-winning churches.

At one Sword Conference at Lake Louise, a businessman from Ohio was challenged. He heard the preachers, read the large sign over the platform that urged people to set out to win one hundred in the next year.

Though he had been saved for some years, he had never won a soul to Christ. His heart made tender by the preaching, he asked God to help him win one hundred in a year.

He left at the close of the week, and on the way home won seven souls!

The next summer he came to the Sword Conference at the Bill Rice Ranch and gave his testimony. During the year he had won—not one hundred but—150! In the years since, he has continued to lead hundreds to salvation.

Mr. Ed Barth is a busy man. He and his brother are turkey growers and have a thriving business, which demands time and work. Still Mr. Barth takes time to witness for Jesus.

† † †

In Kentucky a young man worked in the coal mines. But the mines were not doing well, and the future looked bleak. He left Kentucky and went to Michigan where he hired out to hang dry wall. It wasn't long until he turned contractor and hired men to hang dry wall for him. Later he began to buy property and build apartments. His business grew and became very prosperous.

Then the young businessman heard Dr. Hyles and Dr. Rice preach. Although he had been saved for some time, he knew next to nothing about soul winning. The messages he heard stirred his heart. He decided he would like to try that.

He began witnessing to everyone. He got another young Christian to go with him, and they became a team to visit people in their homes. God blessed their efforts. Over the next months and years, hundreds were saved because they cared about souls.

Mr. Russell Anderson puts in a long day with his business. He has many men working for him. There are demands upon his time. Still he in a year's time has seen as high as 400 come to the Saviour. He wins them because he works at it.

These two examples could be multiplied a thousandfold as a result of some Sword of the Lord Conference somewhere in the U.S.A.

† † †

Dr. Rice commented that "it is wonderfully sweet that, despite my plain strong stand in defending the Faith, denouncing sin and holding up strong standards for Christians, I have so many more calls than I can fill, more open doors than I can enter. How blessed that God's people seek my poor ministry!" When I looked at his coming schedule, I couldn't believe it. He was now seventy-one. Instead of slowing down, letting up, letting go, he was continually going more and taking on more projects.

† † †

This article by Dr. Rice was first printed in *The Harvester* magazine, then reprinted in THE SWORD in March.

"NO MORE GREAT REVIVALS." That slander against God and the Bible and Christianity is being spread in America by many. Who says so?

The atheist for one. Man has become too enlightened to be fooled anymore by the evangelists who preach that man is fallen, that Hell awaits unconverted sinners who reject Christ as a personal Saviour. So says the atheist.

The modernists say so, too. We have learned better, they say, than to take the Bible as authority. No virgin birth, no bodily resurrection, no second coming, so no judgment, no Hell, no need for a new birth. So no more great revivals.

The formal, worldly-minded, compromising pastors and church members say the same thing. No more are they going to have evangelists criticizing well-paying church members who dance, drink, curse, pet and gamble. No more making an issue over evolution or the virgin birth or unbelief in church colleges! People will not stand for that anymore, they say. So down with evangelists and revivals!

Many devout, consecrated people are saying the same thing, however, helping to spread the Devil's lie. Who are they? Defeatist and defeated preachers who never weep when they preach, never agonize in prayer for revival. "No more great revivals," they say; but the truth is, those kinds of people never *did* have a revival— men who rarely win a soul personally, men who never attack sin boldly as Bible preachers did, never preach on Hell or judgment, men who never had and never sought an enduement of power from on High like that which New Testament Christians sought and had, like that found by Wesley, Finney, Moody and Torrey!

How could they have a revival, men who never spent days fasting nor nights in prayer? How could men have a revival who never lost a friend nor a job nor a home nor reputation for Christ? How could easy-going preachers, without sweat, tears, self-denial; men who were never called fools nor fanatics nor publicity seekers nor sensationalists nor troublemakers—how could they have a revival?

So the easy way out is to blame the age or sinners or God and say there will never be any more great revivals. Men without faith, without Holy Spirit power to win souls, defeated men who bear little or no fruit, say there will be no more great revivals. But God did not say it!

OH, IF WE ARE WILLING TO PAY THE COST, WE CAN HAVE REVIVALS!

† † †

When on the tour of Bible lands in February, Dr. Rice got to meet and talk to several missionaries.

> In Cairo it was a joy to sit at the table with a chemical engineer, H. C. Hearn, and family. He works with the oil well industry, but also does missionary work. How he loves THE SWORD! He had ordered extra copies and told me, "Your commentaries on Matthew and Acts are on the way here now."
>
> In Beirut, several missionaries were at our service, and some met our plane. Missionary Hellwege was happy to be distributing 600 copies of *"What Must I Do to Be Saved?"* He makes broadcasts on tape for the whole Arab world.
>
> Pastor Sadaka of Beirut told me of many saved through my sermon-tract, and these had written to him direct.
>
> All thanked me again for THE SWORD, its faith, its Bible content. Let the heathen rage, let modern unbelievers and their compromising friends criticize—but as long as the missionaries, the soul winners and the thousands of common Christians stand by THE SWORD, I shall rejoice and take courage afresh!

† † †

Dr. Rice estimated "that of forty-four years married, I have been away from home thirty years. That is the occupational hazard of the evangelist. I do not repine in loneliness nor fret nor complain. The cross I lifted long ago so gladly, I carry still with joy; but it has never grown light."

Then he joyfully added: "How dear to my heart is the work of the Lord, He knows! To preach, to sing, to write, to witness, to promote revivals and soul winning, to defend the Faith—how sweet!"

† † †

NO, WE DID NOT CHOOSE ANY JAPANESE VERSION. Back in the '60s when we were getting so much literature into Japan, the Sword decided to ask a group of missionaries from the main fundamental groups in Japan, including Evangelical Alliance Mission, Youth for Christ, Conservative Baptists, Bible Presbyterians and some others, to form a committee, get competitive prices on printing *"What Must I Do to Be Saved?"* in Japan, and report what those prices were. Since we had done so much printing and had so much printing done in foreign countries, management knew what a good price was. They wanted to save money by getting competitive bids.

When satisfied with the price, Dr. Rice had the foreign missionary committee translate the booklet in Japanese and supervise its distribution.

Many were disturbed because they had been informed that his tract was printed using the Revised Standard Version type Japanese Colloquial Version, a modernistic version, and these who had been misinformed thought Dr. Rice recommended this version over there.

So all would be properly informed, Dr. Rice gave this information in the June 17, 1966 issue:

> The Revised Standard Version of the Bible is an English, not a Japanese version. In all my books in English we have used Scriptures from the King James Version. Occasionally, on some particular point, perhaps, I have referred to the American Standard Version of 1901.
>
> However, in foreign countries, I leave it to missionaries to decide about the translation. I know not a word of Japanese. Good Bible believers did the translation; and when they used Scripture, they, not I, decided what version to use.
>
> I understand in Japan there are two versions. One is the old Classic Version. But the Japanese language changed so much during the last fifty years that this version was not being read by many people since the language was archaic and stilted. The New Colloquial Version was more in the language of common people. There was nothing in the Japanese language like the King James Version in America.
>
> I am told the New Colloquial Version has many faults, but it is still the Bible the people use and understand. Nearly all Christian literature translated in Japanese uses this new version, I am told.
>
> Being not entirely satisfied, the missionaries have on foot a plan to put out a new translation.
>
> I repeat: there is no Revised Standard Version in Japan. And again I repeat: I made no decision about the Japanese version used in my booklet, leaving that to Bible-believing missionaries there on the field. Whether their decision was wise as to what version they used, I am not well enough informed to judge. But I do know that thousands have claimed Christ through my literature there, using the New Colloquial Version.

Then Dr. Rice went on to explain a certain missionary was making these false reports because he was against one group on the committee, The Evangelical Alliance Mission. Because of his conduct, TEAM had fired him. Then he made an attack on the committee's motives and spread this false report about Dr. Rice's choosing this version for his booklet. This man had also slandered Dr. Rice through the years because he worked with TEAM, both at home and abroad.

And so the world goes!

† † †

Thousands of interesting letters come to the Sword office; this one will make you think. The writer took an issue of THE SWORD OF THE LORD to Cape Kennedy and let some missile workers read a special article by Dr. Rice. Then we learned a little about the life of the writer.

> My first wife divorced me; then I met my present wife. We went to a Presbyterian minister to be married, but he wouldn't marry us. We were unsaved, but he didn't tell us about the plan of salvation.
>
> For eight years I played in a nightclub three doors from a mission called JESUS SAVES. Many times during intermission I would walk on the street and talk to the ministers in front of JESUS SAVES. They told me I should not be playing in this nightclub, this "den of iniquity," but not once did they tell me about being born again.
>
> I played for the Second Division army that completely got annihilated in Korea at this time. I was considered a very good musician and lured many crowds to this club by my talent.
>
> I never drank, smoked nor used profane language; but I was a sinner right along with the crowd.
>
> I wish I could go back and play "The Old Rugged Cross" for all the boys who died in Korea. If someone had just told me about Jesus, I might have had a much better life and might have kept some of your soldier sons out of Hell.

Oh, so many have so many chances to win so many hungry hearts, but we neglect our duty!

† † †

When *Christianity Today* magazine, edited by Dr. Graham's father-in-law, invited publishers to send books for review, we sent Dr. Rice's

Earnestly Contending for the Faith. Now read the review:

> This is an unusual book. The red-white-blue cover carries a pic-
> ture of the author that suggests he is surprised to be there, and
> the Table of Contents contains more surprises. Inside the book
> the author wields "the sword of the Lord," chiefly against
> evangelicals with a finesse reminiscent of Samson.

And that's all! What a scholarly review! Nearly a page is given for
a review of a book by a modernist, Heinz Edward Todt. A mild difference
of opinion is expressed, but not a sneer. "That is left only for Bible-
believing Christians who defend the Faith," Dr. Rice commented; then,
after he had read other reviews in that same edition, he concluded: "This
subsidized evangelical magazine . . . is evidently far more friendly to
modernists than to fundamentalists."

† † †

Dr. Rice, in May, reported that "pastors on the Cooperating Board of
the Sword of the Lord baptized over 6,000 converts last year." On the
Board were pastors of six of the most fruitful soul-winning churches in
the world: Dr. Jack Hyles, Dr. Lee Roberson, Dr. Tom Malone, Dr.
Beauchamp Vick, Dr. Bill Dowell and Dr. Bob Gray.

† † †

It all started when the high school history teacher called the Bible
"a book of fables." The only Christian boy in the class went home that
evening greatly troubled and at the dinner table poured out the story
to his parents.

The godly father immediately gave the boy *Is Jesus God?* (John R.
Rice)—told him to read it, then suggested that he take it to the history
teacher.

Skeptical but curious, the teacher did read the book and finally in the
wee hours of the night flung himself across his bed in tears of genuine
repentance.

So through one book by Dr. Rice, a high school boy's faith was held
intact, an infidel teacher accepted Christ as his Saviour, and an entire
high school was influenced for God!

† † †

During the Sword's Fourth of July week, 1966, at the Bill Rice Ranch,

John R. Rice Tabernacle, Bill Rice Ranch, Murfreesboro

"Hello, Dr. Rice." "Good-by, Dr. Rice." That's about how it was.
He estimated he had been away from home 30 of his 45 years
in the ministry.

the meeting climaxed with the dedication of the John R. Rice Tabernacle. Dr. Hyles gave the dedication message, and Mrs. Hyles sang so sweetly.

† † †

Once when Dr. Rice was invited to a city in Florida for a revival, one of the church members, opposing his coming, said, "He'll come over my dead body."

Dr. Rice did go for the revival. While he was there, this same man died of a heart attack, and his casket was under the banner which announced the John R. Rice revival!

† † †

After investigating thoroughly, Dr. Rice was surprised to learn that only twenty churches in America had baptized as many as 200 converts in a year.

After counseling with Dr. Lee Roberson, Dr. Jack Hyles and Dr. Tom Malone, all of whom had baptized over one thousand last year—all had agreed that it might well be that one hundred or more such churches would set a goal of 200 in 1967, if challenged.

And these three men and Dr. Rice offered to counsel any pastor as to the best way to build a great soul-winning church, and each promised to answer questions and make suggestions as to how to reach that thrilling goal.

Through THE SWORD, Dr. Rice beseeched pastors to prayerfully consider putting soul winning first. "I would like to have a list of every pastor who will take it up with his church and, if the people agree with him, will set a goal to baptize at least 200 converts in the next year."

(Later, we will tell you more about this.)

In order to reach that goal, it was suggested that (1) pastor and deacons and Sunday school teachers set goals for themselves; (2) plan for a regular visitation program; (3) plan where possible to have buses go out to get loads; (4) Sunday morning service should be a great reaping time when those saved through the week could come forward publicly and claim the Lord, then follow Him in baptism.

Dr. Rice stressed that "there are methods we can help you to adopt in winning souls, but no methods will do the work without the power of God as people take the Gospel to sinners."

He also stressed that they were not simply encouraging men to seek a great increase in church membership without getting people born again. "But we believe those who are truly converted should be baptized because Jesus commanded it. And baptism is a clear-cut measure of the soul-winning ministry of a church."

† † †

In 1965, a half-million copies of Dr. Rice's *"What Must I Do to Be Saved?"* were printed in the Japanese language. This year, a missionary sent a report showing that some 3,400 people had claimed Christ as Saviour as a result of that printing and wrote in to them to say so. All were enrolled in a correspondence Bible course for new converts.

Now the missionaries were clamoring for more copies—a million more. The cost of that Japanese printing in Japan would be $7,400.

Dr. Rice wrote the committee: "Go ahead and we will raise the money someway."

Meantime, in Korea, where the Sword had already paid for two large printings of the booklet in the Korean language, came an earnest plea for more. "We can print 300,000 for $2,500 if we authorize the printing now."

Dr. Rice accepted this tremendous missionary challenge and opportunity, and gave the signal to go ahead.

† † †

People, I am sure, often wondered why we pushed so hard to get out gospel literature. Other publishers advertised their literature usually to make a profit; the Sword of the Lord Foundation was a nonprofit enterprise. And even if there were any profit—and believe me when I say there was never any—none of it could go to the editor, his family or the Sword Board of Directors, for the articles of incorporation forbade it.

Why, then, did we press so hard to get out literature? For the same reason a preacher preaches; for the same reason a church advertises its services; for the same reason an evangelistic campaign gives out handbills, tacks up signs, puts ads in the paper or has house-to-house visitation. WE WERE GETTING OUT THE GOSPEL!

And how we thank God for so many thousands saved through this literature and thousands of lives changed.

We knew that God would do through these messages in print the same kind of thing He does through the preaching in the pulpits. In fact, we could reach countless thousands with the Gospel through printed literature that could not be reached through the public platform or even through the radio, as much as we were for churches and the radio ministry.

† † †

"Today noon, after lunch," Dr. Rice wrote, "I spent nearly an hour helping Mrs. Rice make tomato sauce. We have canned many, many quarts of homegrown tomatoes, made tomato preserves, and now we have made tomato sauce with tomatoes, red sweet peppers, onions and seasoned with vinegar, cloves, garlic, cinnamon and celery seed.

"There is a certain enjoyment of having food we make ourselves, vegetables grown in our own garden. It was an excuse to work with Mrs. Rice a little and use my hands while my mind rested."

In their seventies, Dr. and Mrs. Rice were still riding Mac and Lady Grace regularly and enjoying it immensely.

† † †

Now Dr. Rice became "famous" for his "green tomato pie"! Yes, you read it right. Read what the man said:

> We had so many tomatoes on our little farm that before the frost came, we pulled the green ones. Mrs. Rice made some delicious piccalilli or relish. Since the green tomatoes were a little tart, I wondered if they wouldn't make a good pie!
>
> So, with raisins, sugar, margarine and a little thickening, I made a green tomato pie. Mrs. Rice made the crust. She liked the taste so well, she insisted I make some for a meeting of her Garden Club. They liked it. Then she wanted me to make some green tomato pies for the children who had come for Christmas. So this morning we took some of the green tomatoes she had canned and made four big pies for lunch today.
>
> The grandchildren all clapped at Pawpaw's pie. It tasted much like gooseberry pie; but since it was talked up so much, the children thought it was better!

1967 The late Bob Hughes, missionary in the Philippine Islands, Cebu City, wrote of many souls saved and told of a great need for 10,000 *"What Must I Do to Be Saved?"* booklets for prayerful distribution in the Islands. "In the city of Cebu we have 125,000 college students whom we must reach with the Gospel. They will be our leaders here in the Islands soon. If we could only provide them with your booklet explaining the plan of salvation to them!"

Then he asked for twenty-five of each issue of THE SWORD: "They will read them with real interest." Twenty-five SWORDs for 125,000 students!

Of course the booklets and the copies of THE SWORD were sent.

Such requests came all the time. Such requests were never refused.

Already we had sent tens of thousands of dollars to print gospel literature in over thirty-five countries and languages; over $50,000 to one nation—Japan. Dr. Rice said: "We believe money invested in our Free Literature Fund or in our Ministers and Missionaries Subscription Gift Fund or in the Voice of Revival radio broadcast on some sixty-three stations, will do as much for God as in any missionary work where it could be placed."

And the results over the years proved him right.

In giving a later report (than that given in 1965) of *"What Must I Do to Be Saved?"* as printed in millions of copies in Japan, Dr. Rice quoted Missionary Fred Jarvis: "We heard from over 2,800 people who claimed to trust Christ through the first half million copies; we heard from over 5,000 who claimed to trust Christ through the last million copies."

Dr. Jarvis speculated that thousands more had claimed Christ through the other millions of copies in Japan which the Sword sent money for, but they did not have a follow-up report on those since many other missionaries were involved.

† † †

This year seemed blessed of God in that many were saved on the Sword

Tour to Bible Lands. In Athens one member won a man at the hotel's information desk. Dr. Rice won three brothers and two of their employees at a gift shop in downtown Jerusalem. Two of the five came out that night to the First Baptist Church in Jerusalem, where Dr. Rice was speaking, to claim the Lord publicly. (On several tours after this, we found the men still rejoicing in the Lord and always greeted us so kindly.) At the First Baptist Church service, two more young men very eagerly accepted Christ after hearing the message.

Two more members won two more to the Lord. Then Mrs. Rice won the sister of the men at the gift shop.

Oh, they seemed eager to hear the Gospel in Jerusalem! And they were easy to win!

Over the years some wrote asking, *"Why do you go to the Holy Land?"* To make himself clear, Dr. Rice wrote this article for THE SWORD OF THE LORD answering why:

> Paul was a traveling preacher. He had been mobbed and insulted; and the more good he did, the worse the people treated him. But he went right on.
>
> Now he is going to Jerusalem, but he says, *"After that I must also see Rome"* (Acts 19:21).
>
> Why did he want to visit this great city? To preach, of course. But I think there were other reasons.
>
> A man of Paul's intelligence must have had fifty other reasons for wanting to see it. Perhaps the Colosseum was being erected and he wanted to see this giant structure paved with marble, this exhibition hall for gladiators who fought animals and each other. And no doubt Paul wanted to see the Roman Forum, across the street from where he went to his death. And perhaps he (as we) wanted to say that he had walked on the Appian Way. He wanted to see the architecture of that City on Seven Hills, known the world over.
>
> If everybody in the world could be gathered together and it were put to them which two cities they would wish most to see, no doubt the majority would vote *Jerusalem,* then *Rome.* Perhaps that's the way our friend Paul felt.
>
> Why do Christians from America want to see the holy places? Why do Christians spend money visiting Bible lands?
>
> The truth is, not many spend very much money to visit Bible lands. A few devoted ones may spend $1200 to see where Jesus lived and learn firsthand about Jerusalem, Jericho, the Jordan

River, Galilee, Jacob's Well, Mars' Hill at Athens where Paul preached, see where he was imprisoned in Rome, etc.

Good Christians go to the Bible lands for the same reason others take vacations, for the same reason others go to school, for the same reason others buy cars, for the same reason others buy expensive homes, boats, etc.

One will always find somebody who can find fault with any- and everything.

"We must also see Rome"—and Jerusalem and Bethlehem and Nazareth, the places where our Lord lived and died. And we think the Lord is pleased that we pilgrims journey back to see the land of His birth.

Of course we want to preach the Gospel to them at Rome also, to them in the other cities we visit. And, praise the Lord, we have seen hundreds saved on these tours.

(Incidentally, Miss Viola and I always got free tickets from the airlines for taking a group.)

† † †

Missionary Dr. M. H. Paulson had been in the states and was on his way back to Beirut, Lebanon. He had had thousands of the booklet, *"What Must I Do to Be Saved?"* printed in the Arabic language and distributed. As a result, many reported they had been saved.

In 1966 Dr. Rice, while on tour, preached in Beirut at the First Bible Baptist Church and in a fine high school where about sixty people claimed Christ as Saviour.

Becoming so burdened after visiting Arab lands, Dr. Rice took the responsibility of sending $250.00 a month to the Mideast Baptist Missions in Beirut. They had over 10,000 Moslem Arabs on their rolls taking correspondence courses. This work was started by a devout Lebanese businessman. Rev. Victor Sadaka, pastor of First Bible Baptist Church in Beirut, was actively involved, and regularly sent Dr. Rice a report.

† † †

When someone asked Dr. Rice, in the way of arguing, "Why was tobacco put on earth?" could you have given a better answer than this?

Possibly to kill bugs with. It is used in insecticides. But because something is put on earth is no reason to suppose God wants people to eat it.

Why are there so many rocks? Are people bound to eat them?

Why is locoweed put on earth? Are people supposed to chew that
or smoke it? Why nightshade and other poisonous plants?

There is some use for everything on earth; but it doesn't mean
God intended us to use it in the wrong manner and to use it
hurtfully.

† † †

At our annual Sword Board meeting in March, held at First Baptist
Church, Hammond, Dr. Bill Rice was elected as co-editor of THE
SWORD OF THE LORD.

Mrs. John Rice, elated, said:

> My heart is bursting with joy and pride. Bill is my friend, my
> brother, my son.
>
> He was several years in our home as "our boy" after the death
> of his own parents.
>
> The first time I saw him, he was at church, a little lad sitting
> on the lap of his big brother, John R., my sweetheart.
>
> At our wedding he became my little brother, and in youth, as
> in maturity, he was always exciting to be around.
>
> Things moved where Bill Rice moved. Horses, donkeys, cows
> and dogs were ever present. However, he never seemed to enjoy
> our milk goat, Olga, though for a time it was his job to care for
> and milk her. I admit that was not a glamorous job. Olga was
> Joanna's "formula" since our doctor had prescribed goat's milk
> for the baby, and there was no goat dairy in the city of Dallas.
>
> Welcome, Dr. Bill! You are our "fair-haired boy," and we are
> proud that you have been named co-editor. As Dr. Linton, our
> beloved and fun-loving Scot friend, used to say of his contribu-
> tions, "It will be a shot in the ar-r-r-m" for THE SWORD OF THE
> LORD.
>
> Watch things move now!

Dr. Bill was my friend. When he occupied the editor's chair, it became
him ever so well. Dr. Bill was a graduate of Moody Bible Institute, was
on their staff of evangelists for some years. He was a genuine Bible
scholar.

† † †

Dr. Jack Hyles, vice-president of Sword of the Lord Foundation and
Sword Conference director, estimated that in a year's time, over 10,000
preachers attended these Sword of the Lord Conferences on Revival and

Soul Winning all over America. Of course that included some repeats.

On every hand word kept coming where the number of converts in a year doubled or more, because a Spirit-filled pastor made a new start or got a new vision or adopted new methods or set a goal and put soul winning first as a result of these conferences.

† † †

This was the Sword's thirty-third year in business for the Lord. During those thirty-three years, over 13,000 letters had come from those who had claimed to take Christ as Saviour, either from sermons printed in THE SWORD or from literature circulated by means of the Sword of the Lord.

This did not include tens of thousands of others who claimed to take Christ in foreign countries through Sword literature; these wrote to groups of cooperating missionaries who got out the literature; and it is besides tens of thousands of others who, we believe, trusted Christ and claimed Him then in their churches and in revival campaigns but did not write us directly. (We find such people everywhere we go.)

In these thirty-three years, mass evangelism had come back. Where there were no large interdenominational citywide campaigns in America in 1934 when THE SWORD OF THE LORD began, now citywide campaigns were in favor; a good number of evangelists were spending their time in citywide campaigns. And this result was brought about very largely through God's using THE SWORD OF THE LORD, with the help of some others.

THE SWORD OF THE LORD had been the principal Christian defender of evangelism and the principal promoter of evangelists and, many believe, the largest single factor in bringing back mass evangelism in America.

What about the thousands of preachers who got sermon outlines, illustrations and help on vital themes from THE SWORD?

What about something like 150 evangelists who were inspired to go into the work through THE SWORD and the Sword Conferences and the Sword literature and, in many cases, were announced and introduced in THE SWORD?

And what about the thousands of revival campaigns reported in THE SWORD?

And what about the thousands of young men encouraged to go into the ministry through the inspiration and teaching in THE SWORD,

Sword literature, Sword Conferences and literature which THE SWORD promoted?

What about the defense of the Faith, the publishing of sermons and Bible teaching on the great doctrines of the faith, written by the greatest preachers and teachers now living and of the past generation?

These had been thirty-three blessed years. To Christ be all the glory!

There is no way of even estimating the number of people (surely in the millions) to whom THE SWORD had been a guidebook of Bible teaching and living.

Two beautiful verses in Psalms speak of the stars, but they always reminded me of Dr. John R. Rice and THE SWORD OF THE LORD:

"There is no speech nor language, where their voice is not heard. Their line is gone out through all the earth, and their words to the end of the world."—Ps. 19:3,4.

† † †

In the September 22, 1967 issue of THE SWORD, we began what proved to be a very popular column—"Dr. Bill Says." Dr. Bill's writing had a color and charm unmatched, as far as we know, among Christian journalists.

For years he answered questions about the Bible, the Christian life, duty and service. He didn't just skim over with a brief answer; he did a "bang-up" job. If one day we could put those questions and answers in a book, I predict it would be mighty popular and a best-seller.

† † †

In the September anniversary issue, in his article, "Let's Get Acquainted," Mr. Alvin Byers gave some things to think about:

> The first issue of THE SWORD was printed September 28, 1934. In the past thirty-three years, we have printed a total number of 89,927,509 (through September 1, 1967 issue) copies of THE SWORD OF THE LORD. Friends, that is almost one copy of the paper for every two people in the U.S.A.
>
> In 1966 SWORD readers gave $18,973.98 to our Free Literature Fund. This paid for printing Dr. Rice's tract, *"What Must I Do to Be Saved?"* in Korean (300,000 copies) and in Japanese (1 million copies) as well as other projects.
>
> Sword people gave last year $36,662.86 to our Subscription Gift Fund for Christian workers. This paid for more than 18,000 one-

year subscriptions to THE SWORD for missionaries, for foreign preachers and other Christian workers.

Last year you gave $18,158.21 to our Investment Evangelism Fund which is used to retire long-term notes and for operating capital.

Last year 387 people wrote to tell about getting saved as a result of reading Sword literature. This is more than one a day who wrote; there surely were others who did not write.

If you sent a gift or prayed for this ministry, then you had a share in this.

† † †

OUR ADVERTISERS. One of the blessed ministries of the paper is the service it renders in bringing together readers and advertisers who "need" each other.

Theoretically speaking, the income from advertising should pay for the printing and mailing cost of getting out a magazine, and the subscription price should pay for the labor involved in typing manuscripts, enrolling subscriptions, changing addresses, answering correspondence, etc.

Our advertisers are carefully screened. We turn down thousands of dollars' worth of advertising each year that we do not think is beneficial to Christians. So SWORD advertising income pays for only about half the cost of printing and mailing the paper. Yet if it were not for the advertising we carry, the subscription price (52 issues a year then) would have to be priced too high for most people.

† † †

In September Dr. Rice closed a contract for services each Sunday morning at 8:30 on the 50,000-watt radio station WGTO at Cypress Gardens, Florida, just before DeHaan's Bible Class. This made sixty stations from which the Voice of Revival was being heard each week.

† † †

Dr. Rice made this bold—but true—statement in October:

> We honestly do not believe there is another Christian enterprise in America which is run more sacrificially, more unselfishly, without any thought of personal gain, than Sword of the Lord Foundation. The most careful investigation is invited. We doubt if any Christian work is as fruitful for money given.

† † †

Dr. Jack Hyles, in introducing Dr. John R. Rice at the dedication of the magnificent new Sunday school building at First Baptist Church, Hammond, June 18, 1967, said:

> There are a few things I had rather do than preach the dedication message for the building. One is to have my friend John Rice preach it.
>
> Dr. John Rice means a lot to me. He is a pastor to me. He is, in many ways, a father. It has always been significant to me that I get to spend a portion of Father's Day with Dr. Rice, since we are usually together in conferences somewhere. Though I was saved and called to preach before I met him, he has been to me a counselor, a guide, a helper, a friend, a pastor, a father.
>
> He is a great friend of our church and of all God's people everywhere who believe and love the Bible.
>
> As one fellow said to me the other day when Dr. Rice was preaching, *"I guess that must be one of the sweetest men I ever met."*
>
> And I like what Dr. J. Frank Norris said about him: *"John Rice is the finest, sweetest, gentlest man that ever slit a throat or scuttled a ship!"* And that is what he is.
>
> Dr. Rice, we are honored you could be our guest and speaker for the evening.

† † †

WILLS: When asked about making a Will, Dr. Rice gave this advice:

> While there is no specific law on our statute books compelling any individual to make a Will, there are laws that are immediately in force when one dies without leaving a valid Will. These laws, while just and equitable in their stipulations as to the distribution of the average estate, are very rigid and circumscribed.
>
> Inasmuch as a Christian is a steward, accountable to the Lord for his time, testimony and money, it behooves every child of God to so arrange his affairs that what has been accumulated during the lifetime will be used for God's glory.
>
> When the final summons comes, it is too late to make a Will or to change one. Therefore, it is never too early to make a Will, which legally and legitimately sets forth the individual's wishes and desires relative to the distribution of accumulated assets.

He further added:

Have you made your Will? In view of the uncertainty of life, don't put it off. Do it now. And when you do, perhaps you will want to remember to include in your Will the ministry of Sword of the Lord Foundation.

† † †

At year's end, we were asking SWORD readers to join "THOUSAND-A-YEAR CLUB" for 1968, and hoping for a thousand members.

The purpose? A mass distribution of Dr. Rice's famous 24-page booklet, *"What Must I Do to Be Saved?"* which had brought in more than 9,000 conversions from the English language edition, plus uncounted thousands in the more than thirty-five foreign translations. We were hoping for 1,000 conversions in 1968 through the combined efforts of the Sword and the readers.

By signing up as a member of "THOUSAND-A-YEAR CLUB," one was entitled to purchase that booklet at half price. Becoming a member also meant agreeing to distribute 1,000 of them during 1968 to any unsaved person who would promise to read it through, and that the reader would earnestly try to get that person saved and sign the decision form on page 24.

1968 At 7:00 a.m. each weekday the Sword staff gather in the auditorium for devotions and prayer. Then each goes to his particular task. The press starts humming. Others are at the cutting and folding machines and in the photo darkroom. There are computers and IBM typewriters at work. There are supplies to be purchased, ledgers to be kept, packages to be mailed, sermons to be typed, dictation to be transcribed.

It is good to work beside Christians. Blame is taken rather than passed on; patience is long lasting; and there are smiles instead of frowns. Prayers are sent Heavenward during the day to the One who can solve every problem. You hear hymns being hummed instead of dirty jokes being told—as you pass through the various departments.

Finally, at the end of the day, the presses, the stitcher, the folder, the IBM computer stop one by one. Typewriters are covered, desks are cleared for those who will enter shortly to clean. All the work is laid aside for the night. It is evening now—time for our meal, time for a little sleep, time to say, "Thank You, Father, for letting me serve You another day."

Yes, we are proud to be working for the Lord at the Sword of the Lord.

I would not trade these years in the Lord's service for any other job in the world.

There is a story of a missionary in China who was more familiar with things Chinese than any other man at that time. Because of this, an oil company sought his services. He was offered a salary of $10,000 a year. When he refused, the offer went up to $20,000, and then to $25,000; then the missionary was told to set his own salary. In reply he said, "The salary you first offered was large enough. It is not your salary that is too small; it is your job. I have a bigger job than the world can ever offer."

So did I.

As I look back over my years, I cannot doubt God's guidance. There have been weary marches by day, but the pillar of cloud has gone before us. There have been nights of discouragements, but the pillar of fire has shown in the skies above. The work has grown sweeter with every passing day.

But I am forever reminded of how soon the day's end is reached, when not half the day's work is done; that night comes "when no man can work."

† † †

Dr. Rice answered some funny questions, but this one about topped them all: *"Where will the clothes come from for all the people raised from the dead at the rapture?"*

† † †

In February of 1968 the total printing in English of Dr. Rice's *"What Must I Do to Be Saved?"* had reached 15,496,295.

† † †

Just a few of our titles got renamed:

Dr. Rice Has the Answer;
Rebellious Wives and Sluggish Husbands;
Divorce the Week of Marriage;
Out My Kitchen Window;
Closet Skeletons;
Backsliter;
Railed by a Mildbeast.

† † †

February 20, 21, 22, Dr. Jack Hyles and Dr. John R. Rice were in a Sword of the Lord Conference in Tokyo, Japan, sponsored by missionaries and pastors.

About the conference, Dr. Rice reported, "Over 1,000 signed the guest book, including hundreds of missionaries and pastors, during the three days." Then he added, "And people were telling us that 'it works in Japan just as in other countries.' "

He tells about one man coming to him while in Tokyo to show him a worn copy of *"What Must I Do to Be Saved?"* in the Japanese language, saying, *"Eighteen years ago when I was in prison, somebody threw this over the bars into the prison. I read it and was wonderfully converted."*

There is no way in the world to tell how many thousands in countries all over the world have been saved after reading the plan of salvation as given in that little booklet.

Dr. Hyles added this about the Tokyo conference:

> It wasn't easy teaching my soul-winning course through an interpreter. I would make a statement and my Japanese interpreter would make the same statement in Japanese; then the person I was winning in the soul-winning skit would answer, and his interpreter would tell the Japanese people what he had said. Four of us were talking nearly at one time! (I felt like the deacon chairman who said to the board, "We need to stand shoulder to shoulder, back to back, look each other square in the eye and go forward!")

Dr. Hyles did get through the soul-winning course to the 400 who were in attendance. His *Let's Go Soul Winning* book had been translated into the Japanese language, and several hundred bought it for future reference.

At the conclusion of the lecture, some Japanese decided on their own to go soul winning in downtown Tokyo. "It was a thrill to realize that the Gospel was being preached from person to person throughout the city," commented Dr. Hyles.

After visiting all afternoon, the report brought back for the evening service was that forty-five people had been won to Christ on the main streets of Tokyo that afternoon.

At the conclusion of the last service of the Sword Conference, approximately fifty others responded to the invitation to receive Christ.

They say it can't be done, but this proves it can be done—even in Tokyo. People everywhere are lost. Hearts everywhere are hungry. So we need to go soul winning everywhere, don't we?

† † †

Fundamental Christianity lost one of its most militant leaders, Dr. Bob Jones, Sr., on January 16, after several years of declining health. The 84-year-old warrior was one of the last of the "old-time" evangelists. Dr. Rice said, "Dr. Jones was one of the best friends I ever had, and I feel a very deep loss at his going. We were of one mind on evangelism; and what a tremendous help he was in the great Sword Conferences...."

Of course Dr. Rice attended the memorial service at Bob Jones University.

On the tombstone of Dr. Jones' grave, which is located in the center of the campus near the Bridge of Nations, are inscribed the words that belong not only to him but also to the other great men of God of a marvelous bygone era:

A FIGHT WELL FOUGHT,
A COURSE WELL RUN;
A FAITH WELL KEPT,
A CROWN WELL WON.

† † †

SITTING ON A ROCK, WITH HANDS IN AIR: HELP! In Exodus 17 chosen men were selected to fight against Amalek, with Joshua leading. Moses had been entrusted with the rod of God, symbolizing that God's power was with him. He was to go up on a hill and hold up that rod as a sign that they claimed God's power and blessing; then God would give the victory.

But when Moses' arms grew weary, the rod of God faltered in his hands, and the battle went against the children of Israel.

Then Aaron and Hur, there by his side, got a stone, seated Moses on it, and as Aaron stood on one side holding up one arm and Hur on the other holding the other arm, Moses was able to hold up the rod of God; then victory came to the Israelite soldiers under Joshua.

The important thing about a battle is usually, "Who won?" In this case we might have a variety of answers.

One would say, "God won," and that would be true because He actively helped Israel supernaturally to prevail over Amalek. But it is equally true to say that Israel won or that Moses was responsible for the defeated enemy.

But the two that stand out as being responsible in a large measure for Israel's victory over Amalek in Rephidim that day were Aaron and Hur. These two faithful helpers chose the seemingly insignificant chore of holding Moses' hands up over his head. They wielded no sword that day and had no tales of valor on the battlefield to relate that night when weary men gathered about campfires. But their part was absolutely essential, for when Moses' hands were not held high, Amalek prevailed. Without their part, Israel would have fallen victim to the plundering hordes of the Amalekites.

Dr. Rice, in commenting on that story, said:

In some sense I am here holding up the rod God has put in my hands as editor of THE SWORD OF THE LORD. In some sense God wants THE SWORD to be like a lighthouse on the stormy coast to save the ships, like an officer leading others in battle. But more: it seems as if God wants us to be like a prophet on the hill, holding up the rod of God that all His people may have courage to carry on the fight and know God is with them.

My arms grow weary. No one man can make THE SWORD what it ought to be without a staff, editorial counsel, encouragement and the backing and prayers of a multitude of you good Christians.

I believe that God has so arranged that, if THE SWORD were to stop publication or if we should dip our banner in compromise, untold harm would come to the cause of Christ. Many thousands, who are encouraged to be faithful, be against sin and say so, press for soul winning, oppose modernism, would grow faint of heart; and they would grow quiet if we grew quiet, quit if we should quit.

So here I am on the hill of God trying to hold up the rod of God's blessing, trying to inspire people to trust and do right, to win souls, to press the fight against evil, unbelief and infidelity. But my arms grow weary. Human wisdom fails. Human strength gives way. Human resolution and courage may sometimes ebb unless it be encouraged.

Help me, I beg you! Be like Aaron and Hur—holding up the hands of Moses!

† † †

WISE ARE THESE WORDS FROM DR. BILL RICE:

I was preaching in a large Sunday afternoon rally during a Sword Conference. I suppose fifty preachers were lined up behind me on the platform.

At the end of the meeting, as I stepped down from the platform, I was stopped by a middle-aged preacher.

"Dr. Bill," said he, "when you see Dr. John, be sure to tell him how much he has meant to me. It was through his ministry that I surrendered to preach, and I can never thank God enough for him. So be sure and tell him for me."

I turned around and shocked the living daylights out of him by replying, "I won't do anything of the kind—tell him yourself!"

It almost embarrassed him to death. He looked around, and it had obviously shocked all the other preachers who were listening in, too. So I continued: "John Rice works his head off. He prays and he preaches. He writes and he weeps. He spends long hours and carries heavier loads than most of us dream. You say that it was through his influence (reading THE SWORD) that you were called to preach, and you will always thank God for him. Yet you are too lazy to write a letter or too stingy to buy a stamp! Man— you are too sorry to shoot!"

[If you knew Dr. Bill, that was exactly what he said and how he felt!]

I wasn't mad and I said it with a grin, but I wasn't exactly joking, either. As we stood there looking at one another, the man thoughtfully said with an embarrassed grin, "Dr. Bill, you are right. I should have written Dr. John and told him what he meant to me long ago. I am going to write him a letter today."

Need more be said?

† † †

I must have eaten thousands of meals with Dr. and Mrs. Rice. And never once can I recall Dr. Rice's getting up from the table without thanking Mrs. Rice for the good food she had prepared for us. That was true of whatever anyone did for him. He was indeed a gentleman in every sense of the word.

When he got back to the office from a meeting, he was quick to write the pastor a "Bread-and-Butter Letter," thanking him for any courtesy he might have extended during Dr. Rice's stay there.

That was also true of Dr. Bill, who was one of the friendliest people in the whole world.

Let us take note of this and be sure to thank those who do things to lighten our load.

† † †

Dr. Rice called the 5th Sword Convention and Pastors' School at Hammond in March "tremendous, superlative, unique."

The opening crowd in the Civic Center or Colosseum in Hammond was estimated at 6,000.

Then on Tuesday night in the annual Sword of the Lord Pastors' School Banquet in the Sherman House in downtown Chicago, 1,400 enjoyed the $6.00 dinner. Dr. Hyles limited those of his own church, saying, "500 more tickets could have been sold had there been room."

Dr. William Culbertson, president of Moody Bible Institute, was the featured speaker.

Dr. Hyles' effort in always building up and promoting the Sword of the Lord and the staff was wonderfully gracious. He and the church had sent a Greyhound bus to Murfreesboro for all Sword workers. We shut up offices, and some twenty-five went. Rooms and meals were provided at Holiday Inn, orchids were sent to each lady, a basket of fruit to each couple, and tickets were provided for the banquet.

Mrs. Rice was inveigled into presenting an award supposedly won in a contest to a lovely woman present but whose name was a secret. She read the account of the award, then opened the sealed envelope, to find she herself was being presented with a lovely mink stole!

A fourteen-foot-high picture of Dr. and Mrs. Rice stood on the balcony at Sherman House greeting the crowd as they came in. Then the place cards were four-inch-high copies of the same photograph.

The hostesses from First Baptist Church were beautifully dressed. The presiding by Dr. Hyles was masterful. The address by Dr. Culbertson was warm and helpful. And the Sword staff was delighted and grateful for all that was done to make their stay a delightful one.

Some 335 of those pastors signed up at Pastors' school to have a SWORD Sunday on April 21. Our office sent out 30,000 requested samples of THE SWORD with envelopes.

† † †

We could finance THE SWORD if we had a nickel for every Bible Dr. Rice signed for all you good people!

† † †

OPERATION MURFREESBORO. A volunteer project among Sword workers in June was underway. It consisted of reaching every one of the 10,000 or more homes in Murfreesboro with free sample items of Sword literature: one copy of THE SWORD OF THE LORD; pamphlets, *God's Authority in the Home, Government and the Bible;* and *"What Must I Do to Be Saved?"*

The Free Literature Fund bore the expense. Sword workers met at the Sword building on Saturday, collected the material, streets were designated. Usually we worked in teams of two, going forth to "sow the seed."

† † †

Mr. Elmer Klassen from Frankfurt, Germany, had translated Dr. Rice's *Prayer—Asking and Receiving,* the tract, *"What Must I Do to Be Saved?"* and other pamphlets and articles into the German language. The pamphlet on the text, "Be sure your sin will find you out!" (*Trailed by a Wild Beast*) was condensed, then translated, then published twice in the form of a full-page ad in a leading German newspaper, costing $10,000 each time. Much good resulted.

Mr. Klassen and two co-workers visited the Sword in August. A special devotional time was called so Sword workers could meet the party and hear of the good work going on in Germany by way of the printed page.

† † †

We get some real chuckles out of some mail coming to the Sword. For instance: *"You used a Roosevelt stamp to mail your letter to me. Why? Why honor the President who introduced socialism into our government. . .?"*

Blamed "if we do" and blamed "if we don't" by some. As if we could control what kind of stamp the post office issued!

If a fellow didn't have a sense of humor, dealing with the public would have him in a straight jacket pretty quick. People are just plain unreasonable at times.

Yes, we got some real chuckles out of some mail delivered to our address!

† † †

A printing of *"What Must I Do to Be Saved?"* and *Religious But Lost* in Italian was made possible by our Free Literature Fund. Missionary Arthur J. Wiens reported: "For some time now we have been studying the possibility of sending these two tracts to all the priests in Italy . . . probably 60,000. Join us in prayer that we will be able to do that."

† † †

WHAT WAS DR. RICE'S HOBBY?

He was very much interested in only one horse—MacArthur, who took him for jaunts over his 44-acre farm as often as he had time to ride. He enjoyed having Mrs. Rice along on her gaited mare, Lady, who shared barn and board with Mac.

Horseback riding is a most rejuvenating exercise for one who is constantly meeting deadlines. A man can pray as well riding as anywhere—better, maybe, for the open fields and the vaulted sky are an automatic airlift Heavenward. Riding a fine horse over lush green pastureland or through the dry grass or slush and snow of winter is invigorating as well as restful—literally a change of pace, and one much needed by him whose work was indoors at all times. Besides, Dr. Rice had been interested in horses since he was a "very little fellow" and lived on his father's ranch in Texas, where they raised horses, fine horses, for sale.

But that was not *the* hobby.

Nor was it bowling, though he liked to bowl; nor golfing nine holes, though he enjoyed that. And it wasn't cooking; Mrs. Rice was the cook of the family, but she was especially proud of the recipe for ripe tomato ketchup invented by Dr. Rice himself, and of his special kind of pie (something like mincemeat) which he made of green tomatoes, raisins, etc. (already mentioned). Delicious! Dr. Rice helped his wife can if he had any time at home during the canning season. And he made good chili, as many a one who has eaten it could tell—and his pizzas were "out of this world!"

Poetry and song writing went on along with other activities. Often in the Sword office we could hear Dr. Rice trying out the tune of a new song he had written, singing it at his desk or picking out the melody on the piano in his office, given to him by his staff. He would sing it for us in the chapel, polish it and work on it more, send it off to one of his daughters who wrote the harmony, get it back, then publish it.

But none of these was the hobby Dr. Rice claimed as his special interest.

Then what was it? It was woodworking. Pitiful the longing in his voice when he spoke of the need for a place where he could get away for an hour or so to work on things he planned to make! To prove his interest he named the tools and some equipment he had with which to pursue his hobby: a table saw, a sabre saw, an electric sander, an anvil, a power drill and other things. But they lay forever in the boxes they came in—some in the carport at his home and some in the closet in his office.

The dream for a place to work was not a new one. When he and Mrs. Rice were young, they had little money to buy even necessary furniture, so he made high chairs and a hobby horse for his children and a library table, bookcases, chairs and other furniture for the home.

While in Dallas, he constructed his own church building; that is, he made window frames and did any necessary woodwork as well. Now, he thought, if he had a separate shop where he could work alone, he would make chairs for indoor and outdoor use, make cabinets and shelves which were needed. He could enjoy it for the recreation it provided as well as having the satisfaction of making something he needed for an aid to writing a book, such as a revolving bookcase, a kind of Lazy Susan for books. When a reference book is chosen for study in connection with the project, it could be placed in the shelves of the Lazy Susan, for which he had drawn the plans and needed only the time, place and materials to make it.

Dr. Rice never got around to making that Lazy Susan, or anything else. There was always some project ahead of it, some book to write, some meeting to go to, some letters to answer, some research to be done.

But woodworking was his hobby—in his mind at least, if not in the project itself.

In fact, there is a little brick room built behind his house just for that project. But it eventually was used for storage.

† † †

IT WASN'T AN EASY ROAD! Dr. Rice recalled under what conditions his chapters in his large book, *Home: Courtship, Marriage and Children*, were written:

> One full chapter was dictated on a train to a dictating machine hooked up in the Pullman car en route between Chicago and Albany, New York.
>
> Most of one chapter was written by hand until 1:30 a.m. in LaGuardia Airport in New York, as I waited for a plane.
>
> In the airport at Oklahoma City while I waited for a plane, much of a chapter was written on my knee, in longhand.
>
> Then I asked my daughter Elizabeth (now Mrs. Walt Handford) to take a semester out of college to travel with me in big revivals in Chickasha, Oklahoma and Seattle, Washington. She played the piano for the meetings and typed on the manuscript between services. And between speaking about three times a day, I dictated to her the final chapters of the book.
>
> When Libby typed the last chapter, I gave her an orchid, the first she had ever had.

† † †

After introducing Dr. Rice to his members at Tabernacle Baptist Church, Greenville, South Carolina, Dr. Harold Sightler added: "It was one of the great privileges of my life to go with Dr. Rice on a Sword Tour of Bible Lands. I urge you to go if possible. I believe it will do more good than two years in Bible college or seminary."

The hundreds who went with him over the years can attest to the fact that no tour was like a Sword Tour because no other tour had a John R. Rice as its director.

† † †

THIRTY-FOUR YEARS OLD AND GROWING! Did you ever start a publication? And without any money? Probably not; few people are so "teched in the head"!

Thirty-four years ago Dr. Rice was so afflicted. He had a vision of great revivals returning to America. That vision began in 1934 with the birth of THE SWORD OF THE LORD. As a preacher, Dr. Rice foresaw into the next generation the need of old-time preaching, so he decided to do something about it. The Lord encouraged him in this project by supplying day by day the finances to keep going.

Though it had been hard sledding—and you do not know how hard—Dr. Rice kept on seeing visions and dreaming dreams. The need was there.

No other weekly paper was doing what THE SWORD OF THE LORD was doing.

And if you can believe anything I say, then believe this: I honestly do not know any man who was so generous, who worked so hard and devotedly and asked for so little for himself.

Many a time Dr. and Mrs. Rice poured their last penny into this paper. You wouldn't believe what they gave some years to the Lord's work. When income tax men went over his books, they couldn't believe it, either, but the facts were before them. Why would a successful editor not take a cent of pay from the Foundation?

And even more astounding was the fact that he gave back to this work—and other works—twenty, thirty or forty percent of his income from revivals—many times, more.

He was a generous man when it came to the Lord's work, but very frugal when it came to himself. Most of the time in restaurants he would never order a steak; he would not charge to his expense account an expensive meal.

Thinking about it, I don't recall ever seeing him buy himself a thing. I doubt if he owned two suits of clothes he bought for himself. I doubt if he possessed two pairs of shoes he bought for himself.

He would save a string from a box, tear a piece of tissue in two pieces and, in many other ways, save the Lord's money.

And this generosity and saving made it so the Lord kept His promises and blessed this man and the work he did.

Forgive me: I usually did not tell too much about Dr. Rice, but sometimes I yearn for others to know some things I knew about him.

Not only was he unselfish with his money, but he was generous to others in other ways.

Dr. Rice gave himself to standing beside God's men when they were in trouble. Ask Dr. Lee Roberson when the Southern Baptist battle came, who stood beside him. Ask Dr. Roberson when his voice was gone and it looked like he couldn't preach again, who stood beside him and earnestly prayed for and urged SWORD readers to pray for his healing.

Ask Dr. Jack Hyles who wrote him, when the Southern Baptists decided they would rather go along without him than with him, to say, *"Dr.
Hyles, THE SWORD is yours. Use it as you will."*

**"ARE THEY FEEDING YOU WELL?" "WOULD YOU LIKE ANOTHER
GLASS OF TEA?"** He was always solicitous of the other fellow!

I could never measure the things Dr. Rice taught me—like little
courtesies here and there. In a restaurant—"You're a pretty good cook,"
or, driving up to a service station and saying to the attendant, "Do you
know where I could buy some gasoline?" His friendliness always showed,
and it was catching!

I have seen his kindness to bellboys, hotel maids, cab drivers, custo-
dians, little children and common folks. On tours or at banquets, while
others ate, he would get up to see if they needed coffee or water, or he
would lean over and chat with this one or that one who seemed alone
or lonely. He wanted all to have a good time and no one to feel left out.

You know, it is so easy for us to become accustomed to greatness that
we really do not realize what greatness is.

If our Lord tarries, preachers will be building churches and winning
souls and seeking God's power a hundred years from now because John
Rice passed this way.

† † †

In poem form, Dr. Hyles tells us...

HOW TO MAKE ANOTHER JOHN R. RICE

"What will we do when he is gone?"
Why, we'll just make another one.
I think you'll find this will suffice
To make another John R. Rice.

From Paul take all the churches' care,
And stir with David Brainerd's prayer;
Put in some Billy Sunday fire,
With some Bob Gray intense desire.
Of Mueller's faith please add a part,
And Jeremiah's broken heart,
And Larkin minus all his charts.
Throw in a touch of Mark Twain's wit,
With John the Baptist's holy grit;
Add then an R. A. Torrey mind
With all the love that you can find,
Sam Jones' intense attack on sin,
Knute Rockne's strong desire to win;
Add quickly Spurgeon's mighty pen,
The strength of David's mighty men;
Then take Will Rogers' honest face,
And add some Falwell charm and grace;
Some Evel Knievel, but not much,
And Dennis the Menace, a little touch.

Then add Jack Dempsey's mighty arm
To some of Ronald Reagan's charm,
The eloquence of R. G. Lee,
Muhammad Ali's poetry,
Some of Drew Pearson's better side,
With faith from gentle Praying Hyde.
Then add a little Roloff zeal
To J. R. Faulkner's kind appeal,
And then so deftly, quietly blend
A Jonathan-type, a true-blue friend
Who stands beside you to the end.

Then place a large and generous part
Of Dr. Weigle's happy heart.

Add to Bill Harvey's winsome gift
A little of Jack Benny's thrift;
Some Winston Churchill leadership,
Don Meredith's light and folksy quip.

Equip him with Goliath's sword,
And turn him loose to preach the Word.
Then add Lee Roberson's kingly air,
His leadership and godly care;
Adventure from old Lewis and Clark,
The bravery of a Sgt. York.

And let him walk o'er fifty years
With men of passion, power and tears;
With Jones and Riley and Shuler too,
And Gipsy Smith, to name a few;
With Dr. Bob and Ironside,
And others long known far and wide.
Then let him travel all around
With just a pinch of Charlie Brown.

Then give him, to his strength renew
A wife as sweet as Joseph knew,
Who loves our hero through and through,
A brother like John Wesley had,
And don't forget to make him dad
Of six fine daughters all who've been
Long married to fine preacher men;
All six of them so well employ
The Spirit's fruit from Grace to Joy.

Then give him workers by his side
Who will be tested, true and tried;
A Walden, Shappard and a Byers,
As yielded as a pair of pliers.

Then add a touch of Eisenhower,
With Charles G. Finney's mighty power,
The wisdom of dear old Bob Jones,
The preaching of a Tom Malone.
Then add some Theodore Roosevelt,

The courage that MacArthur felt.

And while you make him don't destroy
That charming touch of little boy
That millions get to oft enjoy.

And when you've finished, then, of course,
Please put him on his favorite horse;
And let him give a tender tug
To his beloved General Doug.

Then we can look with high esteem,
For he's the captain of our team;
And we together will have shown
The greatest man we've ever known.

                                   —Written by Dr. Jack Hyles

That is what we will have to do to make another John R. Rice.

† † †

In June, 1968, Dr. Rice went to the Memphis Eye and Ear Hospital for an operation on his right ear.

For some years he had suffered some loss of hearing, and for some time had been wearing a hearing aid. And the famous Dr. John Shea had such a reputation for restoring hearing in some cases that Dr. Rice went to him for X-rays and hearing tests.

The doctor determined that Dr. Rice had better-than-usual hearing, but the channel of communication was nearly closed because the outer canals of his ear had been infected.

The operation included removing all the skin inside his right ear canal, drilling out and making the opening larger. Then he took a bit of skin from Dr. Rice's arm and grafted it into the ear as a lining.

After leaving the hospital on a Thursday, he flew to Fort Worth on the following Monday despite objection from nurses and doctor. Upon his return to Murfreesboro, he developed a severe bladder infection, which his doctor finally controlled with heavy medication.

He lamented: "Very few times in forty-six years of public ministry have I ever missed an engagement, but this week I must cancel out on the First Baptist Church of Hammond and the Sword of the Lord combined conference at Cedar Lake." Dr. Hyles had arranged for another speaker to take his place. The flying to Fort Worth perhaps had affected the ear, so he felt he had better stay on the ground until it had completely healed.

"When I couldn't go to sleep, my mind went over song after song," mused Dr. Rice. "Now I know the meaning of Job 35:10—'who giveth songs in the night.' Between office duties, I have tried to rest, though I am frank to confess it was hard work. I am not a good patient!"

† † †

In July Dr. Rice authorized a missionary committee in Japan to proceed with the publication of another million copies of his *"What Must I Do to Be Saved?"* "This time it was to be a more complete edition, carefully retranslated and with an additional introduction for Japan. It would include a postcard, to bring back a report from those who wanted to be saved or those who have been saved through the booklet and wanted to study Bible correspondence lessons," reported Dr. Rice.

The cost was about $10,000, which the Sword promised to send in three installments.

Missionary Russell Stellwagon said word was going out to 500 missionaries, so "all this edition will soon be gone."

Though this made approximately 6 million copies of this booklet published in Japan, there was still a great demand for it.

† † †

In August Dr. Rice entered Rutherford County Hospital for treatment for that stubborn infection mentioned earlier.

While there, he was rejoicing that he would be able to meet some preaching engagements that were coming up.

But as he thought, he wrote:

> How many, many blessings I would have missed if I never had trouble, sickness, disappointment. How many Scriptures I could not claim nor enjoy!"

Near the end of the long article he asks, "But what about the work that we miss and tasks that seem to go undone?" Then he answered himself:

> All are tempted to feel that we are very greatly needed in God's work. How good to learn that God can raise up any workers He wants to.

We would think that when Moses died, God was really in a tight, but He had Joshua.

God didn't tell a man to talk to Balaam; He had a donkey.

If there was no one else to encourage Gideon, God sent an angel.

It may well be that God is much more pleased with the heart devotion and love and trust that may result from a time of being laid aside, than He would be pleased with all the labor one would feign have accomplished for Him.

I have been thinking about Paul, confined two years in prison at Caesarea. Several times he got to witness to Festus and Agrippa, but we suppose he was not able to preach or win many.

In our human wisdom, we might estimate how much good Paul could have done preaching in those two years; but God knew something better.

And Paul had a great handicap, a thorn in the flesh, which greatly hindered him. We would think he could serve God much better with it removed; but God knew better.

We do not need strong preachers; we need a great God and little preachers, little servants, little men and women surrendered and loving and trusting.

If God allows me to be free this week to take up this work again, I shall thank Him extra for that. But He knows what is best. And I want to be content with whatever He lays on me.

Later: After nine days in the hospital, the stubborn infection was slowly being conquered, but he was still on antibiotics.

Even while in the hospital he called for a tape recorder and made two radio broadcasts, not to mention keeping his mail answered and the sermons selected for THE SWORD.

And the next thing we knew—he was on the road again!

Still later. In October he reported, "Now I am well. Hearing in my right ear has greatly improved, and I hear without a hearing aid."

† † †

A MODEL FAMILY. Rev. Charles Vradenburgh came to the Sword of the Lord in 1952, at Wheaton, Illinois. He proofread SWORD copy and books and did some ads for THE SWORD; was at one time co-editor of the LITTLE SWORD, the employees' paper with a circulation of ninety-two copies; prepared "With the Evangelists" column; and in earlier years, worked in the wholesale and retail sales departments.

In 1954 Miss Lola Munro was employed in the subcription department at the Sword of the Lord.

It came about that Charles and Lola were married (as has happened so often between Sword employees).

God gave them eight lovely children.

When Lola was in the hospital in 1968 with the last baby, the society editor of the Murfreesboro paper, the *Daily News Journal,* became acquainted with the children, who waited in the lobby while their father visited Mother in the maternity ward.

The children were so well-behaved and charming that the society editor asked permission to take pictures of them. And on Mother's Day, 1968, she devoted the entire front page of the Society Section to the Vradenburgh family, displaying characteristic poses of each child individually.

When this is written (1990), all but two have married. The single lady, Rebecca, is assistant to Dr. John Reynolds, who is assistant to Dr. Hutson.

Charles, an ordained minister, held several pastorates, both before and after coming to the Sword of the Lord Foundation. All together he has been a Sword employee for almost thirty years, and though his health is not good, he is still reading proof.

He and Lola reared their children "in the nurture and admonition of the Lord." All made exceptionally good grades in school, and all sing beautifully.

Once when "Becky" was asked if her daddy had promised a dollar for every "A" the children had gotten on their report cards, she very factually but wisely and modestly replied, "Certainly not! If he had promised, he would have been flat broke!"

Lola stayed at home all those years with the children; now that they have left the home nest, she helps me and is typing this book as I prepare it.

Oh, that others would follow the Bible example in rearing their children!

Dr. Rice was so observant and so proud of the children of those on his staff—the Vradenburghs, the Byerses, the Grabys, the Waxes, all following closely his teaching on the home and discipline of children.

† † †

During the first eight months of 1968, we received at the Sword of the Lord some 56,000 letters. And the circulation of the paper was climbing. Praise the Lord!

† † †

Dr. Rice could hardly dictate "Editor's Notes" without mentioning his saddle horse, Mac. This time he filled us in on Mac's behavior:

When that new colt, Trigger, was brought in the other day, Mac
snorted and in great excitement came running up to the truck
to investigate the newcomer.

He must supervise any construction, any destruction, and bosses
all the other horses—in other words, Mac[1] is king of Riceville.

He can open gates, pretend he has his foot caught (for attention), and when the other four horses crowd around for cookies—
wait so patiently and look so disgusted at their greediness!

But he is very jealous when I feed the young horse in his
presence, and he has nipped at Trigger several times to show his
displeasure.

Horses—and some people—are jealous when others are greatly
blessed and favored. Let us be sure to always rejoice when God
puts His soul-winning power on someone else.

On TV yesterday I saw the final services of Dr. Billy Graham
in Pittsburgh. Of course I am very sad with his yoke with
unbelievers, but I found myself greatly rejoicing in those who were
saved there.

General of the Army MacArthur wrote, with some help, this letter
to his rider:

---

[1] When Mrs. Rice died in November of 1989, Mac was taken to the Bill Rice Ranch, along
with two donkeys that Mac claimed as his own. The mother donkey had been around a long,
long time, and was a constant companion to Mac. Mac died three weeks after Mrs. Rice's
death. He was almost thirty years old.

January 18, 1967

TO DR. JOHN R. RICE:

Upon presenting you with my picture, I would like to say a few words. . .

"Trigger" has shared the spotlights and the applause of millions with his famous owner, Roy Rogers.

"Comanche" was greatly loved and prized by Will Rogers.

"Little Sorrell" not only had the honor of carrying General Stonewall Jackson through victorious battles and campaigns but also had the unique and sad experience of carrying him to his tragic and untimely death.

"Cincinnati," the 17-hands-high dark bay, not only bore General Grant to a national victory but—with him on his back—made him look like the conqueror that he was.

The unequaled "Traveller" carried General Robert E. Lee through years of battle without a single injury—and bore him as majestically in surrender as he had done in victory.

"Bucephalus" helped Alexander the Great conquer the then known world.

But my glory and honor is greater than that experienced by any of these famous and heroic steeds. You, my master and owner, are bearing a flag greater than the flag of our nation and fighting a war far more important than the battles of nations. You are the greatest general the Lord has in this day and age. (You will allow me my opinion.) So my pride at being your horse knows no measure.

I would be content to be just your horse. To be your friend and companion and recipient of your kindness and appreciation day by day fills me brimming full of gratitude. I pledge lifelong faithfulness.

Your Tennessee Walker,

"Mac"

† † †

This year we had had letters from 355 people who had trusted Christ for salvation through our English language books and tracts and through THE SWORD OF THE LORD. "We have promised God we will try to do more and get more saved in 1969," added Dr. Rice.

1969 In January, Dr. Rice announced that he was writing a book on the inspiration of the Bible, after years of researching, writing, reading and preaching ardently on this important subject.

As I have already mentioned, in Texas, some thirty-seven or thirty-eight years before, there had been a big fight among Baptists about inspiration. At that time Dr. Rice studied and wrote extensively on it, and the messages were printed in Dr. Norris' *The Fundamentalist.*

Dr. J. M. Dawson, then pastor of the First Baptist Church in Waco, Texas, had delivered a message before the State Baptist Pastors' Conference in which he espoused "thought" inspiration and denied "verbal" inspiration.

After Dr. Rice's series of articles and widespread discussion, Dr. W. R. White, then Baptist State Secretary and later president of Baylor University, came out openly in the Texas *Baptist Standard* espousing *verbal* inspiration. Then J. B. Cranville resurrected the manuscript of B. H. Carroll and had it published by Fleming H. Revell in a book titled *Inspiration of the Bible* which declared ardently for *verbal,* word-for-word inspiration. The two Introductions to that book were written by Dr. L. R. Scarborough, president of Southwestern Seminary, and by Dr. George W. Truett, pastor at the First Baptist Church in Dallas, then the best-known Baptist preacher in the world. Both plainly said that they believed in *verbal* inspiration as they were taught by Dr. B. H. Carroll.

It was now time, Dr. Rice felt, to come out on *verbal,* word-for-word inspiration of the Bible, going more thoroughly into some phases of it than did the material available in other books.

Later: After 10,000 copies of *Our God-Breathed Book—THE BIBLE* had been printed and review copies sent out, the finest praises began coming back to the office: Outstanding Christian leaders of the day were unsparing in their acclaim of its merits, speaking of it in such glowing terms as "the greatest . . ." (Dr. R. G. Lee); "the most exhaustive . . ." (Dr. Samuel Sutherland); ". . . most significant" (Dr. G. Archer Weniger); ". . . crowning achievement" (Dr. Louis T. Talbot); ". . . this masterpiece"

(Dr. Tom Malone); "Your able and vigorous defense..." (Dr. Oswald T. Allis); "...a splendid treatment of this subject" (Dr. Loraine Boettner), etc.

Its 416 large 6x9 pages skim the cream of the best writers on this subject for a hundred years—from Gaussen, Warfield, Carl Henry, Engelder, Laird Harris, Bettex, B. H. Carroll, Edward J. Young and many others.

Dr. Rice wrote other good books before and after this one, but perhaps this is his crowning achievement.

† † †

WILL 1969 BE DIFFERENT? It ought to be. Dr. Rice was hoping that every reader would have a heart examination and make some new vows. Then he suggested:

That the whole family set aside a time every day to have a circle of prayer. "You are concerned that the Supreme Court has forbidden organized and planned prayer times in schools. So am I. But isn't it rather hypocritical to criticize the Supreme Court if you do not have a regular time of prayer in your own home?"

That the family read the Bible together each day. "You wish schools could teach the Bible for the moral uplift of the children and the growth of character. So do I. But isn't it rather insincere to criticize the schools and the Supreme Court if you do not have a regular scheduled time to read it every day with your family?"

† † †

A subscription campaign was on; and Dr. Rice, as usual, wanted to do his part. "I praise the Lord for those whom God used to get the money in my hands and that I can make it available for subscriptions," he wrote. "So I turned in $1,000 Monday, April 14. Some of it came through the book table sales in conferences and some from other sources. How glad I am to see that 500 people can now get THE SWORD OF THE LORD for sixteen months!

(The special then was sixteen months, 69 weekly issues, for $2.)

† † †

In April Dr. Rice returned to Memphis to the Otologic Clinic for his yearly check-up on the right ear. It had shown much improvement.

† † †

OUR LETTER TO APOLLO 8 CREW:

January 22, 1969

Mr. Frank Borman
Mr. James A. Lovell, Jr.
Mr. William A. Anders
NASA Space Center
Houston, Texas

Dear Sirs:

We, the undersigned, wish to join with millions of other Americans in offering our congratulations to you upon the successful completion of the Apollo 8 mission. The perfection of your daring feat gives vast credit to you, the space program and our great country.

As Christians, we recognize that our faith is nothing if it is not practical. Faith that is ethereal has no answers for everyday problems and is of little value. So it seemed especially appropriate that you should read the Bible and pray, attesting to your faith in God and His Word.

It may be that you will be criticized for demonstrating your faith by some whose aim is to totally secularize our society. However, the undersigned Christian Americans want it to be known that we are proud and thankful to have men of character and conviction, like yourselves, in the space program. You have encouraged our hopes that the basic tenets upon which America was founded have not been eroded but still hold firm in the space age.

Congratulations on a job well done. May God bless you. Be assured of our continued prayers for you and every mission to follow.

In Jesus' name, yours,

SWORD OF THE LORD FOUNDATION

(Signed by the Sword President and 32 staff members)

By July, seventy-one stations were carrying Voice of Revival broad-cast. "Hopefully," Dr. Rice said, "we can make it one hundred by the end of the year."

† † †

Dr. Fred Jarvis, head of New Life Missions, distinguished missionary to the Japanese and missions leader, was pleading for 100,000 copies of *"What Must I Do to Be Saved?"* (a translated edition) for Pakistan, saying, *"The field is wide open; we have workers here ready to distribute the booklet."*

No money then was available in our Missionary Literature Fund, but Dr. Rice wanted to go ahead with the project, saying, "Since the missionaries are already there and the organized plan for getting out the Gospel is already set up, every two or three dollars spent should actually bring some lost soul to Christ in that foreign country."

Dr. Rice directed Dr. Jarvis to go ahead with 50,000 copies in the Urdu language of Pakistan, trusting God to bring in the money needed for the project.

† † †

THE SWORD announced the Homegoing of businessman, Mr. R. G. LeTourneau, on June 1. The first $1,000 gift sent to the Sword of the Lord came from Mr. LeTourneau in the 1930's; it was a direct answer to prayer.

A printing bill of over $700 was due and no money at hand. Dr. Rice called his three office girls together to pray with him over this bill.

Then came that $1,000. It seemed just like God dropped it down from Heaven to pay that bill!

† † †

In July at the Bill Rice Ranch, Dr. Bill presented Dr. John with a fine Western saddle of hand-carved leather, a new blanket, bridle, lariat rope and other appurtenances for his saddle horse, General MacArthur. "I am flattered at this beautiful tribute and token of love," said a surprised Dr. John. "Mac carries himself so proudly. This beautiful saddle will become him."

† † †

In one devotional period in July, Dr. Rice talked on the love of the

Holy Spirit and how He is with Christians in life and perhaps stays in the grave with the body at death, relating this about Dr. J. Wilbur Chapman, who, while preaching in Dayton, Ohio, told this incident:

> I was reading the account of an address delivered by Dr. Moorehead at a Bible conference, where he said he believed it was true that, when one became a Christian, the Spirit of God came into him to dwell and will continue to dwell in him always. "I don't know but that in some way—unknown to me—He will continue to abide, even though in the tomb, until the resurrection morning," said Dr. Moorehead. "But if any of my brethren deny me the privilege of this belief, I will say that, when I became a Christian, the Spirit of God came into my life and continues to abide; then when I am placed in the tomb, He will continue to hover over that tomb and will keep watch until the day breaks in glorious resurrection."

Dr. Chapman said:

> I could not read the closing sentences for the tears that filled my eyes.
>
> After hitching the horse to the carriage, my wife and I rode out to the little grave where we had buried our firstborn boy. As we stood there, we said, "Thank God, He is keeping watch!" What peace filled our souls!
>
> I shall never forget going across the country to stand beside the grave of my mother. There I said, "Thank God! Thank God! For thirty years He has been keeping watch. And when the morning breaks, He will lift my boy, my mother up, to be united by the Spirit again—the body in the grave and the spirit in His presence."
>
> That is the work and comfort of the Holy Spirit.

† † †

A GOOD IDEA! A man met Dr. Rice at the S & S Cafeteria in Greenville, South Carolina, whose son was then at Bob Jones University working on his Doctor of Philosophy degree.

Then this same man later wrote Dr. Rice: "Incidentally, his reading your SWORDs was one of the means of his entering the Christian ministry. My father—now gone Home to be with his Lord—paid the lad 25 cents for each copy he read. . . ."

It might be good if other fathers or grandfathers or mothers or grandmothers would see that children in the home regularly read THE

SWORD OF THE LORD, even if it means a few cents out of their pockets.

† † †

Missionary Russell Stellwagon wrote again in June reporting on the *"What Must I Do to Be Saved?"* booklet and the results.

> You will be happy to know that up to the 18th of June, 1969, there were 7,652 decision cards mailed in, and I doubt if to that date over 500,000 or so of the tracts had been distributed. I'll have further information later on.

He informed us in the same letter:

> Next year, at Osaka, Japan will have another World's Fair, "EXPO 70." It is estimated that from 30 to 50 million visitors will be in Japan, and, of course, many millions of Japanese will themselves attend this great Exposition.
>
> Missionaries and others would like to have 2 million more copies of *"What Must I Do to Be Saved?"* at that time. They will cost about $20,000.00. Please help us pray. We must rely on God's people— there is no other source from which we could pay for these soul- winning booklets.

Brother Stellwagon goes on to tell us:

> Japan is in some way the key to all Asia, the most literate and well-developed of all the heathen countries. And they are open to the Gospel in print in an amazing way. We have the missionary friends and organizations already set up to distribute the booklets and to follow up the converts.
>
> Will you tell me if you think we should have them print 2 million copies more, along with a decision card on which the con- verts may report?

I'll give you one guess what Dr. Rice's decision was! He sent out an SOS to SWORD readers, who were always so generous, knowing they could trust Dr. Rice to use God's money wisely.

(P.S. We had had 6 million copies published in Japan heretofore. On the last million copies, before they were all out, the report was that 7,400 had written in to either claim Christ as Saviour or ask for more infor- mation about how to be saved.)

† † †

Dr. Braxton B. Sawyer, founder and speaker of the Radio Pulpit broadcast from Fort Smith, Arkansas, shared with us a letter he had received from one of his listeners after hearing him preach against the liquor traffic on his program.

> Dear Brother Sawyer:
>
> Please let me explain the mind and thinking of a person who is part of the alcohol industry. He is dead to everything except making money. He does worry a bit about seeing friends drink themselves to death, but he figures they should know better. If his customers die, he may even send some flowers or get someone to run his booze joint while he goes to the funeral.
>
> This information is not secondhand; I am an ex-booze and gambling joint operator.
>
> I didn't know I was lost and, if I had died, I would be in Hell this minute. None of the good church people bothered to come tell me how to be saved.
>
> Want to know who did come to my home and invite me to come to church? That's right—one of my old drunken buddies who was saved because someone gave him a gospel tract, *"What Must I Do to Be Saved?"* written by Brother John R. Rice.
>
> After I was saved, I found out I had been selling beer to some of the *church* people around town. We Christians are letting the country go down and down. We are not salty enough to preserve it...
>
> (signed) Roy McArole, Ex-saloon and gambling joint operator saved by His grace forever. Amen!

† † †

THIRTY-FIVE BLESSED YEARS!

September 28 was our 35th year in business for the Lord with THE SWORD OF THE LORD. It then had a little over 100,000 circulation.

In these 35 years there had been over 180 million copies of THE SWORD printed, approximately a billion and a half pages. In these issues were 4,530 sermons, some 1,500 by great men of the past, like Moody, Torrey, Spurgeon, Talmage, Truett, Carroll, Ironside, etc. Over 1,500 of the sermons were directly addressed to the unsaved and, in most cases, had a decision slip.

By now THE SWORD had published more full-length sermons than any other Christian publication. For years Spurgeon published one sermon a week in his *Sword and Trowel.* Talmage had published one sermon a week. And some magazines for a season printed one sermon a week, where THE SWORD published three.

It was acknowledged that THE SWORD was doing more for evangelism in America than any other single factor. It had published more revival sermons, promoted more evangelists, put on more conferences on revival and soul winning, furnished sermon outlines, illustrations and suggestions to more preachers than any other Christian magazine.

Since each week one sermon was addressed to the unsaved, an amazing number of people wrote that they had found Christ through THE SWORD OF THE LORD—some 13,000 through the paper and Sword literature. That was only in America. Thousands more reported their conversion to missionaries on foreign fields.

We were proud of our track record!

✝ ✝ ✝

During this year, Dr. Rice had forty-two engagements for preaching!

✝ ✝ ✝

Are we taking too much time to address envelopes! Here is exactly how one came:

✝ ✝ ✝

When we first moved into our plant in Murfreesboro, there was an auditorium which would seat around one thousand, including about one hundred in the choir. So we could have good-sized Sword conferences in our own "front yard."[1]

Just part of the crowd at one such conference in Sword auditorium in Murfreesboro. All in the back of the auditorium are not shown.

The Sword's 35th anniversary celebration was held in Murfreesboro September 24 through 28. It was a mixture of a Sword of the Lord Conference, an old settlers' reunion and a state fair!

Speakers were: Dr. Bob Jones, Jr., Dr. Jack Hyles, Dr. Bill Rice, Dr. John R. Rice. (Dr. Lee Roberson became ill and could not come.) Then Governor Lester Maddox of Georgia climaxed the five days at a big Sunday afternoon rally.

It began with Open House at the John R. Rice's, where an estimated 500 walked through each room. Then a chili feast in a nearby pasture, under a big tent, with Dr. Bill in charge.

Seats were brought in from the Bill Rice Ranch. There was a piano for special music. Men parked scores of cars in orderly fashion.

The immense crowd thoroughly enjoyed talking and fellowshiping and rejoicing as they ate. Hundreds came; still there was food left. In the chili, 200 pounds of ground meat were used, 100 pounds of beans, 50 pounds of onions and gallons of canned tomatoes. And was it good! Mrs. Cathy Rice and her ranch hands did a wonderful job in preparing and serving the meal.

---

[1] As the work prospered, we kept having to take out more seats for more offices. The Bill Rice Ranch had built the large John R. Rice Auditorium, so we began having Sword conferences there, and continued doing so for many years. We still have an auditorium with 202 opera seats.

Several churches in and around Murfreesboro brought their entire prayer meeting crowd to hear Dr. Bob Jones on Wednesday night, September 24. The evening closed with Handel's "Hallelujah Chorus," beautifully rendered by the Weigle Singers and our own Sword choir.

In the fine crowd on Thursday were sixty-two preachers from several states. What a challenge Dr. Jack Hyles threw out to us all!

On Friday both Dr. Bill and Dr. John spoke. And we had the happiest singing time you can imagine—Bill Harvey, Bud Lyles, the Temple-aires and the Billy Carl-Joanna Rice duet.

And on Saturday, the 27th of September, there was a celebration at the Sword building—Dr. and Mrs. Rice's 48 years of happy married life.

It was also a time of special music: the Weigle Singers from Tennessee Temple Schools; Bill Harvey, Bud Lyles, Jake Hess and the Music City Singers from Nashville, the Master's Men Quartet and the ladies' trio from a church in town, a beautiful duet by Bud Lyles and Pastor Bob Kelley.

Each Sword worker was introduced. All the Sword girls and wives of the husbands were in evening dresses.

Refreshments were served to the crowd that jammed the auditorium.

Hundreds came from fourteen states and Canada, with many delegations driving in from surrounding areas.

The Sword staff had started weeks earlier preparing thousands of circulars, news releases and special mailings. Articles went to leading magazines. Ads were prepared for twenty-three Tennessee papers. Radio and TV gave us fine coverage.

And since we had invited company, our house must be in order. So good custodian Rev. Bill Kirby painted the large 800-seat auditorium ceiling and all the walls, mopped and waxed the floors, shined the woodwork and helped re-cement the large front sidewalk. Restrooms were repainted, the front of the building landscaped, and a red indoor-outdoor carpet installed at the entrance.

An artist had painted a picture of Dr. Rice, and it was hung back of the pulpit. We borrowed bunting from Convention headquarters in Nashville and draped the platform beautifully. We also prepared a booklet about the work and workers to give to all who came to see us.

Extra seats were moved in from an adjoining building, to seat at least 100 more. And there was room for another 78 in the choir.

Hours and hours of free overtime went into the planning and preparation of this event.

Our Sword ladies and the wives of Sword men employees made six dozen cookies each—we had over 2,000 cookies on hand.

There was a four-tier anniversary cake, with a Sword and Bible on the top layer, a picture of Dr. and Mrs. Rice on the second layer, and a picture of the Sword workers on the third.

Since September 25 was Dr. Jack Hyles' birthday, our "party" included him, too. A lovely birthday cake was made especially for him, and the Sword brought his daughter in from Tennessee Temple Schools to spend the day here with both Dr. and Mrs. Hyles.

Later all Sword Board of Directors who were present took Dr. and Mrs. Hyles out to dinner and presented him with a fifty-four-volume set of Spurgeon's sermons and a leather traveling bag. Yet we still felt we did so little for a man who had done so much for the Sword and Dr. Rice.

We had prepared for Georgia's Governor Lester Maddox's arrival on Sunday, the 28th. We had to learn protocol—when to stand, who should meet him at the airport, etc., etc., etc. After all, none of us had entertained a governor of a state before!

The Governor of Tennessee provided a limousine, and Murfreesboro had a police escort for the Maddox party and Dr. Rice, who accompanied him to the building.

Everything went off smoothly. The Governor was most gracious—a true southern gentleman. With him were two or three bodyguards, a couple of pilots, the Georgia State Police, the Tennessee Highway Patrol; and a good many policemen were stationed around the Sword building. (Remember, at this time Governor Maddox was under fire because of his stand on segregation.)

His message was fine and clear, honoring Christ and the Bible.

Several of us were invited to have dinner with his party at a local restaurant at 5:30 sharp. We had a lovely meal and fine fellowship.

How humble was this man of God, yet Governor of the great state of Georgia!

There was a private room for nine, but it turned out more were in the party than expected, so some of the police and bodyguards sat in the next room.

I was deeply grateful for the invitation to eat with, and next to, the Governor.

Later, after I had sent him a write-up from the *Daily News Journal,* this letter came to me:

Executive Department
Atlanta

Lester Maddox
GOVERNOR

Zell Miller
EXECUTIVE SECRETARY

October 8, 1969

Miss Viola Walden
Assistant to Dr. Rice
Sword of the Lord Foundation
224 Bridge Avenue, Box 1099
Murfreesboro, Tennessee   37130

Dear Miss Walden:

This will acknowledge and thank you for your kind
letter of October 7th, with attachment.

It was indeed thoughtful of you to send me the picture.
I am pleased to add this to my scrapbook and am grateful
to you for your consideration in passing it on to me.

The pleasure was indeed mine in being able to be with
all of you in Murfreesboro recently. I was delighted
to be with you and wish to thank all of you for a most
enjoyable experience.

With kindest personal regards, I am

Sincerely,

Lester Maddox

Lester Maddox

LM/afk

Only a few days had gone by when Dr. Rice said, "What about doing this every year?" Right then I "fainted" away! Still, he was the Boss, and Dr. Hyles had said in his Thursday message to "anticipate his wants and needs ahead of time, and spoil him to death!"

So, will we be celebrating our 36th in 1970? Keep tuned...!

† † †

Remember that the Sword of the Lord Foundation had sent money for 20,000 copies of *"What Must I Do to Be Saved?"* in Arabic. A letter from Rev. Victor Sadaka, field coordinator for the Mideast Baptist Mission, Beirut, reported:

> As of August, we had 29 reports of salvation from people in Egypt who signed the decision slip—and we had barely distributed 1,000 copies...
>
> We are aiming to get out our 20,000 copies within a year, and are looking for literally hundreds of decisions as a result, for the message is so clear.
>
> We will keep a separate record of those who send in decision slips, and I will try to give you a monthly report on decisions, which you might want to add to whatever records you keep on the effective ministry of this greatly used pamphlet.

As we mentioned in 1967, $250 a month was being sent for the mission work of this Mideast Baptist Missions, getting out Bible correspondence lessons to thousands of Arabs in Lebanon, Egypt, Jordan, Iraq, Saudi Arabia and Iran.

† † †

JOHN R. RICE HALL, here nearing completion, is a 456-bed dorm at Midwestern Baptist College, Pontiac, Michigan, Dr. Tom Malone, President. It was dedicated on September 29, 1969.

† † †

Two new Sword Board of Directors members were added this year: Dr. Bob Jones, Jr., who had been on the Cooperating Board for some time, and businessman, Mr. Russell Anderson. Both were presented certificates and honored at the regular Board Meeting in September.

Now we were thirteen: Dr. John R. Rice, Dr. Bill Rice, Dr. Jack Hyles, Mr. Alvin Byers, Miss Fairy Shappard, Evangelist Bud Lyles, Dr. Tom Malone, Mrs. John R. Rice, Dr. Robert L. Sumner, Miss Viola Walden, Mr. Nevin Wax and the two new ones.

† † †

On December 1 there came to Dr. Rice a decision slip from his booklet, *"What Must I Do to Be Saved?"* accompanied by this letter, written November 25:

> Dear Brother Rice:
>
> Two weeks ago I was given a tract entitled *"What Must I Do to Be Saved?"* by Evangelist John R. Rice.
>
> Quite frankly, I read this over several times until light shined upon me; then I gave my heart to the Lord.
>
> It was indeed a most joyous occasion for me. I have been a Catholic priest for close on to twenty-five years in Eire, in a Trappist monastery, then in a Benedictine Abbey as well.
>
> When I told my superior of my conversion from the "wafer God of Rome" to the "Christ of the Bible," my life seemed to be in danger. I had to flee in the middle of the night to Dublin, thence to cross the Irish border to Belfast, then by boat to Liverpool, England, where I have now made my way to the little town of Faversham, Kent. I live in digs at the moment.

Then the writer goes on to say he was in need of a suit, since all he had was "Roman clerical attire, which I have to live in at the moment." He said his desire was to secure work and "start life anew for Christ. I did not know Christ until I read your little tract," he again emphasized.

Along with his letter was his certificate of ordination to the Holy Priesthood.

Dr. Rice purchased a suit for him so he could get out of the clerical garb.

Aren't you made to wonder how a Catholic priest of twenty-five years obtained a copy of Dr. Rice's booklet? And further miracle, what caused him to read it? Of course God directed someone to give him a salvation booklet, and this hungry soul read it, was converted, left the priesthood and now wanted to serve the Lord!

We have his name and full address but, not wanting to see him persecuted, will not use it. Dr. Rice wrote some ministers near him, and we trust things turned out good for this "former" Catholic priest of twenty-five years.

What a blessed way to end 1969!

1970 Dr. Rice's goal at the beginning of the new year: "To love the Lord better than ever before and to serve Him with all my heart. I claim the sweet promise of Psalm 92:14, '. . . they shall still bring forth fruit in old age,' and Psalm 92:10, 'I shall be anointed with fresh oil.' "

In January we were able to get a final total on the End-of-the-Year subscription campaign (1969): a little over 21,000 subscriptions received.

† † †

Looks ancient enough to have been dug up from excavation of a Crusader's fort, but we think it was hand-forged especially for Dr. Rice by Dr. Clyde Miller and Pensacola Christian Businessmen's Committee, who sponsored a Sword Conference there. On one side of the blade are the names of Dr. John R. Rice, Dr. Bill Rice, Dr. Jack Hyles, PENSACOLA, FLORIDA, JANUARY 8-22, 1970.

† † †

March 19 was "Sword of the Lord Day" at Pastors' School in Hammond. Board members present: Dr. and Mrs. Rice, Dr. and Mrs. Bill

Rice, Al Byers, Nevin Wax, Miss Fairy, Bud Lyles and I.

At a banquet that night, the theme was "diamond" for Dr. Rice's 75th year (coming up December 11). A lovely make-believe blue diamond revolved in the center of the dining room. Then Dr. Rice was given a beautiful diamond from Dr. Hyles and First Baptist Church.

Dr. Hyles planned a most unusual kind of "congratulations and best wishes." He called over seventy old friends (all older than 75) and taped their greetings: Robert G. Lee, Ford Porter, R. T. Ketcham, Wm. Ward Ayer, Herschel Ford, Colonel Sanders (who said he was sending Dr. Rice certificates for 75 Kentucky Fried chicken dinners).

The speaker of the evening was Bob Jones, III. Then Dr. Rice spoke briefly on "There are ghosts here tonight"—a spine-tingling mention of Dr. Bob Jones, Sr., Dr. W. B. Riley and others who had gone on to Heaven.

† † †

One morning during coffee break, when Dr. Rice bowed his head to thank the Lord, his prayer started: "New paragraph...."

If you were interrupted as many times as he was, you perhaps would say and do some funny things, too!

† † †

Dr. Rice and Dr. Hyles held 18 Sword Conferences for 1970.

† † †

On January 30 it was reported that the Sword had sent the first $10,000 to Japan for printing 2 million copies of *"What Must I Do to Be Saved?"* for EXPO '70 World's Fair at Osaka, to be held in the summer. Another $10,000 was due for this project as soon as we could raise it.

† † †

Dr. Rice stressed again his and the Sword's position:

> Long ago we decided it was the will of God for us to be for all the people who are essentially true to Christ and the Bible and try to win souls, settling that on Romans 14:1, "Him that is weak in the faith receive ye, but not to doubtful disputations." Also, we were influenced by Psalm 119:63, "I am a companion of all them that fear thee, and of them that keep thy precepts."
>
> We will not knowingly have any fellowship with one who does

not believe the Bible is the Word of God or does not believe in the deity, virgin birth, atoning death, bodily resurrection of Jesus Christ and has not trusted Him as Saviour.

We can have fellowship with those who are good Christians but who do not agree on baptism, on some phase of the doctrine of the second coming, and perhaps do not fully understand the Bible doctrine of everlasting life.

I would not endorse a preacher's sprinkling of a baby, nor take part, but I can love and help him win souls.

I would not have someone talking in tongues in my services, but a good Pentecostal Christian who believes the Bible and wins souls is beloved and received, "but not to doubtful disputations."

If one who holds the doctrine of entire sanctification is right on the Bible being the Word of God and right about Christ, salvation and soul winning, then I can fellowship with him, provided it is not a cause of division, strife and argument.

I cannot, in good conscience, support the Southern Baptist Cooperative Program, but many born-again, Bible-believing men do. I can have fellowship with them if they do not make that point of difference a divisive issue.

I could never sit on the platform in a revival campaign with modernists, infidels, unsaved Catholics, Mormons and Jehovah's Witnesses, nor hold membership in a Ministerial Association where they were recognized as good Christians. When others differ with me on such a matter, I reserve the right to say that I think they are wrong. But if they are out-and-out for Christ and the Bible, I can love them and work with them, as long as it does not lead to disputation and strife or misunderstanding.

There is one great center of union: if born-again people believe the Bible, stand up for Christ and the Bible and help win souls, then we welcome their help and want to be a blessing to them.

I am not against Dr. Billy Graham; I am against his yoking up with unbelievers. If Dr. Graham came to town and let it be openly and plainly known that he would fellowship only with born-again Christians who believe the Bible, I would gladly cooperate.

Christ and the Bible are the issue with me and with THE SWORD OF THE LORD. I am for all those who are out-and-out for Christ and the Bible; I am against all those who are not for the Bible and not for the Christ of the Bible. And I will continue to say so while I make soul winning the main thing.

I invite all to join me on this Bible basis.

† † †

Dr. John was overseas, and Dr. Bill was sitting in the editor's chair at the Sword of the Lord. I picked this out of "Co-Editor's Notes":

> Dr. John has been gone just a few days, but I miss him terribly.
>
> As everyone knows who has ever heard me preach—John Rice is the big man in my life. I learned just about everything I know about the Bible and preaching from him.
>
> So many write to ask just what kin we are. We are half brothers. His mother died when he was just six years old. Several years later our father married my mother.
>
> Dad was fifty-eight when I was born, and he died when I was in my teens. So, in a wonderful and delightful way, Dr. John is both my big brother and my father. In him, I have certainly had the best of two worlds! He has given me all of the wisdom and counsel of a father, and all of the affection and companionship of a brother.
>
> For many years he has been not only my teacher but my best friend. I have often wished that everyone could know John Rice like I know him. So many people think of him as tough and hard-boiled and even critical and faultfinding. Actually, he is just about the most tenderhearted, gentle, compassionate and friendly man I have ever known and is anything but critical and faultfinding.

† † †

On the 1970 Tour of Bible Lands, our pilgrims saw about thirty people get saved—Greek Orthodox, Catholics, Roman Catholics and Arab Moslems—greatly renewing the hearts of all.

† † †

Sword of the Lord Foundation received the Bob Jones University Memorial Award for the Defense of the Faith at convocation exercises in May. One side bore the coat of arms of the University; the other, a *bas relief* likeness of Dr. Bob Jones, Sr., and the words: THE BOB JONES MEMORIAL AWARD: FOR THE DEFENSE OF THE SCRIPTURES. (See picture.)

The award—given in honor of the late Dr. Bob Jones, Sr., was presented to Dr. Rice on behalf of the Foundation by Dr. Bob Jones, Jr., who called the Sword of the Lord "a publication that stands against the compromise of scriptural principles in ecumenical alliances and one that has promoted scriptural evangelism, biblical preaching and the winning of souls

Front and back of award shown below

to Christ. It has strongly stood for New Testament principles in affairs of the church."

Dr. Rice served on the BJU Board of Trustees for years and was an honorary alumnus of the school.

† † †

THE SWORD was now reaching into 150,000 homes.

In August, the Foundation purchased a new Goss Web press, which would print and fold in one operation 16,000 copies an hour of THE SWORD OF THE LORD in either twelve or sixteen pages.

For over twenty years Herald Book and Printing Company in Newton, Kansas, had printed THE SWORD, headed by G. H. Willms, one of the finest gentlemen we had ever known. And what a generous heart! He labored faithfully with us, not as a job but as a partner. Our years of relationship were the best.

But sending SWORD copy and the SWORD list to Kansas meant a lot of mailing to and from, and preparing copy three weeks in advance. By doing it in Murfreesboro, this time could be cut to slightly more than one week. Also, the big press was needed for the Sword books, now being printed on a much smaller Harris press, which could not print the paper.

Now the time had come when we felt we could do the printing and mailing of THE SWORD ourselves from our own Murfreesboro plant. We had hoped for years to do this, but it was a tremendous undertaking.

Our fine production manager, Mr. Nevin Wax, had hoped, prayed and worked so long toward that goal.

He had finally finalized some plans, drawing the floor plan, finding what type equipment was needed, deciding the number of additional workers needed, visiting many other organizations with similar equipment, working with the post office and a myriad of other contacts.

After several Sword Board meetings and much prayer, we launched out into the deep, obligating ourselves for thousands of dollars in equipment, employing new workers and remodeling the plant to house the huge Goss Web press.

The $62,770 for the press itself (less a $5,000 gift by the company it was bought from); $26,500 for the addressing machine; $47,300 for typesetting equipment, plus $5,000 for platemaker and line-up table, meant an investment of $141,570—a BIG step of faith. But this was not a large matter for a work so big, which was resulting in so many thousands of conversions and the comforting, inspiring and strengthening of thousands of preachers and missionaries, and reaching into the homes in every state and to ninety foreign countries.

The decision proved to be a wise one. It was much more economical to do the printing here, plus not having to send the mailing list and SWORD copy to Newton each week.

Later the Lord showed us in so many ways that this was also His plan for THE SWORD OF THE LORD.

† † †

Last year we suggested you look for the announcement of another Sword Birthday Party in 1970. Sure enough! It was a musical jubilee, with famous singers, including Tennessee Temple choir, and some mighty fine speakers—five days of blessing (September 23 through 27).

Some new voices were introduced at this party:

REV. LONNIE GRAVES. A gypsy, who had never been to church until he was twenty-five, could not read and write, does not now know his own birthdate, related his life as a gypsy, his conversion, how his wife taught him to read, how he came to a Sword Conference and got on fire for soul winning, how God led and helped him build the largest Free Will Baptist church in the world—one of the most charming personalities we had ever met.

Let's let the gypsy speak:

I was born somewhere in Tennessee. I don't know where nor when. I remember asking my mother one day how old I was, and she said, "Oh, about fifteen." "But, Mom, when am I going to have a birthday?" (I could never remember having a birthday.) She replied, "Son, I think you were born in July. I remember I had two sons born in that month, and I believe you were one of them."

After talking with her for awhile and getting all the more confused, I just decided to choose a date for my birthday. So I said, "Mom, next July 20 I'm going to say I'm a year older than I am now." So since that time, I have on July 20 celebrated my birthday and claimed to be a year older.

We heard at that conference other things about the man which are almost unbelievable:

I slept on the ground for twelve or fourteen years (from the time I was two).

I slept in the front seat of the car for three or four years—after the time I got off the ground!

I went to school for three days; I got two whippings in those three days.

Then gypsy Lonnie told us that at about thirteen, he got lost from his dad—13 miles from where their trailer was parked. What did he do? He had learned how to "gyp" people real good by this age, so he went behind a house, got some ashes, found a coffee can, put a few ashes in it and mixed them with a little water. Then he went to the door and knocked. "Lady, I'm here to fix pots and pans with a mend-all that will fix anything."

Well, it so happened the lady had a couple of pots she was about to discard. He told her for 15 cents a hole (or two for a quarter) he could fix any pot and guarantee it would never leak again. But after he applied the mixture, he told her it had to dry for two hours. (He knew by that time he would be long gone.)

From house to house he went "mending" pans with his cement mix-all that would stay stuck together until it dried, and by that time he would be out of town.

Well, to make a longer story short, he had money to take a bus home, had seen a double feature movie, had eaten so much candy, popcorn and hotdogs that he was sick, and had about $4 left in his pocket!

His stories of his life before conversion were almost unbelievable—but true.

And his conversion was most remarkable. (You should have been here to hear it!) But it was in his booklet telling the story of his life. (And had you been here, you would have received a free copy at the door!)

MR. RUSSELL ANDERSON, businessman, dry wall contractor and builder, a Kentucky coal miner with only a high school education, made it his daily business to seek and to find the lost, and his dry wall business and contracting were second with him. Though a young man, he had already become a millionaire, simply because he had put God first IN EVERYTHING. Russ was one of our best friends; was one of the Board of Directors of the Sword Foundation.

DR. CLYDE MILLER, eminent physician, gynecologist, Christian layman, told of God's dealing with him; reported wonderful stories of soul winning among his patients in the hospital and out.

Example: One day a lady came and explained to him all of her difficulties. She was in a terrible shape. Dr. Miller counseled with her and tried to witness to her.

As was usual, his nurse sent her a bill at the end of the month. But across the back of that bill the lady wrote, *"I refuse to pay the doctor because he told me my illness was due to my sins."*

I wish we had more in the medical profession like him.

On our Sword Tours (he must have gone six times, usually taking each time several of his patients), we could find him out trying to win Arabs to Christ in these foreign lands.

Each year he loaded himself down with gifts for them. This year—1970—he took a dozen baseball bats and softballs to the underprivileged in Egypt and in the Holy Land. You should have seen him carting that heavy package on and off the many planes! One year he took a load of dolls for the little girls. One year his case was loaded down with Bibles and tracts.

Dr. Miller is a very personal friend. The year I had a hip replacement, he came from Pensacola, Florida, to spend several hours with me at the hospital.

Dr. Miller, you're a good man!

Of course, Dr. Rice spoke, as did Dr. Tom Malone. It was a memorable celebration. And how refreshing it was to hear those new voices!

In the afternoons we toured the Hermitage in Nashville, the beautiful home of President Andrew Jackson, hero of the War with the British in 1812. There we saw the old mansion, mementos, letters, the coach or carriage in which President Jackson drove to Washington and returned. A well-organized tour, taking an afternoon.

Another afternoon tour took in the Parthenon in Nashville, an exact replica of the world-famous Parthenon in Athens, Greece. Our guide pointed out en route the Ryman Auditorium where the Grand Ole Opry took place every Saturday night (it moved later to Opryland). The auditorium was built for the Sam Jones revival meetings.

Those on the tour saw the home of Sam Davis, a Confederate hero during the Civil War, located ten miles from Murfreesboro.

Near Murfreesboro they saw the famous battlefield where thousands of Civil War soldiers are buried, and the film describing the great battle.

Every day was filled with blessings. What blessed and happy times we had "back in those days"! Our talented office force worked hard to make each gathering here one to be long remembered.

People came from eighteen states, with over 200 present even in the morning services, held in the 1,000-seat Sword auditorium.

✝ ✝ ✝

In May and June, in a special subscription campaign, some 35,000 new subscriptions were enrolled. Dr. Rice greeted them in his Notes and was careful to make known the position of THE SWORD OF THE LORD which they would be receiving for the next sixteen months.

First, he called attention to the statement of faith at the top of page 1, explaining that "THE SWORD OF THE LORD is an old-fashioned, Bible-believing Christian magazine holding to the historic Christian faith, believing the Bible to be the very Word of God and defending it."

Then he was careful to spell out who we were:

> We are not a separate cult. The Sword of the Lord does not represent any denomination. The best soul-winning preachers of many denominations send sermons to THE SWORD, and the more than 140,000 families taking THE SWORD are in, I suppose, forty or fifty denominations.
>
> This editor is a Baptist, but the work is interdenominational. Thousands of our readers are Southern Baptists, and we love them, but we cannot support their Cooperative Program.
>
> We have some fine, Bible-believing Methodists who take THE SWORD OF THE LORD. We love them although they know we

do not believe in sprinkling babies, and their denominational
modernism is even worse.

We are glad to have the cooperation and fellowship of many
Pentecostal people, although, of course, they know that we do not
believe in their doctrine of speaking in tongues. Yet we thank
God for them and all other Christians who believe the Bible and
want to win souls and live out and out for Christ.

Many people of Holiness faith—Free Methodists, Pilgrim
Holiness, Nazarenes, Salvation Army and others—take THE
SWORD OF THE LORD. We do not agree that any Christian in
this life attains sinlessness or perfection, but we are for good
standards of holy living.

We are for evangelists who preach the Bible and get people
saved. We are for Dr. Billy Graham and for his soul winning,
although we definitely feel it is a sin to yoke up with unbelievers
like Bishop Pike and Bishop Kennedy, and it is harmful and
wrong to send converts to Catholic churches to confess to priests
and pray to Mary and depend on masses to get their souls out
of purgatory.

You see, then, we are trying to be good Christians and to love
God's people everywhere and at the same time lovingly and clearly to preach the whole Word of God as we see it.

You will see great sermons by men of the past in THE SWORD:
Moody, Torrey, Sam Jones, Bob Jones, Gipsy Smith, George W.
Truett, L. R. Scarborough, T. DeWitt Talmage, H. A. Ironside
and others.

You will also find that THE SWORD OF THE LORD works very
closely with the great independent soul-winning churches in
America, and many of the best soul winners and the best Christian leaders are on the Sword of the Lord Cooperating Board and
Official Board.

You will probably see some things in it with which you do not
agree. Then at least you can thank God that you are getting a
paper that has holy convictions and tries to live by them and
preach them even though you may not always agree with them.
Wouldn't you rather have sincere, honest effort to serve Christ
and be true rather than a compromise with no convictions, no
stand against sin and no holy boldness?

So, hello all you dear readers! You are much on my heart. As
editor, I invite you to sit at the table and feast on the good things
of God. If I can help you, I will. And, oh, I need your prayers, and
I want your love and confidence, and I will try to deserve it.

If I can help you, write. Feel free to ask questions or to criticize, just so you write in kindness as a Christian.

† † †

Mrs. Rice: "When I met Dr. Rice (just 'John R.' then), he was 20, going on 21. Five years later we were married, when he was 25, going on 26. Two and a half months later I had the honor of baking his first birthday cake, and it fell! I cried, and he laughed heartily and said, 'I like them better that way'; but I have never been able to produce another one like that!"

† † †

L to R: Dr. Hyles, Dr. Bill Rice, Dr. John R. Rice, Dr. Ian Paisley, Dr. Bob Jones, Jr. Who better to help celebrate your 75th birthday?

DR. RICE'S 75TH BIRTHDAY CELEBRATION. According to the calendar, Dr. John R. Rice would be 75 years old on December 11. Dr. Bob Jones, Sr., used to say, "The calendar doesn't lie." However, those of us who sometimes tried to keep up with Dr. Rice for a week had serious doubts about the veracity of the calendar! He still had the alertness, vigor and stamina of a college athlete.

Feeling that perhaps his 75th birthday was the most important one of his entire life, the staff and the Bill Rice Ranch wanted to celebrate it in a special way. So we agreed to go "all out" to make this one very special for him.

On December 10th we had a great birthday party in the Sword auditorium. (On his actual birthday, December 11, we were more exclusive and kept him to ourselves—his family and associates.)

We invited Dr. Ian R. K. Paisley of Belfast, Ireland, as the principal speaker.

Not since the days of Charles Haddon Spurgeon had Europe seen anything like Ian Paisley and the Martyr's Memorial Free Presbyterian Church of Belfast (North), Ireland. This church was the largest in all Europe. It was not uncommon for the congregation to number well over 3,000 on a Sunday evening.

Also, Dr. Paisley was a member of the British House of Parliament in London. As if that were not enough to keep one man fairly busy, he was also a member of the Ulster House of Parliament in Stormont.

This dynamic man was quite literally a "defender of the Faith" as well as a mighty soul-winning gospel preacher. Twice he had served time in prison for preaching the Gospel to great crowds who thronged to hear him in the open air.

On each occasion he was told that he could avoid serving the jail sentence if only he would agree not to preach in the open again for at least two years. Both times he flatly refused but chose to serve time at "hard labor."

Dr. Bill, Bud Lyles and Al Byers met his plane at the Nashville airport. After a television interview at the airport, he was driven to Murfreesboro to meet Dr. Rice for the first time.

(During this brief visit, Dr. Paisley paid me a compliment! I had asked if he would like a cup of coffee. No, but he would have a cup of tea. Fortunately I knew how to make their kind, since I had traveled in Europe and in Canada. I put on the pot, brought the water to a full boil, added tea bags (one per cup of water) and let the tea boil for a couple of minutes in the pot. Then I served it to him. When he had "tasted," he said, "This is the best cup of tea I have had since I have been in America!!!")

Mrs. Rice and her daughters had prepared lunch. After the meal, Dr. Rice saddled up MacArthur and Trigger, and both he and Dr. Paisley went for a ride around the farm. I think Dr. Paisley thoroughly enjoyed the ride, though he seemed a bit frightened. Never before had he been on a horse, but he had expressed a desire to have his picture taken on one. This photographer granted his wish!

All afternoon the decorating and food committees were busy at the recreation center across the street, readying for the reception following the night service in the Sword auditorium. Mrs. Bill Rice was in charge.

Meanwhile others were decorating the Sword platform.

Come evening, our Sword and Ranch ladies were in lovely formals. The men from both the Ranch and the Sword, with white carnation boutonnieres on the lapels of their suit coats, ushered visitors to their seats.

By 7:15 the photographer had arrived.

On the platform with Dr. Bill Rice, master of ceremonies, were: Dr. and Mrs. John Rice, Dr. Ian Paisley, Dr. Jack Hyles and Dr. Bob Jones, Jr.

At 7:30 p.m. Bud Lyles, masterful song leader, opened the service by leading the congregation in "HAPPY BIRTHDAY" to Dr. Rice. The Rice sisters sang a lovely medley of some of their father's own songs, followed by solos from Bud, Billy Renstrom, a duet by Dr. Rice's pastor and his wife—Rev. and Mrs. Bob Kelley; then other selections by the Rice sisters.

Dr. Bill called Dr. Bob Jones to the pulpit. His tribute to the Man of the Evening caused us almost to burst with pride.

Dr. Hyles was then introduced by Dr. Bill.

Prearranged, Dr. and Mrs. Rice "had a long distance call from a Sword Cooperating Board member, Dr. Archer Weniger." After they left to take it, Dr. Hyles discussed with the audience the plan to present Dr. Rice with a new Buick.

When Dr. and Mrs. Rice returned to the platform, completely oblivious of what had transpired during their absence, Mrs. Rice was asked to make the presentation. She read the note to Dr. Rice and presented him with the certificate for a new Buick.

He could hardly believe it! How could people do such a thing for him! (By the way, the suit he was wearing that night was a gift from Dr. Bob Jones, Jr.; his feet were shod with shoes from Bill Harvey; and the necktie and tie pin were gifts, too.)

At Dr. Bill's suggestion, the Sword staff gave him a Honda motorcycle to ride on his farm. However, it was later returned, unused; it seemed a dangerous plaything for a man 75!

Now Dr. Bill introduced the speaker of the evening.

Dr. Paisley proved all that we had hoped for this great occasion. (Dr. Rice asked me later, "How did he know so much about me, when we just met today?") We heard so many fine comments about his message as people left to go across the street to the reception. He was a very delightful speaker, a man of strong convictions, a man you like from the first.

Hundreds walked across to the reception. There Dr. Rice, Dr. Paisley and Dr. Bill were seated on a throne under a diamond (75th is diamond). With cup in hand and plate in lap, they greeted hundreds between sips and bites.

Other special guests for the evening were: Dr. Monroe Parker, Mr. Bill Mann, Dr. Rice's former advance man for revival campaigns; Dr. Stuart Crane, columnist; Mr. Pano Anastasato of Wholesale Tours International from New York; Mr. G. H. Willms, printer for THE SWORD OF THE LORD, from Newton, Kansas; Missionary Jim Norton, on leave from Japan; Dr. Clifford Lewis of Kansas City; Dr. Ford Porter from Indianapolis—and so many others from distances whom I do not have room to name, and many I didn't know.

A good many local dignitaries were there, including bank president, Mr. Jack Weatherford; Mr. Tommy Martin, known as "Mr. Murfreesboro"; and several local pastors.

On Friday, December 11, sixty-seven special friends were invited to a luncheon at the Southern Diplomat. Among them were: Dr. and Mrs. Lee Roberson; bank president, Mr. Jack Weatherford and wife; Dr. Monroe Parker, Mayor Westbrooks, representing the city of Murfreesboro; and those employees who had come with the Sword from Wheaton, along with Dr. and Mrs. Rice and their six daughters.

Mayor Westbrooks presented Dr. Paisley with a key to Murfreesboro, then stated that, since moving here in 1963, neither Dr. Rice nor the Sword had asked for anything, but rather had helped to make Murfreesboro a better place in which to live.

Dr. Parker composed and read a lovely tribute to Dr. Rice.

Dr. Lee Roberson added some fine comments about him.

A beautiful "Tribute to Dad" by the Rice girls was read by Bud.

Mrs. Rice spoke about her life as wife. Then she said, "They say a woman adds eight years to a man's life, so I am glad that I have contributed eight years to Dr. Rice." (You'll read Dr. Rice's answer in a moment!)

Dr. Bill presented him with a bulging notebook of letters and telegrams (including one from President Nixon).

Dr. Paisley spoke briefly. His talk was certainly a blessed tribute to our Boss.

Then it was Dr. Rice's turn. He thanked all who had made his 75th birthday such a memorable one. Then he added to Mrs. Rice's remark that a woman adds eight years to a man's life: "Well, perhaps I should marry five more times and get forty more years!" But he hastily added that he had stuck with this one forty-nine years, and he guessed he would tough it out!

Dr. Paisley came by the office to bid us all farewell, saying the long trip was worth it; he had had such a good time. He had brought from Ireland a lovely gold-framed picture of a street scene and an arched building over the street, in the center of which was a gold clock which actually told time, run by a battery. It was very unique and very lovely— a treasured gift from the Paisleys. (It still sits on a bookcase in Dr. Rice's office after twenty years.)

On his 75th birthday Mrs. Rice wrote her husband:

> You have earned all the honors we could give you! You have worked day and night, traveled long hours, redeemed the time as you snatched the minutes to work on trains, planes, in airports. And I remember a day when you drove and dictated to a secretary all day long the book, *Bible Facts About Heaven.* I watched the seventeen years when you spent so much time in prayer and work on *The Power of Pentecost.* I was your pupil in the six years you gave a correspondence course through the whole Bible.
>
> I heard your songs in the making. I heard your prayers in the night when you were heard sometimes praying as you slept. "I know thy works," and I am so proud of you.
>
> I remember a time when you were beginning your ministry in Dallas and we had six helpers in the home. One of the young men said to me, "Don't you wish you were a man so you could be a preacher?" I indignantly replied, "I would rather be the wife of John R. Rice than any preacher!" The greatest honor the Lord ever bestowed on me was when He picked me—"little me"—to be your wife.
>
> I have seen you tired but never discouraged. I have heard you bragged on but have not seen you "puffed up." I have heard you criticized but not embittered. I have seen you threatened but

never afraid. I have seen you tried but never faithless. I have seen you harrassed but never complaining.

I trust you will have many more years of service if the Lord tarries, and that thousands more will be saved because of your faithful preaching and praying and going and giving. I'll stay at home and keep the fires burning and the prayers ascending.

As I taught the children, and still think, you are the smartest, the sweetest, and the best preacher in the world. Having married, our daughters may have shifted their allegiance. I still think you are "the most"! And as Brother Joe Boyd would say,

"Excuse me if I do say so"; then he would add, "but you know it is so"!—which you do not know.

Anyway, HAPPY 75TH BIRTHDAY! and many, many more!

YOUR LLOYS

After getting Dr. Rice off the next day for New Jersey, Al Byers, Bud Lyles and I talked about what we might have done differently to celebrate this important event. Each could think of nothing—it had been perfect.

When I said to Al, "The Lord is paying Dr. Rice back for his labor of love through the years," he speedily remarked, "No, it is interest; he will be paid back in Heaven."

Dr. Bud said, "I have a problem. I have been thinking. . . . In twenty-five years, how can we top this celebration?!" (Then Dr. Rice would be one hundred.) I said, "Bud, for exercise, Dr. Rice can push us all down the aisles in our wheel chairs!" Even at our "young" age in 1970, he, at 75, could outdo each of us.

We never thought of him as an old man. He was still young to us. He still golfed with the fellows. He still rode his favorite Mac back to the barn from the pasture, bareback; in a few weeks he had planned to break a colt—little Jill—and get her rideable. He was still going up into the hayloft and pitching down bales of hay for his stock.

God promises long life to those who serve Him; He promises clothes for their backs and food for their bodies. Certainly Dr. Rice never wanted for any good thing.

While musing, the three of us hoped and trusted we would have him twenty-five more years, at least! But God wanted him Home and took him ten years later.

✝ ✝ ✝

In 1970 exactly 367 people wrote to tell us they had been saved through Sword of the Lord literature. These were only the ones who took time to sit down and write that they had been saved. Undoubtedly many, many times that number were saved but never wrote to tell us. No other magazine gets people saved like THE SWORD OF THE LORD does week in and week out.

✝ ✝ ✝

Mr. Al Byers revealed that Sword of the Lord Foundation did more business in 1970 in every category than ever before. It spent over three quarters of a million dollars in getting out the Gospel. More people were reached with the radio message. The circulation of THE SWORD was the largest it had ever been. And more books were sold to bookstores than ever before.

We had received 99,010 pieces of mail (not counting changes of address)—385 letters each working day, or 48 each hour, or a letter every 75 seconds.

Subscription income was more than $200,000. Book sales totaled more than $200,000.

By now the Sword had printed 17,823,470 *"What Must I Do to Be Saved?"* tracts in English and 1 million in Spanish. Since 1970 was the year for the big EXPO '70 World's Fair in Japan, they distributed 2 million in the Japanese language, plus some copies in English.

1971

Get away from it all and relax—that is what twelve of us did in January, aboard the *Homeric Cruiseliner*. We sailed again to Freeport and Nassau from New York.

It was not *where* we were going, but *how* we were going. This was the third time we had chosen a cruise with an Italian crew, who looked after us so well. In fact, there was about one crew member for every passenger!

We left New York on Saturday, January 23, and arrived in Nassau on Tuesday morning. The ship was our hotel, but we could go into Nassau as often as we liked.

How wonderful it was to stroll on the decks or sit as long as we liked in deck chairs! Meals on a ship are out of this world. And to make it more festive, we ladies got to dress three nights in formal wear; and the men, in tuxedos.

On Sunday aboard ship, a preacher in our group preached in a Protestant service. Then each morning our twelve had devotions together, enjoyed each other's company and made our own fun.

Four different preachers in our party preached in four different churches in Nassau on Wednesday night and saw many saved.

One day we went to see the flamingo parade, a beautiful thing with the lovely, pink, pipestem-legged, web-footed, amphibious birds, trained to do some beautiful marching.

Those on this cruise were:

Dr. Bill and Cathy Rice; Mr. and Mrs. Ed Whitley; Dr. and Mrs. Russell Anderson; Dr. and Mrs. John R. Rice; Rev. and Mrs. James Phillips; Viola and Fairy. A businessman, a longtime friend, paid my entire fare.

There was a whole year before us, and we wanted to be fit to serve our readers and our Lord better. Such a cruise always did the job!

† † †

Books and pamphlets by Dr. Rice had reached the enormous circulation of 35 million copies. So deeply and soundly scriptural, so life-changing in spiritual power, so simply and yet pungently written with the zeal and charm of warmhearted evangelism, they had received the praises of spiritual giants and were approved by fundamental leaders everywhere.

† † †

Again this year Dr. Rice went all over the country, being away from the office at least three days each week. He and Dr. Hyles were having between twenty-five and thirty conferences on revival and soul winning a year.

† † †

In "Editor's Notes," Dr. Rice mentioned Dr. Billy Graham having an operation. "He has been ordered by his doctor to take an extensive rest at home. We pray that his health and strength may soon be restored."

Mentioning again their differences, Dr. Rice said: "We have openly protested Dr. Graham's offering Christian fellowship to unconverted people, whether liberal Protestants or Catholic priests depending on the church and Mary and priest for salvation. But we are glad he loves the Lord and preaches the Gospel. And we earnestly pray for his health and for God's help in every way that will honor Christ. Good wishes and God bless you, Dr. Graham."

He never ceased to love and pray for his friend daily.

† † †

When he could catch a few moments, Dr. Rice was at the barn checking on his few cattle and horses. Since boyhood and ranch and farm days, his thoughts were always about the livestock in connection with the weather.

On this particular day he saddled up Jill, the two-year-old black filly he was breaking to ride. He had worked with her until she was about bridle-wise and had quit fighting the bits. "A few more rides and she will be suitable for anybody to ride," he reported. Seventy-six and still breaking horses!!!

† † †

"MAC" ATTENDS SWORD CONVENTION AT HAMMOND! Every year, Dr. Hyles, loyal friend, vice-president of the Sword of the Lord Foundation and Conference director, selected some spectacular way to honor the editor and/or his associates.

At one such annual convention he secretly brought all of Dr. Rice's daughters to be present in the service and sing.

On another occasion I was greatly honored as "Queen for a Day" for my more than three decades of service to the Lord and the Sword of the Lord.

In his seventy-fifth year, Dr. Hyles and the church gave Dr. Rice a diamond ring.

This year, after private scheming and a well-kept secret, Dr. Hyles announced that, "unknown to Dr. Rice, his best friend is here and has come to greet him."

A Sword employee rode into the Civic Auditorium and down the aisle on Dr. Rice's MacArthur! The horse had been brought to Hammond in a trailer and kept through the day on a farm nearby.

"Mac" came forward without undue hesitation as if he were perfectly at home, strutting down the middle aisle before the thousands of people.

Dale got off and Dr. Rice got on and rode "Mac" around in the Civic Auditorium, then sat on him while Dr. Hyles read aloud a poem in the name of this beloved friend, pet and servant, written by Evangelist Bill Harvey.

A Poem With Horse Sense

(Composed by Dr. John R. Rice's horse, General of the Army Douglas MacArthur II, with some help from Bill Harvey)

Now with my hoof I take up my pen
To tell of my life with the finest of men;
We make a fine picture when he's in the saddle,
And everything's right when I feel him a-straddle.
I've heard of play-horses on merry-go-rounds
That ride happy children to steam-organ sounds.
I've heard of war-horses that pull chariots
And small Shetland ponies that ride little tots.
Some horses do pullin' and some even race;
Others just trot with an elegant pace.
Some horses track with a Mountie on top;
Quarter-horses boast of their quick turn and stop.
There's horses for buckin'...I've seen one or two...
They should have been sweeter, for now they are glue.
But of all the horses of which I am one,
I'm sure I'm the one horse that's had the most fun.
My business is carryin', now that's where I shine,

'Cause there's not a rider that's equal to mine.
I'm somebody special when he's up on me;
Why. . . I'm a horse in history!
I make it look regal, I arch my neck well,
I make the Boss proud we can ride for a spell.
I wish there were saddle-bags pressin' my sides
With Bibles and books for a long circuit ride.
We'd head out for Dallas and camp on the way;
We'd make camp at night and ride in the day.
He'd sing to me softly as we rode along
And have by the sunset another new song.
And then we'd make Tulsa; he'd preach where he could,
Gettin' the truth to each neighborhood;
Then on up to Kansas, perhaps Wichita,
Then double back later to old Arkansas.
I'd never once falter or show I was tired;
I'd travel on little, 'cause I'd be inspired.
And when we got back to old Tennessee,
He'd let his sole transportation be me.
No more in the stable to wait his return.
I'm not mad at airplanes, but may they all burn!
I'd never complain with the chief on my back;
Boy, I'd have it made! why, nothing I'd lack.
Some may not believe in predestination
(And all I have studied is some equitation);
But I feel predestined to carry one man,
And I can't help but feel it was part of God's plan.
I wouldn't trade places with Traveler or Trigger
Or any horse anywhere, littler or bigger,
For the pleasure of feelin' the gettin'-on jar
Of the great man that boards me by the name of JOHN R.

    Written for First Baptist Church
    Hammond, Indiana, Annual Preachers' School

Of course the audience was greatly interested, since those who read THE SWORD already knew about "Mac." They often inquired about him, and now there was a great ovation for his horse.

But Dr. Hyles was not the only one to bring about a big surprise. Workers on the staff of the First Baptist Church and of the Hammond Christian High School and the staff of the Sword of the Lord had secretly purchased for Dr. Hyles a new Oldsmobile Cutlass.

Associate Pastor C. W. Fisk, representing the staff, paid tribute to Dr.

Hyles. Then Dr. Billings, principal of the Hammond Christian High School, brought their love. Then Dr. Bill Rice, representing the Sword of the Lord staff, paid tribute.

Then Dr. Rice presented a little gift-wrapped box containing mysteriously the keys to the car and a bronze plaque to go on the dash.

While Dr. Rice was presenting these to Dr. Hyles, the new car was being driven down the aisle of the Civic Center.

Dr. Hyles was pretty well nonplused, almost speechless and, of course, deeply moved. He does so much for others, and it was a joy to surprise him with this gift to replace the old car he used so vigorously in his visitation.

From all over America men had come to ask Dr. Hyles to show them how to lead the people in building a great New Testament church, about visitation program, the bus ministry, the promotion, etc. So he felt led to start having a week of teaching for pastors each year. Now for seven years Dr. Hyles and the First Baptist Church had put on a week of PASTORS' SCHOOL.

God has greatly blessed this PASTORS' SCHOOL. It is amazing how many hungry pastors come and are fed, then go home diligently to set out to learn the business of soul winning, building a New Testament church and reaching the multitudes.

On Tuesday of this year, the church had a reception for Sword of the Lord Board members. First, we were led through a beautifully decorated and prepared "Garden of Eden" lounge where we greeted, one by one, the staff of the great First Baptist Church. Then the Sword Board members stood from 7:00 to 11:00 in a receiving line meeting and greeting the hundreds who came by to shake our hands and tell, perhaps, how they had been blessed by THE SWORD.

Some of the ladies, knowing how long it would be, took extra shoes and changed several times. Or we kicked off our shoes and stood barefoot!

We met pastors from every state in the Union, as well as several provinces of Canada. It was a refreshing time.

All who came through the receiving line got their picture taken with Dr. Hyles.

† † †

Dr. Rice was going to be at home for FIVE days! "What a treasure!" he exclaimed, and went on to say:

> Years ago I heard Dr. Bob Jones, Sr., say, "I don't know why

God called me to be an evangelist. I love home and my wife's cooking. I despise these long nights on train or plane, the lonely hotel rooms, and always being among strangers."

I thought, *That's strange. I feel the same way. Did God make a mistake when He called me and Dr. Bob to be evangelists?*

Then I saw the answer: God does not want any service that does not cost something. He does not call a man to be an evangelist just because he would like to be a gadabout or a traveling salesman. One must forsake father and mother, wife and children, and his own life also, to please God. "And whosoever doth not bear his cross, and come after me, can not be my disciple," Jesus declared. And, "Likewise, whosoever he be of you that forsaketh not all that he hath, he cannot be my disciple."

But how precious when we can have a few sweet days at home!

† † †

In a hotel room in Kansas City, in April, Dr. Rice sought special leading about several things. "I was made sad by the great number of Christian colleges and seminaries giving way to the worldly standards or to the opinions of liberal scholars, or compromising in this way or that. And most denominations are decreasing in membership and baptisms year after year."

He went on to say: "As I thought on these things, I had an overwhelming feeling that THE SWORD OF THE LORD is about the best chance America has to warn people of modernism, to stir hearts for revival, and to call Christians back to the historic Christian faith."

Then God seemed to lay on his heart that "we must set out to have 200,000 subscribers to THE SWORD OF THE LORD by the end of 1971." (A little over 150,000 families were then receiving it.)

Dr. Rice reminded SWORD readers of what once happened to Paul:

> In jail at Rome, and about ready to have his head cut off, Paul's friends seemed to have forsaken him. After he had written for books and a cloak, he said, "Alexander the coppersmith did me much evil. . . . Of whom be thou ware also; for he hath greatly withstood our words. At my first answer no man stood with me, but all men forsook me . . ." (II Tim. 4:14-16).
>
> Where now were Paul's friends whom he had won to Christ? And those who had been blessed by his great preaching—where were they?

When the Lord was arrested, many of His disciples fled. Now He asks the twelve, "Will ye also go away?" (John 6:67).

Dr. Rice was pleading for Christians to stand by him and the ministry of THE SWORD and help build the subscription list. "Unless friends of the Lord Jesus are also 'our fellow labourers,' then we will know something of the broken heart of Paul and Jesus when others forsook them."

Dr. Rice recalled that the path down the years was marked by the death of many a Christian periodical that set out to preach the Gospel to multitudes. "So it seems amazing that for more than thirty-six years God has kept THE SWORD OF THE LORD going."

(And I know how! For years Dr. Rice had made up the deficit out of his offerings in citywide campaigns and by giving his book royalty back to the Foundation.)

He expressed concern that just the week before, the good *King's Business,* the organ of BIOLA (Bible Institute of Los Angeles) had ended because of financial difficulties and lack of support. He recalled that Harvey Springer's *Western Voice* magazine had just recently ceased to be for the same reason. He mentioned that the famous *Sunday School Times,* probably the best-known Christian paper in America, had gone broke and sold out to Union Gospel Press, who combined the *Sunday School Times* with another magazine.

He declared: "THE SWORD has no support from other sources, and our subscription price is less than those of other major magazines but has more material than nearly any of the Christian magazines."

This blessed paper, winning so many, was so dear to Dr. Rice's heart that he wanted the whole world to read it!

† † †

By May, three of his saddle mares had had new colts—Golden Lady, the beautiful golden mare of Arabian-quarterhorse blood which Dr. Bill gave Mrs. Rice; Gypsy (the one I chose to ride), the spirited little black mare, half Shetland, half Appaloosa; and Flicka, the little Welch pony.

Then Daisy, his faithful Hereford cow, the first one he bought, brought them the sixth heifer.

A month later Cleopatra, the little donkey, had a baby also. He was a little larger than a jack rabbit, with much bigger ears.

Then in July "we said good-bye to Geronimo II, the bull, three cows and two calves, as they were hauled off to Nashville. We don't have enough grass in the forty acres for eleven horses (including three little colts), and eleven cows and calves. Besides, I have use for the money!" (I just imagine it went to put on more subscriptions to help reach that 200,000 circulation. He usually put "feet" to his prayers.)

† † †

In July Dr. Rice listed "four ways we can help evangelize America":

1. Enlarge SWORD weekly circulation to 200,000;

2. Get 10,000 families to start daily Bible reading and prayer;

3. Have six or seven tremendous old-time, three-week citywide revivals as a pattern, with the greatest soul winners leading in it;

4. Enlist 100 new churches to set a goal of 200 converts baptized in a year, with visitation and bus ministry to reach multitudes.

A MIGHTY WORTHY OBJECTIVE! Will the four items materialize? Keep on reading...

† † †

This letter was addressed: "To the Sword of the Lord, the Whole Rice Clan—and Their Help."

> FIRST, No. 1, and most important: don't ever (but EVER) let me fail to receive THE SWORD. Bill me and I'll steal my wife's old settin' hen and sell her to pay the bill. (That old widder woman don't need no more chickens no how.)
>
> But seriously—I don't see how anyone who ever met THE SWORD could help falling in love with it. It has helped me more than any other paper. Even if I didn't care for the Rices or their views—but I do—I still would have the sermons of the greatest preachers of modern days to enlighten me on many important points of the Bible.
>
> C. C. Farran of East St. Louis, Illinois

† † †

You may recall that some time back I mentioned that we had gotten out a printing of 600,000 copies of the booklet, *"What Must I Do to Be Saved?"* in Portuguese. (THE SWORD OF THE LORD is published monthly in a Portuguese language edition in Portugal and is circulated in Portugal and in Brazil.)

There was now a great need for more copies of this booklet in that country which was ripe, it seemed, for the Gospel.

With so many needs at the Sword of the Lord—the radio, Ministers' and Missionaries' Subscription Gift Fund, and the big press, mailing machine, typesetting machinery—not much attention had been given to our foreign missionary literature fund.

Nearly every day someone was writing in to say he/she had been saved through Sword literature in the English language, but in the past many tens of thousands had claimed Christ through *"What Must I Do to Be Saved?"* and other Sword literature in foreign languages and lands. One of these was Brazil.

Now, although needs were very great at home, Dr. Rice and the staff felt we must send help regularly to Portugal and to other countries.

The editor of the Portuguese edition of THE SWORD OF THE LORD, saved through the booklet, *"What Must I Do to Be Saved?"* now pled for help to get 50,000 more copies printed.

† † †

Rev. Bob Hughes, a Bible Baptist missionary of Cebu City, Philippines (now deceased), was having blessed results after his return from furlough. On August 29, there were 1,538 in Sunday school and 201 professions of faith during the day.

He wrote that his people were active in soul winning. "We need more of your booklets, *'What Must I Do to Be Saved?'* Will it be possible to send 10,000 for prayerful distribution?"

Then he added that "our preachers have not received THE SWORD OF THE LORD for a long time. . . . If you could send a bundle of fifty of each issue, I will see that every preacher and student in our Bible school gets to read it. I wish it were possible for our preachers to have a copy of each of your books for their library. They have so little, but their desire to serve the Lord is so great. . . ."

Dr. Rice wrote back that we would send whatever he wanted. Soon the booklets were on their way, as were the fifty copies per issue of THE SWORD.

† † †

"Of making many books there is no end."—Eccles. 12:12.

Did wise Solomon look down the corridors of time some three thousand years to 1971 and see the Sword of the Lord Foundation when he made that statement? It fits, certainly.

We were continually reading and preparing manuscripts for new books. Example: In six months' time, sixteen hard-bound books had rolled off our presses, besides monthly radio pamphlets and smaller booklets.

And in September we had just been given this information: "Sword of the Lord Foundation now has in print: 81 hard-bound books, 31 paper-bound titles; 9 booklets; 2 tracts; 85 pamphlets of the 25-cent series and 4 songs in sheet music—totaling 212 titles." Again, this excluded the monthly radio booklets which were not kept in stock.

By now we had grown so large in book publication that a separate building was desperately needed to house the book room, the shipping department and storage. Truck load after truck load was leaving our plant for the post office each week.

The hundreds who visited us each year were amazed at the bigness of our organization—all possible because of God's continual blessing on this soul-winning ministry.

And the running total for these thirty-five years of the Sword's ministry was that 14,811 people had trusted Christ through Sword literature, not including the thousands in foreign lands saved through our literature in thirty-seven languages. These records were kept by missionaries who work with and report to us from time to time, and they do the follow-up on them. We will know in Heaven the grand total!

May we say humbly that Sword literature carries an old-fashioned Gospel, with plain preaching about sin, Hell and judgment, and warning to the unsaved. This literature vigorously defends the historic Christian faith, calls sin by name, demands repentance.

We honestly believe God mercifully blessed Dr. Rice's writings because the books faithfully stood true to the Scriptures. Each day's mail was likely to have from one to eight letters telling of salvation through Sword literature.

What is the measure of a man's ministry? Faithfulness? The geographical extent it covers? The numbers of people to whom he is able to give the Gospel? The churches he established? The souls saved? Those called into service of God in his steps? Can a man's ministry be measured? (We say MAN because Dr. John R. Rice was the Sword of the Lord, and the Sword of the Lord Foundation was John R. Rice.)

Certainly Christians are aware that the influence of a life extends far beyond the short span of years in which that life is lived in this world.

Only at the judgment seat of Christ will all be known of the good Dr. Rice and the Sword literature did and is doing.

We know such a prodigious work and such an extensive ministry will have repercussions in lives of millions for generations to come.

It is unfortunate, very unfortunate, that some great men of past generations did not leave behind them some of their good work in print. And how fortunate we are that we can read now some of the sermons by Spurgeon, Torrey, Moody, Talmage, Sam Jones, Bob Jones, Sr., Billy Sunday and others because they were wise enough to leave us the legacy of their printed messages.

† † †

An earnest request came for more *"What Must I Do to Be Saved?"* booklets in Korea from Dr. Gerald Johnson of the Gospel Fellowship Missions there, a fundamental, long-time friend of the Sword. He said that, if SWORD readers could help in raising the funds, he would gladly take responsibility for printing and distribution. "The Bible Baptist missionaries here in Seoul would like to have 500,000 copies at a cost of over $5,000."

Dr. Rice pledged the money for this printing, and eventually the whole amount was sent.

† † †

In September, Dr. Jerry Falwell started Liberty Baptist College at Lynchburg, Virginia. He flew to Murfreesboro in his plane, placed an order for 10,000 copies of one of Dr. Rice's booklets (taking 4,000 with him and the other 6,000 were shipped). Then we were to send him 10,000 copies a week of various titles which he chose; these he would offer on his nationwide television programs.

How happy we were to be getting out so many thousands of Dr. Rice's booklets all across America!

† † †

This year we began calling for 100,000 sample names to which we would send a few copies of THE SWORD OF THE LORD, in view of getting thousands of new subscriptions.

(As of the first of November, 82,638 names had come in from our good readers.)

† † †

Oh, this changing world! By now we had gone to computer! That meant every subscription had to have his or her name retyped to fit. Imagine changing a whole subscription list of 150,000 or so people!

And Mr. Computer was a funny gentleman! Very greedy. He wanted everything on your stencil that he could possibly get on it.

EXAMPLE:

244720WARN3DN781893 G0673
MR JOHN DOE
7818 MAIN AV
N CINCINNATI OH 44720

If your name was DINGLEHOOPER, you sure were in trouble! He couldn't even call you "MR" and he might have had to leave off your first name! Then if it was DINGLEHOOPER-IPPER, the computer really had to take over; he would deliver the paper to your address, whether your name got included or not!

† † †

By October 1, some 400 churches had agreed to have a "SWORD Sunday." Pastors had written for sample copies and special subscription envelopes so that they could get all the subscriptions they could on this special day. They sent in literally thousands.

How grateful we were through the years for such cooperation among preachers!

We noted that Dr. Jerry Falwell passed out envelopes and took subscriptions on a Sunday morning and again Sunday night and promised 1,000 subscriptions. Also Dr. Curtis Hutson, then pastor of Forrest Hills Baptist Church in Decatur, Georgia, set out to raise a great many subscriptions on this special "SWORD" day, as was true of these other 398 churches.

Mr. Byers checked on the weekly circulation for the last year and found that we averaged 50,000 copies more per week of THE SWORD OF THE LORD in 1971 than in 1970.

What more could you ask for? Advertising was booming, the mail was heavy, letters were coming daily telling of conversions, and thousands of subscriptions were coming in from the approximately 400 churches having "SWORD Sunday."

† † †

"Where there is no vision, the people perish. . . . "—Prov. 29:18.

Nothing truly great is ever done without men of vision. Great business ventures are never successful without leaders with a vision. Behind every important school ever started were men with unusual vision of the need for education. Every great nation has had behind it unusual leaders possessed with a vision of what could be done.

And in God's work, too, we find there is a desperate need for Christians with vision.

Dr. Rice, at 76, still had a great vision, a vision of a world needing salvation. He was gripped with the thought that 115,000 souls per day were going out into eternity and most were unsaved.

† † †

October 1, 1971: DEADLINE DAY. That is the day the first issue of THE SWORD OF THE LORD was to be printed in Murfreesboro. Never before had this paper been done by us, but always by contract with other printers. And in the production department—Oh, my!—the planning, getting experience running the typesetters, making plates for printing, running the new press—the fervor for printing THE SWORD was .n-ning high.

Now it would take only eleven days from the time the copy was turned in until publication date, instead of the previous twenty-one days!

We set a goal to rid ourselves of the debt of the press and related equipment by the end of 1971.

† † †

What a great year! Dedicated workers...increased circulation of THE SWORD...becoming our own printers at last...new equipment...444 decisions for salvation in America during the year...giving Dr. Rice, the "Captain of Our Team," our Boss, to us these long years.

Yes, oh, yes, God was so good to Sword of the Lord Foundation in 1971!

† † †

In December of 1971, Dr. Jerry Falwell, Dr. Curtis Hutson and Dr. Bob Moore were added to the Sword Cooperating Board.

† † †

It is a good thing to keep records. It is a good thing to review the past and see where we have been. But living in the past can be an unwholesome thing. So it is good to set some goals at which to aim for the future.

We thrilled at the blessed reports sent of how God was blessing churches all over the country. Many won and baptized at least 200 converts in 1970. Some did not quite make it but planned to do so in 1971. Others were setting higher goals.

In stressing that churches set a goal to baptize over 200 converts a year, Dr. Rice recalled that, in the great days of his ministry at the Metropolitan Tabernacle in London, Spurgeon had crowds regularly packing the auditorium with room for a reported 5,000. He had many saved and was sometimes called the greatest preacher since Paul.

But Dr. Rice reminded us that, in the best years of Spurgeon's ministry, he baptized an average of about 500 converts a year.

Then he recalled that, in 1970 alone, Dr. Lee Roberson baptized over 2,000 in Highland Park Baptist Church in Chattanooga; that Dr. Jack Hyles baptized over 2,000 in the First Baptist Church in Hammond, Indiana; that Dr. Bob Gray at Trinity Baptist Church in Jacksonville, Florida, baptized 788 converts; that Dr. John Rawlings baptized just under 1,000 converts in the Landmark Baptist Temple, Cincinnati; and that Dr. Tom Malone had already baptized 900 and hoped to reach 1,000 by the end of 1970.

Dr. Rice's comment was:

> How do they do it? They lay aside the formal, stiff services and put soul winning first. They use the Sunday school; they use evangelistic music; the preachers preach for souls and train soul winners; they have strong visitation programs and fleets of buses going out and bringing in those who otherwise would not come. Many of the churches are, in a remarkable way, going back to the New Testament plan like the church at Jerusalem, "And daily in the temple, and in every house, they ceased not to teach and preach Jesus Christ."

† † †

THESE PASTORS BAPTIZED OVER 500 CONVERTS IN 1971:

Dr. Jack Hyles (2,757); Dr. Lee Roberson (2,181); Dr. Tom Malone (1,190); Dr. G. Beauchamp Vick ("nearly 1,000"); Dr. Robert C. Gray, Jr. (936); Dr. Tom Wallace (909); Dr. Curtis Hutson (879); Rev. Bob Moore (852); Rev. Charles Hand (767); Rev. Verle S. Ackerman (722); Dr. A. C. Janney (631); Rev. Ray Batema (604); Dr. Gerald O. Fleming (587); Dr. Harold Henniger (567); Dr. John Rawlings (537); Dr. David C. Hall (537); Dr. Jerry Falwell (510).

Then forty-six other pastors wrote giving the number they baptized—anywhere from 495 down to 200.

We are sure there were many more who may not have known of Dr. Rice's appeal.

This total was a great encouragement, since Dr. Rice had diligently urged pastors over the months to work at winning more and getting them baptized.

1972

The banner above the heading of THE SWORD for January 21 read:

WITH THIS ISSUE, CIRCULATION REACHES 200,000 COPIES.

All during February we celebrated with 16-page issues (instead of 12).

† † †

We were not seeing much of Dr. Rice in January. To Sacramento, to Nashville, back to the West Coast for two days, then north to Fairbanks, Alaska, for a four-day conference, then back to Nashville on Thursday, leaving again for Indianapolis on Saturday.

So it went—day in and day out! His faithful staff kept on being faithful, but how elated when we could hear his office door open!

In these thousands of miles of air travel weekly, he was never late for appointments, never missed his close plane schedule, even when he had to change the clock so often because of time zones.

Remember, he was now 76 years of age! Still, all he was asking for was that "God will keep me well and strong and out on the firing lines!"

† † †

Imagine going to Fairbanks, Alaska, in January!

When Dr. Rice arrived, a literal path of red carpet was rolled out on the snowy airport runway. Pastor Hugh Hamilton and many of the Hamilton Acres Baptist Church members were there to greet him. So was Colonel Taylor, chief chaplain at the Air Force Base nearby. So was the television camera and a man with a tape recorder for an interview. The extended radio interview was put on a 50,000-watt station at the town, North Pole, fourteen miles away.

People were saying it had been a very mild winter—up until the fifty below when he arrived! Parkas—great, thick, quilted coats with hoods— were brought for him to wear.

The church—Southern Baptist—was one of the larger ones in Alaska.

But the pastor, greatly blessed and helped by THE SWORD OF THE LORD, began to put out copies for his people. Bit by bit they became dissatisfied with the liberal Sunday school literature and with the modernism in the Southern Baptist program; so the church took on its own missionary program and dropped all support of the Cooperative Program.

Both pastor and church gave Dr. Rice and THE SWORD credit for their coming out of the Southern Baptist Convention and more than doubling their attendance.

At the closing service, Dr. Rice was presented with a plaque reading:

WARRIOR-SOLDIER FAITHFULLY
CONTENDING FOR THE FAITH.

It had on it not only the presentation plate from Hamilton Acres Baptist Church but a gold-plated Alaskan totem pole and back of it an outlined map of Alaska.

† † †

In January a letter came from Moody Press:

Dear Dr. Rice:

We at Moody Press are proud to send you a copy of the Spanish version of your *Prayer—Asking and Receiving* in its new cover. We are happy at the way the Lord has used this book to bless the hearts of Spanish-speaking believers. We believe the new "package" will increase the outreach.

Sincerely in Christ,
Leslie H. Stobbe, Editor

This made the third Spanish printing. It had been translated and printed also—two printings in Denmark, one in Japan, one in the Ukranian language, and in a total of eight foreign languages, if I recall correctly.

† † †

In February Dr. Rice was for 23 days in Columbus, Georgia at the invitation of 22 independent Baptist churches in the Chattahoochie Valley Independent Baptist Association.

Ahead of time he had printed up 40,000 handbills, listing his sermon subjects for the first week. There had been large newspaper ads; he had been interviewed by two newspapers, had been on two television pro-

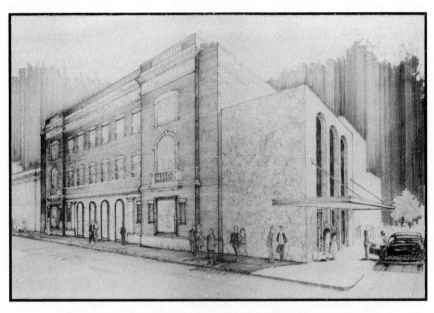

Twenty-two independent Baptist churches joined to invite Dr. Rice for a citywide campaign in Columbus, Georgia. Other churches cooperated. Auditorium seated 2,300.

grams, had spoken at the Lions' Club and three times at the Christian school.

A goodly number were saved—we do not find the final count.

Dr. Rice commented: "How dear to my heart are these citywide campaigns, but I cannot take time for many of them, thus cannot maintain an advance man and an evangelistic party such as I once had, and as is necessary for the best results."

† † †

After a long article on "Let Us Have Peace Among Fundamental, Bible-Believing, Soul-Winning Christians," Dr. Rice summed it all up:

It will be a sad day for America if fundamentalism—the fundamentalism of W. B. Riley, Bob Shuler, James M. Gray, H. A. Ironside, R. A. Torrey and Dr. Bob Jones, Sr.—if that fundamentalism should degenerate to a handful of bitter, sharp-tongued Christians fighting other Christians instead of fighting sin and Satan, modernism and communism.

It is my earnest belief that the great soul-winning churches and pastors in America—I mean fundamental men beyond any question, sound in the faith, premillennial, evangelistic, separated—are not going to go along with fighting, Hell-raising, character-assassination of other good Christians.

I ask Christians to join me in loving compassion toward those with whom we differ and for fellowship with brethren of like precious faith.

† † †

It "comes natural" for a Christian to be interested in music, for Christians have a built-in melody in the heart, you might say. In fact, we don't have a choice about it—we are commanded in Ephesians 5:18, "Speaking to yourselves in psalms and hymns and spiritual songs, singing and making melody in your heart to the Lord." We should have songs in the inside all the time, and songs coming out to bless others.

Dr. Rice was no Enrico Caruso, but God had put a song in his heart.

Early in 1972 he went to a recording studio in Atlanta and prepared an album in which he sang ten of his songs. His voice, after preaching fifty years, was not the best in the world, but the songs at least had rich Bible messages. And he had the assistance of daughters Grace and Elizabeth at the piano and organ, and a guest violinist. Then there were the background voices of Don and Jessie Sandberg, Joy and Roger Martin.

Songs were: "So Little Time," "Oh, Bring Your Loved Ones," "Jesus, Baby Jesus," "When Jesus Comes to Reign," "Oh, Heavy Hearted," "In the Morning," "Here Am I," "I'm Leaning on Jesus, "We'll Never Say Good-Bye," "His Yoke Is Easy."

The album is out of stock, but I hope you can learn some of his seventy songs, which are in *Soul-Stirring Songs and Hymns,* compiled in 1972 by John R. Rice.

† † †

To keep you up to date, in 1972, counting part-time workers, there were 49 on the staff—22 men and 27 women.

† † †

Some of our work was outright unpaid missionary work, which necessarily was supported by no income at all except the freewill offerings of God's people or whatever Dr. Rice could rake or scrape from his meetings and Sword Conferences.

Let me list these missionary causes for which we had raised and spent a quarter of a million dollars in 1971:

1. *Free Missionary Literature Fund.* For many years we supplied free literature to multiplied thousands around the world, as you have read about in previous chapters. This money came from the Free Literature Fund, if we had it to send.

2. *VOICE OF REVIVAL Radio Broadcast* (30 minutes, on 70 stations; some were 50,000-watt) existed only by the gifts of God's people.

3. *The Ministers' and Missionaries' Subscription Gift Fund.* To so many missionaries THE SWORD was a voice from home, a pastor to the pastorless, a comfort to the lonely, a constant inspiration to go out and win souls. Many had small incomes, so we provided them THE SWORD out of the M & M Fund.

Then most foreign countries would not allow their people to send out their currency; in such cases we provided THE SWORD free. At one time, 800 national pastors in Korea requested it. It was so in Japan, in Africa, in India, in the Philippines. Many could not pay the subscription price even if they could get the money out, so these, when possible, were sent a free subscription from this fund.

Sometimes retired ministers in America or shut-ins or men in prison—when they requested it—were sent THE SWORD from the M & M Fund.

Some churches had put the Sword of the Lord missionary causes in their budget. And many individuals were sending good offerings every month. A tax-deductible receipt was sent in each case, since this work is recognized by the government as a nonprofit corporation.

† † †

March was "Letter Month" at Sword of the Lord Foundation. In every issue we were urging readers to write a "thank-you" note to Dr. Rice for what he had meant to them.

I said in one article, "Don't Wait 'Til He's Dead":

> If Jesus tarries, you will read the headlines in *The Sword of the Lord,* "DR. RICE IS DEAD!" Yes, though he is now in remarkably good health and has the energy of a much younger man, yet his age of 76 reminds us that someday he will be going from us.
>
> When this startling headline comes out, many of you who never bothered to thank Dr. Rice for his blessing to your lives, will be desperately sorry that you did not thank him. Thousands who

have been saved from modernism or who have come to know Christ as Saviour under his ministry or who have been called to preach or who have otherwise had tremendous blessings from the Lord through Dr. Rice, have never written to tell him so.

In Matthew 23:27 through 32 Jesus warns the Pharisees that, though they honored the memories of the prophets who had been killed by former generations, they themselves were killing their own present-day prophets.

Charles Spurgeon, the great Baptist preacher of London, is honored and revered by Baptists today everywhere. But during his lifetime he was hated and persecuted by them in England because of his strong stand against modernism.

You hear almost no criticism of D. L. Moody's ministry now. But when he was alive, he was "Crazy Moody." Ugly and wicked letters were circulated against him by his enemies. But today nearly everyone loves and appreciates the man.

Everywhere Billy Sunday is now considered as one of the greatest preachers of a generation past. Even modernists recognize the tremendous impact his ministry had on America. But during his lifetime he often had to be protected by armed police escorts to and from his meetings because of his strong attack on sin.

We strongly believe another generation will rise up to bless the memory of Dr. Rice. The tremendous impact and worth of the books and pamphlets, distributed in over 37 million copies, will then be appreciated. The stand he has taken for the defense of the Faith and for earnest soul winning will someday be recognized by God's people. His sacrificial life will then come into true focus for millions. Though he is now misunderstood by many, someday he will be honored.

It may be that you have said to others a hundred times, "That John Rice! I just don't know what in the world we would do without him. He will never know what he has meant to me and to my family."

And—you are exactly right—he will never know unless you write to tell him!

Now is your opportunity to be grateful for what Dr. Rice is doing. Here is your chance to tell him so while he's living.

We hope he gets 20,000 letters during March. Will yours be one of them?

✝ ✝ ✝

In the first three weeks of Letter Month, we had gotten out 144,407 copies of *"What Must I Do to Be Saved?"* We hoped it would go a quarter of a million copies or 300,000 copies by the close of Letter Month. We will see!

† † †

1800 Plus Letters Some Days! When the final results were in, paper-wise, Letter Month may have been the greatest in our 38 years of existence! We ran over 1800 letters some days—and that's a batch of mail to read! Regularly three or four readers sorted the mail (Dr. John's and Dr. Bill's mail was not opened by the mail department); during Letter Month, the wives of some of our men on the staff were called in to help, and others who were available.

There were letters from the young and the old, the burdened and the blessed, those with suggestions and those with questions, those requesting prayer and those promising to pray.

When we looked at these stacks of letters which came daily, it was hard to realize all the love and gratitude and praise that had gone into writing them.

† † †

In 1970 it was mentioned how we had obligated ourselves for $141,570 in order to buy equipment for printing THE SWORD in Murfreesboro.

God's good people, in these one and a half years since, had already given to this project a total of $67,881.01. And the gifts were regularly coming in.

In the same spirit of gratefulness that prompted Paul to write the Philippians, we at the Sword of the Lord thanked God for those who, through faithful prayer and sending "once and again unto [our] necessity," made possible this great project.

As a Foundation dependent upon gifts of God's people and daily prayer, the tie that binds us to our readers is very close.

† † †

"What Must I Do to Be Saved?" had been printed in the Chinese Mandarin language. Rev. Arnulf Solvoll, who sent Dr. Rice one copy, said, "I have been able to translate and print 10,000 copies."

Then he explained the picture on front of a man landing on the moon: "The idea with the picture on the front is that man are able to get to the moon, but nobody are able by himself to get to Heaven" (using his

language). He then stated, "I am very happy that we now have them ready to put in the hands of thousands of Chinese."

† † †

Hearts were stirred with pity for the awful suffering in Bangladesh, devastated in a recent war with West Pakistan. The new nation was carved from what was once India and then a part of Pakistan. Some 75 million people were living in an area the size of Arkansas, and there were only 80 missionaries. We were told there were only some 35,000 Christians in the entire country.

Missionaries there wrote that they would distribute a million copies of *"What Must I Do to Be Saved?"* in the Bengali language if we could pay for the printing. Dr. Fred Jarvis thought it would cost $9,000 for a million copies, which was less than a penny each. He stated that their hungry hearts needed help and they were open to the Gospel. "With missionaries to carry on the work there and follow up the converts, that is about the least expensive way that anybody could get out the Gospel," Dr. Rice said.

So he committed the Sword for this amount.

† † †

Dr. Rice scribbled all the time! He was the most note-making man I ever saw! And I dared not throw any away. When I would clean off his desk and file some of them, the ones I filed were sure to be the ones he needed! So I would let them lie neatly in one pile on his desk until I was sure they were too old; then I would file them away for posterity—in a file drawer or in the wastebasket!

Once I found a poem entitled "To Jessie." Jessie Ruth (Mrs. Don Sandberg) was his third daughter, his artist, singer and a teacher then at Tennessee Temple Schools. I didn't know when he wrote it to her, nor what the occasion was. Sometimes when he sent Valentines to his six daughters, he would write a poem to each.

At that time I asked him if I could quote this one in my column.

TO JESSIE

Fly away on the wings of plane and train,
Fly away with my love and prayers,
To the woman-child of my heart and brain,
Of my dreams and plans we have shared.
Oh, a sweetheart's love may become a pain
And a husband's heart, though true,
May be Friend, Companion, Protector and Guide
When the fragrance and thrill are through.
Now a father's love is a steady love,
Without fire and passion and pain,
But the little-girl heart isn't grown in his sight,
And he loves but to give, not to gain.
Oh, the years take their toll of the daughter's face,
And the family cares mar her hands;
But the father still cheers to the artist heart,
And years cannot loose the bands.
So here's to the girl with the golden voice
And compassionate heart and purse,
Who pours out to all of her gifted mind
From her father's heart and hers.

—Dad

† † †

Dr. Rice had been in the Holy Land with 68 wonderful people, and it had been a blessed experience for our "pilgrims" all along the way. But he—bless him—was itching to get home. "Oh, speed the hours!" he exclaimed. "I am panting to be home. For one thing, I have a holy interest, a consuming concern about the subscription campaign, about future copy for THE SWORD, about great conferences. I have felt in these days, perhaps more than ever before, how my life is wrapped up in THE SWORD OF THE LORD. Thank God for the burden of it, the privilege of it, the amazing open door to hundreds of thousands through it! Thank God for the impact on tens of thousands of preachers, for its influence on stimulating the crowd of great soul-winning churches; for its defense of the Faith, for its calling out hundreds, even thousands, of young men to preach the Gospel and train in Christian schools."

His thoughts, plans, burden were ever on the paper.

Later he mentions this again: "Some time ago when I was on a tour of Bible lands I felt so desolate to be far from my SWORD readers, and I thought, *How could I ever be happy if I did not have THE SWORD OF THE LORD to pray for and all of you potential friends, all you Christians for whom I am somewhat responsible, to look after!*"

But no sooner was he back in Murfreesboro from the tour than he was off again to Denver, Colorado; Marion, Ohio; Pittsburgh, Pennsylvania; Pontiac, Michigan; then Amarillo, Texas; Claremont, California; and Hampton, Virginia!

Did you ever wonder how he could do all he did and still go as much as he went. His sacrifice was because of his love for God and preachers he was reaching in conferences week in and week out.

But when Dr. Rice was home, amid such heavy duties he usually took time for a brief walk out to the barn if only to pet Prince Charley and Jean and Flicka's sorrel yearling colt and Cleopatra the donkey and her yearling baby, Elmer. Often he would saddle up MacArthur for a few moments' ride around the pasture to check on the cows. To do that was a tonic to him.

† † †

How grateful we were for some 36,000 subscriptions in the subscription campaign which closed in June. An editorial note in THE SWORD welcomed the "newcomers" to the SWORD family.

† † †

After writing an article, "Southern Baptist Convention Approves Liberal Commentary," he predicted that he would receive many bitter comments, many slanderous charges, and be accused of the basest motives.

"We know from experience that there will be a variety of responses, some bigoted, some wholly unchristian, some in shocked unbelief, but some in earnest gratitude for the truth presented."

Dr. Rice went on to say:

> There is no intolerance like religious intolerance, no bigotry like religious bigotry. There have been few mass murders like St. Bartholomew's murder of Protestants by the Catholics. There have been no systematic persecutions of Christians like the Spanish Inquisition, like the burning at the stake, the beheading

and torture of Christians by Catholics. And Protestants themselves have not always been blameless.

And it must be remembered that persecution by Catholics was not usually against those who doubted Bible doctrine. Rather, it was on those who defied the Catholic church or who would not accept its dictums as the will of God nor its officers as God's appointed rulers.

So there are many Southern Baptists who will never speak ungraciously about a man who denies the deity and virgin birth of Christ, the inspiration of the Bible; but one who threatens the Baptist program or threatens the authority of the leaders, so stirs that men who are otherwise normally sensible, fair and compassionate, become angry and blinded and do wicked things they would not do in other situations.

There is no idolatry like denominational idolatry!

† † †

Dr. Bud Lyles, our radio assistant, wrote a note to Dr. Rice, after attending the Sword Conference at the Bill Rice Ranch:

> In the thirteen years I have been associated with you and this ministry, I have attended many, many Sword Conferences. But the one at the Ranch last week was by far the greatest I have ever seen there, and probably the greatest I have ever attended.
>
> I thought Dr. Roberson had a fresh touch from the Lord and got the conference off to a flying start. Dr. Bill surely rang the bell on Tuesday afternoon. The program and preaching on Thursday would have been a high point in any conference anywhere in the world. But in my opinion, it lifted this conference out of this world....
>
> When Dr. Hyles spoke Thursday on "Anointing With Fresh Oil," what a blessing to see one man run down the aisle, fall on his face and weep out to God.

Dr. Bud's expression was mine also.

We had the largest attendance at a Sword Conference we had had at the Ranch. Many had to stay in local motels. Scores were new people. And many vowed they would return again and again!

After hundreds of Sword Conferences over the years, you would think they would become routine. Not so. It seemed they got better each year!

† † †

Christian booksellers from all over America and beyond, and principal publishers and suppliers for these bookstores, gathered this year—July 30-August 3—at Cincinnati. Among the publishers with booths displaying their wares was always the Sword of the Lord.

There were all kinds of seminars on the affairs of Christian bookstores and getting out the Gospel. Dr. Rice was the devotional speaker Monday through Thursday from 7:30 to 8:30 a.m. He felt it a tremendous privilege. And of the more than 2,000 registered, perhaps a thousand gathered for that time of devotion.

Then in the Sword booth, he was on hand to autograph some 500 copies of his newest publication, *A Christian's Wells of Joy,* which he was giving to book dealers.

Ethel Waters was there and sang so well at age 76. Dr. Rice commented: "She sang several songs, including her favorite, 'His Eye Is on the Sparrow.' She took that song of trust apart, wept over the pieces, kissed them, laughed, then put them back together. Although her golden voice quavered a bit on the high notes, her love for Christ, her enjoyment of testimony wavered not a bit."

† † †

Dr. Rice mused while the fire burned:

> In reading over the accounts of God's blessings for several years through the Sword of the Lord, I was reminded of when two teachers in Southwestern Baptist Seminary of Ft. Worth, along with the pastor of the Gambrell Street Church, came to warn me that leaders had planned to have the county Baptist association censure me, have it published in the *Baptist Standard,* have the doors closed to me for revival work in all Southern Baptist churches, so that, they said, I "would never have another revival in a Southern Baptist church—" simply because I kept speaking out against the evolution taught in Baylor University, where I had graduated.
>
> God wonderfully answered. Many Southern Baptists were not willing to go along with their plan; so doors continued to open to me to preach the Gospel.
>
> But more than that; I now found God leading me to great independent citywide campaigns. He used my poor efforts to organize new independent Baptist churches with the hundreds who came out of my big campaigns in Decatur, Sherman, Bridgeport, Bowie, Wichita Falls, Dallas and elsewhere in Texas.
>
> Then I remembered the wonderful blessings of God in the

Galilean Baptist Church in Dallas. In the midst of the Depression and starting within two blocks of a great Southern Baptist church with 3,000 in attendance, God helped us build a church, pay cash for the lot and all the building material, and see many thousands saved. In one six-month period we had a record of 1,005 professions of faith.

I read again accounts of the time when Dr. J. Frank Norris set out to block a revival campaign in a church in Binghamton, New York and elsewhere, and how, instead of blocking it, the campaign expanded to a great citywide meeting. More and more doors were opening, and I had calls for citywide campaigns in Buffalo, Cleveland, Miami, Chicago, Seattle, Winston-Salem, Oakland and elsewhere.

I read again what a struggle we had starting a new paper and the burdens of keeping it going and getting subscriptions.

How I praise God for the nearly 200,000 homes that now get THE SWORD OF THE LORD each week!

I can only say that God has cared for my needs, has opened doors and has raised up friends. I have much evidence that He has greater things to do for us in the future.

Thank Him for the more than 15,000 who have written to tell us they were saved through my printed sermons in English, aside from tens of thousands saved in foreign countries through my foreign language editions of booklets and other thousands in my revivals.

† † †

In October he was announcing expansion plans:

Goal 1: 250,000 paid subscribers;

Goal 2: 1,000 churches undertaking to get THE SWORD to every resident family in the church;

Goal 3: 500 churches attempting to win and baptize at least 200 converts in a year;

Goal 4: 10,000 families reporting having daily family Bible reading and prayer together;

Goal 5: $250,000 in gifts for the various Sword missionary projects.

† † †

THE LORD MET US HERE! Weeks and weeks of planning, praying and working yielded the desired harvest when pastors, bus workers and Christian laymen from thirty states and Canada streamed into Murfreesboro for our 38th Anniversary Conference.

Original plans for a Busmen's Banquet, September 27, with a maximum seating arrangement for 150, had to be revised and a second banquet hall rented and staffed to take care of the 344 people making reservations.

Jim Vineyard, bus director of the First Baptist Church, Hammond, spoke at both banquets.[1]

Our Sword auditorium was filled, and extra chairs had to be brought in. The crowd continued to grow, with more chairs being put out for each service. Starting Wednesday evening at 6:45 with Dr. Rice speaking, and closing Friday evening with Dr. Jerry Falwell—a total of twelve services in the auditorium—the crowd averaged well over 800 per service, with an estimated 300 preachers attending.

Fully one-half of the audience had never been to a Sword Conference before, and many had never seen Dr. Rice nor Dr. Hyles.

Dr. Falwell surprised Dr. Rice in the final service as he challenged those present to give toward the expansion program before Christmas. Many responded with gifts and pledges totaling over $11,000.

Dr. Rice was saying that we would have to add a great balcony or get a larger auditorium for our conferences in Murfreesboro, adding, "Look for plans for next spring and next fall."

† † †

Encouraged by many Christian leaders, the Sword reprinted the large 590-page memorial edition of the *Life of D. L. Moody* by his son. Tens of thousands of copies were printed after Moody's death some seventy years before. Then it was no longer available. In secondhand bookstores all over America people had bought up used and worn copies.

It may well be the most read and most loved biography in the English language.

† † †

During 1972, Dr. Rice and Dr. Hyles held 28 Sword Conferences across America, always stressing: how to win souls; how to get your prayers answered; how to have Holy Spirit power; how to have a visitation program; how to build soul-winning churches.

As a result, thousands of pastors made a new start, got a new vision,

---

[1] A few weeks later our banquet speaker, Jim Vineyard, wrote, "Rejoice with us—we have averaged 4,256 on the buses for the month of October, using 113 buses."

adopted new methods and, above all, put soul winning first in their ministries.

Dr. Hyles estimated that, in these many conferences, they reached some 10,000 preachers a year.

Here in Murfreesboro we planned two big conferences a year in the Sword auditorium—one in the spring and one at anniversary time in September.

† † †

Dr. and Mrs. Rice and I were the guests of Rev. and Mrs. Bob Ware in Orlando, Florida a week before Christmas. Dr. Rice was to speak at Tabernacle Baptist Church on Sunday, and we were asked to come early for a visit to Disney World.

It was well worth our time. Since that was eighteen years ago, many other attractions have been added, but we were elated over what we saw then.

You probably have your favorites, but ours were:

COUNTRY BEAR JAMBOREE, a hilarious cast of wilderness bears performing in a foot-stompin' western hoedown, with duets, quartets, solos, etc.

THE HALL OF THE PRESIDENTS was simply miraculous. All thirty-six American Presidents "came to life" on stage in a dramatic show about our nation's founding and its great leaders. The most realistic "people"—our Presidents—are right there on stage. A spotlight flashed on each as he was introduced, and these life-size Presidents actually turned toward the one being introduced, twiddled their thumbs, moved their limbs—words cannot describe this wonderful attraction.

THE HAUNTED MANSION, where we came face to face with 999 happy ghosts, ghouls and goblins in a "frightfully funny" adventure. Seats moved us about, ghosts sat with us and screamed (so did the people)!

20,000 LEAGUES UNDER THE SEA saw us sailing with "Captain Nemo" aboard the "Nautilus" to lost undersea worlds.

On and on we walked, saw and laughed.

One of the greatest attractions was AMERICA THE BEAUTIFUL— when the scenic wonders of America surround you in exciting 360-degree Circle-Vision. Hundreds of us, standing in a round room, were riding in the fire engine as the sirens blew, and we turned corners on the way to the fire. We rode down the trolley car in San Francisco; flew with the pilots over our beautiful nation; visited Mount Vernon; saw the Statue of Liberty, the Capitol, Lincoln's home and his tomb, and many other beautiful spots in our great land.

Those were the five attractions we enjoyed the most.

We had been to Disneyland in Anaheim, California, but to us, Disney World was much more interesting.

Oh, yes, Dr. Rice rode the Merry-Go-Round! And Brother Ware had him pose for a silhouette portrait which he planned to hang in his office at the church.

Mrs. Rice and I flew home, leaving Dr. Rice to go on to his next engagement.

Immediately I drove to Dallas—713 miles—in one day. After such a long drive, I could barely walk.

This caused me to have an exciting experience—two appointments with an acupuncturist. Each visit was an hour and a half. The first saw me with thirty-three needles in all parts of my body; the second, many more—I didn't ask the doctor this time the number. Don't judge me too quickly: one will try anything for some relief.

And it just may be that their treatment—as old as the Chinese—works. It did for me. I got up from the second appointment, walked straight to my car and drove home—in two days this time, stopping occasionally to stretch, but no pain and no trouble this time.

† † †

In the early days of America's western history, when every man carried his law and order on his hip, it was a common sight to see the town marshal nailing up "WANTED" posters with the butt of his six-shooter. When the crime was severe enough—such as horse steal-ing, cattle rustling or murder—the poster would read, "WANTED, DEAD OR ALIVE!"

We were always nailing up our "WANTED" poster, but unlike the posters of yesteryear, we wanted our subjects ALIVE! Instead of horse thieves, cattle rustlers and murderers, we wanted SWORD SUBSCRIB-ERS! We wanted our readers to be the town marshal in their commu-nity and round up the names and addresses of good Christians and bad sinners and see that they got THE SWORD OF THE LORD.

Getting subscriptions was foremost on the mind of Dr. Rice and his staff. His appeals and those of his assistants were so inviting that we were able to 'round up' thousands of subscriptions every subscription campaign.

† † †

I have been reading some about this great prayer-warrior George Mueller. Oh, how the Lord must have loved him! Not only was he a preacher of the Gospel, but he ran an orphans' home.

I saw a comparison!

During Mueller's lifetime, it was a day-by-day faith for food. A former orphan wrote, "I was in schools Nos. 2 and 3 eight years. When someone asked me if we were ever short of food while there, I said, 'Never one meal was missing; neither did we think there would be, for we know in whom we trusted.'"

The orphans were not told when supplies appeared to be failing; never-theless, they knew that everything they ate, wore and used, came in answer to prayer, and they were well able to believe God would supply all their needs.

When he was 91, Mueller recorded that he had read through the Bible considerably more than a hundred times.

Unlike C. H. Spurgeon, his friend and contemporary, Mueller was no orator. It was his great spiritual power that carried his message to hearts. Spurgeon himself, referring to one of Mueller's addresses, said, "There was nothing particular in it. The diction and structure of the discourse were not above the average Sunday school teacher. *But there was the man behind it.*"

Mueller estimated that at least 30,000 of his prayers had been an-swered on the very day, even in the very hour, in which they were made.

In the five orphan houses at the time of Mueller's death, there were 2,050 orphans.

Perhaps the most impressive tribute to him was the manifest grief of the orphans. In the funeral sermon, his son-in-law referred to "those dear fatherless and motherless children who, when I faced them this morning at nine o'clock, so filled the air with their sobs that I scarcely knew when I should begin." And when hundreds of the older orphans walked in the funeral procession, so many were observed to be still in tears that even strong men were affected by the sight.

At age 93 he died. Before his death one of his friends said to him, "When God calls you Home, beloved Mr. Mueller, it will be like a ship going into harbor full sail."

There's a similarity there.

Dr. Rice's spiritual children—myriads of them—loved him so dearly. They too were fed weekly with manna from Heaven through his work.

And it was day-by-day faith that kept the Sword and the employees knowing God could and would do great things in time of crisis.

And, oh, how many answers he got directly to so many prayers! God supplied money and paper for THE SWORD and books the very day they were prayed for—and needed, even during a great paper shortage. And all knew that God had sent what was needed, and when it was needed.

I am sure Dr. Rice read through the Bible scores of times, and he knew by heart literally hundreds of verses.

It was the Holy Spirit's power on his ministry that made it so he could accomplish so much in eighty-five years.

And what a void he left when he took off for Heaven! Literally the whole world mourned his passing.

And what a grand Homecoming he must have had, when thousands who had gone before, met him at the Gate to welcome him in!

And there will never be another like him.

† † †

By the second week in December, the subscription list had grown to 247,000—and still coming in. He and the staff were earnestly praying for 250,000 by the first of January.

† † †

Five hundred forty-two people wrote in 1972 that they were saved

through THE SWORD and the literature. That is, of course, in the English edition and does not count the thousands who claimed Christ in foreign countries.

1973   Dr. Rice was rejoicing that he was to have two full weeks and a day at home! But not wanting to be misunderstood, he explained:

I do not complain about travel, travel, travel, waiting in airline terminals...carrying heavy suitcases...selling subscriptions...announcing the books...living in motels...packing up the books to ship home...going, going, going all the time. I do not complain that when I get home there is always more work than I can get done...more letters than I can answer...pressure for getting copy ready for THE SWORD...radio broadcasts to make. But I do rejoice in having two weeks here. I am sure the Lord wants me to rejoice in the fellowship of my family and workers.

† † †

One after another Southern Baptist Convention pastors were writing that they and their churches were leaving the Convention and becoming independent since they could no longer support the Cooperative Program nor use the Southern Baptist Sunday School literature. Many were saying they could not conscientiously lend their support to the Convention because it supported liberalism, modernism and unscriptural issues, as Dr. Rice had proven in articles being run in THE SWORD.

† † †

The January 12th issue announced that 263,513 SWORDs were going out that week to every state in the Union, to every province in Canada, and to more than ninety foreign countries. But Dr. Rice reminded himself that, "every time we get a bunch of subscriptions in a big drive, it all has to be done over in a year. We must get renewals for all of them." He went on to explain:

In a local church, when a person is saved and baptized, it is not necessary to get him to renew his membership at the end of every year. The member remains on roll until he moves, passes away or joins another church.

Here at the Sword of the Lord each subscription expires at the end of the term (unless they are automatic renewal subscribers), and it is imperative to get each subscription renewed.

† † †

The New Life College in Benares, India, was training full-time workers to win souls in the closed lands of Bhutan, Nepal and Afghanistan. Nationals of India could go into these countries, and they had asked for books for their library, which Dr. Rice sent, grateful for another open door to get out the Gospel.

† † †

Dr. Rice was lamenting that he hadn't written a song in more than a year. "Oh, for a fresh anointing for this!"

† † †

Word came from Beirut that some 500 Moslems had been converted through Sword literature which was being spread in the Arabic language through our gifts to Rev. Victor Sadaka and the Mideast Baptist Mission there.

† † †

A check for $10,000 was mailed to Bangladesh for printing a million copies of *"What Must I Do to Be Saved?"* there. The literature fund didn't have enough in hand for that, but we made it up temporarily so the literature could get out.

† † †

Before, we mentioned the Italian translation of his *Religious But Lost* booklet. Now we learned: "After a test mailing to a good many priests, missionaries in Italy found that Catholic priests may be won to Christ through the Italian translation of your booklet. We want to print and mail it to every Catholic priest in Italy: it will cost some $2,500."

His booklets were being used mightily in foreign lands. For one thing, they were thorough. For another, missionaries trusted Dr. Rice and knew his teaching was sound.

Had the Sword been financially able, I am sure thousands more could have been won to Christ through the widely-spread *"What Must I Do to Be Saved?"* which, we suppose, has been used of God to win more people than any other gospel tract.

† † †

In February Dr. Rice had just returned from a meeting in Sherman,

Texas. He was used of God to organize Central Baptist Church there in a big revival in 1931. Now he reported "that more than thirty people were present who had attended that campaign 42 years ago and most

of them were saved and baptized in that meeting. The Sunday school
is running some 550 in attendance now."

He went on to say: "Last night in the Ramada Inn restaurant at Sherman a waitress approached me to remind me that she was saved and
baptized by me when she was twelve. Another man came to say he was
saved listening to Voice of Revival broadcast as he drove his truck from
Oklahoma City. A woman came over to my table to report that she was
saved through my sermon-tract, 'What Must I Do to Be Saved?' All this
while I was trying to eat my evening meal!"

But I am sure he was delighted to be interrupted to hear such
good news!

† † †

We were having spring and September (Anniversary) Sword Conferences in our own opera-seated auditorium in Murfreesboro.

The building was crowded with people from many states. When we
later had to remove so many seats for offices, we could still invite our
friends to Murfreesboro "to see our plant in operation," if they came
to our Sword Conference at the Bill Rice Ranch, nine miles west of us.

This year's speakers there were: Dr. Wally Beebe, Dr. Curtis Hutson,
Dr. Jerry Falwell and Dr. John R. Rice.

DR. CURTIS HUTSON: In telling about Dr. Hutson's work, Dr. Rice
related this incident:

> A preacher walked into Dr. Hutson's new 2500-seat auditorium
> and remarked, "I'd hate to be responsible for filling this church—
> you'll never do it!" Dr. Hutson grinned and replied, "When a
> farmer builds a barn, he builds according to the crop he expects
> to harvest. I know how much sowing has been done around here."
>
> (At the time they were having some 2300 in attendance each
> Sunday morning.)

Dr. Rice had both ears open when this preacher spoke, thinking God
might have even greater things planned for his future. He liked it when
he said, "I feel that this generation of saints is going to answer to God
for this generation of sinners. We cannot answer for those who lived
before our time, but we will certainly answer for those whom we now
see and pass every day." He knew Dr. Hutson had a soul-winning heart,
and that was so necessary for the work at the Sword.

DR. FALWELL: When Dr. Falwell was once asked why his church

was so successful, he answered, "God honored a combination of faith-fulness to His Word, continuous dependence upon prayer, and hard work. We have prayed as though everything depended upon God; and we have preached, visited and worked as though everything depended upon us."

(On their sixteenth anniversary in June, 1972, 19,020 people gathered to thank the Lord for sixteen years of blessings at Thomas Road Baptist Church, Lynchburg, Virginia.)

DR. WALLY BEEBE, better known as "Mr. Bus," started and revitalized bus ministries all over this country—at Trinity Baptist Church, Jacksonville, Florida; at Thomas Road Baptist Church, Lynchburg, Virginia; at First Baptist Church, Hammond, Indiana; and he set up his simple system in other churches having anywhere from 40 to 3,000 in Sunday school.

(Jim Vineyard had been the Bus Banquet speaker in 1972; this year it was to be Dr. Beebe.)

And Dr. John R. Rice, the "Captain of Our Team," was to M.C. the banquet and speak several times during the conference. No Sword Conference was ever complete without him. We think his messages got better and better as the years went by. Many people drove from all over America to be in a service where Dr. Rice was preaching.

✝ ✝ ✝

Needless to say, I was thrilled when I received this letter from my Boss:

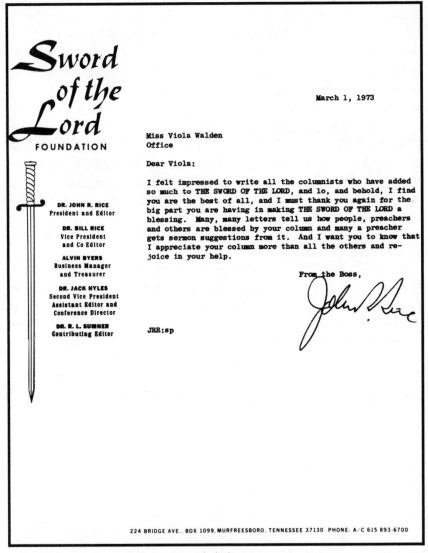

Sword of the Lord
FOUNDATION

DR. JOHN R. RICE
President and Editor

DR. BILL RICE
Vice President
and Co-Editor

ALVIN BYERS
Business Manager
and Treasurer

DR. JACK HYLES
Second Vice President
Assistant Editor and
Conference Director

DR. R. L. SUMNER
Contributing Editor

March 1, 1973

Miss Viola Walden
Office

Dear Viola:

I felt impressed to write all the columnists who have added so much to THE SWORD OF THE LORD, and lo, and behold, I find you are the best of all, and I must thank you again for the big part you are having in making THE SWORD OF THE LORD a blessing. Many, many letters tell us how people, preachers and others are blessed by your column and many a preacher gets sermon suggestions from it. And I want you to know that I appreciate your column more than all the others and rejoice in your help.

From the Boss,

John R. Rice

JRR:sp

224 BRIDGE AVE., BOX 1099, MURFREESBORO, TENNESSEE 37130 PHONE: A/C 615 893-6700

† † †

Dr. Rice was always elated when he could spend a few days at home—not to rest but to work. On this particular day, the first of eight he would spend in Murfreesboro, he wrote:

> I rode MacArthur. Then dinner at home. I came back to the office for three hours of hard work—research and writing. Most

people who do not edit a paper would have no idea how much work is involved. How many times last night I consulted the Encyclopedia Britannica, the World Almanac, the big book by Bruce Catton on the Civil War, *This Hallowed Ground,* and the Bible, in preparing a message. Hours alone, time to study, meditate, make notes, look up facts and figures and wait on God—these are essential to the best kind of writing.

Then his editorial recalled how Christmas Evans, traveling one Sunday on a lonely road to attend an appointment, was convicted of a cold heart and said:

I tethered my horse and went to a sequestered spot, where I walked to and fro in an agony as I reviewed my life. I waited for three hours before God, broken with sorrow, until there broke over me a sweet sense of His forgiving love. Then I received from God a new baptism with the Holy Ghost.

As the sun was westering, I went back to the road, found my horse, mounted it and went to my appointment. I preached with such new power to a vast concourse of people gathered on the hillside, that a revival broke out that day and spread through all Wales.

Dr. Rice commented:

This is what all of us need and must have—a fresh anointing for any work we do for God, whether it be preaching or writing.

After these few days at home, I found, along with the refreshing of body, a new zeal, a new fervency, to get out the Word of God! Oh, may God keep the fountain flowing! How sad if I should become so occupied with the work that the freshness was gone in my enjoyment of the Lord, if the lilt was gone from my song, if the work ever got to be prosaic and dull!

† † †

A goal of 300,000 SWORD weekly circulation was announced by January, 1974; but we were now asking for 50,000 subscribers in the March-April 10-Club Subscription Campaign.

† † †

During Letter Month an amazing amount of mail was received—3,800 pieces one day, 2,600 pieces another, causing the staffers to get behind on mailing out books, thanking givers and answering questions. For this, Dr. Rice apologized to his readers. Even though at times we were running three shifts and trying to catch up, we were still behind. Funny—but that was a good feeling! This meant we were having contact with you, our readers.

† † †

He had arrived in his office about 10:00 a.m. from a conference in Springfield, Missouri. No sooner had he gotten seated at his desk when the long distance calls started coming, asking for him. We were trying to serve him coffee and a roll; of course the coffee got cold. I was a little fretted. "How come people from all over the country know when he steps in his office!" But then I realized, after two or three calls, that they were needing help desperately and had no one else to counsel with.

One was from a pastor wanting a Sword Conference; another, a woman from a distant state disturbed about her salvation; another was a local call. Scores regularly looked to him for help. And Dr. Rice never turned down an opportunity to help one in need.

And no matter how pressing his duties, when visitors dropped in at the Sword of the Lord, he showed them every courtesy. I cannot recall anyone's coming to the office and desiring to meet him who was told he was too busy.

This was also true of his staff. His door—to his office and heart—was always open. If Al or Ron or Scottie or Miss Fairy or Bud needed to see him five or ten minutes before he had to leave to catch a plane, he never said he was too rushed. As a result, many times I had to go to the airport to finish the last bit of work necessary before he caught that flight.

God bless his memory!

† † †

His analytical mind had figured that in one recent week the printing of THE SWORD OF THE LORD took 102 miles of paper—enough to run from Murfreesboro to Chattanooga! How we needed more storage and office space!

The Board of Directors of Sword of the Lord Foundation gathered together. Here we were—with the great blessing of God upon us—yet nowhere to turn, with an increased staff, no place for storage of paper needed to take care of the increased circulation, no storage for paper for books whose sales had tripled in recent months. Lord, what shall we do? You have blessed us so mightily; now what will we do about these blessings?

THE SWORD had 87,000 subscriptions when we moved to Murfreesboro eleven years before; there were close to 300,000 in 1973. Volume of sales was then about $60,000; the first six months of 1973 we had sold in both retail and wholesale $198,642.94. There were thirty-one workers eleven years ago; now the staff numbered eighty-two.

By the Sword's fortieth anniversary (September, 1974) we hoped to be running 350,000 circulation; then the goal was 500,000.

Our Stewardship Department was in a rented building on Highway 41, then more recently had moved to a property adjoining the Sword. Another department was housed in a temporary trailer in back of a rented house. The tons of paper used constantly for the increased circulation were crowding out the already crowded basement. Some was being stored in a warehouse in town.

Now we must decide how best to take care of this emergency.

The Sword president called in an architect, who readily saw the crowded condition and began working on plans. Some of the parking area east of the present building could be used for a two-story-and-basement administration building.

The architect said glass would be no more expensive than brick and would give so much more light. After altering the plans here and there, it was finally decided what would best suit our urgent need.

Builder Gordon Lynch, a fine Christian who had helped build the existing plant, estimated the cost to be some $306,000.

The artist's drawing of the new Administration Building, to be added on the east side of the present auditorium.

Dr. Rice commented: "By faith we want to look at the opportunities rather than at the difficulties. We don't know where we will get $306,000 for His building but, with Caleb and Joshua, we will look at the opportunities, not at the difficulties."

† † †

After reading an article in THE SWORD on the second coming, the rapture became so real to one dear lady that she began putting water out for her dog at night in case the Lord should come! And she was concerned about her unsaved husband and asked Dr. Rice if she should stock up groceries for him to have after she was gone!

Is His coming that real to you?

† † †

We checked once and discovered that, if all the sermons printed in a year's issue of THE SWORD OF THE LORD were available in book form, it would cost over $80 for the book.

† † †

In April Mr. Elmer Klassen wrote from Germany that *Prayer—Asking and Receiving* had just been printed in Dutch. "It will be offered to readers [of this paper in Germany] in April, and I anticipate a good response."

He also reported that "another printing of 100,000 *'What Must I Do to Be Saved?'* has been done in German and we are doing another translation and printing in Dutch."

† † †

Dr. Rice was never content to ask for just 10,000 or 20,000 or 25,000 subscriptions. With little faith, we on the staff might suggest one of those figures, but he was always striving for that 50,000 mark during a campaign!

Here again a campaign was on in April, and you can see the high mark (opposite page).

This time the offer was 10 subscriptions for $20. Remember, that was seventeen years ago. Dr. Rice was showing that "for $20 you can buy one pretty new dress for your wife; or one medium-priced pair of men's shoes; or one pair of dress slacks, OR 10 YEARLY SUBSCRIPTIONS TO THE SWORD!"

Then he asked, "What will happen to the lives of those to whom you send gift subscriptions? How many will be saved? How many will be strengthened spiritually? How many will become soul winners? How many will surrender to full-time Christian service, to preach, to go to the mission field, or attend some good Christian college for further training?

"We do not know, but you have a responsibility to reach as many as possible while there is still time. Be a SWORD missionary by sending subscriptions."

From the time he put to press the first issue of THE SWORD until his death, each issue burned with his commitment and concern for the dear readers of THE SWORD. Every letter he dictated, every sermon he preached, every article he wrote, was geared to this thought: "How can I use the material to help my Christian friends and the unsaved who might read it?"

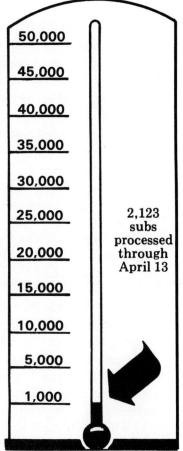

2,123 subs processed through April 13

† † †

In April we had just returned—124 of us—from the Sword Holy Land Tour.

This year an unusual number of preachers were on the tour. One of the sweetest incidents was on the last Sunday, when our own Rev. Ron English preached at the Bible Baptist Church at Jerusalem. A number on the tour went to hear him, while others went on to Masada.

One woman held up her hand for prayer. After Ron had made the way very plain, she came forward at the invitation to claim the Lord.

Then a wonderful story came out.

This Lutheran from Wisconsin was hungry-hearted and wanting to get saved. She thought if she could go on a tour of Bible lands with some good Christians, perhaps she would find the way of salvation. After considering other tours, a Catholic neighbor, who subscribed to THE

SWORD OF THE LORD, told her about Sword Tours and said, "Why don't you go with Dr. John Rice?"

This lost Lutheran woman sent in her payment.

Her hungry heart was waiting. That Sunday morning she got her soul secured, her salvation settled, and how excited she was when she came to tell us about it!

When she got saved, she wept for joy. But then she asked Mrs. Rice rather anxiously, "Do people cry when they get saved?"

A day or two later she said to Dr. Rice, "In the Bible it says, 'Seek, and ye shall find,' and I sought and I found!"

What a blessed memory she will always have of this Sword Tour of Bible Lands!

Isn't it wonderful that God used a Catholic woman who took THE SWORD OF THE LORD to bring an unsaved Lutheran woman into this tour so she could find the Lord!

Another sweet incident happened in Rome.

One of the places to see was the famous Church of St. John the Lateran. We especially wanted our pilgrims to get a glimpse of the tremendous Statue of Moses sculptured by Michelangelo.

After crowds had dispersed and we could see it close up with the lights focused on the statue, Pete Rice drew our Italian guide aside and talked to her about the Lord. Soon she saw her need and turned to trust the Saviour. Later she went to tell Dr. Rice what she had done.

Oh, everywhere there were hungry hearts!

Other incidents happened on this particular tour.

Up on Mount Tabor, in the Plain of Megiddo, a Catholic monk, "Father Joseph," met us warmly, as he had done in the past. He plays the organ and sings beautifully. And each year he looked forward to our coming and always sang for us. He embraced Dr. Rice and kissed him on each cheek, so glad was he to see him.

He had told us before that he loved the Lord and liked to sing the old hymns. This dear monk especially liked our "old-fashioned" group who loved the old hymns also. He thought Sword Tours was very clearly different from other groups, even other religious tours, because we dressed modestly and looked and talked like Christians. God bless this sweet Catholic monk!

One of the three bus drivers said to me, "None of your people smoke, do they?" He was glad none did, for after a great struggle, he had given up cigarettes.

As we started the morning tour each day, the captain of each bus (45 to a bus; several years it took four buses for Sword Tours) always had prayer and usually sang a chorus or a verse of a song. This impressed those drivers and those guides.

Sword Tours was well respected in every country. After seventeen tours, people looked forward to our coming at the hotels, in the restaurants, in the shops, as well as the guides and bus drivers, whom we came to know and love so well.

† † †

This year Dr. Rice employed someone to head up the newly established Stewardship Department. In connection with the Stewardship Department, the John R. Rice Associates was founded.

During the National Sword of the Lord Conference on Revival and Soul Winning at Cobo Hall in Detroit, Dr. Rice preached a sermon on the new birth, which was later televised nationwide. It was the John R. Rice Associates who paid these bills.

Through the years this special group of friends have helped to pay for such projects as the new Administration Building and offering THE SWORD OF THE LORD through national magazines, such as *Reader's Digest, Saturday Evening Post* and *Grit.* Thousands found Christ through the gospel presentation on television and in print through the magazines, and scores of others were dealt with by our office staff when the calls came in on our special telephone hookup.

Today the John R. Rice Associates help give THE SWORD OF THE LORD to people around the world. Since Dr. Rice's Homegoing, money given by John R. Rice Associates goes into our special gift fund, which Dr. Rice called the Ministers and Missionaries Fund. Thousands of subscriptions to THE SWORD OF THE LORD have been given to people around the world from this special fund.

† † †

Y'ALL COME AND BRING THE FAMILY! Y'all come and ride with us during the July Sword Family Conference at the Bill Rice Ranch. The beautiful 1,500-acre Ranch includes a portion of the old Natchez Trace. Come saddle up! You might ride Golden Chain, Sunburst, Red Flame or any one of the 100 other horses stabled there. It's a ride through history as you make your way down through Sunshine Valley to Altar Mountain; take a look at the grave of a Civil War Confederate soldier;

and enjoy the Cowboy Cookout Breakfast at the chuck wagon. From the hearty breakfast at 6:30 a.m. to the last "Amen," we promise you a thrilling time.

That's the way we began advertising for Sword Family Week at the Ranch in Murfreesboro in 1973. And we roped in a "full house," as usual.

† † †

It pleased me to read again a letter from Dr. Wally Beebe, a tremendous friend to the John R. Rice family and to me personally. I now serve on his board, Beebe Evangelistic Association, which makes me proud.

His letter is long, so I cannot quote it all but highlight the main points.

> As I think about what Dr. Rice means to me, I think of one word—"influence." He has influenced my life a great deal. . . .
>
> It is hard to separate the two—the Sword of the Lord and Dr. John R. Rice—as I think of the influence they have been on my life. Dr. Rice and the Sword have been to me a teacher, an exhorter, an encourager. He personally is the greatest Christian I have ever known.
>
> The second influence they have been to me regards my mother. . . .
>
> I sent this cultured and refined woman a six-months' subscription when I had no money, one who felt I became a fanatic when I was saved. . . . Mother would receive "that Baptist paper" and comment that she had received "my subscription gift." This went on for some ten or twelve years. She would receive THE SWORD off and on through Dr. Rice's influence on me to send it to her. . . . She had heard me preach, and I had given her literature to read, and I would witness by the hour to her, yet she was not saved.
>
> Two years before she died, Mother wrote me that she believed she finally understood how to be saved through "that Baptist paper. . . ."
>
> I was fortunate enough to be with her the day before she died. . . . Holding her hand, I again dealt with her about the Lord and asked if she was really saved. Again she related the experience of trusting Christ by reading a sermon from THE SWORD OF THE LORD.
>
> Yes, what my preaching and witnessing could not do and what other sermons of preachers could not do and the literature of others, THE SWORD OF THE LORD did in the life of my mother. It won her to Christ!. . .

In Danville, Illinois, where Dr. Rice, Dr. Hyles and Dr. Malone were preaching, Dr. Rice instilled in me the vision of a large and aggressive church that was constantly multiplying. It was there where I first felt you could still be a fundamentalist and have a large church.

Then Dr. Beebe recalled how we published his first book, *All About the Bus Ministry,* which book has been used to start literally thousands of bus routes around the world.

He went on to reveal that:

Dr. Rice has always been an encouragement to me. I have come to him for advice on almost every move I have made in the Christian realm. . . . I would shudder to think where I would be and what I would be doing if it were not for Dr. Rice. I am certain there are thousands of people who would be in Hell rather than Heaven if it had not been for the influence of this man upon my life.

† † †

"Dr. Rice—bless his heart—will come to the rescue of anybody who stands for God anywhere—I don't care who he is. If I had my life to live over and could be born with any daddy in the world, I'd say, 'Let me be John Rice's son.' "—Jack Hyles.

† † †

"Since editorial labors are so heavy, I have been continually burdened lest I should grow stale and dry in my preaching," Dr. Rice wrote. "So, long ago I promised Him that, when needed, I would complete the commentary on the book of Matthew so as to tie myself down to daily digging in the sweet Word of God. Again I did the same thing with the book of Acts, then Luke.

"Oh, to keep our hearts warm and our souls fed not only with the letter of the Word but with the sweet moving of the Spirit. So I must take time for that, along with these other duties," he went on to say.

Then he told about Spurgeon asking his congregation, "Have you ever read the *Ancient Mariner?*" Spurgeon commented that "it was one of the strangest imaginations ever put together, especially that part where the mariner represents the corpses of all dead men rising up to man the ship—dead men pulling the rope, dead men steering, dead men spreading the sails. What a strange idea that was!"

Then said Spurgeon: "But do you know that I have lived to see it done! I have gone into churches; I have seen a dead man in the pulpit, a dead man as a deacon, a dead man handling the plate, and dead men sitting to hear."

Dr. Rice wanted to be sure he did not become "a dead man" in spirit, with nothing to move his heart, nothing to cause a tear. Oh, how he kept pleading to God for a warm heart!

† † †

Dr. David Wood, who now writes the column, "Soul Winning With David Wood" in THE SWORD, wrote in 1973:

> Just this morning a young man came into the office and asked me which school I graduated from. My answer was one that I had given often—"THE SWORD OF THE LORD." This is the honest testimony that is upon my heart. If it were not for the ministry of you, Dr. Rice, and THE SWORD OF THE LORD, I do not know where I would have gotten leadership necessary to build an evangelistic, Bible-believing, fundamental church.

† † †

By now Dr. Rice was burdened to write a verse-by-verse commentary on I and II Corinthians. In fact, he had already dictated the first draft on I Corinthians and was then working on the second book. And what a lot of work it was!

† † †

This exciting news was in July 27 issue: "The last five days we have had forty-five people write to say they were saved through our printed literature."

† † †

In July Dr. and Mrs. Rice, Dr. and Mrs. Curtis Hutson, two daughters and son; Dr. and Mrs. Russell Anderson and their three daughters, and I were on the cruise ship *Mardi Gras,* sailing to San Juan in Puerto Rico, the small island of St. Croix in the Virgin Islands, then to Nassau in the Bahamas.

Dr. Rice stated: "On Sunday morning when I preached aboard ship in the interdenominational service, twelve or more claimed the Lord.

L to R: Miss Viola Walden; Tommie Sue Anderson; Sherry Hutson; Dr. Rice; Mrs. Rice; Donna Hutson; Mrs. Geri Hutson; Dr. Hutson; Tony Hutson

Besides, Russell has won three, and Dr. Hutson won a cab driver. Russell figured that, counting those saved Sunday morning in the service on the *Mardi Gras,* there were twenty-two or twenty-three professions of faith won by our group."

It was a vacation/work week. Dr. Rice worked on his commentary on II Corinthians and dictated two full-length sermons for THE SWORD. When Dr. Rice worked, guess who else worked! But the cruise and our crowd were a lot of fun. We already knew well the Andersons; now we got better acquainted with the Hutsons, who would later become very important to our lives.

† † †

FILM STAR SAVED THROUGH SWORD BOOKLET. Rev. Bill Matthews was a pastor in Shawnee, Oklahoma. At this time his church was sending a letter to everyone who entered the two hospitals there and with it, enclosing Dr. Rice's *"What Must I Do to Be Saved?"*

A Mr. Tim Hold, who resided there then, was in the hospital and received one of Dr. Rice's tracts. A nurse called the pastor and asked that he personally visit the man, which he did. Then Rev. Matthews wrote:

"Tim told me he had read the tract and...'for the first time I understood that you are saved *to* something as well as *from* something.'

"He showed fruits of salvation, and was concerned about things that *had been* in his life."

Then he wrote these words on his picture which hangs in Rev. Matthews' office: "I am also saying 'thanks' for letting God use your life in the field of the printed page. I pray this will encourage you to keep working for God, and may those of us who believe in the great salvation provided by our Lord pray and work while we have time."

Then Tim Hold died of bone cancer at age fifty-four. The paper gave this information about him:

> Hold made 149 movies. From the time he quit making them on a regular basis, Hold pursued a variety of activities. At the time of his death, he was advertising manager for KEBC, an Oklahoma City radio station.
>
> Hold starred and played alongside the biggest names in show business—John Wayne, Gene Autrey, Roy Rogers, Rita Hayworth, Ginger Rogers, Orson Wells and a host of others.
>
> He teamed up with John Wayne in the production, *Stagecoach*. Hold, Humphrey Bogart and Walter Houston starred in the smash hit, *Treasure of Sierra Madre....*

Thank God for reaching another one through this mightily used 24-page salvation booklet!

† † †

The Flint, Michigan, *Journal* for July 19, 1973, carried this news note:

BAPTISTS WILL OPERATE PRIVATE ACADEMY

A fourteen-grade private academy intended to emphasize discipline, religious training and academic excellence will be opened in the fall by two Baptist churches in Burton.

The school, to be called the JOHN R. RICE BAPTIST ACADEMIES, will be officially introduced at a dinner at Sweden House on Tuesday.

Sponsoring churches are Good News Baptist Tabernacle and

Bentley Community Baptist Church, both congregations unaffiliated with Baptist organizations.

The churches expect 250 pupils for the opening semester, said James A. Morris, Bentley pastor.

† † †

The number of contributions for the new Sword addition were increasing weekly; and at the last of July, 188 had sent in a total of $59,755.97 in cash, and pledges were another $40,049.00. The estimated cost was $306,000.

We had no money—except as God sent it through His people. Several months had gone by since the architect and builder had been consulted. Now we desperately needed that new administration building to care for the work and workers, scattered all around us as it was. As he discussed it further, Dr. Rice said:

> I have often wondered why God didn't raise up some wealthy friend who would be able to finance all the many projects for which we are responsible. It would be so nice not to have to keep going to our friends with the need for the worldwide Free Literature Fund, the Ministers and Missionaries Subscription Gift Fund, the radio broadcast, now our new need for this additional building.
>
> But today I began thanking the Lord that we have these special needs constantly pressing upon us.
>
> First, I am thankful for problems that remind us that this work must have the daily blessing of God in order to be effective. If we should cease having to depend on Him, how sad would be our plight! This immediate matter before us will draw us closer to the Lord as we depend on Him to provide.
>
> Second, the urgent need provides another opportunity for thousands of friends all over the world to help. Abraham Lincoln said, "God must have loved the common people: He made so many of them."
>
> Sometimes we plain folks wonder how we can really do something for the Lord. But the Lord said, "Despise not the day of small things."
>
> Jesus was much more pleased with the widow who gave her mite to God than He was with the rich man who gave a great deal more. She had given all she had.
>
> Jesus one day took a boy's lunch and fed a multitude of more than five thousand. The boy gave Jesus all he had.

Elisha was met one day by a widow whose boys were to be sold as servants. All she had in the house was a pot of oil, but given to the Lord, it multiplied to meet her need.

If you will help with what you can and thousands of others like you will help, then there will be enough.

† † †

SOME ENCOUNTERS AS A TRAVELING MAN!
You thought you had troubles! Top these few days with Dr. Rice!

Dr. Hyles and I flew from Decatur, Illinois, to Chicago. I was scheduled to take a Delta flight from Chicago to Nashville; but when I checked in, I found the Delta flight was cancelled. They tried to get me an Eastern an hour later: it was full. Nothing to do but fly me to Atlanta, then back up 200 miles to Nashville.

When I changed in Atlanta, the Delta flight had been delayed, so I took a Southern flight back up to Nashville. But my bags didn't make all those changes. Where were they?

Arriving in Nashville, I went to my car in the parking area and found I had left my lights on two days, so the battery was down. I called a service station. They got me started, and I arrived in Murfreesboro late and so tired!

After two days, I flew to Atlanta on Southern Airlines and changed planes to another Southern flight to Greenville, South Carolina. The plane again from Nashville to Atlanta was late. All had already boarded the Greenville flight. Rushing, I got on, but my bags didn't get transferred.

The pastor who met me brought me more than thirty miles to Anderson to the motel. I had no pajamas, razor, toothbrush, nor Bible. He loaned me a razor. I slept without pajamas, and I borrowed a Gideon Bible from the motel room.

I remember well how in my early ministry, the work of a traveling evangelist was so heavy. A Model-T car, rough roads and mud, and often flat tires had to be patched and then pumped up by hand. I remember so well those days, with some poverty, having to make friends anew all the time, and living in the least expensive accommodations. We were happy, and I was aware that God meant all this for my good.

Now in recent years, I usually fly. But it is quite a burden to change planes, wait in airports, pack the baggage; then in the conferences to pack and unpack the books, set up the book table, announce the books, get subscriptions and sign hundreds of

Bibles, as well as preach two or three times a day.

But the Lord seemed to tell me I must never think I am beyond those ordinary vexations that trouble poor souls everywhere. His lovingkindness and watch care are beyond expression and always present.

Once when a pastor said to me, "I wouldn't like traveling all the time, being away from home, eating and sleeping in strange motels, always among strangers," I answered, "Like it? What has that to do with it? I am in the will of God. It is a style of life. I have given myself to it for Jesus' sake."

Yes, there are some burdens for those who make traveling for Jesus a way of life.

† † †

In 1973 Dr. Rice said about his pastor:

Dr. Bob Kelley

Rev. Bob Kelley has been my pastor and the pastor of most of the Sword employees for many years, and he has been mightily blessed of God. Franklin Road Baptist Church has grown to an attendance of 600 or 700 regularly, sometimes up to 1,000.[1] We see souls saved week after week, and hundreds have been baptized.

Brother Kelley is a remarkably strong Bible preacher. He is a graduate of Tennessee Temple Schools, has a beautiful singing voice, is robust and manly. He is a former football player with Austin Peay College. His standards of Christian life are plain, sharp and well-defined. He is out-and-out for the fundamentals of the faith, is without compromise, without fear, yet with a culture, restraint and clarity in his preaching.

Brother Kelley's preaching, vision and spiritual wisdom fit him to preach in the greatest churches in America and in tremendous revival campaigns. I have used him in Sword Conferences. He preached at

---

[1] On later special drives, the church has reached 2,000 or more.

Highland Park Baptist when Dr. Roberson was pastor, and many other preachers have vied for his services.

His family consists of lovely April, a devoted, modest, beautiful wife who sings with her husband, and three children, Star, Dawn and Daye.

When Dr. Rice was in town, he went to hear his beloved pastor. I asked Dr. Kelley recently for a word about Dr. Rice for this book.

HIS PASTOR SPEAKS:

Dr. John R. Rice was one of the greatest, most respected, most unique men I have ever known. He was a big man who never sought to be big, a brilliant man but right at home with the ignorant. He never had to demand respect; he got it because of his godly life and loving compassion. He loved people, and people loved him.

Then he had a vast knowledge of the Word of God. He was like an artesian well—the Bible just flowed out of him. I have never known any man who could better apply Scripture to the problems of life than Dr. Rice. He was filled with the Word of God. I have seen him with his head bowed in deep study of the Word, and he wept as God spoke to him. What a love for the Bible!

One thing I must mention is that he would make all men, big and small, feel like a king when they were around him. He was always interested in your life, your family, your needs. Little children loved him. His "grandpa" image couldn't be beat. They would run to him, and he would set them on his knee, like Jesus with children.

He was greatly loved by this pastor and church. Our people knew he was always for the pastor and church. He never once hurt me or this ministry—He *was a big man!*

How many times in my ministry I have been asked, "Bob, isn't it hard to be the pastor of Dr. John R. Rice?" My basic answer is always the same, "No, it's wonderfully easy."

From my very first day as pastor of Franklin Road Baptist Church, Dr. Rice manifested a deep love for his pastor and his local church. He often told me, "Pastor, traveling like I do, I can't be as faithful as I would like, but I love you and our dear members."

Dr. Rice proved that statement in so many ways! He prayed diligently that God would always bless his home church. He gave faithfully, systematically and generously. During one of our building programs he became so heavily burdened that he contributed, before it was over, $16,000.

Dr. Rice loved souls, and every Sunday he was home he looked for those to whom he could witness. He was always asking, "Pastor, how many were saved last Sunday?"

The week before the last attack, he was in the service at Franklin Road Baptist Church. Though he was enfeebled by several heart attacks and strokes and handicapped by impaired hearing and eyesight, at the end of the service he stopped a little girl and asked, gently, "Honey, are you a Christian?" His great, overwhelming concern, through all the years, was always that people not only hear the Gospel but be urged to accept Christ as Saviour.

† † †

BURIED WITH *"WHAT MUST I DO TO BE SAVED?"* BOOKLET. Rev. J. W. Joiner, Sr., retired pastor of Marshall, Texas, had in his church in Silsbee, Texas, a Mr. Howell Fisher.

When Mr. Fisher became interested in soul winning, his pastor taught him a soul-winning course and introduced him to Dr. Rice's *"What Must I Do to Be Saved?"* booklet. Mr. Fisher bought them by the thousands and, everywhere he went, passed them out. "Only God knows how many souls have been saved by those pamphlets passed out over these years by our brother. He always had a good number in his pocket and car," his pastor wrote.

On January 14 Howell Fisher went to be with the Lord, and Pastor Joiner preached his funeral. Now here is his report:

> When my wife and I walked up to the casket in the funeral home, I noticed something immediately and called my wife's attention to it. In the lapel pocket of his coat was one of your *"What Must I Do to Be Saved?"* booklets, pulled up just far enough for the full title to show.
>
> As possibly 250 to 300 people passed that casket at the close of the service, that pamphlet witnessed once again to the saving grace of our Lord. Howell was buried with that message in his pocket.

† † †

IT'S A FRAME-UP! No, we were not talking about Watergate, but about a huge map that had been framed and placed on the west wall of the Sword auditorium. We were telling pastors we would like to frame

It's a Frame-up!

**Put Your Church
on the SWORD Map!**

them and their churches on this colorful map, when they agreed to have a "SWORD Sunday."

This map was hung so all who attended the Sword Conference in September could see those churches that were helping spread THE SWORD. And it served to be a constant reminder to Dr. Rice and his Sword team to pray for these in our 7:00 a.m. morning devotions.

(Ron English, circulation manager, reported joyfully that 360 churches had set a date to have a "SWORD Sunday" and had ordered about 30,000 copies of THE SWORD for samples.)

† † †

CONVERTED CONVICT SET FREE. . . Here is only one story of thousands that could be told about the ministry of Dr. Rice's sermon-tract, *"What Must I Do to Be Saved?"*

A man in Japan was in constant trouble with the law. Finally, he was committed to prison with a life sentence.

Then someone gave him a copy of Dr. Rice's booklet in the Japanese language. He read it, believed the message, then accepted Christ. So transformed was his life that the jailer went to court to plead for his release.

The converted convict was set free.

While walking in a park, he came upon a man sitting on a bench. He stopped to talk with him. The bench-warmer told how he had become despondent over his drunkenness and had attempted suicide by slashing his wrists. In the hospital, he tried again to kill himself, feeling there was no way out of his thirst for alcohol.

But the new convert said, "Yes, there is," and showed him Dr. Rice's tract.

The alcoholic read it, then said, "It can't be true!"

"Yes, it can and it is," replied the new friend. "Come with me. We will see a missionary together."

The missionary affirmed the truth of the tract and helped the alcoholic to trust Jesus as Saviour.

Some time later, Dr. Rice was in Japan for meetings. One night after he had preached in a tent, many Japanese came to get saved. Dr. Rice and others dealt with each carefully. A young Bible college student stood to one side waiting patiently. Afterwards he came to meet Dr. Rice. Missionary Fred Jarvis told the story you have just read. He said to Dr. Rice, "Here is your spiritual grandson, saved through your tract given to him by another who had come to know Christ through the same tract."

As the young Japanese preacher listened to Dr. Jarvis talk with Dr. Rice, he held up his hands toward Heaven and, speaking exultantly in Japanese, said the only words Dr. Rice could understand, "Allelujah! Allelujah!"

† † †

Dr. Rice was asking, "What Would Christians Do Without THE SWORD?"

> If there were no SWORD OF THE LORD, Christians of this generation would probably never read a sermon by Charles Spurgeon, D. L. Moody, H. A. Ironside, Bob Jones, Sr., T. DeWitt Talmage, George W. Truett, nor Billy Sunday. Most of the books of these men are out of print. We sadly find the Sunday School Board of the Southern Baptist Convention does not now print the messages by Dr. Truett nor Dr. B. H. Carroll.
>
> Pilgrim Publications gave me a $365 set of Charles Spurgeon's Metropolitan Pulpit sermon books for the simple reason that we have kept Spurgeon alive in America by printing his sermons.
>
> So if you want the great impact of the great soul winners of

this and the past generation, you will have to get it from THE
SWORD OF THE LORD.

† † †

After choosing a fine sermon for THE SWORD by Dr. Bob Jones, Sr.,
"You Can Do Anything You Want to Do," Dr. Rice reminisced about
their friendship.

> Dr. Bob was born in 1883 and died in 1968 at age 84. He was
> one of my very dearest friends. What a joy it was for me to use
> him in great Sword of the Lord Conferences and revivals, to unite
> with him in the tremendous citywide campaign in the Chicago
> Arena.
>
> What a solid, trustworthy, unwavering friend he was to this
> editor and to THE SWORD OF THE LORD! I can remember more
> than once when he sent a gift of $500 or so and said, "Please send
> THE SWORD OF THE LORD to some preachers."
>
> He was most gracious in his kind words about me. In the
> biography of Dr. Jones, written by R. K. Johnson, "Lefty" Johnson
> said, "Later Dr. Bob commented, 'I think that Dr. Rice and I are
> more thoroughly agreed on all "principle" matters than any other
> men in the world. I depend on him more, believe in him more
> strongly and would risk him further than any other preacher in
> the world; for he would stand by a friend and die for his Lord.' "
>
> In a letter from Dr. Bob Jones to this editor, published in THE
> SWORD OF THE LORD August 1, 1958, Dr. Jones expressed his
> pleasure at my extensive review of the propaganda book,
> *Cooperative Evangelism,* put out in defense of Dr. Billy Graham's
> compromise by his worker, Dr. Ferm:
>
> "Dear Brother John: Since reading your review of the book,
> *Cooperative Evangelism,* I appreciate you in the service you are
> rendering more than I ever have; and you know how I have always
> appreciated you."
>
> Dr. Bob asked me to go with him all over America in one-day
> and night stands and asked me to speak again and again on
> "Cooperation and Separation," and then he asked me to give the
> same message at Bob Jones University, and I did. It is published
> in pamphlet form and has been widely spread ever since.

† † †

It was now the first of November—getting fairly close to the closing
of that subscription campaign. We were praying for 50,000 subscriptions.

Dr. Rice was in New Jersey, then in California, then in Maine, then in Wisconsin; but he never missed a day calling home to check on the number of subscriptions received that day. "Can we get 50,000?" he would ask again; then he would answer his own question by saying, "Yes—provided Christians are willing to invest a few cents per week; provided readers feel themselves debtors and will pay their honest debt; provided they all do as the Holy Spirit directs; provided they will not procrastinate." He was sure we could; then there was doubt we would!

The Sword of the Lord was ever on his mind, day and night, traveling and when at home, playing or when working.

Now the last of November the Boss man was saying: "When I think of the more than 270,000 homes receiving THE SWORD OF THE LORD, I feel ashamed that I asked for only 50,000 subscriptions during this campaign."

(I looked ahead to find the final count of subscriptions: "over 60,000"!!!)

† † †

By November, our carefully kept records showed close to 17,000 had received Christ as Saviour as a direct result of this work, not counting the many thousands in foreign lands which were reported to missionaries. God keeps a very accurate record, and one day we will total it up. Then we will know exactly the number saved! Oh, the lives changed, the homes blessed, the preachers set on fire, the downtrodden encouraged—as a result of the Foundation!

We actually believed that money put into Sword of the Lord Foundation got more souls saved, revived more Christians, called out more preachers, did more to maintain soundness in the faith and kept more people and institutions from modernism, than the same money put most anywhere else in the world.

† † †

"Stedfast!" "Unmoveable!"

What do these words bring to your mind?

Well, perhaps Gibraltar, that great rock so long fortified by England to guard the Strait between Spain and Africa that joins the Atlantic Ocean and the Mediterranean Sea. This peninsula of rock, so firm and unyielding, has become the synonym of that which is steadfast and unmovable. *"Firm as the Rock of Gibraltar,"* we say when discussing something that is absolutely reliable.

But when I think of "stedfast and unmoveable," I think of John R. Rice, who was steadfast and unmovable until his last breath.

Even physically he had changed not nearly as much as one would think. At age 77, the "Captain of Our Team" was still in excellent, vigorous health. You would never in this world believe he was three-score, ten and seven.

An Ohio woman wrote, *"I always laugh when Dr. John writes in 'Editor's Notes' about riding a horse—that dear, feeble old man!"*

She thought it likely that someone saddled the horse, helped Dr. John into the saddle, then let him ride it around the corral! As a matter of fact, that "dear, feeble old man" went into the pasture, caught MacArthur, slapped a saddle on his back and galloped him all over the farm! And sometimes rode him bareback!

Oh, he was not the athlete he was when he was forty and still in football playing condition. He no longer challenged us to a race up the stairs (thank goodness!), and at the airport he probably walked a little slower than he had twenty years before. But that "dear, feeble old man" was on the go from early morning until late at night every day, carrying the workload that might be expected of several strong, middle-aged men, ate heartily, slept soundly and was in excellent physical condition.

A Tennessean would probably have said that Dr. John Rice was "bright-eyed and bushy-tailed!"

Steadfast! Unmovable!

1974 In the first issue of THE SWORD in 1974, Dr. Rice's heart was running over with thanks for blessings of the past year—and there had been many. "And the mercy of God in the past guarantees that He will be merciful still in this new year. I look forward with great joy to 1974, expecting more and greater blessings, which could be our last to do work for Him."

† † †

Our Board of Directors now consisted of:

1. Russell Anderson
2. Wally Beebe
3. Al Byers
4. Curtis Hutson
5. Jack Hyles
6. Bud Lyles
7. Tom Malone
8. Bob Moore
9. Bill Rice
10. John R. Rice
11. Mrs. John R. Rice
12. Fairy Shappard
13. R. L. Sumner
14. Viola Walden
15. Nevin Wax

And on the Sword Cooperating Board were:

1. Gary Coleman
2. Jerry Falwell
3. Robert C. Gray, Jr.
4. Monroe Parker
5. Ford Porter
6. Lee Roberson
7. Harold Sightler
8. G. B. Vick
9. Tom Wallace
10. G. Archer Weniger

† † †

By now THE SWORD OF THE LORD circulation was over 300,000, and we hoped to "hold our own."

Maybe some of you do not understand that, when we have a great influx of subscriptions, they must all be renewed one year later or regretfully be taken off the list. So every month when thousands expired, we had to continually try to get these back on and keep working at getting new ones.

But think of reaching 300,000 families, or more than a million people each week with the Gospel! (It was figured at least three in a family read the paper.)

† † †

In an article concerning "controversy," Mr. William Petersen of *Eternity Magazine* was surprised at how many controversial articles a certain evangelical letter contained. Listing them, he reported that it first spoke against denominationalism, then dealt with sex, and went on to discuss divorce and separation. It continued with an article concerning dieting, another one on the place of women in the church, and discussed women's dress. It also featured an article about speaking in tongues.

Then Mr. Petersen lifted the curtain and let the readers know he was talking about the First Epistle to the Corinthians.

Makes us realize, does it not, that the Bible faces up to real problems—with more courage than we sometimes show.

And Dr. Rice, in a new commentary on *The Church of God at Corinth*, carefully and clearly explained these "controversial" issues raised by the Apostle Paul not only in the book of I Corinthians but also in II Corinthians.

This church was the New Testament church plagued with the most problems. Yet reading Paul's letter to this church today is not much different from reading letters needed now in the majority of our congregations. The problems are the same. And—bless God—so are the solutions!

The Church of God at Corinth by Dr. Rice gives detailed discussion of divisions, carnal Christians, inspiration of the Bible, the judgment seat of Christ, those who commit fornication, when to dismiss a member and when to restore him, going to law, marriage, remuneration for preachers, the Lord's Supper, women's long hair—a glory; men's long hair—a shame; the tongues heresy, etc.

Then the Second Epistle to the Corinthians answers more questions: dealing with Paul's apostleship and questions of fellowship, relationship, happiness and service.

No pastor is well equipped to lead his people without a thorough knowledge of I and II Corinthians. And what's good for the pastor is good for all his people. If you don't have this commentary, we suggest you purchase it.

† † †

When someone asked Dr. Rice, "Would it be wrong for a ministerial student to take part of his tithe for his schooling?" he answered:

> There is an honest difference of opinion on this among good Christians.
>
> When I was a student working my way through college and seminary, I personally did not feel it right for me to use my tithe for my own schooling. So in my case it would have been wrong because of my convictions.
>
> However, you pray and ask God for clear leading.
>
> I gained a great deal of confidence, joy and assurance of God's blessing because I carried on the tithing practice, Mrs. Rice and I giving more than twenty percent of our income while we were in the seminary and living in great poverty.

† † †

HE TELLS HOW LIFE FEELS AT 78:

> David exhorted himself to remember: "Bless the Lord... who satisfieth thy mouth with good things; so that thy youth is renewed like the eagle's."
>
> When Moses was 120, "his eye was not dim, nor his natural force abated."
>
> Caleb, one of the faithful spies who went into the promised land at Kadesh-barnea and returned with enthusiasm, along with Joshua, to recommend that they go in speedily and take the land, was 40 at the time. Forty-five years later, when they had entered the land of Canaan and fought most of the battles, Caleb came to claim Mount Hebron, saying, "...I am as strong this day as I was in the day that Moses sent me; as my strength was then, even so is my strength now for war, both to go out, and to come in. Now therefore give me this mountain..." (Joshua 14). By God's mercy, this old man at 85 was as strong for battle as when he was young.
>
> God renewed the youth of Abraham so that he could have a child when he was 100.
>
> God renewed Zacharias when he was an old man and, in answer to prayer, gave John the Baptist.

Psalm 90:10 indicates that 70 is a normal lifetime.

I am still, with enthusiasm, preaching, editing and winning souls. My bones may be a little stiff, and sometimes I may be slower to remember a name, but preaching is still great joy. I work hard and sleep well.

I still have big plans for THE SWORD OF THE LORD and other work for the Lord for as long as He sees fit to leave me here and allows me to be active.

Once the Scripture blessed me mightily, which said, ". . . young men shall see visions"—and I did. Oh, the holy ambitions, expectations and dreams of my heart as I served God when a young man! Now I can delight in the rest of the verse, ". . . old men shall dream dreams."

The power of the Holy Spirit is as much for the old as for the young, and the concern about the work of the Lord should be as great when the hair is gray as it ever was with the first dew of youth.

Psalm 92:14 is always a comfort: "They shall bring forth fruit in old age. . . ."

And much of that sweet old hymn, "How Firm a Foundation," is based upon the promises of Isaiah 46:4, "And even to your old age I. . . will bear; even I will carry, and will deliver you."

That means more now than it did in youthful days.

The song puts it in these words:

> E'en down to old age, all My people shall prove
> My sovereign, eternal, unchangeable love;
> And when hoary hairs shall their temples adorn,
> Like lambs they shall still in My bosom be borne.

How full of riches the Bible is for every age and circumstance—old or young, in poverty or wealth, in sickness or health!

And now, how does life look at 78? It looks grand! I am claiming Philippians 1:6, "Being confident of this very thing, that he which hath begun a good work in you will perform it until the day of Jesus Christ."

Let me ask you: What makes a man obsolete?

Some business concerns make it a rule that when one reaches a certain age, he must retire. Thus they throw away mellowed experience. England held onto Disraeli, to Gladstone, to Balfour so long as they lived. Their value could never be measured by years.

What makes one old? Is it gray hair? A faltering step? A stooping posture? Or is it when the mind loses virility? And where is the sage who can speak with real wisdom in his early thirties?

In the light of eternity, we should judge a man's life, not in the sum of his days nor the span of his years, but in what he has accomplished.

Each of us is ambitious to remain everlastingly youthful—to play gaily at 60, to be interested in all of life at 70, to keep one's wits at 80. But years are the artificialities of calendar makers. If the spirit is young, the years are not even remembered. If the spirit remains young, one can sing a song at 78 as at 17—but at 78 it will have more meaning.

What a sterling example of this we had in Dr. Rice!

† † †

"LET'S GO FISHING." Dr. Rice tells these incidents of childhood, then makes an application:

> "Let's go fishing," Dad said. It was about 1911, near the little cowtown of Dundee in West Texas. Our grain was already cut with a binder, chopped in the field and the thresher had come, the oats had been stored for feed in the winter, the wheat had been sold. No work was pressing.
>
> So "Let's go fishing."
>
> We hitched the big black horse Prince to the sturdy buggy and drove out seven miles to the Little Wichita River, taking along a frying pan, some meal to roll the fish in that we hoped to catch and fry, some bread, and some bacon in case we didn't catch any! Yes, and some potatoes. We had with us a shotgun, for we must get some bait—a cottontail rabbit or a crow.
>
> How pleasant it was beside the deep pools where the river was just barely flowing! Trees shaded all about.
>
> We caught catfish and sometimes perch, and cooked them over an open fire. Then we sat around the campfire, and Dad told stories of his cowboy days, about 1877-78, when there was not a fence between Fort Worth and Denver. He told about the open range, Indians and cattle drives to the North.
>
> We had thanks over our meal and, after awhile, laid out bedrolls and slept under the stars. As I went to sleep or waked in the night, I could hear old Prince—hobbled but never straying far from camp and us—cropping the grass about.
>
> After such trips we would go home the next day hoping to have

some fish for the homefolk after having a fine refreshing in the midst of a summer's work.

Going fishing has a good sound to those who have enjoyed such vacations.

Once Jesus came along by the Sea of Galilee and, wanting to preach to the people, asked permission to sit in a boat shoved out a little way from shore. There He preached to the multitude.

He then turned to the disciples and, in effect, said, "Let's go fishing" (Luke 5).

But instead of fishing for fish, Jesus called these fishermen to a far greater task: they were to fish for men. They were to be His soul winners. In Matthew 4 He said, "Follow me, and I will make you fishers of men."

That, too, is our great task. No one can be a soul winner until he puts Jesus first. If you want to go fishing with Jesus for lost souls, then Christ must be the Master, and His work must come before all else.

† † †

Mrs. Hilda Allen, "our girl Friday" to me and Dr. Rice for 30 years, until she retired in 1988

YOU DON'T ALWAYS HAVE TO GO TO A FOREIGN FIELD TO BE A MISSIONARY. If God called one to the Sword of the Lord, that one truly was in missionary work, as we tried to show in this brief article, run in 1974:

Standing with an open Bible under a palm tree, expounding the Gospel to naked savages, nursing the leper, yes; even being headmistress of a school in another country, is missionary work, but being a secretary—no!

Rarely today does one stand up and testify that he/she is called to be a secretary. What has that got to do with preaching the Gospel to every creature?

Now, by being a secretary we mean a personal assistant, one who helps another do his work.

Abraham's secretary made the marriage arrangement for his son Isaac. Joshua was Moses' secretary before he succeeded him as Prime Minister. Samuel was Eli's personal assistant, and he also succeeded "the Boss" as leader of God's people. Elisha obviously did well as the great prophet's secretary, and he must have helped in other ways apart from pouring water for Elijah to wash his hands. There are many more secretaries, or assistants, mentioned in the Old Testament; but let's move on to the New Testament.

Mark was called to deal with travel agents and catering in a missionary team. He too had a setback, but he later proved to be an invaluable secretary for Paul (II Tim. 4:11).

On another occasion Paul's secretary is named (Tertius), but usually Paul added a postscript to what an anonymous assistant had written. A verse at the end of Second Thessalonians shows that Paul dictated, but personally signed, important letters.

It is obvious that the Mediterranean would not have been evangelized so rapidly had Paul not had personal assistants, or secretaries, as we call them today.

That good lady Phoebe is described as one who "has been a succourer [helper] of many, and of myself also," says Paul. Oh, for a few modern Phoebes!

Secretaries are not just typists who reproduce mechanically what is dictated, but they are men/women willing to do anything and everything to help the cause. Drawing water like Elisha; arranging the catering and making ship reservations like Mark; keeping accounts more faithfully than Judas—these and other matters need to be done by willing hands.

Secretarial work is "missionary" work.

The Sword of the Lord Foundation is truly a missionary work. One who comes to work here must come with the same dedication as one has who goes to the mission field. We require separation from the world. . .a sacrificial spirit. . .a holy dedication of self to Christ.

Sword of the Lord Foundation won through literature 631 people last year (1973) in this country, and many more on foreign shores, which records are kept by local missionaries. . .and HEAVEN! Multitudes, more than can be numbered, write us of lives changed through this ministry. Indeed it is a missionary work as great as any in a foreign land.

God has given the Sword many dedicated hands. Some have been with us thirty, forty years or more. Dr. Rice's work was greatly expanded by talented men and women "secretaries" and he knew it—and let others know it. Continually he publicly praised those who willingly gave themselves to this ministry.

And he would do special favors like: money to help on buying a house; paying another's hospital bill after a cancer operation; a dinner and making it a special occasion when one had been with the work for a certain length of time; buying new dresses for "Secretary's Week" for several employees; a Caribbean cruise after years of faithful service; buying a new suit for a diligent worker; a free trip to the Holy Land—I could never name all he did for his staff. I am just showing how much Dr. Rice appreciated his assistants, or "secretaries."

No wonder his employees loved him and were so devoted to him!

† † †

PREACHERS ON TRIAL. Some occupations have built-in hazards, such as that of the coal miner, the deep-sea diver, the steeple jack, the astronaut. Everyone knows that the men who follow these pursuits are in at least some degree of danger most of the time.

Contrasted with these, the work of the ministry would appear to carry with it no danger at all. For physical hazard, the ministry stands just about at the bottom of the list, and the minister is considered one of the best risks any insurance company can handle.

Yet the ministry is one of the most perilous of professions. The Devil hates the Spirit-filled preacher. Satan knows that the downfall of a prophet of God is a victory for him. And the preacher's dangers are likely to be spiritual rather than physical.

In his giant volume, *Bible Giants Tested,* Dr. Rice reviews the lives of eight characters from the Bible. Both the successes and failures, the victories and defeats of these "giants of the faith" are explained with simplicity—Jacob, Caleb, King Saul, Jehoshaphat, John the Baptist, Elijah, Peter and Paul. The chapter on Jehoshaphat is one of the most glaring illustrations of the sin of associating with apostates to be found anywhere.

THIS BOOK OUGHT TO PRODUCE 20TH CENTURY GIANTS FOR
GOD (still available).

† † †

Two years before, a second printing of 200,000 copies of *"What Must
I Do to Be Saved?"* was done in the Korean language. Now Missionary
Gerald Johnson of Seoul says, "Soul winners come to us asking for the
booklet, but we no longer are able to supply this need. It is now completely out of print."

He had checked prices for a new printing. "The lowest estimates given
me were: For 100,000 booklets the price is a little under 2 cents a
booklet—$1,823.00; for 200,000, the price is a little over 1 1/2 cents a
booklet—$3,342.00."

Dr. Rice told Missionary Gerald Johnson we would undertake to raise
the $3,342.00 for the salvation of many souls in Korea.

† † †

FORTY YEARS! Sword of the Lord Foundation was 40 years old this
year. THE SWORD OF THE LORD was a mighty power for Christ,
entering one-quarter million homes weekly. Most people did not realize
the floods of good literature released from these premises, but we knew
it was a ton a day for Sword books, 18 tons per week for THE SWORD
OF THE LORD.

Dr. Rice alone had been used of God in sending out an almost un-
paralleled amount of Christian literature. A friendly comparison:

Dr. G. Campbell Morgan, a great minister and writer mightily blessed
of God, saw 29,720 copies of his greatest work sold. Some 22,629 copies
and 29,018 copies of other great volumes by him were sold. Fleming H.
Revell printed 1,200 to 1,500 copies of these at a time; whereas, Dr. Rice's
Prayer—Asking and Receiving had by now 20 printings in 31 years and
was still going strong. From 10,000 to 20,000 copies were printed at a
time! Total already distributed: 232,500.

Another great preacher and author of more recent ministry, Dr. H.
A. Ironside, wrote and published a total of 900,000 copies of books,
pamphlets and tracts. Dr. Ironside, long pastor of Moody Memorial
Church, Chicago, wrote commentaries on many books of the Bible, and
they were very, very popular. His work was scattered widely. We thank
God for him and them.

BUT. . . Dr. Rice's total volumes had reached heavenly heights—some

40 million copies! They had been and will be read by more millions. His books challenge, stimulate, comfort. They bring salvation and lead to soul winning, to revival, to Bible study. They magnify Holy Spirit power.

† † †

POTENT POWER OF TRACTS. The late W. B. Riley, many years ago, said: "There will be more people in the redeemed throng when asked the question, 'What led you to Christ?' who will reply, 'a tract,' than will point to Spurgeon, Wesley or Whitefield or even to the Apostle Paul."

You have heard of Hudson Taylor, the founder of the China Inland Mission; John Bunyan, author of *Pilgrim's Progress,* and John Huss, the great Christian reformer—they all were saved through reading a tract.

So we pushed on with Dr. Rice's *"What Must I Do to Be Saved?"* which had already won its thousands, and in years to come, perhaps other thousands.

† † †

When Dr. Rice could not finish his commencement message at Indiana Baptist College, Indianapolis, the last of May, people present from all over the country were very concerned, thinking he was seriously ill, perhaps with a heart attack. He said he was only affected by an upset stomach, a hot robe and the heat.

After a brief hospital visit, he flew home that same night, was at his office the next morning, and then went on to California.[1]

† † †

Mr. Peter Gunther, General Sales Manager of Moody Press, conceived the idea of a D. L. Moody Award that would honor the person who had made the greatest contribution to the industry in these three basic areas: publishing, distribution and promotion of the industry. A committee of six spent much time considering facts and gathering information to determine who should receive D. L. MOODY AWARD FOR DISTINGUISHED SERVICE IN THE FIELD OF CHRISTIAN LITERATURE.

> The gentleman selected has been the publisher and director of a weekly publication for over 40 years, whose publication distribution has reached a maximum of 300,000 weekly, with distribu-

---

[1] We honestly believe he suffered his first mild heart attack at this time, with several others coming over the next few years.

tion in all fifty states and 99 foreign countries. He has authored 159 books and pamphlets, with a total distribution of over 40 million, with 10 million being in 35 countries around the world. His hard-backed *Prayer—Asking and Receiving* has had a press run in excess of 225,000, and has now gone into Spanish. One sermon perhaps for which he is most well known, *"What Must I Do to Be Saved?"* has had a publication in excess of 20 million in English, 6½ million in Japanese.

He is currently on many, many radio stations promoting the sale and distribution of Christian literature. He is a regular exhibitor at Christian Booksellers Association, has been a speaker on several occasions, and just two years ago devotional speaker at the annual CBA Convention, with every opportunity promoting Christian literature and Christian Booksellers Association.

It is indeed a privilege and an honor for Moody Press to present the D. L. Moody Award on this 25th anniversary of CBA to Dr. John R. Rice, Sword of the Lord, Murfreesboro, Tennessee!

Mr. Floyd Robinson
Sales Manager for Moody Press
1974

† † †

The greatest gathering of fundamental Bible believers in the history of America assembled in Indianapolis August 12 through 18 for the first National Conference on Revival, sponsored by the Sword of the Lord. In the Greater Indianapolis area, some one hundred independent churches cooperated.

In days gone by, Moody and Billy Sunday would have had to erect a huge tabernacle to house such a gathering, but the new and spacious Indiana Convention Center, seating 8,000, was available.

Speakers included the best known pastors and evangelists in the

**A portion of the vast crowd that filled the Indianapolis
Convention Center for the Conference**

nation, and two of the best soul-winning missionaries—Robert Hughes
of the Philippines, running over 5,000 in their Sunday school, and Jim
Norton of Japan. Both brought a breath of Heaven from the mission
field to the Mission seminar.

Mayor Lugar proclaimed August 12 through 18 "Sword of the Lord
Week." Many dignitaries came to one or more sessions, including the
Governor and Lieutenant Governor.

† † †

It was nearing the end of 1974. Our concern was the shortage of paper
in supply houses. The supplier had said they could not get enough
newsprint for us to continue to run 16 pages weekly for 300,000 copies
of THE SWORD, "that your contract was for 250,000 copies a week."

We "bothered" the Lord again about this, reminding Him that He had
no paper shortage.

Not many days hence word came that 250,000 pounds of newsprint
was available, equivalent of six semi-trailer loads. Some company had
ordered it, then could not pay for it, and we could have it!

Praise God from whom all blessings flow!

† † †

We always hoped and prayed for more people to be saved through our literature each year. But how thankful we were that a total of 551 people wrote us during 1974 to say they had been saved through THE SWORD and Sword books. Of course, we believe many others were saved who did not write. (Our own office force won 79 in personal work here in Murfreesboro, in addition to the figure above.)

† † †

How good God has been to bless the Sword of the Lord so abundantly. In the past ten years our wholesale book sales, which were $47,700 in 1964, increased to $290,267 in 1974—more than six times as much as they had been!

The circulation had likewise doubled and doubled again.

1975 We realized that more nickels would have clinked onto our desks had we printed some things other magazines printed or had we run some ads other magazines had run; but our standards were not made of elastic bands! We would rather print 8 pages of THE SWORD OF THE LORD that could safely be left around for children and students to read and could stand the scrutinizing eye of our Lord, than to print 16 pages of material which might hurt or ruin an immortal soul. Dr. Rice had said, "When our Foundation ceases to uphold our reputation and principles, may the name THE SWORD OF THE LORD appear on the obituary list of magazines."

That was always our policy while Dr. Rice was editor; I trust it will continue to be the policy as long as there is a Sword.

† † †

"Let's have this year a thousand letters from those who write to us and say, 'I here and now take Christ as my own personal Saviour after reading. . .' some message in THE SWORD or some Sword book," Dr. Rice stated the first of the year.

Why not? For every week a sermon to the unsaved was printed, followed by a decision form. And thousands of new subscriptions were coming in. Surely some were for/from the unsaved.

Too, we were offering Dr. Rice's famous tract, *"What Must I Do to Be Saved?"* for $2.00 a hundred. Thousands had already written that after reading the salvation message, they had received Christ.

† † †

I never knew a more thankful person in all my life than Dr. Rice. In February he wrote this short article:

"IN EVERY THING GIVE THANKS."—I Thess. 5:18.
In the motel room here in Florida is a big bowl of fruit, provided by loving hands. On the desk here is a lovely bouquet of

flowers with a card of loving welcome from the First Baptist Church here in Ruskin, Florida.

I am reminded how many things there are all about us every day for which we ought to be thankful.

When at home I go down to the office about 6:30 in the morning. Already Miss Viola has the daily paper from the evening before on my desk, and an apple! Then Mrs. Hilda Allen sharpens my pencils, brings a pitcher of fresh water, then provides me with what she calls my "beauty pill"—a vitamin tablet! She thinks it is good for me, and I am glad she thinks so. Then at 10:00 a.m. and 2:00 p.m. she fixes coffee for me and Miss Viola, and serves rolls or a piece of cake.

I left my desk the other day; and when I came back, there were some beautiful jonquils from Miss Willie Brummitt [now deceased]. She is always on the lookout for flowers for my desk.

When I ate breakfast at home Saturday, I had eggs and country-cured ham provided by Mr. Ed Whitley from Wilson, North Carolina [also deceased]. My heart is ever grateful. But it is far better to have people's love and their care for me.

A little more than a week ago, Rev. James Mastin presented me with a lovely engraved wall plaque:

> **To Dr. John R. Rice in appreciation**
> **for the many years of leading**
> **churches in New Testament soul**
> **winning, and for the influence on**
> **our church, Central Baptist Church,**
> **Milwaukee, Wisconsin, 1975.**

Back at my study are keys to the cities of El Paso and Hammond, Indiana; then the great sword presented by the Christian Business Men of Pensacola, the wall plaques, the clock from Ireland, given to me by Dr. Paisley; citations, degrees, pictures, the Japanese doll sent by missionaries; the wood carving from Indonesia, and other thoughtful and loving gifts.

In the nature of the case, one who carries the load I carry has many burdens. But I have so much to make me happy, so many friends who love me.

Mrs. Rice and I have been well, wonderfully well, these 53 years of married life. There has been no serious illness among our children and grandchildren.

We had a meeting last Friday night of the old-timers who came

twelve years ago with us from Wheaton, Illinois. How wonderful
that God has preserved them and their families! And how grateful
I am for their loyal, faithful work!

So I give thanks to God. And I hope you will remember to do
so also.

† † †

RED-HOT, REVIVAL-TYPE PREACHING. (A look into the past.)

We had just printed a 585-page book, *Preaching That Built a Great
Church,* and I was anxious to tell the whole world about it; therefore
I wrote an article which read in part:

In July, 1932, Dr. John R. Rice came to Dallas, Texas, and,
without money, a building, organization and backing, began an
open-air revival at Tenth and Crawford in Oak Cliff. That revival
lasted 13 weeks. Hundreds were saved, and the Fundamentalist
Baptist Church of Oak Cliff was organized.

During those days it was one 12-week revival after another, in
many sections of Oak Cliff and Dallas proper. And I think I
attended every service!

My, what blessings! My, what crowds! My, the people who
walked the aisles for Christ! I had never heard such powerful
preaching as Dr. Rice did night after night. I saw some mighty
answers to prayer in those days! I thought then—and think now—
Dr. Rice was (is) the world's greatest preacher, the greatest Boss,
the most courteous gentleman!

In just **20 months,** out of these open-air revivals in Dallas, over
900 people had joined the church. The Tabernacle-type church
where God blessed so mightily in seven years was designed by
Dr. Rice (see picture on page ____). For awhile we had a sawdust
floor, until money could be raised for a cement one. We had
homemade benches—these too designed by Dr. Rice. But with God
blessing so mightily, who cared whether they were hard benches
or padded pews! Most of the services saw a packed auditorium.

Well, this was the early ministry in Dallas of Dr. Rice, when
he was 37 to 44 years of age. Known familiarly now these forty
years to America as "The Sword of the Lord man," I knew him
also as pastor of a great church (1932-1940). Then—as now—
he was called "a plain, old-fashioned preacher of the Gospel,
an ardent fundamentalist, one who believed all the Bible; the

uncompromising foe of modernism and unbelief and of sin in every form."

How could he, in the midst of the terrible Depression and one block from the second largest Southern Baptist church in Texas, begin an independent Baptist church, and see it grow in 7 years into 1,700 members with over 7,000 professions of faith? By the kind of preaching in *Preaching That Built a Great Church.*

These 29 stenographically reported messages are the best of his early sermons just as they fell from his lips. This is the real Rice, this, indeed, is Rice speaking!

† † †

"Maybe I ought to tell you," Dr. Rice confessed, "about a love letter handed me in Buffalo recently. On the outside was drawn a heart with the words: 'TO JOHN RICE WITH LOVE TO YOU.' Inside it said:

'Dear John Rice,

'I love you very much
You are very cute to me.
You sing very good to me.
You preach very good to me.
Do you want my phone number? Here it is _____.'

"Then it was signed with another heart and the words: 'WITH LOVE TO YOU. Lisa Booker, eight years old.'

"The affection of little children is very sweet to me," said he.

† † †

After quoting John 10:16, Dr. Rice made a contrast.

> Joe Trigger is our registered Tennessee Walking horse. My, what a magnificent animal! Over sixteen hands high, high-headed, with a flowing blond mane and a tail reaching nearly to the ground. A beautiful saddle gait, fox-trot pace, single-foot.
>
> I bought Trigger for Mrs. Rice to ride alongside my fine Tennessee Walking saddle horse, MacArthur.
>
> When I first brought Joe Trigger on the place, he was not at all well received. MacArthur was king of the farm and knew it. All the other horses respected him and followed his leadership. But Joe Trigger, so anxious to be friends with Mac, had to keep his distance. Mac saw to that. The new horse was not allowed in the bunch, so he grazed 50 to 100 yards away until they

gradually came to recognize him as a member of the family, with all the rights they enjoyed.

Sometimes we, like MacArthur, are not quick to recognize Christ's other sheep! All over the world He has multitudes of born-again people who are dear to His heart, who are redeemed by the blood of Christ, who love Him and are loved by the Saviour. Jesus reminds us, "Other sheep I have, which are not of this fold: them also I must bring, and they shall hear my voice; and there shall be one fold, and one shepherd."

How easy it is to be a Pharisee when we ought to be Christlike. Oh, this fundamentalism that is sound in doctrine and hard in heart! Oh, this Christian faithfulness to truth without tears, compassion, forgiveness; without open arms of fellowship and a heart big enough to take in all of God's people!

Does that strike a note in your own heart? convict you of your own attitude?

† † †

In March, Dr. Rice was granted the Doctor of Humanities degree from Hyles-Anderson College. Many years before, the Los Angeles Baptist Theological Seminary had bestowed upon him the Doctor of Divinity degree. Later, Bob Jones University gave him the Doctor of Literature degree. Then the San Francisco Baptist Theological Seminary granted him the Doctorate of Sacred Theology. The Sioux Empire College had given him a Doctor of Humanities degree also. Then in 1974 he had the very great honor of being awarded the D. L. Moody Award for "distinguished work in Christian literature," the first such annual award given by Moody Press.

Dr. Rice's grateful comment was: "We understand, of course, that these are the recognition of friends who love us, and so we accept them as a token of love and gratitude for the work God has helped us to do. But as Dr. J. B. Gambrell said, 'A doctor's degree is a very beautiful ornament, but it doesn't make any more pork! It doesn't make a preacher!' "

† † †

AN INTERESTING COMMENT: "Money is safer in my home than my SWORD OF THE LORD paper. I had a young man and woman here for dinner Sunday. The woman asked if she could have THE SWORD paper. I told her no, as I hadn't read it yet. But when they were gone,

I asked my wife, 'Where is my SWORD paper?' She said, 'The young lady took it.' "

† † †

144 SAVED IN 2 MONTHS! Yes, in April, 77 people wrote in to say they were saved through reading Sword literature; and in May, 67 others wrote to tell us the same good news.

† † †

This is a very interesting letter:

"Just received 3/14 SWORD. Happy to see 'Let's Go Soul Winning With Jack Hyles.' I think he's the greatest. I always look for him second. First, I look for something by R. A. Torrey, my grandfather." (It was signed by Victor Torrey.)

† † †

This letter shows again the power of a booklet:

Six years ago I was on the other side of the world—a sailor on Destroyer DD-466. I was outside God's love, up to my neck in sin, and totally disgusted with life and myself. We were on patrol in the Gulf of Tonkin.

The week before we had pulled into Subic Bay to take on fuel and ammo and a few new men. One was a young seaman named Glen Simpson who placed in my hands a small booklet of yours which changed my life.

It was evening, and I went up to the main deck to read it. The words were food to a starving man. The booklet was called *"What Must I Do to Be Saved?"*

I came to the Lord that night and left all my sins at His feet.

For the next two years I was fed through the mail by the people at Sword of the Lord. Not long after I had sent in the decision page of the booklet, you sent me a Sword Bible and someone else paid for my subscription to THE SWORD OF THE LORD.

What more can I say—except thank God for you and your people who are now my people!

The Scripture was fulfilled which says: 'He raises the poor from the dust, and lifts the needy from the ash heap. To make them sit with princes, with the princes of his people' (Ps. 113:7,8).

Love in Jesus,
(Signed) David E. Morgan

† † †

Have you ever read more touching letters than these quoted in this biography? And most of these dear ones were saved after reading the remarkable salvation booklet, *"What Must I Do to Be Saved?"*

But here is one paragraph from a letter written by an Episcopalian lay reader:

> Because of your excellent sermons and writings in THE SWORD, I have begun to feel fire in the pulpit on a Sunday. I am lay-reader in charge of St. Peter's Episcopal Church, a small mission in Blairsville. Your sincerity and love have warmed my heart and given me a desire to tell of my Saviour to others, and not just rely upon the dead sermons I am supposed to read....

† † †

In 1965 Dr. Rice could locate only 20 churches in America that claimed to baptize over 200 converts. Twelve were Southern Baptist churches. Dr. Lee Roberson and Dr. Rice talked about it. Dr. Roberson thought that, if they could get pastors and people to set a goal, they would be more apt to work to reach that goal. So he suggested that 200 churches ought to baptize at least 200 converts in a year's time.

Many pastors did set a goal, then set out to reach that goal. Seventy-six attempted that goal the first time it was announced in THE SWORD.

Then in 1973 THE SWORD published a list of some 90 churches that had baptized 200 or more.

In March of this year 123 churches were listed showing the number of converts reported baptized—from 200 up to 7,273. There were an Evangel Temple, two Christian churches, a Bible church, a Brethren church, a Church of the Open Door—all of them winning and baptizing over 200 converts. There was a Landmark Missionary Baptist Church, 36 Southern Baptist churches and 80 Bible Baptist or independent Baptist churches. We felt sure there were others, but these were the ones we knew about.

† † †

REPORT ON KOREAN SWORD LITERATURE. In 1971, the Sword of the Lord and contributors had provided $5,000 for printing 500,000 *"What Must I Do to Be Saved?"* in Korea. Then in 1974 the missionaries were begging for more copies. Money was sent to print 200,000 more.

Missionary Gerald Johnson of the Gospel Fellowship Missions, acting as our agent, reported:

> We thank the Lord for your telling SWORD readers of the great need for printing a new Korean edition of *"What Must I Do to Be Saved?"* We are most grateful to all who contributed to this printing of 200,000 booklets.
>
> As soon as they were printed, requests began coming from pastors, evangelists and lay Christians from every part of Korea. Our office staff is kept busy sending out the booklets.
>
> I am amazed at the response. For example, in the last three days we received 35 postcards with a signed statement that each of these people received Christ as their personal Saviour after reading the booklet. . . .
>
> In Korea many know something about the Bible, but they have not heard the pure Gospel. Therefore, your clear presentation is meeting a real need. With the demand as great as it is, I'm afraid this edition won't last too long.
>
> Thanks again, Dr. Rice, and thanks to all who, out of love for the lost, helped in the printing of this edition.
>
> Sincerely in Christ,
Missionary Gerald Johnson

† † †

When it rains, it pours. And it sure was a good rain! By now we were receiving so many good letters that we couldn't print them all.

One woman wanted to know what church in her area of New Jersey would teach the Scripture like Dr. Rice. I wrote her commending three churches within reach that advertised in THE SWORD. Then came a most wonderful response.

The lady, wife of an executive with an engineering firm, attended one of the churches, which was crowded that day. The minister preached to the unsaved, and several claimed the Lord; then some were baptized.

"The invitation was to accept Christ as Saviour," she said, "but I had already taken Christ as my own personal Saviour through THE SWORD OF THE LORD and Dr. John R. Rice. Did I need to go forward again?" (That was the first time she had ever seen anyone baptized by immersion. She had been baptized as a baby in the Catholic church.)

In the same letter she told how, as she read THE SWORD and the Scriptures, she had gotten "a serenity beyond anything I had ever thought possible."

The pastor had given away Dr. Rice's booklet, *Saved for Certain,* to every stranger brought by a member. But she said, "Nobody brought me. I came by myself, so I didn't get the book. Some of us have to make it alone." Of course we sent her the book and wrote her about following Jesus in baptism AFTER conversion.

† † †

Then came a letter from a dear cowboy friend in Colorado, a trick rider in rodeos all over the West. He was rejoicing and reminding Dr. Rice that it was through THE SWORD that he read the Gospel, learned how to be saved and was wonderfully saved.

Two or three books could be filled with such letters. We laughed, we cried, and we praised God for every one!

† † †

I said before that Dr. Rice never asked God for a piddling number of subscriptions, anything under 25,000. Now in April he was saying, "I would love to have 70,000 subscriptions, new and renewal, in this earnest effort now"—the Spring Subscription Campaign.

† † †

THE SWORD OF THE LORD was and is one of the two most influential gospel papers ever published in the history of the world. The other was *The Sword and the Trowel,* edited by the great Charles Haddon Spurgeon.

Of course, everyone in Spurgeon's day did not read his paper. But thousands of the most ardent soul-winning preachers and defenders of the faith did. And everyone today does not read THE SWORD OF THE LORD. But we are convinced that the greatest Bible-believing preachers of our day do read it. The greatest soul-winning pastors and evangelists alive today are friends of THE SWORD OF THE LORD, and their sermons are published in it.

† † †

Who would have ever believed it possible—build a fine brick-and-glass 3-story building and pay for it as it went up! That does seem unbelievable; but, then, Dr. Rice is an unusual man. Now in his 80th year, he seemed to have greater vision, zeal and determination than ever.

When he suggested building a much-needed addition to the Sword plant and paying for it as it was built, many eyebrows were raised in question, "Can we do it?" Dr. Rice's answer: "No, we can't do it alone, but with God's blessing and the help of His people, together we can do it."

So the building was begun; and by May, 1975, it was almost completed. Already $302,955 had been paid to the contractor and architect. And by July 3, all the money needed was in hand!

We felt visitors would be impressed immediately with the businesslike atmosphere of an efficiently run Christian organization that honored Christ in appearance and actions.

LATER: As we entered the new building, we felt we were set free from the restraints that had held us back from growing; now we could set goals, reach more people for Christ, bless more hearts and encourage more Christians than ever before possible.

The gifts of God's people had not erected a monument here in Murfreesboro, but a new mission house with Dr. Rice at the helm and the world at heart.

† † †

He always had a burden for ministerial students. So this year he made a special effort to get good literature into their hands. Now he was going to several colleges with huge amounts of books and letting students buy them at cost, or below cost.

In just a few weeks' time, he was invited to: Grace Theological Seminary at Winona Lake; Grand Rapids Baptist College; Hyles-Anderson College; Tennessee Temple Schools; Piedmont Bible College; Pensacola Christian College; Liberty Baptist College and Thomas Road Baptist Church at Lynchburg, Virginia; Clearwater Christian College, Clearwater, Florida; Midwestern Baptist College, Pontiac, Michigan; Calvary Baptist College, Kansas City, Missouri.

Since he took no royalty on his books, the Board allowed him to make a special offer now and then to these students in Christian colleges. There is no telling what these books did or will do to the ministry of those ministerial students and others.

† † †

Word came on Monday, September 29, that Dr. G. B. Vick had passed away suddenly. Dr. Rice had preached at his church, Temple Baptist Church, Detroit, the day before.

Dr. Vick had been a friend of Dr. Rice since 1926, and had been on our Sword Cooperating Board for a number of years.

✝ ✝ ✝

Part of the crowd attending Dallas National Sword Conference

After the unusually successful conference held last year in Indianapolis, Dr. Rice, with the aid of his staff and the counsel of other good men, set out to find the mind of the Lord concerning where the next National Sword Conference could be held.

Several major cities were seriously and favorably considered, but finally Dallas was picked, and the Convention Center seating some 10,400 secured. The time was August 3 through 6.

After much prayer, Dr. Rice chose the speakers: Jack Hyles, Jerry Falwell, Jack Van Impe, Tom Malone, John Rawlings, Ed Nelson, Bill Dowell, Bill Rice and, of course, he himself was on the program.

The Sunday night crowd saw approximately 8,000 in attendance, while other services ran from 4,000 to 7,000. In one service some 500 preachers were present.

There was a choir of 350 voices. Bill Harvey[1] did a masterful job with the music.

Some 115 exhibitors bought space in the exhibit hall, which helped to bear the great financial load.

The mayor of Dallas made a special presentation and gave Dr. Rice a plaque declaring him an honorary citizen of Dallas.

Many declared the Sword Conference in Dallas a grand success.

Atlanta was being considered for the National Sword Conference the week of August 22 through 27, 1976.

† † †

Dr. Roger Voegtlin is pastor of Fairhaven Baptist Church at Chesterton, Indiana—a tremendous church with several thousand members. Dr. Rice was with him in October.

When introducing him, the pastor told his people how, when he was ten years old, he went to Airport Baptist Church in Chicago to hear Dr. Rice preach in a revival. Then he confessed: "What I preach to you on the home, I got from Dr. Rice. What I preach to you on prayer, I got from Dr. Rice. What I preach to you on soul winning, I got from Dr. Rice." Of course, he meant he had gotten some help in those fields; but we know that, as an earnest student and preacher, he got much more from the Word directly.

† † †

On December 11, we celebrated in the Sword of the Lord auditorium Dr. Rice's 80th birthday. A great crowd came from 20 states.

There were four glorious and historic hours of celebration, with Dr. Jack Hyles bringing a special birthday message. Assisting in the preliminaries were two outstanding Christian businessmen, Dr. Russell Anderson and Dr. John Beiler, and Christian movie producer, Ron Ormond.

Adding to the excitement and thrill of this birthday evening was the premiere of Dr. Rice's new film, "The Land Where Jesus Walked." Much of the filming was done in the Holy Land on Dr. Rice's 1975 Tour.

Mr. Ormond presented Dr. Rice an "Oscar," a small gold moving

---

[1] The freedom Bill had came from working in the Salvation Army and singing with his twin brother in the Army meetings. He had the culture of fine training in Southwestern Baptist Theological Seminary, the experience with some of the greatest men of God, including years with Dr. Hyles and Evangelist Joe Boyd. Bill regularly sang in Sword Conferences.

picture camera which still sits on his office piano.

I just wish we had space to print the full message by Dr. Hyles, "Happy Birthday, Barzillai." Barzillai was also "fourscore years old" (II Sam. 19:32).

He showed how similar our Barzillai—John Rice—was to that Barzillai who celebrated his 80th birthday with King David many years ago. Nothing could have been more fitting.[2]

In that message Dr. Hyles was honoring "the greatest man I have ever known, Dr. John R. Rice." Looking directly at the Captain of our Team, he reminded him that there were several Bible greats who served God faithfully at the age of 80, and now was no time to quit!

> Moses was 80 when he went before Pharaoh. Aaron was 83 at the time of the Exodus. Anna was 84 at the birth of our Lord, as she consummated her wait for Him. Abraham was 86 at the birth of Ishmael and 100 at the conception of Isaac. Caleb was 85 when he declared himself as strong as he was at 40 and completely fit to fight at the age of 85. He was 85 when he said, "Give me this mountain."
>
> But, as far as I know, only one man in all the Bible told us the very day he was 80, and that was Barzillai.

Then Dr. Hyles thinks of men of more recent years:

> Tennyson produced his famous poem, "Crossing the Bar," at age 80. Michelangelo painted the ceiling of the Sistine Chapel on his back on a scaffold at near 90. Phillips Brookes, one of the world's renowned preachers, was still preaching at age 84. Justice Oliver Wendell Holmes set down some of his most brilliant opinions at age 90.
>
> John Wesley preached his last sermon when he was 88. George Mueller lived to be 94 and was still preaching to large crowds at age 86. Sir Winston Churchill continued to sit in the House of Commons until 1964, when he was 90. At the age of 85 he held a one-man exhibition of his own paintings at the Royal Academy.
>
> General Douglas MacArthur remained an active general in the army until the year of his death, at age 83. Henry J. Kaiser, builder of roads, dams, ships, automobiles, planes, factories and resorts—at age 84 was still overseeing his television network and the Kaiser hotels in Hawaii.

---

[2] The full message was run in December 26, 1975 issue of THE SWORD OF THE LORD.

At Dr. Rice's 80th birthday celebration (l to r): Mr. John Beiler, newly elected to the Sword Board; Tim and Ron Ormond, who directed and photographed "The Land Where Jesus Walked"; Mrs. John R. Rice; Dr. Rice; Dr. Jack Hyles, who spoke at the celebration; and Dr. Russell Anderson, trusted friend and great helper of the Sword

I would like to remind you that Thomas A. Edison was 81 when he obtained his last patent. Charles Weigle wrote his last song when he was 92. He was 95 when he died.

Dr. Rice, if Mueller can make it to 94, you dead sure can! We haven't got time for you to die!

† † †

This poem was written by Ferman Sauve in his 92nd year:

> *I am not old, though folks may say*
> *That I am aging every day;*
> *Though I am weak at times, I know*
> *That in my weakness I can go*
> *To Christ who strengthens me; and so*
> *I am not old.*

I am not old; though sight grows dim
I still can feel the hand of Him
Who leads me o'er the darkest way,
Still guiding that I may not stray;
So with assurance I still say:
        I am not old.

I am not old; though up in years
Life's twilight holds for me no fears
Because I know my destiny
And that my Saviour waits for me,
Renews my strength each day: you see
        I am not old.

I am not old; true, this old shell
Of mortal clay in which I dwell
Shall fall when trials of earth are o'er;
Yet I, within, shall upward soar
And go on living evermore:
        I am not old!

Over 2,000 friends sent greetings, and many sent gifts to the Sword of the Lord or for subscriptions.

† † †

EDITOR'S 80TH BIRTHDAY SUBSCRIPTION CAMPAIGN. It is now fall and time for another subscription campaign.

When some of us walked right into his office one day and flatly asked, "Dr. Rice, what would you like for your 80th birthday?" do you know what he answered? "80,000 subscriptions!"

Now we had never before in one campaign gotten 80,000 subscriptions. Always before, we had undertaken what we thought was "possible." *But Dr. John R. Rice has never been 80 before, either!*

That was a mountain we thought we couldn't tunnel through.

Well! We loved our Boss, and we wanted always to please him. But, good-night! 80,000 subscriptions! That seemed impossible!

Now we began trying to figure out how the Lord could do it! "Say we have 300,000 in our subscription files—and we did. That means if only one-fourth of our subscribers send one subscription, Dr. Rice's wish would be granted!" Our faith grew a little bit.

Then "some of our 'Old Faithfuls' surely would want to send a list of ten names for ten subscriptions for Christmas." A little more faith!

"And we are allowing our subscribers to get subscriptions at rock-bottom prices—one to nine for $3 each instead of $5." The impossible had now become more possible!

But what increased our faith the most was Dr. Rice's praying for 80,000 subscriptions and believing when he prayed! Nothing is impossible to him that believeth!

At an age when most men had already been turned out to pasture to live out their retirement in ease and comfort, Dr. Rice was pushing ahead with a greater vision than ever!

After asking for that gigantic bunch of subscriptions, he wrote: "I laid upon Circulation Manager Rev. Ron English and Editorial Assistant Dr. Viola Walden the burden to get 80,000 subscribers for THE SWORD OF THE LORD in this 'Birthday Campaign.' "

Is that "passing the buck" or what!! So now you know who was to carry the ball and get those 80,000! But the "Captain of Our Team" was an important man in our lives, so Ron and I planned to toot our birthday horns loud and clear for several weeks.

Let's get started raising those 80,000 subscriptions for his 80th birthday! (Read results in February, 1976.)

† † †

Two Sword staff members had a very unusual experience in October. Mike Baldwin and Max Lambert ran a bus route for our church, Franklin Road Baptist Church. On a recent Saturday they had gone to a new part of the city house to house and collected seven or eight black children on the bus and had a lovely service. Best of all: all these children on the bus that day claimed to trust Christ as Saviour.

That evening two of them, a brother and sister, were run over by a car and killed. Mike and Max, hearing of the deaths, went back to the community, found the house where the two lived and tried to comfort the loved ones. Relatives had gathered, and fourteen of them trusted Christ on the spot.

Later the family of the two killed called the church and asked if one of these men would come to the funeral and say a word about the children trusting Christ. Mike went, and there at the funeral fifteen others got saved!

Dr. Rice, by example and precept, had caused the staff of this

Are we seeing double? No, a talented friend drew this likeness and Dr. Rice posed beside himself during the celebration. The portrait hangs in the Sword lobby.

organization to be concerned and on the lookout for the lost.

Thank God, Dr. Rice's Sword team were soul winners!

✝ ✝ ✝

In December Mrs. Rice and I had driven down on a Saturday with Dr. Rice to Chattanooga. He was to speak Sunday in two services at Trinity Baptist Church there.

It was a blessed morning service.

Soon after lunch Dr. Rice began having shortness of breath and was in a great deal of distress. We prayed, talked about what should be done, and waited. His doctor already had him on some medication, which often gave him some relief from his shortness of breath. After taking a tablet, the trouble remained. Very reluctantly, he asked me to call the pastor, Dr. Thompson, and explain the problem and see if he would release him from the night service.

Of course Dr. Thompson understood and agreed to preach in his stead.[3] He had me drive home. By nightfall he was feeling better.

Again we believe this was another mild heart attack. But he came to work the next morning, and things went pretty well for awhile. Of course some of us were distressed by his frequent shortness of breath, but he was convinced it was nothing serious and would not give in.

† † †

Our carefully kept records show that 712 people wrote in 1975 saying they had trusted Christ as Saviour through our literature. Some were saved through sermons in THE SWORD: many through the booklet, *"What Must I Do to Be Saved?"*; some through other printed messages to the unsaved. How we rejoiced in that!

---

[3] We could count on one hand the number of times Dr. Rice had ever missed an engagement in his years of travel. That was something he would never, never, never do unless it was an emergency, as this seemed to be.

1976 Dr. Rice dearly loved that tender Gipsy Smith and often used his sermons in THE SWORD. His preaching revealed his gentleness. Although a simple Gypsy, he was a man of culture and a great blessing everywhere he went.

Once Dr. Rice called the Gypsy, who was in Chicago, to ask permission to publish a certain sermon in THE SWORD. In his gentle voice, he said: "Why, my dear, I do not see any reason why not. Yes, you may!"

† † †

From February 6, 1976 SWORD:

> *BULLETIN*
>
> *81,822 SUBS!*
>
> *The Sword Staff is happy to announce the greatest victory ever in our recent subscription campaign. We received a grand total of 81,822 subscriptions, new, renewal and gift, in response to the campaign honoring Dr. Rice on his 80th birthday. We extend our sincere thanks to those of you who prayed, gave and renewed, making it possible for us to exceed all previous records. We consider you part of the ever-growing Sword family, and we thank God for you.*
>
> *Ron English, Circulation Manager*
> *Viola Walden, Editor's Assistant*

† † †

"They just told me Friday (March 12) that already, before Letter Month is over, we have had orders for over a half million copies of my booklet, *'What Must I Do to Be Saved?'* ordered during this Letter Month,"

Dr. Rice reported. "That means this year we will run a good deal more than two million copies distributed in the English language."

† † †

In March I read this: "Thirty-six wrote in the last five days to tell us they had been saved through Sword of the Lord literature." Nothing rejoiced our hearts more than to have such good news.

† † †

At Pastors' School this year, Dr. Hyles passed out SWORD envelopes and got 974 subscriptions, though it seemed almost everyone there was already a subscriber. But he asked those who received it, to renew. What a friend!

† † †

Guess what! Same song, second . . . third . . . fourth . . . fifth verse! Subscription campaign time again! Talking to Ron and me, Dr. Rice said, "Let us get in the next few weeks 50,000 more subscribers to THE SWORD." We had hardly gotten our breath from the 80th birthday campaign; now here our Boss was planning another in the spring. Remember, he always started counting at 50,000!

† † †

S O S. When ships are in trouble at sea, they send out an SOS distress signal to alert any other ships nearby that they need help. When an airplane is in trouble, the pilot sends an SOS distress signal by transmitting on his radio, "Mayday! Mayday!" which means, "Come help me!" When a man is drowning, he sends out a distress signal by screaming "Help!" There are many variations of distress signals, but all have essentially the same meaning—"Come and help me!"

Now Ron and I were sending out our distress signal: "Help us with subscriptions!" The Boss man, the "Captain of Our Team," was asking for 50,000 close on the heels of the 80,000 for his 80th birthday just six months before. He would be busy at other things, leaving the getting of them largely to his circulation manager and personal assistant! But Dr. Rice never washed his hands of a campaign. Indeed, he was always in the thick of it and wrote many articles and made many mentions of it in "Editor's Notes." And I think it was he who got the bulk of subscriptions, while we just assisted him.

One of his favorite verses was Psalm 81:10, "I am the Lord thy God, which brought thee out of the land of Egypt: open thy mouth wide, and I will fill it." And he was continually asking for *BIG* things, believing, trying to do that bigger thing for Christ to please Him.

Our offer this time was 4 subscriptions for $15 or 10 for $30 and Dr. Rice's new book, *The Charismatic Movement* (20 chapters), free.

† † †

Happy Warrior Room, joining Sword auditorium

The Happy Warrior Room is full of pictures, articles and memoirs which trace the life of Dr. Rice from his boyhood to the worldwide ministry he eventually had. It was the creation of Mrs. John R. Rice and Miss Willie Brummitt and was first opened to the public during the spring conference of 1976 here in Murfreesboro.

† † †

We had just returned from another successful and fruitful Sword Tour with 132 pilgrims (many others had wanted to go but had to be turned away because of lack of hotel space in Cairo).

We know of eight happy conversions during the tour. Mrs. Rice won a young woman on one tour bus. Another, who indicated she was unsaved,

in the midst of singing old songs and praising the Lord on the bus, came
to the front rejoicing that she had found Christ. Joseph, a serious,
cultured guide in Israel who told Dr. Rice privately that he had been
deeply concerned to learn more about the Christian religion, was won
by our own Ron Zywotko.

Before leaving our beautiful Intercontinental Hotel in Jerusalem, Dr.
Rice talked to the young photographer at the hotel, who had for years
taken pictures of our group, and he happily trusted the Lord. In writing
about it, Dr. Rice commented: "He went to Miss Viola (his dear friend)
and said, 'Do you know what I did?' then told her what he had done!"

What a variety of 132 people and religions! Baptists, Presbyterians,
Pentecostalists, Nazarenes, Mennonites, Lutherans and Reformed made
up the 132. Two Sioux Indians were among us. There were 14 preachers.

Though we had been to the Holy Land scores of times, each trip
brought back delightful memories. Dr. Rice baptized each year in the
Jordan those who wanted to be but had not been previously baptized,
and many were won to Christ year after year. Those fond memories will
never fade.

† † †

"90 'ODD' WORKERS"! I doubt if there was any organization in
America that had as many talented people as Sword of the Lord Foundation. Almost any of them could do any task assigned to them, whether
it was their "talent" or not. This included clever articles.

I was looking through back issues of THE SWORD and found this one
by a wonderful Sword employee in the book department, Mrs. Gen
Womack.

Though clever, it gives forth much information about those who make
up this organization.

> Dr. Rice sometimes tells people there are 90-"odd" workers at
> the Sword of the Lord. At a recent conference, Al Byers asked
> those 90 "odd" workers to stand and introduce themselves.
>
> Since then I have been thinking about the "odd" workers at
> the Sword of the Lord.
>
> There are some "odd" women here who have given up the com-
> forts and joys of a husband and family to give themselves com-
> pletely to the ministry of Dr. Rice and the Sword of the Lord.
>
> Some of the "odd" ones are men with families who have left
> lucrative positions in the business world to bring their wives and

children here to serve the Lord with less pay than they received before.

Other "odd" people owned their own businesses "back home," yet sold out lock, stock and barrel to work here for the Lord.

One of the "oddest" groups and the one to whom I really must take my hat off, are the young girls, right out of high school, who have never been away from the protection and care of their loving parents. Yet they come, many times hundreds of miles, not really knowing what is involved, where they will live, what kind of friends they will find or the kind of work they will be doing—yet they blindly trust their heavenly Father to lead them each step of the way.

We have some very "odd" secretaries! Several ladies are executive secretaries who could command their salary and work conditions in the biggest and most influential offices of the land. Yet they work for much less because of their dedication to this work.

Another group of "odd" ones are the men who are ordained, God-called preachers of the Gospel who feel their lives can count for more in eternity by investing them in this worldwide ministry than in a small local ministry. We have several who fall into this category.

Some of our very special "odd" people are a few handicapped. Although their crutches and hearing aids are very much in evidence, they are giving what they can of themselves and their talents to this ministry.

Some "odd" ones are our part-time working mothers. They work from 4 to 6 hours each day to help keep their children in the Christian school. They faithfully carry their work load here, then cheerfully hurry home to their many and varied duties as loyal wives and mothers.

Praise the Lord for the "odd" people, both men and women, whom you see at the Sword of the Lord offices. The ladies all wear knee-length dresses in modest styles. No pant-suits, no mini-skirts, no revealing necklines and bare backs. Our men are very handsome with their short haircuts and hairless faces. Each man comes to work clean-shaven and dressed appropriately for his work. We have decent Bible dress standards at the Sword of the Lord.

Another thing about us "odd" people: we believe and practice Bible separation in our daily lives. We have the same standards at home or up town as we do in the office. You will not find our "odd" folks at the Hollywood movies up town or in a bar or other questionable place. Instead you will find these "odd" fellows and girls up town passing out gospel tracts or studying at the Bible institute, or at some church- or Sword-related activity.

Visitors to the Sword building will notice a sign which welcomes them but also says, "Visitors—No Smoking." The "odd" workers, of course, do not need to be reminded, since no one who works for the Sword of the Lord has a tobacco problem.

You say, "That surely is an 'odd' gang!" Yes, I agree! As you pass a machine you very probably will hear some "odd" fellow singing, "Oh, say but I'm glad, I'm glad. . .," and it's from the heart. We really ARE glad! A recent visitor who has worked for many years in a factory among worldly people remarked about the fact that everyone looked so happy here and, furthermore, seemed to be so happy!

Yes, Dr. Rice is right! There are 90 "odd" workers at the Sword of the Lord! I have often heard preachers explain away the term "peculiar people" in Titus 2:14. They say, "That does not necessarily mean that God's people should be odd."

Well, I'm not so sure! The 90 "odd" workers on the staff at the Sword of the Lord headquarters in Murfreesboro prove that being "odd," as the world thinks, is not so bad after all. I, for one, am proud to be one of the 90 "odd" Sword of the Lord workers.

† † †

BACK AGAIN AT WINONA LAKE. In 1945, 1946 and 1947 Sword of the Lord had tremendous conferences at Winona Lake, Indiana. Now we were having perhaps 25 Sword Conferences a year all over the United States. But it seemed wise to have once again another large mid-summer conference at Winona Lake to reach a multitude of friends in the Indiana-Illinois-Michigan-Ohio area and beyond.

The conference was held July 12 through 16. Speakers were: Dr. Tom Malone, Dr. Jack Hyles, Dr. Greg Dixon and Dr. John R. Rice.

Great crowds attended the oldest of the large conference grounds in America. Night after night the Rodeheaver Auditorium was filled, with people standing around the walls. A tremendous presence of the Holy Spirit was sensed in that place.

Winona Lake extended another invitation in 1977.

† † †

A great National Sword Conference was held in Atlanta, Georgia, August 22 through 27. Speakers were: Drs. Jack Hyles, Jerry Falwell, Jack Van Impe, Lee Roberson, Bill Rice, Charles Billington, Harold Henniger, Curtis Hutson, E. J. Daniels, Bob Gray, Cecil Hodges, Greg Dixon, Russell Anderson, "Mr. Bus"—Wally Beebe—and John R. Rice.

The estimated crowd the beginning night was 6,000. Night after night multitudes thronged the Atlanta Civic Center. All the speakers rejoiced at the tremendous attendance. We know people were present from nearly every state, also from Australia, Canada, Ireland and one came from Palestine.

How wonderful to see pastors from far and near committing themselves wholly to out-and-out soul winning, making that priority in plans and labor.

When Dr. Rice spoke on the Christian home, perhaps a thousand men, heads of families, stood to wholly give themselves to Joshua's vow, "As for me and my house, we will serve the Lord."

There was great movement among the scores of preachers attending. Each speaker spoke with power and liberty. And what unity, what friendliness, what cooperation among these godly preachers and leaders in the immediate area!

† † †

It had already been decided that, in 1977, the Sword's National Conference would be held at Cobo Hall, Detroit, seating 12,000.

† † †

This year several sad things happened. Dr. Bill Rice suffered a severe stroke; Dr. Oliver B. Greene and Dr. Ford Porter went Home to Heaven, as did Dr. Rice's long-time friend and classmate at Baylor, Rev. L. O. Engelmann, a missionary to Mexico.

† † †

WHAT WAS IT. . . A "WHAT?"!? It most likely was. Dr. Rice's greatly used tract, *"What Must I Do to Be Saved?"* was referred to very possibly in a story released by a certain local newspaper reporter when he reported the return of several items stolen from the apartment of a faithful soul-winning couple, members of a local Baptist church. The report stated: "Among the things returned was a pink booklet containing questions and answers about religion, such as, 'What must I do to be saved?' On the inside of the booklet's cover the thief had scribbled these words in pencil: 'Sorry. Pray for me.' "

We reasonably hoped that the message of our pink tract-booklet touched the heart of the thief and resulted in not only the return of the stolen goods but the salvation of his soul.

† † †

In September Dr. Russell Anderson turned in a list numbering 2,156 new families to receive a one-year subscription to THE SWORD OF THE LORD, and along with the names, a check for $6,468 to pay for these subscriptions.

† † †

Another highlight of the year was a Bible study cruise September 11 through 18 on the *M/S Southward* in the Caribbean Sea, with stops at Jamaica, Grand Cayman Island in the West Indies and Cozumel, Mexico. Sixty-two people went to hear Dr. Rice teach the book of Revelation two hours a day. My, how they were blessed!

† † †

We worked hard when we attempted once to get 40,000 subscriptions in one campaign—and did it. For Dr. Rice's 80th birthday last year, we aimed at 80,000 subscriptions—and reached it.

Now, during the present fall campaign (October 15 to December 11), Dr. Rice and his staff felt God would give us 100,000. We had never asked for such a big response before; we do not know of any Christian magazine in America that had. But God is delighted when we ask of Him *BIG* things.

In addition to a reduction in subscription price, we added this fall the "100 Sub Club." And I'm telling you, preachers and laymen alike were sending in 100 subscriptions for $250.00 like you never saw! I had never seen the pastors and our readers more enthusiastic.

We put pictures of the 100 SUB CLUB members in each issue as they came in. Why? Because the scriptural command is that we give "honour to whom honour is due." We felt that those who sent in 100 subscriptions should have special honor.

David was inspired of God to list 37 mighty men and their great exploits in defending and building his kingdom. They earned that honor.

Paul told Timothy, "Let the elders that rule well be counted worthy of double honour."

Paul named sixteen and gave worldwide fame to certain friends at Rome whom he greeted (Rom. 16).

Our Lord was so pleased with the sacrifice and love of Mary of Bethany who anointed Him with precious ointment that He said the story of her loving gift would be recorded and spread throughout the whole world.

So these who were helping us reach the 100,000 goal by Dr. Rice's birthday December 11 were our heroes, our Hall of Fame, our friends on whom we could rely and for whom honor was due.

Of course Dr. Rice was the first to join the 100 SUB CLUB, and Russell Anderson and Dr. Jack Hyles and Dr. Lee Roberson! Then came great lists from Dr. Falwell, Dr. Ed Nelson, Dr. Gary Coleman, Dr. and Mrs. Bill Rice, Dr. Tom Wallace, Dr. and Mrs. Pennell, Dr. Clyde Box, Dr. Tom Berry, Dr. Greg Dixon, Dr. J. R. Faulkner—joining those who had large churches or works. Hundreds of others were sending 100 or more subscriptions, including a good many on the Sword staff. Rev. John Powell sent 530 subscriptions.

By the middle of November, some 15,000 subscriptions had already come through the 100 SUB CLUB alone.

Such interest encouraged us that "maybe" such a goal was possible.

LATER: I looked ahead into 1977 and in January found this first item in "Editor's Notes": "This morning I got a full account of paid subscriptions coming in up to December 31, 1976, in our fall campaign—AN AMAZING TOTAL OF 100,605!"

† † †

On December 11, 1976, an interested group gathered at the new Sword retirement home called Sunset Square, a block west of the Sword plant, to see the fourteen beautiful apartments, plus the apartment and office for the manager. There was even space for a beauty shop (to operate on Saturday only) and a guest room.

It has all security measures and luxurious comfort for retirees.

Those lovely people who would come to live there would be provided a ride to the Franklin Road Baptist Church.

There was a long list of interested parties.

† † †

Dr. Rice reported that the Sword "did a business of over two million

Inside courtyard at Sunset Square

dollars in 1976." That was income from subscriptions, book sales, commercial advertising and gifts. He then quoted, "Being confident of this very thing, that he which hath begun a good work in you will perform it until the day of Jesus Christ."

† † †

How grateful we were to hear from 667 people who wrote that they were saved through our literature in 1976! It is very likely that, for everyone who trusted Christ and wrote us about it, there were others who trusted Christ and didn't write us but who went to some church and claimed Him.

That made over 18,000 who had written us that they had trusted Christ through our printed sermons and Sword literature published in 38 languages around the world.

† † †

The Sword had a "fun" party, and it was really fun—singing, mimicking, skits, etc.

Our Wholesale Book Department made a reading out of the books we publish. These letters in caps are names, or parts of names, of Sword publications. Read with that in mind, and laugh with us, as we split our sides laughing when this was read! You should have heard Dr. Rice! He enjoyed having fun. And it thrilled him to see the talent and cleverness of his staff.

One day as I was looking FROM MY KITCHEN WINDOW down the GOLDEN PATH that leads from my HOME to the FIVE PILLARS OF THE TEMPLE I saw the BUILDER OF BRIDGES BUILDING AND BAT-TLING until BEYOND THE SUNSET. It was long past my tea time so I said, "FILL MY CUP" and sat waiting for SOME GOLDEN DAYREAK. I must have dozed off in sleep, for I saw much to my surprise, SKELETONS COME OUT OF THE CLOSET!

As I watched spellbound from the shadows, there seemed to be BLOOD AND TEARS ON THE STAIRWAY. Soon, COWBOY BOOTS came clomp-ing along, and I could not tell to WHOSOEVER AND WHATSOEVER they might have belonged. However, the person wearing them told me SEVEN SECRETS and that he would have a REWARD FOR JERRY. He also showed me some APPLES OF GOLD he carried in his VEST POCKET (for his COMPANION).

I said, "Sir, have you seen SOME DOGS I HAVE KNOWN?" and he said, "Yes, as a matter of fact, TWO DOGS about got my PEACE OF MIND just down the road a bit, but I ran from the GRIDIRON TO THE GOSPEL and GOD'S IDEAL WOMAN put me on the GOOD SHIP COURTSHIP and we sailed away to the RIGHT WAY IN MARRIAGE with ROMANCE AT RED PINES."

As I sat, still in the shadows, THE EXILED PRINCE came along. He said he had just had a wonderful ADVENTURE IN ANIMAL LAND. SCAMPER SQUIRREL had found a COFFER OF JEWELS by the CHURCH OF GOD IN CORINTH. At first he could not decide whether to COME OUT OR STAY IN, but he ran home to tell his mother. She was sitting on the porch reading 742 HEART-WARMING POEMS out of the SWORD SCRAPBOOK. He was so excited it sounded as if he were SPEAK-ING WITH TONGUES; but when she had finally succeeded in TAMING THE TEENAGER, she admonished him to DO RIGHT and told him a STRANGE SHORT STORY about a little boy who once thought that HELL IS NO JOKE. Of course Scamper knew he must tell the SOUTHERN BAP-TIST LEADERS that the WORST THING THAT CAN HAPPEN TO YOU would be to be TRAILED BY A WILD BEAST. He wanted to LIVE HAP-PILY EVER AFTER, so reported the loot to the FOUR BIGGEST FOOLS IN TOWN.

About that time some CHRISTIAN TEENAGER GUYS AND GALS came running along with a CHARISMATIC MOVEMENT. They wanted to catch HERBERT W. ARMSTRONG to tell him HOW TO QUIT SMOK-

ING and to keep from MISSING GOD'S LAST TRAIN. The last I saw of them they were going down the PATHS TO RUIN with a WHAT MUST I DO TO BE SAVED? tract in their hands, shouting, "JESUS MAY COME TODAY."

The DANGEROUS TRIPLETS came along, then UNEQUALLY YOKED together. I asked what their problem was, and they said, "THIS WOMAN THOU GAVEST ME is a REBELLIOUS WIFE and it is ECUMENICAL FOLLY to try to KEEP THE HONEY IN THE HONEYMOON any longer!" I said, "Oh, please, don't get a DIVORCE: you have a LOT of ECUMENICAL EXCUSES left yet, so COUNT YOUR BLESSINGS and remember that you are NEVER ALONE AND NEVER FORSAKEN!"

As the dawn approached I became hungry and reached for a slice of BREAD FROM BELLEVUE OVEN just as a MAN SENT FROM GOD came hurrying along, muttering to himself, "WHAT IT COSTS TO BE A GOOD CHRISTIAN these days! It seems everyone is carried away by FALSE DOCTRINES! It's no use trying to BUILD AN EVANGELISTIC CHURCH when everyone is busily USING FORMS AND LETTERS and going to HEAR JACK HYLES! To say nothing of asking DR. RICE MORE QUESTIONS! If they would only BAPTIZE MORE CONVERTS and do GOD'S WORK meant FOR PREACHERS ONLY, they would be ALWAYS REJOICING and OBTAIN FULLNESS OF POWER!"

As he walked away, MISS VIOLA CAME THROUGH THE BIBLE LANDS after having the WORLD'S BEST HOLIDAY SEEKING A CITY. She said it was the WORLD'S MOST POPULAR GAME, but you had to COMPEL THEM TO COME IN and tell them ALL ABOUT THE BUS MINISTRY and THE SECOND MAN. All she wanted to do was tell them the TRUTH ABOUT THE CHRISTIAN LIFE and HOW TO GET THINGS FROM GOD.

As the sun broke over the MOUNTAIN PEAKS I realized I must COME BACK TO BETHEL. DAVID AND BATHSHEBA would be waiting for me by the CHRISTIAN WELLS OF JOY as they were planning to sing a SWORD SPECIAL SONG. They also had 10 MESSAGES they needed to give to the BOSSY WIVES AND WOMEN PREACHERS and those with SKIMPY SKIRTS AND HIPPIE HAIR, to tell them HOW TO COPE WITH YOUR PARENTS.

As I hurried home, I felt my evening, though strange, had been profitable. I now knew how to be a GRAND SUCCESS and what to do when I had an OPERATION. I would work a CROSSWORD PUZZLE and read the 300 books on the Sword book list!

Did I tell you we've got talent!

1977 In March Dr. Rice listed six great 50,000-watt stations carrying the Voice of Revival broadcast: XPRS, San Diego...WCRJ, Jacksonville, Florida...WOR, New York City ...WRCP, Philadelphia...WSM, Nashville...WOAI, San Antonio, with intentions of soon going on another one in Albany, New York.

† † †

"Ladies, you are invited to attend the Sword's first Women's Jubilee Retreat. Nine famous women have prepared 14 hours of blessing, teaching, problem-solving, heavenly refreshing, fun and fellowship just for you."

That's how we announced our first get-together for women only at the Sword of the Lord in March, bringing in such speakers as Mrs. Jack Hyles, Mrs. Lee Roberson, Mrs. Marlene Evans, Mrs. Bill Rice, the Rice sisters and Dr. and Mrs. John R. Rice.

And they came from 25 states—throngs of women, godly women, earnest women, hungry-hearted women.

We announced the jubilee would be in the Sword of the Lord auditorium, which seats 800 or a little more with chairs. Soon we found we had far more than this one auditorium could handle. We reserved then the gym at Franklin Road Baptist Church, filling it. The same program was heard at both places.

We estimated 1600 ladies attended.

After it was over, many insisted that it be a yearly affair!

Mrs. Lee Roberson wrote back: *Thank you for one of the best times I've ever had!*

This was the first of many Sword Women's Jubilees. Dr. Rice tells why he felt these jubilees necessary at this time in our generation:

> In America and other civilized countries several trends have brought disaster to women. One marriage in every three ends in

divorce; so marriage is not a place of security and permanence for good women.

The Women's Lib Movement plays down the Bible command that wives should be subject to their husbands; so a woman is left without a responsible and respected head for the family.

The John Dewey philosophy of education and Dr. Benjamin Spock have helped take away any philosophy of discipline and control of children; so a permissive generation of spoiled brats do not honor motherhood nor other authorities.

In the church, generally preachers have gone away from the Bible standards of morals and responsibility to God. And you can't have the moral standards of Christianity without Bible Christianity.

Large numbers of women have left the home to work so families can have two cars or more luxuries. And the sanctity of the home is largely gone. That means that wives and mothers in America are adrift morally and spiritually. Cigarettes, abortion, birth control, extra-marital sex, have left American womanhood in great need of spiritual help.

We need to restore the family altar... authority of husband and father... permanence of marriage vows... the glory of motherhood... the blessing of large families.

These are reasons why the Sword of the Lord feels a great need to hold seminars to help Christian women.

One beautiful feature of the Sword Women's Jubilee was the crowning of the Jubilee Queen by Dr. Rice. That lady was the one bringing the largest number. The happy queen was photographed with Dr. Rice, received a dozen red roses and a beautiful crown to keep as a souvenir. Then she was awarded an all-expense-paid trip to the next jubilee where she crowned the new queen.

He was invited to bring the jubilee all over the United States. The years it was held at Highland Park Baptist Church, Chattanooga, over 3,000 ladies attended.

This was a very popular addition to the Sword's ministry.

† † †

In March of 1977, Dr. Curtis Hutson resigned as pastor of Forrest Hills Baptist Church, Decatur, Georgia, which had "the fastest growing Sunday school in the state," and was so recognized by *Christian Life Magazine* in its annual listing of "100 Largest Sunday Schools."

Dr. Curtis Hutson and Dr. John R. Rice

A Sunday school official in Chicago noted: *"Dr. Hutson is giving up what many ministers work a lifetime to accomplish."*

The resignation was prompted by his growing burden for evangelism.

Like a Horatio Alger success story from rags to riches is the thrilling story about how God spoke to this postman and part-time preacher in a Sword Conference in Atlanta, in 1959. There he got the vision of Spirit-filled Bible preaching, of personal house-to-house soul winning, and of how to build a great New Testament church.

He went back to Decatur to put into practice what he had learned in a three-day Sword Conference conducted by Dr. Rice and Dr. Hyles.

Do not say about the work of Spurgeon, Moody and Wesley, "It can't be done now!" Dr. Hutson knows better!

From the little frame building, the church blossomed, ran over, a new building was started, it ran over before they got out of the basement; they built another new building, and it ran over. In March of 1972 they entered the marvelous new auditorium seating 2,500, with over 1800 present that day. Their Sunday school regularly ran over 2,000, with 50 to 80 saved per Sunday. The church led the state in baptisms from 1972 to 1977, baptizing over 800 per year.

At the time Dr. Hutson resigned, they were averaging 3,031 in Sunday school.

It is thrilling to listen to this amazing preacher, with his charming style—and smile; one in touch with God in a very sweet and marvelous way.

Dr. Rice was invited many times to speak at Forrest Hills Baptist Church, and was deeply impressed with the work there and with the pastor.

Dr. Hutson had been elected to the Sword Board of Directors a good while before his resignation.

God works mysteriously and miraculously. Who would have thought in just three years this successful pastor, then evangelist, would succeed Dr. Rice as editor of THE SWORD OF THE LORD!

Dr. Hutson speaks from week to week to great audiences and is invited to the largest churches. His desk is stacked high with invitations. And he is carrying on the Sword Conferences and has some Sword Women's Jubilees.

✝ ✝ ✝

On May 27 we had ground-breaking ceremonies for a big new building on the Sword of the Lord property. The Stahlman-Hollobaugh family of Pennsylvania had provided an irrevocable trust for the Sword of the Lord of over $300,000, hoping that, if we could build a new building for the book publishing, it could be in memory of the beloved wife and mother who had recently died.

Our purpose for this building was to take care of the book ministry, housing the retail and wholesale books, warehouse and shipping.

Prominent leaders in the community were present at the ground breaking (building pictured on page 233).

✝ ✝ ✝

So you would never wonder about Dr. Rice's stand on abortion—and I can't believe anyone would wonder—here is his brief statement made in July, 1977:

> The unborn baby is a human being. He has already come alive. He has a heart, a brain, blood vessels, nerves, muscles. To kill that helpless unborn one is murder. If a woman has a right to decide to kill her baby **before** he is born, she would have the same right to kill him **after** he is born.
>
> Women who kill their babies want the pleasures of a harlot without the duties of a wife and mother.
>
> Most doctors who perform abortions do it, not because they think they are serving mankind, but because they are getting paid for it.
>
> An angry God will hold that innocent blood against America of millions murdered yearly with the approval of lawmakers and doctors and the connivance of wicked women. They must meet God as murderers.

† † †

If you were looking at a map and were to take your pencil and draw a circle within a 100-mile radius around Detroit, you would find that there are more independent, fundamental, soul-winning pastors and churches within that circle than in any other northern city in the United States. So it seemed wise to have a National Sword Conference in Detroit this year.

On the program at Cobo Hall Arena, Detroit, July 31 through August 5, were pastors with the largest churches in the world. Their congregations collectively would number over 51,000 on Sunday morning and together would baptize over 16,000 converts in a year's time. Four were in full-time evangelistic work.

John R. Rice...Jerry Falwell...Jack Hyles...A. V. Henderson...Lee Roberson...Gary Coleman...Greg Dixon...Jack Van Impe ...Ray Batema...E. J. Daniels...Curtis Hutson...Bob Gray...Tom Wallace...Truman Dollar. Wally Beebe held a giant bus seminar. Russell Anderson and John Beiler were in charge of the men's meeting each afternoon.

The 500-voice choir was directed by Mr. Vic Bledsoe of Temple Baptist Church, Detroit. Bill Harvey had charge of the congregational singing.

One hundred seventy-five exhibitors set up beautiful displays of Christian materials and soul-winning helps.

A professional television crew filmed Dr. Rice on Wednesday night as he preached on "You Must Be Born Again." This message was to be part of a one-hour special to be presented in the fall during prime viewing time on 250 TV stations with a total audience of 188 million people.

Dr. Rice's comment on the Detroit Conference was: "In many respects it was one of the very best we have ever had. Although that giant auditorium was not full, the crowds, we thought, were comparable to those in Indianapolis, Dallas and Atlanta, and the spiritual impact seemed stronger. Although the preaching was aimed at Christians, there were 37 public professions of faith, and many others were saved outside the services."

After Dr. Lee Roberson spoke, more than 30 people publicly surrendered themselves to full-time Christian service.

The man in charge of the personal work committee told Dr. Rice he had never seen so many preachers coming forward to confess backsliding and coldness and seeking the power of God on their ministries.

† † †

Before him was a request from Sam Moore, head of Thomas Nelson Publishers, the largest Bible publisher and distributor in the world, to prepare notes for a complete reference Bible. Should he, at his age, undertake such a tremendous task?

Dr. Rice made this comment:

> The Scofield Reference Bible is the best in the world and has been enormously useful. However, in some places it is too dispensational. It left the historic position of Spurgeon, Chapman, Moody, Torrey, Billy Sunday, etc., for the Plymouth Brethren position on the Holy Spirit.
>
>
>
> I feel inadequate for the task, yet it may be God wants the long years of study, memorizing, the writing on doctrinal answers to Bible questions, preserved in simple form in a reference Bible for the use of multitudes in the future.
>
> The actual work on the Rice

Reference Bible was not started until after his first heart attack in 1978. But in two years he was able to finish it. Unfortunately Dr. Rice never got to see it in its final form. It was released through Thomas Nelson, Inc., Bible publishers of worldwide prominence, in February 1981, two months after his death.

In March, I received this gracious letter from the publishers:

Publishers since 1798 **THOMAS NELSON INC.**

March 24, 1981

Miss Viola Walden
Sword of the Lord
224 Bridge Avenue
Murfreesboro, TN 37130

Greetings Dear Friend,

It seems as if it were only yesterday when we first sat with you and Dr. Rice to discuss the possibilities of his Bible. At that time we knew we had a long road to travel, and many sacrifices would be made in order to complete the project. But now its happened. Dr. Rice's golden teachings are now in print for all the world to read, understand, and believe in Jesus Christ.

I am truly lost for words to express my gratitude for your kindness, devotion and professionalism which you displayed to me while we worked together on Dr. Rice's Bible. Sincerely, I praise you and your staff there at the Sword, for the tremendous job that has been done. Likewise, I give thanks to my Lord for the opportunity of meeting and working with Dr. Rice and the Sword of the Lord these past two years. Blessings upon you, the staff at the Sword, and the ministry of the Sword of the Lord. And may God truly use this new Bible, The Rice Reference Bible, to bring sinners to Christ and bring Christians to a greater knowledge of His Holy Word.

Enclosed are some copies I wish you would pass on to these most deserving folks: Mrs. Allen, Mrs. Pope and Mr. Vradenburg. Please express to them my appreciation. And of course, there is a "special" copy for you. Also I'm sending two extra copies in case we might have overlooked someone. If not, then please place them in the hands of someone in need of a good Bible.

God bless you my friend, I hope our paths cross again in this life. But if not, see you in Heaven along with Dr. Rice, where we will shout and sing, and give God praise forever more.

In my Master's service,

R. Jefferson Miller
Bible Editor

RJM/lm

THE SWORD EMBLEM. The Sword of the Lord is mentioned in Judges 7:20: "The sword of the Lord, and of Gideon," the battle cry which helped deliver Israel from the Midianite hosts. "The sword of the Lord" is found in Isaiah 34:6; 66:16; in Jeremiah 12:12; 47:6, etc.

Again and again the Lord speaks of "his glittering sword" or "my sword" or "I will bring the sword."

Forty-three years ago we got the idea from the immortal Spurgeon's paper, *The Sword and Trowel*: then when we found it scriptural, we used it.

We believe the Sword of the Lord has two symbolisms:

1. The defense of God's people, God's work and the historic Christian faith. We are commanded to "earnestly contend for the faith . . ." (Jude 3). Paul commended the Philippians because they were partakers with him in "the defence and confirmation of the gospel" (Phil. 1:7). He said again, "I am set for the defence of the gospel" (vs. 17).

Paul boasted that "the weapons of our warfare are not carnal, but mighty through God to the pulling down of strongholds" (II Cor. 10:4).

Timothy was commanded to "war a good warfare" (I Tim. 1:18); to "fight the good fight of faith" (6:12); urged to endure hardness as a good soldier of Jesus Christ" (II Tim. 2:3).

The sword scripturally represents the work of a Christian in opposing sin and defending the Faith in the warfare against Satan.

2. Presents the Bible itself. We are commanded to put on the whole armor of God "and take the helmet of salvation, and the sword of the Spirit, which is the word of God" (Eph. 6:17). Hebrews 4:12 tells us, "For the word of God is quick, and powerful, and sharper than any two-edged sword."

So this magazine, THE SWORD OF THE LORD, is an exposition of the Bible. It is a Bible-preaching, Bible-teaching, Bible-defending magazine.

The name may be offensive, just as is any attack on sin and any defense of the Faith, to some weak-kneed, compromising, pussyfooting Christians. Also it sometimes is offensive to the unsaved and to modernists. But in this, when it displeases weak, sinful and unbelieving men, it pleases God.

† † †

The Sword of the Lord Foundation staff wished to thank our friends far and wide on our 43 years, so we got our heads together and sent this message through the pages of THE SWORD OF THE LORD.

We're Sad About 'Nothing'!

To our Sword friends—

As we look back, forty-three years doesn't seem to be a very long time. In fact, it doesn't seem possible that almost a half century has slipped by since we first started THE SWORD OF THE LORD with a couple of typewriters and a printer who couldn't spell any better than the stenographers!

That they have been interesting years, no one can deny.

A recital would include the Depression of the thirties—Hitler—Pearl Harbor—World War II—rationing—scrap drives—the birth of United Nations—atomic bombs—television—jet planes—Social Security—vistadome trains—50-cent dollars—high taxes—astronomical government debt—home permanents—astronauts—walking on the moon—impeachment of a president—assassinations—and a host of other good and bad events and inventions that have impressed us.

So much for the past!

But not without acknowledging our everlasting debt to our thousands of friends across the country and around the world—wonderful folks who have kept us increasingly busy—who have enabled us to "keep on keeping on." Many of you have ordered every book we sell; others have greatly sacrificed, "beyond the call of duty," to help get out the Gospel through Sword literature. Scores have joined hands with us in becoming members of John R. Rice Associates. Others have given so liberally to our cause. All of you have made this business a pleasure, and burdens lighter. Thank God for your friendship!

We are very proud of you and appreciative, too, for your day-by-day cooperation, consideration, love, support and prayers.

We trust God will give us many more wonderful years together in His service.

With this hearty handshake through the mail goes our appreciation for your friendship and for the privilege of serving you.

Gratefully yours,
Sword of the Lord Foundation Staff

† † †

We would have had to close shop in three or four days' time without mail, and how well aware we were that this line of communication kept us going.

† † †

Since Dr. Rice would be 82 December 11, he was asking for 82,000 subscriptions by December 15. THE SWORD went many years before it got as many as 82,000 total subscriptions. And now we are asking for that many in 8 weeks!

Dr. Rice's aim was that in a few years we could reach 500,000 circulation. "And we hope that others who have a like mind and concern for the work of God will help us get that number for Jesus' sake," said he.

One businessman started off the drive with 1,000 subscriptions and challenged other businessmen to do likewise.

With 5 yearly subscriptions for $20.00, we were giving free the large commentary, *"Behold, He Cometh!"* Will we get that number? (Tell you later.)

† † †

At the annual Sword of the Lord Board meeting, Dr. Bill Rice, because of his declining health, asked to be relieved as associate editor. This made us all sad, but we knew he could not function in that position after his stroke.

† † †

Letters kept coming, week after week, from those telling us their experience.

One wrote: "It was through this paper that I had a personal experience with the Lord, and now I know Him as my Saviour, as do my wife and six children also" (R. F. of Hammonton, NJ).

After ordering 1,000 *"What Must I Do to Be Saved?"* booklets, Mrs. P. of Big Prairie, Ohio, wrote: "I can't thank whoever it was enough for leaving your pamphlet in a rest room in a truck stop somewhere in our travels. My husband and myself are long distance truck drivers.... After reading your booklet, there was little question in my mind I needed salvation. Thank God, your booklet made it all happen! I immediately asked God to forgive me. And I'm here to tell you, He did in an instant! It's been so wonderful ever since. My life has done an about face...."

Mr. Seavolt wrote that he went "to a funeral last month and in his sermon, the pastor said this sister (the deceased) got saved in 1953 while reading THE SWORD OF THE LORD."

In just one issue of THE SWORD, there were dozens of such letters. Of course I have no room in this book for them all.

We were convinced that the simplest, most obvious thing one could do toward winning a loved one was to send him a subscription to THE SWORD OF THE LORD, or give him Dr. Rice's famous gospel tract.

† † †

Dr. Rice now has in print seven large commentaries—all he was able to finish before his death:

King of the Jews (Matthew); *The Son of Man* (Luke); *Filled With the Spirit* (Acts); *The Church of God at Corinth* (I, II Corinthians); *"In the Beginning..."* (Genesis); *The Son of God* (John); *"Behold, He Cometh!"* (Revelation). All have 400 to 500 pages.

All are still in print. Every Christian who privately studies his Bible will find in them great blessing.

† † †

If you were away from home over half the time, good home-cooked meals would taste mighty good. Dr. Rice was continually bragging on Mrs. Rice's cooking (as well he might!). "Last night we had chicken and dumplings, made like my father taught her."

After mentioning having green corn, his granddaughter, Holly Martin, age 3, had one ear of field corn with some rows missing. When she asked why, Grandfather said it happened because the weather had been so dry. She handed the cob back to her grandmother and said, "After it rains, cook it again."

† † †

In September Dr. Rice was thinking back over 43 years. Would you like to know his thoughts? Read on.

"What hath God wrought!" were the first words Alexander Bell uttered when he made his telephone connection and spoke over the phone the first time.

Oh, the wonders of God! And how He has worked with THE SWORD OF THE LORD!

September 27, 1934, the first issue was published. We had no paid subscription list. Five thousand copies were given free on the streets of Oak Cliff and sent to a few friends. A second-class mailing permit could be gotten only after THE SWORD had 500 paid subscriptions.

We worked on, building bit by bit.

And what a contrast that first printing was to the more than 300,000 circulation we averaged last year!

Forty-three years ago when the first issue came out, there were an editor and two secretaries. As editor, I was only part-time, for I was an evangelist and pastor. My, the long hours of hard work! Once each week the three of us worked until around 1:00 a.m. in the morning getting the last copy ready to meet a deadline for a four-page paper. At first the subscription price was 50 cents a year.

Now, instead of three workers, we have 95. When we started, this editor worked—as now—without salary, and two secretaries worked for almost nothing. Now we have a payroll of over $12,000 a week. Newsprint alone for THE SWORD runs over $6,000 a week.

Through these years, some 18,000 have written in to say

they found Christ through our literature.

And we look back through these years to the preachers touched and stirred with holy fires beginning to burn in their hearts for souls, influenced by THE SWORD. How many are now pastors of great churches, or missionaries, to whom God gave a spark of divine fire through THE SWORD and our ministry!

Yes, "What hath God wrought!"

† † †

"TRICK OR TREAT"! Some children had knocked at a door on Halloween night, saying, "Trick or treat!" When some little "treats" were handed out, one little tyke said, "Now I have something to give you," handing the man a copy of Dr. Rice's *What Must I Do to Be Saved?* The one given the tract wrote: "That made the evening for us!"

† † †

It was interesting to read about Dr. Rice's **"Prayer List"** near the end of the year. He told how he prayed earnestly every day for the subscription campaign, for God to bless his sermon telecast at Cobo Hall, "You Must Be Born Again," which was later to be on some 200 television stations; mentioned his daily praying for his children and grandchildren, how he took his Sword staff before God....

> And I have a list of about 90 other Christian men I take to God daily by name. I find it hard to drop any one of them from my list. Dr. Beauchamp Vick, Dr. Ford Porter, Dr. Oliver Greene—now in Heaven—keep coming back to mind each time I pray through my list. Sometimes I stop and thank God the three are with Him now, and certainly don't need my prayers—but they are still on my heart and in my mind.
>
> I occasionally, as I pray, stop and thank God for that particular person.
>
> Some whom I pray for daily are not now the intimate friends they once were. One who tries as hard as I do to be true to Christ and is bold in his preaching, must displease some and lose some friendships.
>
> Is it strange that Jesus was betrayed by one of His disciples?
>
> Is it strange that the Galatian Christians turned away from Paul, to try to follow the ceremonial law again?
>
> Is it strange that Demas forsook Paul, having loved the present world?

Is it strange that David's son Absalom rebelled and tried to kill his own father? But Jesus said that sometimes "a man's foes shall be they of his own household."

Oh, but some of these are still dear to me and to God, though they do not now feel as close to me as they once did. I wish it were not so.

In praying the other day, when I came to one name, I said to the Lord, "Let me stop here and cry awhile before I continue on, Lord."

I feel I must not cease to pray for them, to wish them well, and trust God to continue blessing them, even though pressure from other sources, sometimes from other friends, has caused this one or that one to break away from the fellowship we once enjoyed.

But what a joy to love everyone who is doing God's business! If I can have some part in moving Heaven in their behalf, I want to continue to do that.

As an onlooker, and frequently joining in his prayer session, I can vouch that every word printed above was true. He prayed for his enemies as often as he prayed for his friends.

† † †

On December 11, 1977, Dr. Rice turned 82, and continued to amaze friend and foe alike with his zeal and persistence in going about the King's business.

The most amazing thing about this man was, he appeared to be more than just one man. He was an *evangelist* whose messages tenderly called sinners to the Saviour. He was an *editor* and for 43 years had published THE SWORD OF THE LORD. An *author* with 185 titles to his credit, his books and pamphlets had already been circulated in 52 million copies and in 38 languages. A *radio preacher,* Dr. Rice was being heard on a network of 50 independent stations that reached into every part of our nation.

He was receiving more invitations each week for speaking engagements than he could possibly accept. He, Dr. Jack Hyles and other good men were kept busy with some 25 Sword Conferences each year. Dr. Rice usually left on Saturday afternoon, started the conference on Monday morning (the pastor wanted him for both services Sunday), and closed on Tuesday or Wednesday night.

When he was not preaching, you would find him back in his motel room dictating answers to his correspondence or writing for THE SWORD. Dr. Rice maintained his book table where he set up the books, sold them, signed Bibles, autographed the books, took care of the money, saw that any books that were left over were packed up and shipped back to Murfreesboro; then he set out for home.

When the wheels of that big bird touched down in Nashville, you might think he would set his face toward the little farm that sat just outside Murfreesboro, for a time of relaxation and rest. Not so. His heart was yearning to get back to his desk at the office, to check his mail and get editorial copy ready for the next issue of THE SWORD.

As president of Sword of the Lord Foundation, he had almost 100 staff members. Heads of the various departments were responsible to him. During the short time he could stay in his office, there was a steady stream of supervisors going in and out, coming to him for advice or giving him their reports of the week's work activity.

But Dr. Rice seemed to thrive on hard work. You never heard him complain.

That is a pretty true picture of a busy man, the "Captain of Our Team."

✝ ✝ ✝

Another sample letter on another day. Multiply it by the hundreds. Oh, what a joy such reports brought to his soul!

Missionary Tom Eckman from Argentina relates this story:

> Recently I have been working with an Argentina couple, Jose' and Marta Fernandez, trying to lead them to the Lord. Since I couldn't provoke a decision from them. . . I gave Jose' one of your *"What Must I Do to Be Saved?"* booklets in Spanish. Last night he came to our Bible study and during the service asked me if he could be saved. He read your tract (translated into Spanish) and wanted to pray the prayer on the back of the pamphlet to receive Christ. He did, and he knew he got saved.
>
> I looked at Marta (who at this point had tears in her eyes) and asked her if she would like to be saved. She prayed the same prayer you have on the booklet, and she knew she then and there got saved!
>
> Praise the Lord for the way He used your gospel message in Spanish!

✝ ✝ ✝

Without discussing it with him, we had a man sit in a room and record on a cassette tape Dr. Rice's devotional messages to his staff at 7:00 a.m. each morning he was in town. Devotions took from 12 to 15 minutes, including two verses of a song and prayer.

After taping enough to fill a book, we got them typed out, corrected, then presented them to Dr. Rice for publishing.

The book was called *Golden Moments With Dr. John R. Rice,* and it was 300 pages in length (not now available).

† † †

In writing an article for THE SWORD entitled, "The Riches in Gospel Tracts," Rev. John Wilder told this story, among others:

> A Michigan couple living in the country walked one day along the highway that ran in front of their home. In a patch of mud on the shoulder of the road they saw a booklet. It was the John R. Rice tract, *"What Must I Do to Be Saved?"* Apparently some careless motorist, uninterested, had thrown the booklet from a car.
>
> But the Holy Spirit had not finished with its message. The man and his wife read the tract and opened their hearts to Christ. They wrote to Mr. Fred Hawkins, who had distributed the tract (and put his name on the back) informing him of their new salvation.

Oh, the miracles of grace that often spring from a bit of paper bearing the message of salvation!

† † †

It was sweet, yet amusing, to read one letter from a Georgian. After congratulating Dr. Rice on his 82nd birthday, he told of reading everything in THE SWORD OF THE LORD—"Everything! Even the page numbers!"

† † †

LATER: During the 82nd Birthday Campaign, nearly 8,000 renewed their subscriptions to THE SWORD for five years or more, becoming what we called 5-STAR SUBSCRIBERS. Instead of subscribing for the regular price of $7, they got the paper five years for $20. To these were sent a precious little gold Sword pin. We thought they deserved it.

LATER STILL: There were 54,000 one-year subscriptions during the Birthday Campaign. Nearly 8,000 were 5-year subscriptions; actually, then, we had a total of some 86,000 yearly subscriptions counting these

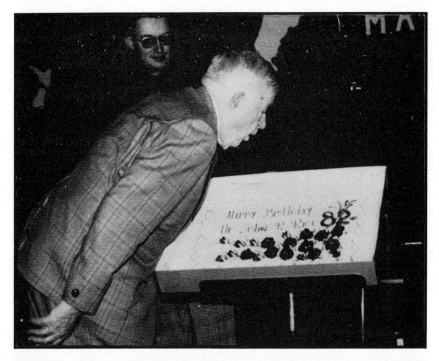

On Dr. Rice's 82nd birthday: blowing off the roses—well, do you see any candles?!

for several years each. This report was made in January, and subscriptions were still coming in. We feel sure the Lord answered our prayer once again in this matter.

1978

JOHN R. RICE TELEVISION SPECIAL. In January, Dr. Rice's message, "You Must Be Born Again," preached at Cobo Hall, Detroit, was telecast on some 106 stations. Sword staff manned nine toll-free lines to take calls from those who heard the broadcast and wanted to be saved.

(Another 52 TV stations aired the message in April.)

Letters and calls flooded Sword mail room. Some 16,000 people wrote for the book, *You Must Be Born Again,* prepared especially for this telecast. In almost every city where the message was shown, television counselors were sent these names for follow-up.

Some 831 people were won to Christ in conversation with our staff, after the two telecast dates.

† † †

THOSE WOMEN'S JUBILEES. 1,648 were registered at the Sword Women's Jubilee, held at Franklin Road Baptist Church, Murfreesboro, March 2 through 4. Women came from half the states. One carload drove 1,063 miles from Connecticut through snow, sleet and rain.

The Rice sisters, Mrs. John R. Rice, Mrs. Jack Hyles and Mrs. Cathy Rice dealt with the problems, burdens and needs of Christian women. Many holy vows were made, many tears were shed.

The Queen brought 63 from Chattanooga and was crowned by Dr. Rice, given a dozen red roses and a beautiful tiara. Thirty-five were crowned as Princesses, having brought from ten to thirty-five each.

These Jubilees were proving to be such a blessing to women everywhere. In Louisville in April, some 500 ladies attended. Then in Orlando, Florida, in October, plans were made for between 400 and 500 guests, but registration at the door swelled the number to 820.

† † †

SPECIAL BULLETIN. On March 8 Dr. Rice was rushed to the

coronary care unit of Rutherford Hospital with a heart condition. A wire was inserted in a vein from the neck down to the heart, to make possible instant connection with a pacemaker should it become necessary. A week later the thin wire was removed.

After a two weeks' stay, he was released. His speaking dates were cancelled up until April 20.

An elevator was hurriedly installed to his second-floor office, eliminating his climbing 17 steps three times a day.

s. mouse first joined us in Wheaton as "night manager," then somehow followed the crowd to Murfreesboro! "They wouldn't let just any ding-a-ling in the hospital to see Dr. Rice, but never once was I asked to leave," he bragged! See Dr. Rice smile at his old friend!

He was a real "fan" of s. mouse and got a charge out of his articles, written when he was "night manager." (He wouldn't tell you what the s. stood for until you placed an order! And he couldn't shift the typewriter key to cap any letters!)

And do you know what! That rascal could sell Sword books! But since he was always lousing up the phone orders, we finally got rid of him—for awhile at least, by sending him to a cheese factory in Wisconsin!

We had loads of fun even doing hard labor, and Dr. Rice heartily entered in and always enjoyed the fun the most.

Maybe s. mouse will speed his recovery!

Jokingly he said, "Some of my boys (on the staff) talk of taking me fishing. I agreed if the fish didn't waste time getting on the hook!" He wouldn't waste time at ANYTHING!

Once again he was praising his faithful staff. "I don't know of any Christian organization that has as much talent, loyalty, experience, energy and devotion. The work will go on with or without me. I get reports, say a brief yes or no, plant an idea here and there—and they take it from there."

LATER: After seeing the doctor again in early April, he was allowed back at the office two hours a day for three weeks, then after another check-up, he would be given further instructions.[1]

✝ ✝ ✝

I do not believe Jesus discouraged the use of humor, do you? There was gaiety in His company, and the ripple of a smile doubtless accorded with the twinkle of His eyes.

Remember—He was the Guest who saved the wedding party at Cana. When He speaks of "swallowing a camel" (if you can picture the humps of the camel going down the throat of a haughty Pharisee), it would seem He encouraged the use of humorous pictures.

There must have been a genial laughter in His voice as He pictured the importune widow who finally broke down the old judge, who at last granted the woman's request in order to get rid of her.

Did He not enjoy describing the guests at the feast who always pushed to the head of the table, then were coldly invited to take a seat at the lower table?

How about the man who protested that he was asleep in bed with his children when he was awakened at night by a friend in need of bread—is there not a touch of humor in that picture?

Since our Lord used humorous situations, it seems God's busy people are certainly entitled to occasional laughter as well as tears.

And Dr. Rice had plenty of both—with tears probably outweighing the laughter.

✝ ✝ ✝

---

[1] The doctor had as well let him come back full time, for from his recliner he was making notes on his new Rice Reference Bible, keeping in touch with his seven noble Bible Consulting Editors, planning campaigns and selecting SWORD copy.

Dr. Rice was scheduled to speak at Pastors' School March, 1978, but the doctor forbad him to travel so soon after the heart attack. But hold onto your Stetson—and see what happened!

His horse MacArthur made his second trip to Hammond.

On the night Dr. Rice was to speak, one of the Sword men rode Mac proudly down the aisle of the Civic Center. Mrs. Rice was the only one Mac knew in that vast crowd, so he walked straight up to the edge of the platform, reached his head over and rested it on her shoulder, as he so often did to Dr. Rice.

But wait! What else? General of the Armies Douglas MacArthur II was declared D.H.S. *(Doctor of Horse Sense)* and brought home the beautiful certificate to prove it!

In addition, the church sent to the Captain of our team a fine Stetson hat, beautiful patent leather cowboy boots, a spangled suit with sequins, a handsome western tie, a bowstring tie, a fine western shirt and a belt.

Dr. Rice was loved so much, as has been evidenced throughout this volume. And it was because he gave so much!

At this gathering in Hammond, Mrs. Rice was given a new Monte Carlo Chevrolet. "I thought it a disgrace for a preacher's wife to win a car named after a gambling center—Monte Carlo—but she seems very much at home with it," Dr. Rice chuckled!

† † †

He had written to pastors that he was compelled to cancel all two- and three-day conferences because of his health. "The work, the travel, the crowds, signing Bibles, rushing to meet engagements and planes are too heavy a load for me now." He had never before cancelled engagements; now he knew that he could no longer continue that heavy schedule.

† † †

DR. BILL RICE DIES SUDDENLY. Dr. Bill had been incapacitated for two years. He could walk a bit, could speak with difficulty and was paralyzed in his right hand and arm.

On May 29 God had taken him Home, and I had lost a very, very dear friend. He had done a marvelous work through the ministry of the Bill Rice Ranch. He had held great revivals. He had done an outstanding missionary work with the deaf and was loved and admired by scores of noble people. Dr. Bill had been co-editor of THE SWORD OF THE

LORD. Although he and Dr. Rice were half-brothers, they were extremely close-knit.

The memorial service was held on June 1 at the Bill Rice Ranch, with perhaps 1200 in attendance.

Good-bye, Dr. Bill, for a little time. Heaven is sweeter, and we grow more homesick for Home as we think of so many loved ones like you who will be there to greet us.

† † †

MURFREESBORO, TENNESSEE: For many years Sword Conferences had been held all the way from Moody Church, Chicago (seating 4,040); from the Church of the Open Door in Los Angeles, of similar size; to Massey Hall, Toronto; to Winona Lake in Indiana; to Toccoa Falls in Georgia; to Siloam Springs in Arkansas; and in principal churches all over America, as well as at the Bill Rice Ranch and in our own Sword auditorium in Murfreesboro.

But for years Dr. Rice had a great burden to have NATIONWIDE gatherings in large centers in America. So the last four years saw the Nationwide Sword Conferences at Indianapolis, Dallas, Atlanta and Detroit. This year's conference at Murphy Center on the campus of Middle Tennessee State University, in Murfreesboro, would be number 5.

Murfreesboro was certainly the center of activity in the Christian world July 31 through August 4. Tennessee had never had a religious program of such distinguished preachers. No Southern Baptist Convention, no Moody Founder's Week conference, no Winona Lake in the old days of Torrey, Chapman, Billy Sunday, ever had as strong a program of mightily used soul winners as Dr. Rice was having in these nationwide conferences.

This one was really a convention of "delegates." According to University rules, no one was allowed to invite the general public as such. So this was not a mass meeting; it was a meeting of registered "delegates," or representatives, or special friends of the Sword, **broadly interpreted.** And the registration was for adults only.

It was not surprising that the big bulk of those attending were from outside the state, as we knew ahead of time would be the case. Southern Baptist headquarters are in Nashville nearby. Church of Christ people are very strong throughout the state. Between Chattanooga on the border of Georgia and Indianapolis on the north, the independent, fundamental churches are small and few.

In all, there were 4,002 registered "delegates."

Perhaps this was the most effective of the five **nationwide** conferences. Two or three services ended with hundreds of preachers and Christian workers kneeling and giving themselves to a new dedication. In one service, 27 young men surrendered to the ministry.

Two buses were given away to churches bringing the largest number— Victory Baptist Church, Bowling Green, Kentucky, 135 miles away, brought 572 people; Metropolitan Baptist Church, Madison, Tennessee brought 553.

A golf cart and a driver for the cart were provided for Dr. Rice so he would not have to walk anywhere in that large Center. There was a room so he could rest or study or have a cup of coffee. He could not attend all the services.

The displays by Christian organizations offering services and materials to the churches and to Christians were a fine part of the conference. At one booth, a distributor won eight souls during the conference.

Murfreesboro merchants were proud of the Sword for that week. We made a good impression on the town.

† † †

Thinking back to the old days, we read this by Dr. Rice:

> In the rough pioneer backwoods of West Texas, in a little community that didn't even have a Sunday school, much less a church, in many miles, I taught a country school, though I was only nineteen. Every day I put a Scripture verse on the blackboard and had the children memorize it.
>
> I was strict and God blessed the school, but there was some opposition in that drinking, dancing, bootlegging, frontier community where no one went to church and only a very few had been saved. But in the midst of that unfavorable atmosphere I found a sweet promise which seemed to be just for me. I claimed it then; I have claimed it many times since, and am depending on it today—Isaiah 54:17: *"No weapon that is formed against thee shall prosper; and every tongue that shall rise against thee in judgment thou shalt condemn. This is the heritage of the servants of the Lord, and their righteousness is of me, saith the Lord."*
>
> On that verse God has wonderfully prospered my ministry, has delivered me from those who would have destroyed me; has raised up THE SWORD OF THE LORD and continues to bless it among

many enemies of our strong defense of the Faith and our sharp evangelistic preaching. Praise the Lord for that promise! How safe and sure it is!

† † †

The Sword now had two corporations; the nonprofit Sword of the Lord Foundation and the new corporation, Sword of the Lord Publishers, publishing books. It has to pay taxes on any profit in the book publishing, so it seemed wise to put that in a separate corporation and in a separate building, though there was no change in the methods and plans of the Sword of the Lord. The new Stahlman-Hollobaugh Sword publishing building would be owned by the book publishers, and the investment could be depreciated year after year against the taxes. But the two were legally connected.

† † †

In September, it was announced that Dr. Curtis Hutson would succeed Dr. Bill Rice as Associate Editor. He was already writing a soul-winning column for THE SWORD, and some of his sermons had also been printed. Now he would write more, would counsel with the staff, help get subscriptions and be on the field in revivals and Sword Conferences.

"Dr. Hutson will not be just a figurehead, not simply a contributor. He will help bear the heavy responsibilities of editorship, publishing and promotion as a full-time partner," Dr. Rice announced.

† † †

In September alone, 55 people had written that they had found Christ as Saviour through either sermons in THE SWORD or through other Sword literature. That made 637 this year. Add to that the 831 who saw the telecast of Dr. Rice's message on prime time TV, called long distance and were saved over the phone, bringing the total to 1,468 who had claimed Christ through the influence of the Sword in nine months.

1979 Some of our most highly prized possessions here at the Sword of the Lord offices are the bound volumes of old issues of THE SWORD since its beginning September 28, 1934. Reading many of these old issues is like reading pages out of the book of Acts. What a blessing to see the hand of God on this paper down through the years! And how valuable they have been in my research!

Occasionally someone will accuse us of changing our editorial position to accommodate some special issue of the day.

I can honestly tell you that this is not true. THE SWORD stands exactly where it stood in its beginning. The editors have changed but not the content of THE SWORD. Persecution, opposition and criticism have failed to alter the course of THE SWORD.

† † †

This very interesting letter was addressed to:

Ms. Waldron,

Can't you nail Dr. John R's feet to the floor to keep him quiet before he works himself and all the rest of you to death?

The first thing I look for in the Big Sword is "Editor's Notes" to see if he is behaving himself. But he isn't.

† † †

Sword Tours for 1979 was full by the first of the year. We could only take 160, and already on hand were applications for that many, with more than 30 wanting to go with us April 19 through May 4. How sad to have to turn them down!

† † †

GRACE'S ILLNESS AND DEATH:

Dr. and Mrs. Rice's oldest daughter, Grace Rice MacMullen, became ill in 1979. This was a great shock to us all.

We were returning from the Holy Land and were spending the night in New York. About midnight the phone rang. Dr. Rice answered. A sweet voice said, "Daddy, I want to tell you and Mother first. The doctor says I have cancer and may not live."

Their firstborn! Both sat for awhile, neither saying a word. After a bit, Mrs. Rice asked, "Daddy, is it going to be all right?" And Dr. Rice answered, "Yes, it's going to be all right."

I overheard the conversation and surmised the problem, then was told what Grace had relayed to them.

The next day Dr. Rice went on to his scheduled meeting and Mrs. Rice joined Grace, who had already been admitted to the hospital for breast surgery.

After it was over, the doctor thought she would live only about six months. But Grace temporarily recovered and lived until October, 1981. Death came to her ten months after her dad had died in December of 1980.

† † †

"SON OF SAM" ASKED FOR THE SWORD OF THE LORD. Surely you remember David Berkowitz, known as "The Son of Sam," the man who killed a score of people in New York.

On February 5 this note came from Dr. Tom Wallace:

Dear Dr. Rice:

I thought you'd want to know about a letter I got from David Berkowitz. He's in prison at Attica, New York. He wrote:

"I would like to ask you to please send me a copy of THE SWORD OF THE LORD newspaper. I used to read this newspaper. I think it is located in Tennessee. If you could send me a copy, I would appreciate it."

Dr. Wallace sent him a subscription.

† † †

On this Sword tour in Jerusalem, Dr. and Mrs. Rice, Ron and Brenda English and I went shopping for a birthday gift for Ron. A taxi took us to the Jaffa Gate. Just inside we walked into a bazaar and, lo, here were old Arab friends! They had before owned a store at the 8th Station of the Cross on the Via Dolorosa. Dr. Rice made a point to see them each time he was in Jerusalem, but this year we found they had moved. Now

we had located them by accident close to the Jaffa Gate!

Dr. Rice, a few years back, had gone into their store and had the joy of winning the three Razzouk brothers.

Those in the picture are Samir Razzouk, Michel Behnam (an employee), Dr. Rice, Anton Razzouk ("Tony") and George Razzouk. Mrs. Rice had earlier won their sister while visiting their gift shop.

After returning from the Holy Land, a preacher told how in Damascus a few years before he had met a young man from Jerusalem (it was "Tony"); when he asked if he was a Christian, "Tony" replied, "Yes, Dr. John R. Rice won me to the Lord in Jerusalem."

On this visit, Dr. Rice had asked "Tony" how he was getting along spiritually. He answered, "I'm doing well. I am a better Christian than ever. I read THE SWORD OF THE LORD every week, read a page in the Bible each day, and pray."

It was a happy reunion with these friends! Those on Sword Tours over the years had already won over one hundred souls in Palestine.

† † †

On this year's tour to Bible lands, Dr. Rice dictated to me some fifty of the 107 stories in *John R. Rice Bible Stories*. I was amazed once again at his knowledge. His briefcase did not reach him while overseas, so he was some time without a Bible. But do you know, he described every detail of those characters as if he had a Bible before him and was reading from it! After returning home, I checked up on him as I began transcribing those stories! Sure enough. It was just like he said! What a mind! Even at age 83!

† † †

SWORD WOMEN'S JUBILEES REACHED 2,273
LADIES IN 24 DAYS.

From March 15 until April 7, three jubilees were held in three major cities: Houston, Texas; Murfreesboro, Tennessee; and Jacksonville, Florida. A total of 2,273 ladies had attended these sessions sponsored by Dr. John R. Rice and the Sword of the Lord.

Murfreesboro, Tennessee is where it all began. In 1977 Dr. Rice decided that God would have him prepare and sponsor a meeting designed especially for women. The first jubilee was planned and held in the hometown of the Sword. The crowd enlarged to such an extent that two sessions had to be established; one at the Sword building and one at Franklin Road Baptist Church.

Since that first outstanding meeting, ten other jubilees had been held across America up to this time. God has blessed them greatly. Literally thousands of ladies have attended and enjoyed and learned from the teaching given by the speakers.

There is no other program like it for women. The Christian home, soul winning, child training, prayer and personal problems are soundly dealt with using the Word of God as the final authority.

Many speakers have blessed many hearts, speakers such as the six Rice sisters and their mother, Mrs. John R. Rice; Mrs. Lee Roberson, Mrs. Jackie Dark, Mrs. Beka Horton, Mrs. Jack Hyles, Mrs. Marlene Evans, Mrs. Cathy Rice—just to name a few. Some subject titles:

I've Been Looking for the Lord. Can You Help Me?
A Woman's Most Dangerous Weapon
Who's Afraid? I Am!
Good, Better, Best
A New You for a Surprised Him
Making Your Marriage Magnificent!
Child Rearing With a Guarantee
Please Be Patient: God Isn't Finished With Your Husband Yet
When a Woman Must Forgive the Unforgivable
Good Kids Don't Just Happen
How to Handle Depression
Femininity in Appearance
Measuring With a Rubber Ruler
You Can Be Somebody

SPECIAL FEATURES. Crowning of the Jubilee Queen, which honored the lady bringing the largest number; a lovely reception to welcome the hundreds who attended; a boxed lunch; two coffee breaks; an outline booklet with a brief summary of the messages.

The Sword Women's Jubilee began on Thursday night and ended at noon on Saturday—14 hours of blessed teaching.

In these Women's Jubilees scores of ladies asked Dr. Rice to pray earnestly that God would give the baby they so desired. And God answered that prayer over and over again. Dr. Rice explained:

> We have so much encouragement to pray on this matter. Sarah prayed for many years, and God gave her Isaac. Hannah prayed earnestly, and God gave her Samuel. Zacharias and Elisabeth prayed long years until they got John the Baptist. Rebekah was barren for twenty years; then we are told that, when Isaac prayed, God gave her twins, Jacob and Esau.

THREE TESTIMONIES. A pastor's wife trembled at the great expense of going from Texas to California to a Sword Jubilee. But she went, then wrote: *"Thank God, it cured six years of rebellion and unhappiness!"*

Another: *"I have received greater joy in these past weeks since attending the jubilee than I had before experienced in my Christian life."*

"Our feet haven't touched ground yet!" excitedly wrote another.

† † †

In chapel one day at Hyles-Anderson College, the student body elected Dr. Rice "President," and on the next page are the pictures to prove it!

He was campaigning for the "Independent Fundamental Party" and seems to have won by a landslide victory, having carried all the states!

We were always proud when others showed their affection for the "Captain of Our Team."

† † †

MOTHER, KEROSENE LAMP AND THE SWORD. A lady from Tab, Virginia, gave us a touch of spiritual nostalgia by sharing fond memories of her mother and THE SWORD OF THE LORD:

> My mother has subscribed to THE SWORD OF THE LORD for as many years as I can remember. One of my earliest recollections of bedtime stories was when she put us children to bed (13 of us)—the boys upstairs and the girls downstairs.
>
> Before we went to bed, Mother would have her clan gather on

Chapel "election" at Hyles-Anderson College

the stair steps. She would take her seat with the kerosene lamp by her side and read us sermons from THE SWORD OF THE LORD. Talk about bedtime stories! Those were the greatest. I treasure those precious memories.

† † †

The aim of any Sword Conference was to revamp the spiritual life of those who attended and fit them for Christian service. Our national Sword Conferences had a growing reputation for providing the best-known speakers in America representing fundamental, Bible-believing churches. The hundreds of aggressive, soul-winning churches springing up all over America were living examples of the success of Sword Conferences. When just one preacher got stirred to have the power of God on his ministry and returned to his church as a leader determined to win souls and encourage Christians in Christ, there was no telling what God could do.

After a similar Sword Conference one pastor went home to insert an ad in the paper: "Come Hear the New Pastor of First Baptist Church Next Sunday."

Had the present pastor suddenly resigned? left town? died? No. He had been changed. He really had become a new preacher. No longer stale, in a rut or defeated, he had been revived in heart, refreshed in spirit, and had gone home from the conference a new man. And during the months ahead, the church became a new church under the leadership of this "new" pastor.

And that was the purpose of a Sword of the Lord Conference.

† † †

COLUMBUS, OHIO. The Nationwide Sword Conference at the Ohio State Fairgrounds in Columbus, Ohio, July 2 through 6, was everything we had hoped for. Some of the finest preachers in America were on the program. The attendance increased nightly until the Fairgrounds auditorium was filled.

Geraldine and "Ricky" were there—one of the most delightful couples to charm audiences of every age. Geraldine, a ventriloquist, continually uses her talent for God. She and "Ricky" have blessed millions on Christian television programs and in prominent churches throughout America.

BIRMINGHAM, ALABAMA. "It was in many ways one of the most blessed of all the major conferences" was Dr. Rice's evaluation of the Sword Nationwide Conference at Birmingham, Alabama, July 30 through August 3. Hundreds of preachers attended. The noble men of God spoke with great blessing and power.

The musical program for the two conferences was planned with great care. Dr. Al Smith directed in Columbus, and Dr. Earl Smith in Birmingham.

In both conferences, women enjoyed the afternoon women's seminars; dads were moved by the preaching program; teens were attracted to the giant youth rally. Exhibitors were on hand to display materials on every phase of church-related work, schools, printing and publication, music, bus promotions, puppets, etc.

† † †

HAWAII. Many could not go with the Sword Tours to the Holy Land this year because space was not available (we took 160); so we planned a second tour, this time to Hawaii, hoping some of these "leftovers" could go.

Upon arrival at Honolulu International Airport on the Island of Oahu, a fragrant flower lei was placed around each neck—the traditional welcome to Hawaii. As I recall, some 40 were in our party.

At a briefing at our lovely hotel, men were told coats were forbidden on the island, to be replaced by Hawaiian shirts! That included Dr. Rice, who was never seen without a coat!

Sword Hawaiian Conference on the Fundamentals of the Faith combined a delightful visit in that great vacationland with two lectures daily by Dr. Rice.

What do fundamentalists believe, and why? How do we know Jesus is coming again? What does the Bible say about the eternal security of a believer? What about Bible prophecy? Is the Bible to be taken literally? Yes, but how do you know that?

The purpose of this 8-day conference was to show the Christian the why and what of the great fundamentals.

The two lectures daily were after breakfast and after supper, giving plenty of time for sightseeing.

Both Dr. Rice and his pastor, Dr. Bob Kelley, spoke in a church in Oahu on Sunday.

† † †

SEEING THE SIGHTS. A ship took us to Pearl Harbor to view the *USS Arizona*, the mighty battleship, sunk in 50 feet of water when Japanese aircraft bombed military installations in Hawaii, touching off the Pacific phase of World War II. Oil still seeps from her tanks, a memorial to the 1,102 men still entombed within her shattered hull.

The Navy treats *USS Arizona* as if she were still a commissioned vessel. An honor guard daily raises and lowers a flag from the platform over her exposed superstructure.

As we neared the ship, William Conrad, a movie star tourist on the ship we were on, threw a large wreath overboard in honor of the dead.

It was, to say the least, a solemn occasion.

We saw Waikiki and Diamond Head, shopped in the International Market, and saw more Japanese tourists than the population of Hawaii!

We learned that sugar cane now tosses its tassels over more than 200,000 acres. And did you know that in Hawaii sugar cane fields have traffic lights and the moon sometimes shines so brightly they have rainbows at night!

Let me expose my ignorance! I thought pineapple grew on trees. Imagine my surprise when a guide took us to a huge field to see them growing on the ground like cabbage!

If sugar cane is still king, the pineapple is queen. Every stop we were offered complimentary glasses of pineapple juice or sliced or crushed pineapple.

It was a "learning" vacation long to be remembered.

† † †

PUSH, PUSH, PUSH! these many years had been Dr. Rice's watchword. There had been deadlines to meet, letters to write, broadcasts to prepare, books to publish, SWORD copy to prepare, revivals or conferences to plan. . . .

Now his strength was somewhat lessened, and he must allow others to do much of the work that he had long done.

It would have been impossible to continue even his limited speaking schedule had it not been that a good man volunteered to travel with him as companion-protector, paying his own expenses.

For six months he got a wheelchair for Dr. Rice when it was a long walk to the plane. He protected him from large crowds who wanted him to sign Bibles. He drove him to and from the church and sold books at the book table. He saw about getting them to and from airports. He got him a lean-back chair in the motel room so he could breathe better at night. This was indeed in God's plan, allowing Dr. Rice to win a few more souls, to bless a few more people.

Though there was so much to do here in the office, he never felt like giving in to his frailty, so kept on the road as long as he could. Of course good sense made him now limit his engagements.

† † †

On his birthday, December 11, Dr. Rice was to be out of town, so we celebrated with him on the 7th.

The Sword staff prepared a lovely banquet and invited the good people from Sunset Square retirement home. An excellent program was planned and carried out.

Each department had a group picture taken with Dr. Rice.

His sister, Mrs. Ruth Martin, came from Nederland, Texas. Mr. and Mrs. Peterson from Hawaii were here. Dorothy was his cousin, daughter of his mother's sister. He saw her in Hawaii for the first time in many years. Having these three was an added blessing.

There were telegrams read. Dr. Lee Roberson and Tennessee Temple Schools had prepared a tape with singing of his favorite songs and a happy birthday greeting.

Of course there were gifts and more gifts. It was a happy hour.

† † †

In 1979, we had a report of 647 being saved through Sword literature, plus 60 saved through our "Loveline" (saved over the telephone)—a grand total of 707 saved through Sword agencies in the last year.

That added up to a grand total of 20,250 saved through Sword ministries over the years!

For over 59 years Dr. &
Mrs. Rice walked hand
in hand in life's
greatest rela-
tionship. When
God chose...

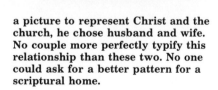

a picture to represent Christ and the
church, he chose husband and wife.
No couple more perfectly typify this
relationship than these two. No one
could ask for a better pattern for a
scriptural home.

1980

In the April, 1980, issue of *Saturday Evening Post* was a message by Dr. Rice on the resurrection of Jesus Christ. And in the same issue was a full-page ad of Sword books.

† † †

Dr. W. A. Criswell wrote a most kindly letter, addressing it to "Dear gracious friend, Dr. John R. Rice." One paragraph read: "Through the years you have been such an inspiration to me. We can meet and make new friends, but we cannot go back and make old friends. Thank you for the many years of friendship we have enjoyed."

Strange, that nearly at the same time came another letter from Dr. Adrian Rogers, then president of the Southern Baptist Convention, and who succeeded Dr. R. G. Lee at Bellevue Baptist Church, Memphis:

> Dear Dr. Rice:
>
> You have been a blessing to my heart and a strength to my life for almost thirty years. I believe that some of the basic convictions I have were first born in my heart from reading THE SWORD OF THE LORD as a nineteen-year-old college student. Your books, your life and your convictions have been a strength and a testimony to me. You have stood like the Rock of Gibraltar, yet with a love and a compassion and a tenderness that I have seen in few men.
>
> I love you, as do multiplied thousands. I am grateful to be counted as one of your friends.

† † †

In a little over one month, 2,300 copies of *John R. Rice Bible Stories* had been sold. It was our most expensive publication, at $9.95.

† † †

For several months, once each month Dr. Curtis Hutson was preparing an issue of THE SWORD OF THE LORD and writing "Associate

Editor's Notes." Little by little we found Dr. Rice releasing some responsibility to others. Dr. Hutson had arranged his schedule so he could spend one week a month in the office.

† † †

MANY HANDS MAKE LIGHT WORK! When the lights in the auditorium went out suddenly, a Chinese man in the audience said: "If all of us will raise our hands, maybe lights come back on." Sure enough! All raised their hands, and the lights went back on. Then he explained: "It all goes to prove the old Chinese proverb: 'Many hands make light work'!"

The work of Sword of the Lord Foundation most certainly was a team effort. Well aware of the importance of his staff, Dr. Rice often expressed his appreciation to each in person or with some gift and a handwritten note. He was well aware that no man, though superstar, worked alone; it took many hands to make light work!

Some of the best people in the world—and the most talented—have been employed at the Sword offices over the years. When God led someone our way, we felt that one very important. New employees were given a booklet explaining our rules, our hours, our standards, etc. In it Dr. Rice had written a word of welcome:

Maybe when you came to us there was no brass band to meet you—or even an official welcoming committee! Maybe you thought people weren't too interested in whether you were here or not—but they were. In fact, we thought about you and prayed about you long before you came. You see, there was a special need in our work for a certain someone to do a particular job. We held consultations and had prayer and lo and behold—God sent us you! So here's a great big welcome. We hope you'll be wonderfully happy here, and we're counting on great things from you.

Employees with the Sword 25 or more years: Standing, L to R: Al Byers, 32 years; Rex Graby, 31 years; Sarah Pope, 31 years. Seated: Terri Graby, 31 years; Viola Walden, 56 years; Rose Gibson, 38 years; Mary Koehler, 35 years; Marcella Byers, 31 years.

This picture was taken in 1984 of those who had been with the Sword of the Lord Foundation 25 years or more. All moved to Murfreesboro from Wheaton in 1963. These eight are still on the staff and their years of service to 1990 listed. Besides these "old-timers," we work alongside 56 others who are likewise dedicated Christians.

† † †

In devotions one morning, Dr. Rice surprised his staff when he said: "For the first time in my life, I have recently considered retiring." He named over some issues he had fought for, some men he had held onto, but were now compromising. And his heart was sad. Seldom had we seen him any way but "UP."

This shocked all of us. We had expected him to be sitting at his desk in the office until the day he died.

One sweet couple on the staff ordered him a dozen red roses that day, while others came by to comfort him.

He held on eight more months; then God took him Home.

† † †

On April 5, Dr. Rice was admitted to Rutherford Hospital. When it was determined he had had a heart attack, he was moved to the coronary care unit.

After a few days Dr. Garrison reported that he was about back to the place he was physically before entering the hospital two weeks before. He had reduced from 182 down to 164.

After 16 days he was released with instructions he could be in the office only an hour or two each day.

He was greatly touched by this poem-prayer sent by Naomi and Ralph Pierce:

> *Dr. Rice. . . .*
>
> *We read a little squib today—*
> *We saw it in THE SWORD;*
> *It said you were admitted*
> *To the coronary ward.*
> *We saw it just about the time*
> *That we sat down to sup,*
> *So while we said a little prayer*
> *Your name we lifted up.*
> *We didn't try to tell the Lord*
> *Of all you say and do;*
> *We didn't think that this would help*
> *'Cause He already knew!*
> *We simply sent a humble prayer*
> *That He'd look after you.*
> *We're just so sure He's seen you walk*
> *And watched the path you've trod,*
> *And knows your inner heart's concern*
> *For those who know not God.*
> *So we just sent a simple prayer*
> *And did it mighty quick;*
> *We marked it "Top Priority"—*
> *DR. RICE IS SICK.*

Who wouldn't be touched by such love of friends!

While at home, he spent most of his time in his big lean-back chair. There he remained most nights also. He could breathe better while his head was elevated.

In his "Notes" he wrote: "The English poet, Alfred Lord Tennyson, a devout Christian, expressed the way I feel about death:

> *Sunset and evening star,*
> *And one clear call for me:*
> *And may there be no moaning at the bar,*
> *When I put out to sea,*
> *But such a tide as moving seems asleep,*
> *Too full for sound and foam,*
> *When that which drew from out the boundless deep*
> *Turns again home.*
> *Twilight and evening bell,*
> *And after that the dark!*
> *And may there be no sadness of farewell*
> *When I embark;*
> *For, tho' from out our bourne of time and place*
> *The flood may bear me far,*
> *I hope to see my Pilot face to face*
> *When I have crost the bar.*

† † †

To the 5 million readers of the *National Enquirer,* ten of Dr. Rice's pamphlets and a year's subscription to THE SWORD OF THE LORD were offered in a full-page ad to any who would call or write the Sword. A toll-free 800 WATTS number was listed.

After the ad had come out (May 27), 1,633 phone calls were received in a short period of time. Manning the phones were soul winners from the Sword staff. In each case they said to the caller, "Now may I ask you a most important question? If you should die today, do you know you would go to Heaven?"

It had been surprising how many hungry and empty hearts were out there. In answer to that question, one dear soul responded, "No, I wouldn't go to Heaven. I am 75 years old and dying of cancer. Can you please help me?" After being dealt with, she happily trusted the Lord.

Protestants, Catholics, one Moslem and more than one defeated preacher were counseled.

From call-ins and letters, 1,285 said "Yes" to the Saviour. Fundamental pastors all over the country, who had been contacted ahead of time, were given their names for follow-up.

We were beginning to get response by mail and expected some 12,000 to write.

Continually we were reminded of lost people all about us.

Some were a little critical that we wanted to put an ad in a worldly magazine like *National Enquirer*. But this had been prayed through. And the fact that the people who read the *National Enquirer* wanted Christian literature and were eager to accept Christ showed that it was a wise choice. And we were reminded that of Jesus it was said: "There drew near unto him all the publicans and sinners for to hear him," and the Pharisees and scribes murmured, "This man receiveth sinners, and eateth with them."

† † †

After his most recent heart attack, Dr. Rice made his first public appearance (though he did not speak) at the Sword Women's Jubilee in Chambersburg, Pennsylvania, May 8, 9, 10. His oldest daughter Grace MacMullen gave her stirring testimony of her bout with cancer. Though she was in great pain, she encouraged and enlightened the hearts of those present. Grace had been chairman for the Women's Jubilees. After she became so ill, Dr. Rice asked another daughter, Mrs. Joy Martin, to chair the Jubilees. (Grace died in October, 1981, and is buried at the Bill Rice Ranch cemetery.)

† † †

On June 12 he flew to the Women's Jubilee at Wadsworth, Ohio, but due to his physical condition, asked Dr. Hutson to speak in his place. He did greet briefly the 540 registered.

† † †

Meet Honey, newest member of the family.

On Father's Day, his daughters gave him an apricot-colored 5-week-old poodle, whom he named Honey. When he could come to the office, Honey came with him. Commenting on this precious gift, Dr. Rice said: "He has trouble getting Mrs. Rice 'housebroken.' He thinks Miss Viola is an angel from Heaven [because I walked and fed him]. When someone

accidentally stepped on his foot, he came screaming to me. He chews up Mrs. Rice's house shoes. Every Kleenex he can get his paw on, he tears to bits. He plays with the end of a rope and chews on it.

"Honey is a beautiful little thing, and we are going to have much pleasure with him."

Dr. Rice got to enjoy him from May to December.

Honey was such a comfort—and company—to Mrs. Rice after Dr. Rice's death.[1]

† † †

Missionary Gerry Johnson of Seoul, Korea had, several years before, been provided funds to print *"What Must I Do to Be Saved?"* in the Korean language. Hundreds had been saved through it.

In May Missionary Johnson wrote that Korean Christians were requesting the booklet for use in evangelism and soul winning. "Would it be possible to assist us in another printing? Inflation has taken its toll in Korea and the cost has risen, but still the monetary cost is cheap compared with the value of precious souls. I have compared estimates for the cost of printing 100,000 copies, and the lowest estimate given me is $3,965.00. What do you think, Dr. Rice?"

Brother Johnson was authorized to go ahead with the printing. (LATER: In July the check was sent for the printing of 100,000 Korean *"What Must I Do to Be Saved?"*)

† † †

In tribute to Dr. Rice, his church, Franklin Road Baptist Church, gave him his roses before he died. On May 18, the pastor and people honored him with a special "John R. Rice Sunday." It was a grand time for the great evangelist. He was vibrantly happy as we sang his songs, remembered his victories and celebrated his accomplishments.

As a monument to its most famous member, there hangs in the lobby of Franklin Road Baptist Church, a beautiful hand-painted portrait of the "man sent from God whose name was John."

† † †

---

[1] When Mrs. Rice died, the daughters wanted me to have him, since I had looked after him for ten years and he had stayed with me every time Mrs. Rice went out to speak. He is very precious, comes to the office with me daily and knows every employee—not by name, but by smell! They love him, too. He knows Dr. Hutson's voice, and when he calls me on the intercom, Honey beats me to his office.

ATLANTA: The Sword Conference in Atlanta August 18 through 22 was a grand success. Attendance in the great Civic Center grew nightly until the auditorium filled to capacity. It was estimated the number of pastors involved in the four days was over 500.

It started with a banquet. In that meeting 101 pledged to be in the "Gideon's 300 Club," agreeing to keep THE SWORD in the full membership and to send subscriptions to new members.

The conference program included messages by Jerry Falwell, Lee Roberson, John Rawlings, Russell Anderson, Cecil Hodges, Bob Gray, Al Janney, Jack Hyles, Walt Handford, Curtis Hutson and John R. Rice.

The choir, directed by Lloyd Smith, was a tremendous feature. It presented not only the "Hallelujah Chorus" but "Down From His Glory," with Ray Hart taking high tenor. The genial Al Smith directed the music, and it was of the finest order.

A number of pastors from the Atlanta area and beyond acted as chairmen in the morning and night sessions, doing a fine work.

Many agreed this was one of the greatest conferences the Sword had held in numbers, in program and in impact.

Dr. Rice limited his activities, letting Dr. Hutson take responsibility of leadership.

On the last night when Dr. Rice spoke on "Other Sheep Have I Which Are Not of This Fold," emphasizing Christian fellowship and brotherhood and opening the door to every born-again believer to sing, "I'm so glad I'm a part of the family of God," by Bill Gaither, he received a long, standing ovation.

† † †

In the male teachers' lounge, where Dr. Rice had been speaking at Tennessee Temple Schools, a man rose and said to Dr. Rice:

> Brother Rice, you won me to Christ at Dayton, Ohio, when I was eleven. On the way to the platform you stopped in the crowd, put your arm around me and talked to me. You asked, "If you should die today, are you ready to go to Heaven?" I had to answer, "No." You urged me to settle the matter then and there. I waited for the invitation time. There was a pause, and you called out from the platform, "Where is that red-headed boy?" I knew you meant me, and I came forward and claimed the Lord openly.

I have been preaching now for thirteen years. I am preparing to go to the Philippine Islands for mission and pastoral work.

This was Rev. Mel Brown, who had written Dr. Rice so often, but had never expressed the above to him.

† † †

You will appreciate this kind word from Rev. Elmer Towns on Dr. Rice's one-day visit to Liberty Baptist College, Lynchburg, Virginia:

John R. Rice Came to Liberty Mountain
By Elmer Towns

One of the greatest days in the life of Liberty Baptist College was when John R. Rice visited the campus August 25, 1980 to speak in chapel. Dr. Jerry Falwell has always exposed great men of God to the students; so that is why Dr. John R. Rice has been to Liberty Mountain almost every year since the school began.

Even though Dr. Rice is limited in speaking engagements by a major heart attack two years ago and another one in March of this year, Dr. Falwell arranged for a jet to fly him to Lynchburg. He was driven to the campus and preached to over 3,000 students.

When Dr. Falwell was called unexpectedly to Birmingham, since I had been a friend of Dr. Rice's for many years, he asked me to introduce him.

I had heard that Dr. Rice was in poor physical condition. However, when he stepped off the jet, he looked spry and his eyes twinkled. Even though he had lost a lot of weight, his handshake was firm, and he was able to walk, although a wheelchair was available.

Well over 3,500 were present to hear him. Several married students and faculty brought their children, realizing that may be the last time for them to hear the great John R. Rice.

As he began to climb the stairs, the audience stood silently. Then as he took a seat on the platform, they broke into spontaneous applause.

When I introduced Dr. Rice, I noted he was "the most powerful pen of the 20th century." No other man has written and sold more books, pamphlets and tracts than he. His books have sold without the help of the influential New York public relation firms and their advertisement. God has allowed Dr. Rice to be the most powerful pen in the 20th century because he has stood true to the Gospel.

I told the student body that our commitment was to the "hot poker" principle. Just as the poker is heated when placed in the fire, so these young men would become firebrands for God when they were exposed to the life and spirit of great men of God.

My prayer is that these young men will catch the spirit and vision of Dr. John R. Rice and go out and accomplish the same tasks for the glory of God.

For almost thirty minutes Dr. Rice's voice was strong and he stood erect. Only towards the end of his sermon did his voice seem to grow weary.

On some occasions the students of Liberty Baptist College shout "amen" during chapel. However, that day was a different time and a different place. Then I realized why they were so quiet. They were straining to hear every word. Whereas on many occasions when Dr. Rice speaks, there is a revival atmosphere; that day was a quiet, reflective service. The students were respecting one of the greatest men of God living today.

During the message Dr. Rice still had a keen sense of humor. As he told anecdotes, the audience laughed with him. He gave illustration after illustration of how God had answered prayer. I thought of the great testimony of a man who has moved Heaven and earth on his knees, sharing with the students the secret of his power.

As he left the platform, the applause rang throughout the gymnasium. I heard them applauding until we went out the side door and entered the car. The doctors had requested that he not sign Bibles and greet the crowd.

As we got into the car, a student asked Dr. Rice, "May I have a copy of the sermon notes from which you preached today?" He smiled and said they were not very complete. The boy got them anyway and knew he had an historic document.

† † †

Twenty-one years later, Voice of Revival was still being aired on 72 stations, with four of them being 50,000-Watt stations.

† † †

A WEEK AT HYLES-ANDERSON (Sept. 22-26). Hyles-Anderson students are encouraged to have preachers as their heroes, and Dr. Rice was a favorite of them all.

After speaking to 2,000 students for a week, when he left on Friday, the lane was lined on both sides with probably a thousand students, each with at least two balloons, which were released into the air as he passed by.

† † †

In 1980 Southwide Baptist Fellowship honored seven Giants of the Faith, chosen because of the outstanding leadership they have displayed during their years of untiring service to God. Most of us are content to live the average life of the average Christian, giving the average service in the average way. When someone steps forward with determination and says, "By the help of God, I'm not going to settle for average," things happen.

These men have made things happen all their lives. God's Honor Roll of the Giants of the Faith were: Dr. John R. Rice, age 84; Dr. Lee Roberson, age 70; Dr. B. R. Lakin, age 78; Dr. John Rawlings, age 68; Evangelist Lester Roloff, age 66; singing evangelist Howard Jewell, age 76; and Dr. Jacob Gartenhaus, age 84.

† † †

On November 17, about 2:00 a.m., my phone rang. Mrs. Rice said Dr. Rice was not feeling well. I rushed to the house. Even in his distress, he wanted to know if I had pencil and paper so he could dictate some words. (He likely thought he might go to be with Jesus at this time.)

First was a letter to Mrs. Rice. (See page 502.) Then he dictated this brief word to me:

November 17, 1980

Dear Viola:

Secretary, Assistant, Beloved Partner in the Lord's Work:

I have learned to depend on your judgment so much concerning copy for THE SWORD OF THE LORD and other matters. You are a remarkable friend, bound to me with tender ties of long association. No one else could have been the strength to me in this work as you have been.

God bless you richly as you continue to serve where the Lord has put you. I love you very much. And it may be God will draw you even closer to me in the Holy Land.

Gratefully,
John R. Rice

I will forever prize that letter. He had said time and time again, "Reckon the Lord will let us work together again in Heaven?" I assured him that I was going to ask the Lord for that privilege.

He also dictated a brief word to Miss Fairy, another longtime helper.

Come morning, he was feeling better and seemed to continue improving, with only an occasional flare up.

† † †

On December 11 the Sword staff prepared a lovely dinner in the Sword auditorium, to celebrate his 85th birthday. Dr. Tom Malone flew down for the occasion, which pleased Dr. Rice, for he has always considered Dr. Malone his great friend.

Telegrams, phone calls, letters came from far and wide.

Though he was in a wheelchair, he seemed to delight in all these expressions of love.

At this luncheon, we sensed that he might not be with us much longer. (He died two and a half weeks later.)

Then on December 12, some friends gave a Christmas party for all Sword employees at Ramada Inn. When Dr. Rice was asked to say a

L to R: Grace,
Elizabeth,
Mary Lloys,
Jessie,
Joanna,
Joy

Above: The six Rice sisters blend voices across America.

Right: Taken shortly before Dr. Rice's death, with all his girls and Mrs. Rice.

Left: December 11, 1980, at his birthday party. Dr. Tom Malone flew down for the occasion. Dr. Rice died 2½ weeks later.

few words, he was wheeled to the mike and spoke briefly—his last spoken message on earth. He did not stay for the full program, but on the way home, he remarked, "Wasn't that a good party?"

† † †

His Christmas letter for 1980, written some days before his death, read:

My dear Friends everywhere!

"Tidings of great joy!"

I wish I might bring it with the rustle of the wings of the angel who first whispered it to Mary, then in a dream gladdened the heart of Joseph and took away the blackest fear a coming bridegroom ever faced, making Joseph happy again! I wish I could tell it with the tremulous radiance that the angel brought to the shepherds in the field that first Christmas night. Oh, if the heavens were filled again with the heavenly host to sing, "Glory to God in the highest," so your heart would burn as theirs, half with holy fright, half with glad believing!

As I lie in my recliner or walk around or sit in my office chair and think of the goodness of God these 85 years, my heart runs after my friends, my beloved brethren, my fellow-workers. God bless each of you at this Christmas time! May all that love can give, all that need may ask, all that a good heart can crave, be yours. But most of all, may Christ Jesus our Saviour, our Lord, our Beloved, that name above every name, be your Christmas Joy, your New Year's Prosperity, your ALL-IN-ALL! My heart's love and yearning can ask no greater for you.

I trust that you have as much to be thankful for as I have. A good home, my wife, children and grandchildren—and great grandchildren, too! Kindness of friends everywhere, the loyal help of some of the best assistants ever given a man. For these I praise my Heavenly Father this holiday season. Oh, for a heart to praise Him as I ought! I acknowledge my debt, I receive my gifts with godly joy, I trust.

In this hour I want God to assure my friends of my love and gratitude for your encouragement, your love, your prayers, your precious letters.

This year I was slowed down once again with another heart attack. But I am 85 years of age! And how well and strong I have been through all this time! Up until just a few years ago I could still beat my sons-in-law in both golf and bowling! Oh, God has blessed me in so many ways. Of course I yearn to be about my

Father's business, but He knows all about it; I am in His hands to use—or not to use—as He now sees fit. I often find comfort in these inspired words: "Even to your old age . . . even to hoar hairs will I carry you: I have made, and I will bear; even I will carry, and will deliver you" (Isa. 46:4).

I still, from my arm chair, "preach" in great revival campaigns. I still vision hundreds walking the aisles to accept Christ. I still feel hot tears for the lost. I still see God working miracles. Oh, how I long to see great revivals, to hear about revival crowds once again!

Talking about revival in a Christmas message to friends? It would be no Christmas to me without the sense of the breath of God upon me still, weak and frail as I am. I want no Christmas without a burden for lost souls, a message for sinners, a heart to bring in the lost sheep so dear to the Shepherd, the sinning souls for whom Christ died.

I will have the comfort and company of my faithful wife, my sweet girls' arms around my neck, grandchildren to be proud of and to hear tell of their plans for God's service; I will give and receive presents and surprises, and carols will be heard the day long, along with feasting and fellowship with family and workers. All this will be sweet, of course. But may food be tasteless and music a discord and Christmas a farce if I forget the dying millions to whom I am debtor; if this fire in my bones does not still flame! Not till I die, or not till Jesus comes, will I ever be eased of this burden, these tears, this toil to save souls.

Now may 1981 bring help in all trouble, a lifting of all burdens, grace for every duty, supply for every need. May the Saviour bless you today and always. May the Holy Spirit never leave you. May the Father's watchful care never fail.

In Christian remembrance and best wishes to my friends scattered in every state and in all nations.

John R. Rice

† † †

When Paul was near the end of his course, he gazed with pride on a younger man who was strong in the faith and learned in the Word, knowing that his ministry would continue in Timothy and knowing he was capable of carrying on the work which the original apostle had so nobly begun.

Some time back Dr. Rice had chosen his Timothy, Dr. Curtis Hutson.

He had been looking over this greatly used man of God for some time, though Dr. Hutson was unaware he was being watched. Then later at a board meeting when names were being considered as to on whom the mantle was to fall, Dr. Hutson was chosen. Though some on the Board did not know him well, they certainly relied on Dr. Rice's wisdom and choice.

Dr. Hutson is a ministry product of the Sword of the Lord. He was a successful pastor of a great church, then an evangelist. Then God led him to become Associate Editor of THE SWORD OF THE LORD and learn the heartbeat of Dr. Rice. Then on January 3, 1981, he became editor.

I have no doubt that he will continue to carry on in a mighty way, taking this ministry to greater heights. That is the way the Lord works. There is a Joshua for every Moses, if we earnestly seek the Lord's provision and direction in these matters.

I am glad to report that ten years have gone by, and Dr. Hutson's editorship still stands squarely upon the foundation built by Dr. John R. Rice, with some 70 employees loyally supporting him.

"Howl, fir tree; for the cedar is fallen."—Zech. 11:2.

December 29, 1980, an axman dressed in black went into the forest of men. In the past he had cut down many a tall tree of a man—Spurgeon, Moody, Finney, Bob Jones, Sr., Billy Sunday, R. G. Lee—but this time the axman aimed his blade at one we all knew and loved and honored and depended upon. He struck again and again until the cedar which had stood the blast of trouble and trial and abuse dropped into the dust and the sound of the fall resounded around the world.

The saddest words the Israelites ever heard were "Moses my servant is dead." The saddest words Fundamentalism will ever hear: "John R. Rice is dead."

We look forward one day to renewed fellowship where the gates swing outward never.

1895-1980

A RECAP OF HIS LAST FEW DAYS

We were all fearful of it, yet somehow never expected it. Dr. John R. Rice would live on, and on, and on. . . .

Doubtless it was best; but it was a sharp gash to the heart when he laid down his burdens and would no more walk amongst us.

Just a few details of his last days.

On December 16 he had read on and off all night lying in his recliner, with Mrs. Rice nearby. She had prepared his breakfast; and when she went to wake him, he did not respond. The Ed Martins, who lived next door, were called, then the ambulance, then the office.

After working over him for some time and seeing they could not wake him, the paramedics rushed him to the hospital, where he never regained consciousness, as far as anyone knows. It seems he was the victim of a massive brain hemorrhage.

He lay in the coronary care unit for two weeks. In that period of time, when his daughters would talk or sing to him, he would sometimes move a hand, and once or twice tears came to his eyes, but no other response.

On Sunday, December 28, he developed a high fever, got an infection, his breathing became very labored. . . and around 2:00 a.m. on Monday morning, December 29, an angel of the Lord came into the room, took Dr. John by the hand and whispered, "John, let's go Home!" I'm thinking there must have been a choir somewhere sweetly singing, "Steal away, steal away, steal away Home to Jesus"!

It was the family's wish that he be brought home for the last time, so he lay in a beautiful casket in the living room from Monday night until Tuesday noon.

His memorial service was at 1:00 p.m. on Wednesday.

A church auditorium, completely encircled with memorial wreaths and packed with nearly 1200 mourners, marked funeral services at Franklin Road Baptist Church, Murfreesboro, his home church. The three-hour program of eulogizers included prominent clergy from across the nation—a veritable who's who in fundamentalism. Each of Dr. Rice's sons-in-law spoke briefly, along with Drs. Bob Kelley, his pastor, Lee Roberson, John Rawlings, Bill Rice III, Pete Rice, Jerry Falwell, Tom Malone, Curtis Hutson and Jack Hyles.

Solos were rendered by Bill Harvey, Ray Hart and Don Holmes.

Some 1200 attended his funeral at Franklin Road Baptist Church, Murfreesboro.

A funeral scene on the Bill Rice Ranch at Dr. John R. Rice's burial. His two brothers are buried to his right in picture.

A special choir sang "The Hallelujah Chorus," and the Rice sisters sang some of their father's own songs.

Many described the service as the most unusual they had ever attended. It was a victory service...graduation...coronation.

He was laid to rest at the Bill Rice Ranch alongside his two other preacher brothers, Joe and Bill, and facing the John R. Rice Tabernacle.

Yes, to rest. No more sleepless nights. No more rushing off to catch a plane for engagements. No more tears over sinners. His right hand is closed because there are no more heroic words for it to write for THE SWORD OF THE LORD. His lips are shut, for there are no more sermons for him to preach. His heart is quiet; it will never break again. The sword which clave to his hand has dropped at last.

AT REST.[1]

There is no time that we could set for parting. We who must remain are never ready for such pain. Even our prayers would be "Not yet! Not yet, dear God—another day, with us let our loved one stay." We must believe, when falls the blow, that, wisely, God has willed it so.

Knowing Dr. Rice as I did, I know he felt in the words of the poem by John Oxenham,

> *Lord, when Thou seest that my work is done,*
> *Let me not linger on,*
> *With failing powers,*
> *Adown the weary hours—*
> *A workless worker in a world of work.*
> *But, with the word,*
> *Just bid me Home.*
> *And I will come*
> *Right gladly—*
> *Yes, right gladly*
> *Will I come.*

How can anyone sum up this godly giant's life and ministry in a few short pages? Admittedly, he did more for our Lord than a dozen ordinary preachers, and left a record unmatched by any other man of this century.

No one can take his place. Certainly the work goes on. God's movements are not dependent upon personalities. But the man is not alive who can take the place of John R. Rice!

---

[1] Yet if there's work to do in Heaven, he may be dictating for the Jerusalem Sword of the Lord! I know if Jesus has some work to be done, Dr. Rice would volunteer!

Dr. Rice, thank you for your beautiful life, your wonderful example and your prayers for forty-six years. See you soon, Sir!

† † †

From the One Who Knew Him Best—His Wife...

My husband was well known through his ministry as a writer, a preacher and a friend to preachers, but you may not know how faithfully he served the Lord in his position as a husband and father.

While preaching and teaching others to love and serve the Lord, he never neglected his own. If he had succeeded ever so well with his public ministry and failed with his family, he would have felt himself a failure. He set out to teach his children to love and obey the Word and live by it, to pray and to diligently follow every good work. He expected them to make good grades, to be good workers, to attend all the services of the church and to set a good example for others. We won five of the children to the Lord when they were five years old. A friend won one of them.

He made home a happy place where we sang, made music and enjoyed each other. Meals were always a happy occasion at our house, a special time for food, fun and fellowship. Our daddy wanted every meal served nicely with tablecloth, napkins and preferably with bone china. Every member of the family was expected to be present if at all possible. We started first with a good breakfast, followed with Bible reading and prayer, where everyone took turns at both reading and praying. The records in my Bible show where we have read the Bible through twenty times together.

He taught them to swim, dive, water ski, ice skate, play tennis and softball. He liked to play as well as work. There are no words to describe this man as a husband and father. We all agree he was ever the greatest.

At noon our daddy *always* came home for lunch when he was in town. He wanted to be with his family and have a twenty-minute rest in his reclining chair.

Then came the big climax, when we were all home for dinner. What a happy time of sharing events of the day, exchanging jokes, singing and making melody in our hearts! After dinner there were music and games. Dr. Rice played with his children—chess, checkers, Rook, "42" (a Texas domino game), Monopoly, Careers, or he would take them bowling.

The following letter was dictated on November 17 at 2:00 a.m. After he had given me this message personally, then he dictated it to Miss Viola as he wanted others to know his heart. Thank God for this precious letter he wanted to share with others!

November 17, 1980

Dear Mother:

We have had a wonderful life together. God's mercy has been extended to us over eighty-five years. These last two months, since I was in the hospital, have been a revelation to me. How kind you have been, constantly seeing that I was covered at night so that I did not get cold. And you have prepared for me the very finest of things to eat. How patient you have been and wonderful.

You have been a wonderful wife, a wonderful mother. We have loved the Scriptures, and you have helped make them a blessing to me. You have a good name among the people of God, and you have deserved it.

I hope the remaining years—whether few or many—will be very happy.

I rejoice with you in our wonderful children. Your prayers have held them up and those of the grandchildren, especially those called to preach. I rejoice with you in the great work they will do.

I greet you with a heartfelt kiss of love. You have been a wonderful partner-wife to me.

We will sing at the last:

> *On Christ the solid rock I stand;*
> *All other ground is sinking sand.*

The dear Saviour will make you happy and care for you all the way.

John R. Rice

How the Rice Daughters Feel...

(Written in 1981)

Grace
MacMullen

THE QUEST FOR EXCELLENCE

One of the things I remember most about growing up was Daddy's insistence that we do things right. He might want them done in a hurry, but he still wanted them done the best way. "I don't want to pay you for for doing work twice," he would say in the office. "Do it right the first time."

At the dinner table we often used words carelessly and were reprimanded for it. If we said, "This girl said...," without an antecedent for the word *this,* he would stop us and say, "What girl are you talking about?" If we said something meaningless, such as "and stuff like that," we were immediately reminded that "stuff" was too indefinite to mean anything.

I remember once I wrote him a letter scribbled hurriedly in pencil. He wrote back instructing me that I was too important and he was too important, for me to write letters in pencil.

The biblical basis for the whole thing, of course, is, "whatsoever ye do, do it heartily as to the Lord" (Col. 3:23).

I am so glad he pushed us to do our best. Even now, I can't do a sloppy job without thinking how displeased he would be. I miss him terribly but thank the Lord for the privilege of having John R. Rice as my dad.

Grace
(Now in Heaven)

† † †

TRIBUTE TO MY FATHER

Mary Lloys
Himes

Wise in so many ways, fun to be with, to play with, to cook for or to eat with, a great preacher, prolific author, great Bible student, loving but stern father, devoted husband to my mother, fond "Pawpaw" to my children but almost naive sometimes in his relationship to people: that was my father.

He was my teacher, encourager, pastor, boss, consultant about important decisions, favorite author and radio preacher and intercessor and prayer partner. His example in loving people, trying things new from exotic foods ("If many people like a dish, it must be good") to new sports or games, and developing new tastes and abilities like writing music, will always be before me, though he has gone to Heaven to be with the Lord. Of course, we miss his presence, but rejoice with him in that great Homegoing.

Mary Lloys

† † †

Elizabeth Handford

Daddy! Daddy! How many times his name was a talisman against fear. A childish nightmare, a dangerous throat infection, an elusive algebra equation, a tempestuous boy-girl friendship, a distraught searching for the will of God concerning school: whatever it was, Daddy could fix it! He might not know the exact answer—though likely he would—but he always knew where to find the answer. He seemed always to know exactly what it was God wanted us to do in the situation, and he was willing to explain it so even a child could understand.

And he was always the same. You could count on Daddy. You knew what his response would be in time of stress or joy or trouble. Others have groped for words to express their appreciation of Daddy's life. We've smiled to hear them mention universally the same great strengths of character we valued in him as his children.

I know what my Heavenly Father is like. I know how He grieves over my sin, but how He yearns over me and works to make me happy and successful. I know what my Heavenly Father is like because my father introduced me to Him in ways words could not express.

Do I know how fortunate I was to be able to call him Daddy? Yes, in some measure, at least. And I count it one of the greatest of the blessings of a blessing-filled life.

Elizabeth

† † †

MEMORIES OF DADDY...

Jessie Sandberg

My earliest memories of Daddy are somehow associated with the times I was in trouble. I remember his praying for me when a firecracker went off in my hand, his reassurances that my face would be all right again after I fell off a sled and landed on my face, his comforting words when I was afraid.

Later, it was the fun we had with Daddy that became most important. I remember our giggling and hiding together in the bushes when the whole family played a game of "kick the can." How many hours Dad spent with us playing tennis, ice skating, playing softball and bowling and how many *more* hours were spent singing or reciting poetry or discussing great books.

Even later it was the spiritual support and advice which Dad provided that became important. Whether it came to a problem about standards, advice about a boyfriend or an interpretation of a particular Scripture, Dad always had the answer.

Thank God for the memories of a wonderful father!

Jessie

† † †

A TRIBUTE TO MY DAD

Joanna Rice

The world's greatest dad? Yes, I think so. The functions of a family have been listed as education, religious training, production, recreation, security and nurture. How lovingly and wholeheartedly our parents together performed these functions for my sisters and me. Our education wasn't just a matter of going to a good school; it included animated discussions on every subject, wide exposure to books, art and music, fantastic motivation to measure up to God's expectations of us. When it came to religious training, Dad was the expert! He led me to the Lord, won many of my friends, read, explained, memorized and lived God's Word daily with us. His Spirit-filled prayer life helped me to know I, too, could have what I wanted and needed.

He could demonstrate homemaking skills as well as any woman, whether it be sewing on a button, canning peaches or making donuts, and none of it was beneath his manly dignity. How I cherish the times of recreation with my dad—tennis, skating, table games, volleyball, bowling, even golf!

Security came from knowing I had eternal life, knowing the Scriptures, knowing I was loved. Love, the very necessary ingredient, was always evident, frequently indicated by words, but also by the chastening rod (Prov. 13:24). Thank God for the world's greatest dad—Dr. John R. Rice! "And all thy children shall be taught of the Lord; and great shall be the peace of thy children" (Isa. 54:13).

Joanna

† † †

Joy
Martin

THANK YOU, DADDY

"Joy, give us a few words to describe your dad."

A few words... to describe a precious relationship that began on Mother and Dad's sixteenth wedding anniversary, September 27, 1937, and lasted for forty-three years, absolutely full of vivid pictures in my mind!

SALVATION—Hoopeston, Illinois: I am four years old, taking a nap with my evangelist-dad on a Sunday afternoon. I am musing over Dad's morning message and the children who responded at the invitation. "Joy, are you wondering if you are old enough to be saved?" Daddy gently explains the Scriptures. I bow my head and ask Jesus to forgive my sins and save me. Sweet relief for a four-year-old!

Thank you, Daddy, for leading me to Christ.

MUSIC—Wheaton, Illinois: I am seven years old. Mother and Daddy insisted on piano lessons beginning when I was four. Now at seven, I am delightedly "composing" a song for my own enjoyment, accompanying myself. I think, *What beautiful sounds I am making! What fun to press down these black notes! Sounds like the ocean.* When my sisters protest my irritating "music," Daddy suddenly looks up sternly. "Girls, you let Joy alone!"

I am a self-conscious fifteen-year-old, the youngest of six girls. My older sisters all seem brilliant and gifted. Comparing myself to them, I feel untalented, awkward, homely. How does a busy preacher-father sense my need to be accomplished and creative in something? "Joy, I want you to start taking voice lessons at the Conservatory immediately." Does he think I have a glorious voice? No, but he discerns my need to achieve. How does he know that music will be a major part of my life—in the church my husband pastors, in the university where I teach, in the jubilees where I lead the music, in the most private corner of my heart— "Singing and making melody in my heart to the Lord"?

Thank you, Daddy, for my music!

COURTSHIP AND MARRIAGE—Wheaton College Days: I am twenty-one and in love with a serious young man who is Daddy's assistant pastor. When Roger comes "to court," Daddy teases him out of his reserve. So often the big twelve-room house is full of people, so Roger and I go outside to talk. One day I suggest that Daddy might buy a swing for the front porch for Roger and me. To my surprise, Daddy instantly agrees—"But I don't know how I will explain this to your mother, Roger!"

Daddy sees the "inevitable" coming, but dreads to lose "the last little robin in the nest.". . . Greenville, South Carolina. . . When Roger finally, after four years, asks for my hand in marriage, Daddy gives his blessing and Mother says, "Oh, this is so sudden." Three months later Daddy helps me pick out trousseau dresses and watches me whirl around misty-eyed in a white lace wedding gown. Just before walking me down the aisle, he quips to Roger, "I'll help you get away, Roger. There's still time!" Minutes later he joins our right hands, and we repeat our vows. . . Twenty years later—I think about the fine, godly man I married.

Thank you, Daddy, for teaching me to save all my kisses for the man who became my husband.

Thank you for setting an example of what a loving husband is.

Thank you for making me be sure Roger was God's choice.

Thank you, Daddy—you tied a good knot!

PARTING—Rutherford Hospital, Murfreesboro, Tennessee: December 29, 1:30 a.m. We stand around Daddy's bed, waiting for the angels. My sisters and I know it can't be long. We cry a lot, our minds and hearts full of little mental etchings of Daddy's touch in our lives. But we smile through our tears—there are such happy, happy memories. We hold his hand; his eyes are closed, but we kiss him as we have done so many hundreds of times. We say one last time, "I love you, Daddy." Two quick sighs, and then he is at Home.

Thank You, Jesus, for these precious years with Daddy.

"A FEW WORDS. . . ABOUT YOUR DAD." Too many words already for the space allotted me—but not nearly enough words to describe the great man I call Daddy.

Joy

✝ ✝ ✝

Dr. W. A. Criswell gave us this testimony of the influence this Texas evangelist had on his life as a young boy:

When I was a boy living in a small village in the northwestern panhandle of Texas, Dr. John R. Rice and another man came to town and conducted a tent revival meeting for our Baptist church in the little village.

In that revival meeting I gave my life to

being a preacher. I was twelve years of age. Dr. Rice talked to me, took time to visit with me, was very interested in me and kind to me; he encouraged me in the work and faith of the Lord.

When you're older, people have somewhat of an influence upon you, but nothing comparable to that influence that people have upon you when you are young and pliable.

The friendship of Dr. Rice to me has always been precious. I have had a moving affection for him through all the years since I was a small boy. Dr. Rice believed in the things that I believe in. He preached the Gospel that I try to preach. He believed in the inerrancy of the Holy Scriptures. He believed in all the great truths that are revealed to us in the Bible. And he was evangelistic and sought to win people to Christ. In all of those great areas of doctrinal commitment, my heart has always been committed, and I've tried to exhibit them, present them, preach them in my own ministry.

May God bless and sanctify the memory of Dr. Rice to all the millions who knew and loved him now and forever.

> Dr. W. A. Criswell
> First Baptist Church
> Dallas, Texas

† † †

"Greatness!"

When we think of the life and ministry of Dr. John R. Rice, we are talking about greatness!

Dr. Rice was great in his concern for others. Soul winning was the theme of his life. He preached sermons, he conducted conferences, he wrote books, he edited a paper—all with one theme: soul winning!

Dr. Rice was great in his influence on pastors and churches. Thousands of churches were touched, yes, were changed by the spoken and written ministry of Dr. John R. Rice.

Dr. Rice was great in his courage. He was not always popular in his battle against sin, but he was always courageous. Those of us who knew him noticed that he never let these battles embitter his soul. In the midst of the hottest conflicts, he maintained his Christlike attitude.

Dr. Rice was great in his writings. Thousands of articles, hundreds of books, millions of gospel tracts have been distributed around the world with one end—the salvation of the lost.

Dr. Rice was great in his friendship. He made friends, he prayed for his friends, he assisted his friends, and he was loyal to his friends. I am indebted to Dr. John R. Rice and his friendship extended over these many years. He was unfailing in his willingness to help others. Many of us owe much to him for his fervent, faithful praying in our behalf.

The story of this great life is only partially known. The full significance of his work and life will be revealed at the judgment seat of Christ.

Our prayers are for Mrs. Rice and the family.

Dr. Lee Roberson

† † †

"ONCE IN A GENERATION"

This morning I was told that Dr. John R. Rice had gone on to be with the Lord and it was a very, very, very distinct loss to me. I know that at his age we should be ready for his going on to be with the Lord and, when it comes to my feelings about him, I'm not exaggerating—I envy him being at the place where he's always wanted to be—with the Lord Jesus Christ.

Now, Dr. John came into my life—our paths crossed—in 1930, when I entered a seminary in Fort Worth, Texas, and Dr. Rice and, of course, his family were living right there on Seminary Hill. Since then, thank God with all my soul, our paths crossed again and again. Not often enough to please me, but then he's been busy and I've been busy. His Holy-Spirit-inspired counsels to me—and I'd ask them from him by phone, by letter, in person—have helped me enormously all along the way. First, in my work as a pastor—we were pastors together in Dallas for a little—then in the years of my evangelism. He was my ideal in many ways. His very presence stirred my soul. His works-filled life was and shall continue to be a source of challenging motivation to my life. THE SWORD OF THE LORD has blessed me from its very start. I never miss an issue of it.

Dr. Rice was a man who comes, perhaps, once in a generation. The Holy Spirit had endowed him with many talents. As a gifted author of most helpful books, as a noted, effective pulpiteer—matter of fact I can say a giant of the pulpit—as a pastor, as an evangelist, as a protagonist and a leader of noble causes—many, many times sacrificing himself. Above all, as a Titan in the realm of soul winning. Tens of thousands, aye, hundreds of thousands have been saved, reclaimed, added to the churches under his impassioned appeals. Truly, hundreds of others will join me in my own fervent, unreserved testimony that I am the better man because John R. Rice came into my life.

Beyond any of these things, great as they were and are, John Rice was a Christian through and through—a gentle, compassionate, Spirit-filled Christian, sacrificially going out of his way in many ways to help us lesser people. May I say from the depths of my soul, thank you, Lord, for giving us John Rice for so many years. God, please, the prayer of my soul, bless his wife and wonderful children and grandchildren and may they carry on the superlative tradition of this giant of giants in Christ's name. Amen.

—Evangelist Hyman J. Appelman

† † †

Dr. Theodore H. Epp, founder and director of Back to the Bible Broadcast, expressed his gratitude for Dr. Rice and his ministry throughout the past fifty years:

My acquaintance with Dr. Rice goes back to seminary days in the late 1920s in Fort Worth, Texas. He was conducting a gospel radio broadcast in Fort Worth; and as a member of a quartet from the seminary, we had the privilege of singing for him on a few occasions. I found Dr. Rice to be one of the kindest men I ever had the privilege of associating with—an association which lasted for more than fifty years.

When Back to the Bible Broadcast was less than two years old, we invited Dr. Rice to conduct a month of radio evangelistic meetings. These programs were released on three stations in three states in the heart of the nation.

During that month we distributed thousands of his tract booklets entitled *"What Must I Do to Be Saved?"* At least one thousand souls testified to their salvation as a result of this evangelistic outreach. We repeated this venture of thirty days of evangelism by radio in 1943, when Back to the Bible was then heard on twelve stations. Again hundreds testified to being saved during that month.

Dr. Rice was a giant among preachers and a prolific writer of many books, and his many conferences on evangelism had worldwide effect. He talked evangelism, he wrote evangelism, he lived evangelism, he was active in this passion of his soul until God said, "It is finished; well done, thou good and faithful servant."

He made a deep imprint upon the Back to the Bible Broadcast, and in his last communication to us assured us of his constant prayers and love for this ministry.

I cherish his memory as one of the kindest men I have met—always outgoing toward others. We always appreciated his fellowship and his deep fervor for the souls of men. He was a constant challenge and was most helpful in keeping alive in us the ultimate goal of winning souls, for he that winneth souls is wise. And Psalm 126:6 became most precious to me because I heard it quoted from his lips many, many times: "He shall doubtless come again with rejoicing, bringing his sheaves with him."

As God said to Joshua concerning Moses, "My servant is dead; now therefore arise, [and] go," and, "as I was with Moses, so I will be with thee: I will not fail thee, nor forsake thee" (Josh. 1:2,5), so God must be speaking today to a younger generation, "John R. Rice, my servant, is dead; but now you go—and as I was with John R. Rice, so I will be with you." So let us arise and be doing, remembering Psalm 126:6.

† † †

Elected Officials:

I was so very sorry to hear about Doctor Rice. His service to God during his lifetime has benefited so many. And his work will be long remembered. He has touched very many lives. I know this has been a difficult time for you. Honey and I will keep you in our thoughts and prayers.

> Governor Lamar Alexander
> Tennessee

Nancy and I were saddened to learn of the death of your husband, John. His life and his great faith were an inspiration to millions through the years. In this hour may the peace of God comfort you and your family. With warmest personal regards.

> Ronald Reagan

It was with deep sorrow that I learned of the passing of your husband. Dr. Rice has been the titular head of the fundamentalists in this country and one of the most powerful pens through his 45 years with the Sword of the Lord and the numerous books he has written. My heartfelt condolences are with you and your six daughters during this time.

> United States Senator Howard Baker, Tennessee

Dr. John R. Rice was a dedicated and talented Bible scholar and writer whose insights will be sorely missed by the readers of THE SWORD OF THE LORD and his many other written works. His evangelical beliefs were shared not only in Tennessee and the Southeast, but in every state of our nation and more than 100 countries of the world.

Although his death is an extreme loss to his family, friends and faithful readers, they can be proud to reflect that Dr. Rice spent his life spreading goodwill and good news to all men. His was a full and fruitful life and one which should set an example for all citizens.

United States Senator Jim Sasser, Tennessee

I'm certainly sorry to hear of the passing of Dr. Rice. He has been one of the outstanding people who have come to our community during the past few years. We have enjoyed very much having him as a citizen. The organization which he brought to our city has been outstanding in its contribution to our community. We have enjoyed having the Sword of the Lord people. They have all been good citizens. We are sorry to have to give up Dr. Rice.

Mayor W. H. Westbrooks, Murfreesboro

† † †

SAVED CHISELING DR. RICE'S FAVORITE VERSE!

"I could almost hear him clapping his hands in Heaven!" exclaimed Rev. T. A. Powell of Virginia. Shortly after Dr. Rice had entered into Glory, Powell and his family visited the grave. When they had climbed up the hill to the gravesite, they found a workman on his knees, inscribing Dr. Rice's favorite Scripture, Psalm 126:5,6, on the stone.

In chatting with the man briefly, Powell discovered he had never been saved. As they knelt together by the tomb, the worker poured out his heart in surrender to Jesus Christ.

Powell's statement referred to Dr. Rice's joining in celestial celebration. In truth, his influence was still reaching men for the Master!

† † †

May 31, 1981, on the 15th anniversary of its opening, the Christian Hall of Fame added one new original oil portrait to its collection of great Christian leaders, bringing the total to 101.

The Christian Hall of Fame, housed in the Canton Baptist Temple, Canton, Ohio, is a collection of original oil portraits which trace the progress of biblical Christianity from the time of the closing of the New Testament canon in approximately 100 A.D. until the present.

Sometimes it's hard to understand why certain things must be.
But there's a reason for it all beyond
our power to see. You wished no one
a last farewell—no chance to say
good-bye. You were gone *before your
death,* and only God knows why.
Your smile is gone for now; your
hand we cannot touch. Thank God for precious
memories of one we love so much. It breaks our hearts
to lose you, but you did not go alone, For part of us
went with you the day God called you Home. In that
blessed land called Heaven, we all once more will be,
United as we were on earth, for all eternity.

> Sadly missed by "Miss Viola"
> Your personal secretary for 46 years

HIS WRITINGS

"And his works do follow him...."

THE AUTHOR:

At his death at the end of 1980, Dr. Rice had over 200 different titles in print with a combined circulation exceeding 60 million copies. Many of these volumes are considered Christian classics.

When you begin to total up the writings which have flowed from his pen, you begin to wonder if Solomon was referring personally to him when he wrote, "Of the making of many books there is no end"!

The sum total of the ministries of the man tell an almost awesome story. It seems incredible, impossible, that one man could accomplish so much for Christ in one lifetime.

"Twentieth Century's Mightiest Pen" is a plaudit earned not only by output but also by outcome.

From the time Dr. Rice began his writing ministry until the hour of his death, a total of 22,923 letters came to him saying the writer found Christ through his books or booklets or a sermon published in THE SWORD OF THE LORD. This does not include the tens of thousands saved in his crusades, those coming to Christ through the radio and TV ministries or the thousands professing Christ through the foreign language editions of his writings.

Dr. Rice left a goodly heritage to each of us through the printed page.

A list of his books follows:

HARDBOUND BOOKS

A Know-So Salvation
Always Rejoicing!
All About Christian Giving
Amazing Power of the Gospel in Print
"And God Remembered..."
"Behold, He Cometh!" (Revelation)
Bible Doctrines to Live By
Bible Giants Tested
Blood and Tears on the Stairway
Charismatic Movement, The

Christian's Wells of Joy, A
Christ in the Old Testament
Church of God at Corinth (I, II Corinthians)
Coming Kingdom of Christ, The
"Compel Them to Come In"
Dr. Rice, Here Is My Question
Dr. Rice, Here Are More Questions
Earnestly Contending for the Faith
Evangelist and His Work, The

False Doctrines Answered
Favorite Chapters of the Bible
50 Years of Soul-Stirring Illustrations
Filled With the Spirit (Acts)
Five Pillars of the Temple
God in Your Family
God's Cure for Anxious Care
God's Work: How to Do It
Golden Path to Successful Personal
    Soul Winning
Gospel That Has Saved 16,000 Souls, The
Great and Terrible God, The
Great Truths for Soul Winners
Hallelujah! Sermons on Great Songs
Hands of Jesus, The
Here We Are in Bible Lands
Home: Courtship, Marriage and Children
Immanuel: "God With Us"
I Saw These Come to Christ
I Love Christmas
"In the Beginning..." (Genesis)
Is God a Dirty Bully?
Is Jesus God?
John R. Rice Bible Stories
King of the Jews (Matthew)
"No Man Cares for My Soul"
Our God-Breathed Book—the Bible
Power of Pentecost
Prayer—Asking and Receiving

Revival Appeals
Ruin of a Christian
Scarlet Sin, The
Seeking a City
Son of God (John)
Son of Man (Luke)
Soul-Saving Sermons for Sinners
Success-Prone Christians
Sweet Family Ties in Heaven and Hell
Ten Messages That Changed 10,000 Lives
Twelve Tremendous Themes
Watching Jesus Die
We Can Have Revival Now
"What Must I Do to Be Saved?" (sermons)
What It Costs to Be a Good Christian
When a Christian Sins
When Skeletons Come Out of Their
    Closets!
Whosoever and Whatsoever When You
    Pray
Why Our Churches Do Not Win Souls

Compiled

742 Heart-Warming Poems
Coffer of Jewels
Sword Book of Treasures
Sword Scrapbook (Vol. 1)
Sword Scrapbook (Vol. 2)

PAPERBOUND BOOKS

Amusements for Christians
Angel's Christmas Message
Bible Baptism
Bible Facts About Heaven
Bible Lessons on Revelation
Birth of a Saviour
Bobbed Hair, Bossy Wives and Women
    Preachers
Church That God Blesses, and Why
Come Out—Or Stay In?
Dr. Rice Goes to College
Electrocution of Raymond Hamilton
Fires From Many Altars
For Men and Women
Four Songs on the Second Coming
Golden Moments With Dr. John R. Rice
Great Controversial Subjects
Great Men of the Bible
Ho! Israel, Repent!
How to Get Things From God
How to Have a Real Christian Home
How to Make a Grand Success of the
    Christian Life
I Am a Fundamentalist

Lodges Examined By the Bible
New Solos and Duets
Preaching That Built a Great Church
Predestined for Hell? No!
Resurrection of Jesus Christ
Second Coming of Christ in Daniel
Seven Secrets of a Successful
    Christian Life
Songs of John R. Rice
Soul-Winner's Fire, The
Southern Baptists and Wolves in
    Sheep's Clothing
Southern Baptists, Wake Up!
Success-Prone Christians
Tears, Blessed Tears
Was Pope John Paul I a Born-Again
    Christian?
What Is Wrong With the Movies?
What's Wrong With the Dance?
When a Christian Sins
You Must Be Born Again

Compiled
Apples of Gold

Beautiful for Thee   Poems That Preach

BOOKLETS

Abortion
Adultery and Sex Perversion
All Have Sinned
All Satan's Apples Have Worms
American Heritage
Are You Going to Heaven?
Attack on the Bible
Backslider, The
Banquet Invitation, R.S.V.P.
Beware of False Prophets
Biggest Job in the World—Soul
    Winning
Born Again, Then What?
Can a Saved Person Ever Be Lost?
Christ Is Coming, Signs or No Signs
Christian and the Holy Spirit, The
Christian Faces Sex Problems, The
Christmas Pageant
Christ's Literal Reign on Earth From David's
    Throne in Jerusalem
Church Members Who Make God Sick
Churches and the Church
Come Back to Bethel
Correction and Discipline of Children
Count Your Blessings
Courtship and Dangers of Petting
Crossing the Deadline
Dangerous Triplets
David and Bath-sheba
Dear Catholic Friend
Divorce, the Wreck of Marriage
Double Curse of Booze, The
Eight Gospel Absurdities if a Born-Again
Soul Ever Loses Salvation
Eternal Salvation
Evolution or the Bible—Which?
Fall of a Preacher and His Restoration
Father, Mother, Home and Heaven
Four Biggest Fools in Town
Four Great Heresies
Fullness of the Spirit
Giving Your Way to Prosperity
God's Authority in Home, Government and
    the Bible
Good Man Lost—Bad Man Saved, A
Guys and Gals
Healing in Answer to Prayer
Hell! What the Bible Says About It
High Cost of Revival, The
Hindrances to Prayer

How Great Soul Winners Were Filled
    With the Holy Spirit
How Jesus, Our Pattern, Was Filled
    With the Holy Spirit
Hyper-Calvinism—a False Doctrine
Jehoshaphat's Sin
Jesus May Come Today!
Last Judgment of the Unsaved Dead, The
Lot
Missing God's Last Train for Heaven
Neglect, the Shortest Way to Hell
Negro and White
Never Alone, Never Forsaken
Open Your Mouth
Our Loving Friend—the Holy Spirit
Our Perfect Book, the Bible
Personal Soul Winning: How to Do It
Rebellious Wives and Slacker Husbands
Religious But Lost
Saved for Certain
Sermon From a Catholic Bible
Some Great Bible Characters
Soul Winning
Southern Baptist Leaders Approve
    Liberal Commentary
Southern Baptist Leaders Now
    Committed Liberals
Speaking in Tongues
Spectators at the Cross
Steps for New Converts
Storehouse Tithing
Sunday or Sabbath
Sword Special Songs
Tears, Blessed Tears
Tears in Heaven
Tobacco: Is Its Use a Sin?
Trailed by a Wild Beast
Unequal Yoke, The
Verbal Inspiration of the Bible and Its
    Scientific Accuracy
"What Must I Do to Be Saved?"
    (large print)
What Was Back of Kennedy's Murder?
What Will Happen When Jesus Comes?
Why Pray?
Why Preach Against Sin?
Winning Your Loved Ones
"Woman Thou Gavest Me, The"
Wonderful Jesus

PAMPHLETS-TRACTS

Christian Cooperation and Separation
Ecumenical Excuses for Unequal Yokes
Sin of Formalism, The

These Bible Christians Fell Through
  Compromise
"What Must I Do to Be Saved?"

A Disclaimer

Some of the valuable men in this volume who worked with Dr. Rice and the Sword of the Lord Foundation have either gone to other fields of service, or, sad to say, have disappointed us in ways we do not wish to discuss.

But that was the case of a few even in Bible times.

My mind goes back to Demas, a "fellow labourer" with Paul (Philemon 24). He had been a dependable disciple, or else he wouldn't have been traveling with Paul, who selected his coworkers with the utmost care. Yes, the man who traveled and served Christ with Paul had to measure up to the highest standards.

And Demas is favorably mentioned several times in the Bible; but in II Timothy 4:10 we read: "Demas hath forsaken me, having loved this present world. . . ." In the original language, "forsaken" meant to let someone down, to disappoint, to abandon, to desert.

At a crucial time, when Paul most needed him, Demas got more interested in his "Fifth Avenue" chariot, or in his home entertainment center, or in his weekend camping out in the desert—"Having loved this present world."

Then John Mark was chosen to accompany Paul on his first missionary journey. John Mark proved undependable and "returned to Jerusalem." (Later, John Mark did prove useful, for Paul said in II Timothy 4:11, "Take Mark and bring him with thee: for he is profitable to me for the ministry.")

For history's sake, it seemed necessary to include these who were once our "fellow labourers," who loved the Sword of the Lord, but are no longer connected with the Foundation.

CHRONOLOGY
(Not all events listed)

1895-1931:   Early life on Texas soil

1932:   Open-air revivals in Dallas
Founding of Fundamentalist Baptist Tabernacle, Dallas

1934:   Birth of THE SWORD OF THE LORD, with its
emphasis on evangelism

1935:   The Rice-Oliphant Debate, of great statewide interest

1936:   Hinderers fail to stop revival at Binghamton, New York
Fundamentalist Baptist Tabernacle destroyed by fire of
unknown origin

1939:   Tragic death of P. B. Chenault; Dr. Rice conducts funeral in
Waterloo, Iowa

1940:   Leave Dallas after eight years, for Wheaton, Illinois to enter
full-time evangelism

1941:   Conducts "Radio Revival" for Dr. Theodore H. Epp, with over
one thousand conversions

1942:   Answers to definite prayer related

1943:   Conference on Evangelism, Bethany Reformed Church,
Chicago
North Minneapolis union campaign
Huntington, West Virginia, campaign with twenty
churches
Partnership of Evangelists formed to promote union
campaigns

1944:   Singer J. Stratton Shufelt joins team
"EVERETT-(Wash.) FOR-CHRIST" union campaign
CHRIST-FOR-GREATER-BUFFALO campaign
Expresses "thanks" to his office staff

1945:   To Evansville Rescue Mission
CHRIST-FOR-GREATER-CLEVELAND union campaign
Beginning of Sword of the Lord Conferences
Winona Lake, Indiana Sword Conference
Sword Book Club announced
50,000 subscriptions on his 50th birthday

1946:   W. F. (Bill) Mann joins evangelistic team as Advance Man
             for union revivals
             To Miami, Florida with 44 churches
             "LIFE BEGINS" campaign in Chicago Arena
             True Evangelism book (Lewis Sperry Chafer) exposed
             Sword literature being mightily used in wartime
             Harry Clarke, formerly with Billy Sunday, joins Rice
             evangelistic team
             To Dayton, Ohio with 100 preachers cooperating

1947:   Sword of the Lord Foundation becomes a tax-deductible
             corporation
             San Pedro, California united campaign under big tent
             Winston-Salem, North Carolina union campaign in huge
             tobacco warehouse
             Greenville, South Carolina campaign causes many to
             right wrongs
             Dr. Rice grievously afflicted with sciatic rheumatism

1948:   Stays closer at home base, planning for future

1949:   Great tent campaign, Springfield, Missouri
             Sword of the Lord Conference at Lake Louise Conference
             Grounds, Toccoa, Georgia
             Other conferences at Cedar Lake, Indiana; Siloam Springs,
             Arkansas
             Bob Jones University ministerial students required to read
             THE SWORD OF THE LORD

1950:   Presque Isle, Maine union campaign
             Japanese attacker on Pearl Harbor converted
             Began to flood Japan with *"What Must I Do to Be Saved?"*
             booklet
             Sword Staff of Evangelists formed; Dr. Bill Rice, Director
             "I got it from John" (Bill Rice)

1951:   A ten-week revival through THE SWORD OF THE LORD
             That first Moncton, N. B., Canada campaign
             1800 Japanese pastors offered THE SWORD OF THE
             LORD free

1952:   SWORD OF THE LORD nears 100,000 circulation
             D. A. (Scotchie) McCall becomes Promotional Secretary of
             Sword Foundation
             Fairy Shappard's ministry with Sword of the Lord
             Foundation
             Rapid Growth and Expansion
             Takes first vacation since 1935!
             Sword Cooperating Board formed
             Back to Moncton, N. B., Canada; many saved

1952 (cont.)	Feels God wants him to spend more time editing the paper
1953:	Flicka, his beautiful small sheep dog, writes her master! Bill Rice Ranch (Cumberwood Christian Retreat), Mur- freesboro, added for Sword of the Lord Conferences "Ma" Sunday sends in 25 SWORD subscriptions
1954:	"Yesterday I gave away $4,101.90" THE SWORD, a mighty defender against modernism, false cults, worldliness

1955:	Declares his deep love for preachers; invests $34,216 in their
	    ministries
	Organizes Calvary Baptist Church in Wheaton
	Liberal McCormick Theological Seminary, Chicago, puts
	    all SWORD OF THE LORD issues on microfilm

1956:	Goes to Japan and Korea Booklets translated and printed in many languages and lands Sadly, Sword Book Club is discontinued

1957:	500,000 *"What Must I Do to Be Saved?"* booklets distributed
	    at shrines during Japanese New Year
	Zondervan Publishing House takes over all publishing and
	    wholesale distribution of Sword books
	Dr. Rice's near-fatal accident
	Withdraws support of Dr. Billy Graham, but still loves him,
	    still prays for him
	Dr. Bob Shuler, great Methodist, writes defending Dr. Rice;
	    tells how God gave him grace to stand alone
	Letters tell of anxious sinners finding the Saviour
	Al Byers joins Sword staff as Business Manager and
	    Treasurer

1958:	"Praying for my evangelists—one by one" Puzzles—and more puzzles! Project almost got out of hand! Speaks on Moody Bible Institute station; offers free booklet, *Bible Facts About Heaven*; 7,000 respond!
1959:	"Voice of Revival" broadcast is born Many being saved in Japan through salvation booklet
1960:	Family drives 300 miles to Wheaton; five get saved! She lived among a hundred Christian women, yet was unsaved. Dr. Rice easily wins the dear soul
1961:	Very exciting letters from SWORD readers Books which most influenced his life
1962:	He takes notes as Dr. Bob Jones, Sr., preached; read them!

1962
(cont.)

Executive Board expresses thanks to Dr. Rice
Battle at Sword between Sabers and Scimitars!
More blessed letters
How to defeat the modernistic poison in Southern
    Baptist seminaries
Dr. Jack Hyles becomes Sword Conference Director
Sword Tours to Bible Lands

1963:

Sword of the Lord Foundation moves to Murfreesboro,
    Tennessee

1965:

Editor not for sale
Statement of Faith of Sword of the Lord Foundation

1966:

Results of Sword Conferences
Answers slander, "No more great revivals"
Challenges pastors to baptize at least 200 converts a year

1967:

Many saved on Sword tour to Bible Lands
An estimated 10,000 preachers attend Sword of the
    Lord Conferences in year's time

1968:

Sword Conference in Tokyo
What was Dr. Rice's hobby?
Recalls under what conditions he wrote *Home: Court-
    ship, Marriage, and Children*
How to make another John R. Rice
Ear operation in Memphis
Another million *"What Must I Do to Be Saved?"* for
    Japan
A Model Sword Family
Read his saddle horse's letter to the Boss

1969:

Important book written, *Our God-Breathed Book—THE
    BIBLE*; outstanding Christian leaders praise it
Letter to Apollo 8 Crew
Two million more booklets for Japan
Sword's 35th anniversary celebration, with Georgia
    Governor Lester Maddox as one speaker
Catholic priest for 25 years signs decision slip from
    "What Must I Do to Be Saved?" then writes how he
    must flee country

1970:

Dr. Rice's 75th birthday celebration; Dr. Ian Paisley comes
    from Ireland
Sword of the Lord Foundation receives Bob Jones University
    Memorial Award
SWORD now entering 150,000 homes
To 35,000 new subscribers, Dr. Rice explains Sword's doc-
    trinal position

1975   Second National Sword Conference held at Convention
(cont.)   Center, Dallas
               80th birthday celebration
               Perhaps another mild heart attack

1976:   The "Happy Warrior" Room opened to visitors
               "90 'odd' workers"!
               Third National Sword Conference in Atlanta
               Teaches Book of Revelation on cruise in Caribbean
               Campaign yields 100,605 subscriptions!
               Sunset Square retirement home
               First Sword Women's Jubilee Retreat
               Cobo Hall Arena, Detroit, scene of fourth National Sword
                   Conference
               John R. Rice Reference Bible

1978:   The John R. Rice television special
               Rushed to hospital in Murfreesboro with heart attack

1979:   Killer "Son of Sam" requests THE SWORD OF THE LORD
               Other National Sword Conferences
               Hawaii Conference on Fundamentals of the Faith, Dr.
                   Rice speaker

1980:   Back to hospital
               JOHN R. RICE SUNDAY at home church
               Another great Sword Conference at Atlanta
               Goes to speak at Lynchburg, Virginia
               Seven Giants of the Faith honored at Southwide
               Baptist Fellowship meeting, Louisville
               Dictates notes at 2:00 a.m. from armchair
               Sword Staff honors Dr. Rice on 85th birthday
                   December 11
               His last Christmas letter to SWORD OF THE LORD
                   readers
               Mantle falls on Dr. Curtis Hutson
               John R. Rice goes Home December 29

A recap of his last days
Tributes from wife and daughters
Other tributes
Dr. Rice added to Christian Hall of Fame
A farewell to my Boss
Listing of all Dr. Rice's writings
A Disclaimer